PLANTS FOR A FUTURE

Edible & Useful Plants For A Healthier World

Ken Fern

Permanent Publications

Published by
Permanent Publications
Hyden House Limited
Little Hyden Lane
Clanfield
Hampshire PO8 0RU
England
Tel: (01705) 596500
Fax: (01705) 595834
Overseas: (international code + 44 - 1705)
Email: permaculture@gn.apc.org
WWW: www.permaculture.co.uk/

Distributed in the USA by:
Rodale Institute Bookstore
611 Siegfriedale Road, Kutztown, PA 19530
Tel: (800) 832 6285 Fax: (610) 683 8548

Design and typesetting by Tim Harland.

Printed by Hartnolls Limited, Bodmin, Cornwall.

Printed on Totally Chlorine Free (TCF) Environmentally Friendly paper.

British Library Cataloguing-in-Publication Data.
A catalogue record for this book is available from the British Library.

ISBN 1 85623 011 2

DEDICATION

This book is dedicated to Robert Hart for his vision and the inspiration he has given me.

Through inspiration we can gain a vision for the future. Thus I also dedicate this book to my young son Ajna and to all other children, that there may still be a beautiful world when they grow up.

CAVEAT EMPTOR

To the very best of my knowledge, all the information on edible plants contained in this book is accurate and true. However, I cannot guarantee that everybody who eats the plants mentioned here will react positively to them. Even amongst the more commonly eaten foods, for example, there are plenty of instances where people react badly to them. There are many people who are allergic to strawberries and will come out in a rash if they eat them. Some people develop a rash if they touch the stems of parsnips. Potatoes become poisonous if they turn green and eating large quantities of cabbages can adversely affect the thyroid gland.

However, in general I am sure that the overall health of people will be greatly improved by bringing more diversity into their diet. Therefore I strongly recommend the following procedures when adding a new food to your diet:

1. Make sure that you have identified it correctly – and that you have used the botanical name to do this.

2. Try no more than a small taste of the new food at first. If there are no side effects then increase the quantity at a later meal.

BIOGRAPHY

In 1974, whilst employed as a bus driver in London, Ken Fern obtained a small plot of land in Surrey with the idea of becoming self-sufficient in food and of providing a cash income with the surplus. After a couple of years of growing an acre of vegetables by hand he decided that there must be easier and more environmentally friendly ways of growing food. It was at this time that he read the book *Forest Farming* by Robert Hart and James Sholto-Douglas, and this convinced him that the future of food production lay in perennial plants.

This is how Ken started his experiments with alternative food crops. With this experience coupled with his travels around the gardens of Britain, he has acquired a vast wealth of knowledge about how well these plants can grow. As a result, he has now developed a database of 7,000 species of edible and useful plants.

In 1989, he moved to Cornwall and helped set up a demonstration site at Penpol. Over 1,500 different species of plant are being grown here and an educational charity, called Plants For A Future, has been established to promote and spread the work of the project.

Ken is considered to be a leading expert in his field, and has written many articles on the subject. He gives lectures, runs courses and gives practical demonstrations on useful plants.

PHOTOGRAPHS

All photographs are by Ken Fern unless stated otherwise.

FRONT COVER PHOTOGRAPH

Hemerocallis fulva 'Kwanso'. The DAY LILY. The most exquisite tasting and beautiful flower you could possibly eat. See page 94.

BACK COVER PHOTOGRAPHS

1. *Berberis georgii.* A highly productive fruit for the woodland edge. Its acid flavour being adored by children. See page 55.

2. *Allium sativum ophioscorodon.* Tasting identical to common garlic, the curious growth habit of serpent garlic makes it a talking point in the garden. See page 107.

3. *Hibiscus syriacus.* A beautiful autumn flowering shrub. The flowers make an attractive mild tasting salad and the leaves have a delicious nutty flavour. See page 189.

4. *Typha latifolia.* A very invasive plant, but with a huge variety of edible and non-edible uses. It is also a superb plant for wildlife. See page 134.

CONTENTS

PLANTS FOR A FUTURE
The Project

This book contains information on a great many alternative food plants and otherwise useful plants. It also offers alternative methods of growing these plants in ways that are in harmony with the local environment and can help to improve the overall health of the planet.

Whilst many of the plants discussed here are reasonably well known in this country (even if their uses are not so well known), a number of the plants are much more experimental in their nature.

It is hoped that the book will stimulate interest in these plants and help people to increase the range of foods in their diet. It is also hoped that it will encourage people to experiment with some of the plants in this book and thereby help us to increase our knowledge of them.

For the past few years I have been involved with a charity called 'Plants for a Future'. This project has been gathering information on the many useful plants that can be grown in temperate climates and has also been gathering together a collection of these species. The intention is to become a resource and information centre that is able to supply the plants and give information on how to grow them.

There are many areas of research that we want to carry out, but are rather limited by availability of funds and facilities. We would like to be able to gather information on how well (or badly) the plants grow in different parts of the country. We need to look more closely at different systems of growing plants, especially integrated woodland plantings and in particular looking for low-input and low-labour systems. We are also beginning to look at the possibilities of selective breeding for improved cultivars.

These are all areas where you, the grower, can play an active role. It would be very useful for me if you could keep records of the plants you are growing. Of how well, or badly, they grow with you. Of how well they crop, and whether that crop is worth eating.

Any information we receive will be added, where appropriate, to our database of the plants. This database is made available on a donations basis to all who want a copy.

If you would like to help in this task of increasing our knowledge of these plants, then please get in touch with:

Ken Fern
Plants For A Future
The Field
Penpol
Lostwithiel
Cornwall
PL22 0NG

FOREWORD

by
Joy Larkcom

Twiddling the knobs of the radio many years ago I lighted on a man extolling the virtues of eating chickweed. 'The world's full of nutters', I remember thinking dismissively. I would never have guessed that twenty years on **I** would be the nutter, gathering buckets of ground elder, chickweed and nettle tops for the 'Wild Food' menu of a pricey restaurant in London's Covent Garden. (No customer, apparently, ever ordered the menu... but that's another story.) The point is that we are all more imprisoned by our prejudices than we care to admit.

It is probably true to say that almost every plant in the world, from forest and woodland trees to the plankton in the ocean, provides food for some species, or has the potential for being used as fibre, fuel, dyes, medicine or some practical purpose. Yet only a tiny handful have been selected for improvement. With the kitchen garden in mind our forefathers chose, among others, the cabbage tribe and lettuce... and what assets they have proved. But what would have happened if they had picked on wood sorrel or plantain or hawthorn?

Ken Fern is one of those rare people with an open mind coupled to a scientist's curiosity and powers of observation. He has made it his business to investigate our native plants, seeing what is practicable to gather or grow to enliven our narrow modern diet. He has found an enormous number. Many of these are now being grown by 'Plants For A Future', the charity established in Cornwall to research useful temperate climate plants.

Ken's curiosity extends beyond the culinary value of these plants to the limitations of our traditional cultivation methods. He is an enthusiast for permaculture, a practical but philosophical approach to gardening where natural, sustainable systems are used rather than the almost adversarial approach most of us adopt, where anything not clearly a friend is considered a foe and eliminated – often with the expenditure of a great deal of energy. In permaculture perennials are looked on more kindly than annuals (unless the latter are self-seeding), fewer plants are labelled and treated as weeds, and useful plants are woven into the garden, into borders, hedges and ponds, even into the grassy areas and corners that cry out for ground cover. This is easy to do without sacrificing the beauty of a garden, for so many edible plants, especially those less known, are beautiful.

I personally have learnt an enormous amount from the 'Plants For A Future' leaflets, in which, up to now, Ken has distilled what he has learnt. His enthusiasm and pertinent, honest observations make his writing as easily digested as the edible plants he loves and writes about. I'm delighted that this treasure trove of information has now been marshalled between book covers and so made more accessible and preserved for future generations. Gardeners young and old, conventional and curious, will thus be encouraged not only to enrich their own diet, but to consider new ways of blending the wild and the tame, the marginal and the mainstream, in their own gardens, balconies and windowsills.

Joy Larkcom

Joy Larkcom is a pioneer organic gardener and known worldwide as an author. She is a recent Garden Writer of the Year and has also been awarded the Royal Horticultural Society's prestigious Veitch Memorial Medal.

INTRODUCTION

If Only Carrots Grew On Trees!

I was picking the first crop of apples off trees that had been planted just two years ago. Although there were only a few pounds of apples on each tree I knew that the yields would increase annually until they averaged out at about 100lbs per tree each year. All I would have to do was come along in the autumn and harvest the apples. I could, of course, also spend time pruning the trees, cutting the grass under them and performing various other jobs, but even if I just sat back and left the trees to their own devices they would still produce apples for at least the next 50 years and probably considerably longer.

The many hours spent preparing the soil, sowing the seeds and keeping the plants weeded that was necessary in order to grow a good crop of carrots, and then trying to find ways of keeping them free of carrot fly, slugs and various diseases seemed so much more hard work. Especially when I would then have to do it all again next year and the year after that and the year after that...

It was 1977, I was a bus driver in London and the thought of driving buses for another 40 years before retiring and then waiting to die did not appeal to me. I had bought a small 1¾ acre field some two years previously and, filled with a yearning for the 'good life', had decided to try my hand at self-sufficiency and earning a living from the land. Two years of growing an acre of organic annual vegetables by hand convinced me that there must be some better way of producing food! It was so much hard work – you would clear the land of its weeds, sow the seeds that you wanted to grow and then spend all your time trying to prevent the weeds from re-establishing themselves. I started looking at various alternative methods of cultivation, minimum and no-digging techniques for example, but my dissatisfaction with annual crops remained.

Reading a book called *Forest Farming* by James Sholto-Douglas and Robert Hart was an eye-opener. Although this book did not really deal much with temperate areas of the world, it did show that there are many tree crops that can be grown to produce foods for people. Not only is there less work involved in growing trees but the potential yields are also much greater than from annual crops. Further research showed that there were also many other alternative food crops, some of these were annuals but a large number of them were perennial plants. Without knowing it, I was beginning to discover permaculture.

What is Permaculture?

Much of the philosophy of permaculture is not new but draws on the wisdom of many cultures and systems of growing and utilising plants that have been in existence for thousands of years. The word has two main derivations. The first comes from **perma**nent **culture**, a recognition that solutions to the world's problems are as much social as they are physical. The second derivation is from **perma**nent agri**culture**.

This indicates that, amongst other things, permaculture is a method of plant management that tries to emulate the natural ecosystems of the planet, to work in harmony with nature rather than seeing her as an enemy that must be subdued.

The Productive Woodland

For a good example of this, one need look no further than a native woodland. Who feeds it with artificial fertilizers? Who sprays it with fungicides and herbicides, and why isn't everything eaten up by insects?

The diagram shows a typical woodland with its wide range of plants and habitats. Year by year this woodland produces masses of plant growth feeding a host of mammals, birds, insects etc. A wide range of plants grow side by side, sometimes competing but more often occupying subtly different niches in the woodland. For example, some plants have deep root systems and obtain many of their nutrients from deep down in the soil in areas beyond the reach of other plants. When their leaves drop to the ground in the autumn and decompose, many of these nutrients are made available to other members of the plant community. Other plants have shallower root systems and these obtain their nutrients from nearer the soil surface.

Similarly, there are gradations of height in the woodland. Some of the plants are tall trees, some are smaller trees or shrubs, climbers make their way up the trunks of the trees whilst smaller plants that are able to grow in the shade of the trees are found on the woodland floor. Some of these smaller plants, such as the bluebell and wild garlic, come into growth early in the year, before the trees have leafed out, and complete most of their annual life-cycle by early summer before the tree shade closes in.

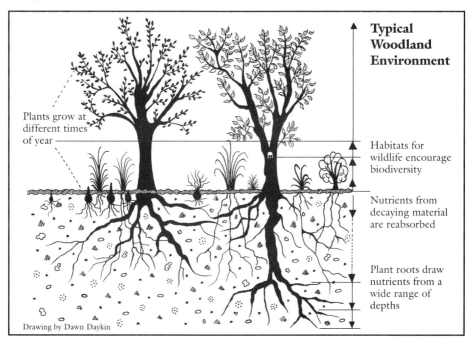

Typical Woodland Environment

Plants grow at different times of year

Habitats for wildlife encourage biodiversity

Nutrients from decaying material are reabsorbed

Plant roots draw nutrients from a wide range of depths

Drawing by Dawn Daykin

A woodland garden can be a very attractive place in which to grow a wide range of edible and other useful plants.

Thus there are different niches for plants to occupy in the soil, above the ground and in time. The canopy of trees creates a sheltered and more stable environment inside the woodland. Temperature fluctuations are less extreme than in an open field and there is less wind and frost so plants are less subject to the vagaries of our weather. Because of all the different available habitats, a wide range of creatures are able to live in the woodland. In general, the more diverse the numbers of species that live in an ecosystem then the more stable and also more productive that system becomes.

When rain falls on a woodland its force is broken by the trees and other plants and it thus reaches the earth more gently. The rich carpet of organic matter on the floor of the woodland can then absorb the rain and allow it to soak into the soil. Thus the rain enhances the water table instead of running off into the rivers and thence to the sea, taking valuable soil and nutrients with it. A woodland, therefore, acts as a regulator, soaking up water in wet seasons and releasing it at a steady rate all year round.

Remove the woodland and much more of the water runs straight off the surface and into the rivers, thence straight out to sea. Heavy rain falling on cultivated soil will also wash away that soil and the nutrients it contains. I live in a particularly beautiful village with a stream flowing through it. Whenever we get even moderate rainfall (a pretty common event in Cornwall!) the stream turns brown with all the soil that it is carrying out to sea. This is the natural fertility of the soil that is being carried away – or to put it more succinctly it is our children's future that is quite literally being washed out to sea.

The end result of heavy rainfall onto cultivated land is a rapid rise in river levels with the threat of flooding that this brings. As an example of this, there is strong evidence to suggest that the regular flooding that occurs in the Ganges delta in Bangladesh is caused by deforestation more than 2,000 kilometres upstream in the Himalayas.

There are also various fungal and bacterial activities taking place on the root systems of the woodland plants. These increase the plants' abilities to take up nutrients from the soil and also produce nutrients for the plants to utilize. So we see that a woodland is not only high-yielding and self-sustaining, but it can also lead to a gradual build-up of fertility until an optimum level is reached and this is then maintained.

A Field of Wheat

Just compare this woodland with a field of wheat illustrated in the diagram below. Here, all the plants have the same nutritional requirements, their roots occupy the same levels in the soil and will only be able to obtain nutrients from this one level. Any nutrients that have been washed lower down into the soil will be lost to the plants in the field and will eventually find their way into the water system either to be washed out to sea or to pollute our drinking water.

Genetically very similar, these plants are all susceptible to the same pests and diseases and all have the same climatic requirements. If one suffers, they all suffer. The system is dependent on large inputs of fertilizers, herbicides, pesticides, fungicides etc. The soil becomes little more than a medium to hold the plant up, and it is deteriorates as soil structure and depth are destroyed. It is not only in tropical countries that this is a major problem – the Fenlands are some of the most fertile land in Britain, and they are losing 30 mm of topsoil every year due to erosion.

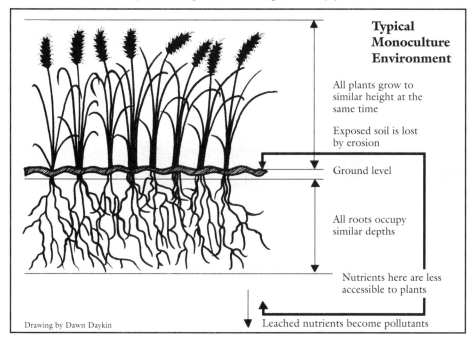

Typical Monoculture Environment

All plants grow to similar height at the same time

Exposed soil is lost by erosion

Ground level

All roots occupy similar depths

Nutrients here are less accessible to plants

Leached nutrients become pollutants

Drawing by Dawn Daykin

Having been ploughed in the autumn the top soil in this field was then washed away by every heavy rain shower all through the winter.

The monotony of the barley field in the foreground is contrasted by the developing diversity at the Plants For A Future site in the middle background.

Yields of wheat have increased dramatically over the last hundred years, from around 1 ton per acre at the beginning of the century to 3 tons or more now. But is this sustainable? No it is not! In fact when you take into account all the energy that is expended in making the farm machinery, in fuelling it, in making the fertilizers etc. and all the other things that need to be done in order to produce the food and bring it to the consumer, almost 10 times more energy is actually used up in producing food than the food itself yields in energy! This ridiculous state of affairs is only possible due to the current abundance of fossil fuels, but how long are they going to last?

Of course, whilst the acre of wheat produces about 3 tons of food that we can eat, our native woodland seems to produce very little in the way of food for us. We might find some hazel nuts and chestnuts in the autumn, some blackberries and other fruits in the summer, but they are not going to keep us supplied with food all year round unless we want to eat the acorns, crab apples etc.

The simple solution is to design woodlands – and other models of natural systems such as bog gardens, ponds and meadows – that **do** contain edible species. There are well over 20,000 known species of edible plants in the world, plus many more that have yet to be documented, and more than 5,000 of these can be grown outdoors in Britain – I wonder how many of them you have ever eaten?

The Value of Diversity

Research has shown that before the dawn of agriculture, when people were hunter gatherers, somewhere between 200 and 1000 different species of plants would be eaten by a person in any one year. With the advent of agriculture, however, things changed rapidly. It seemed so much simpler to grow and manage a field of one annual cereal crop than it was to grow a range of different grasses for their seeds. Some species responded more easily to cultivation and these soon became the favoured crops. In a relatively short space of time the variety of foods people were eating dropped dramatically, and along with the move to agriculture came the first recorded evidence of human degenerative diseases such as arthritis. Nowadays fewer than 20 species of plants supply about 90% of all our plant foods.

One of the great dangers of this loss of diversity is that, as we become more and more dependent on fewer and fewer species, so the potential for disaster increases. We often hear about famines in tropical areas of the world, but the temperate zone is not immune from such disasters. There was the potato famine in Ireland in the 19th century when blight wiped out the potato crop, causing millions of people to die or leave the country. Can you imagine what would happen if our wheat crops were destroyed by disease?

Whilst writing this introduction I came across an article in the Spring 1994 edition of *Kew* magazine. It was talking about a group of chimpanzees that live in a small area of forest, called Gombe, in Africa. The forest is a reserve and is surrounded by cultivated land. The article continued:

Outside Gombe, the local people are struggling to live off perhaps 30 different types of foods, mostly introduced species of plants grown in drought conditions on easily eroded soils... But the chimps seem to be expert botanists, knowing exactly where and when the next crop of fruit will be. There may be only six major plant foods each month but, over the year, more than 150 species are used.

Some of the fruits they eat are delicious and they can certainly teach us a great deal about a balanced diet and preventative healthcare. But although a lot is known about the chimps' social behaviour, our understanding of their botanical knowledge and its significance to us is in its infancy. Few of their food plants have been tested for nutrients or medicinal properties.

It seems that the chimps are more intelligent than we are! Instead of fighting with the land to grow our food crops, would it not make more sense to try and design methods of growing plants that were based on the natural systems around us? There is certainly no shortage of promising species to choose from, as I hope this book will demonstrate. Once established, these systems would require very little input in order to remain productive and would have the potential to greatly out-yield any of the annual crops we cultivate today. Thus we will end up with a situation of less work for greater returns – surely the dream of all gardeners!

Since 1980 I have been carrying out considerable research into temperate-zone plants and their uses. As a result of this research a project called 'Plants for a Future' came into being in 1989. This non-profit-making project is based in Cornwall, where we grow about 1,700 different species and cultivars of useful plants. We have also set up a database of almost 7,000 species of edible, medicinal and otherwise useful plants that can be grown outdoors in Britain. The project is very much in its infancy (the average tree in our woodland was about 1.5 metres tall in 1996) but it is already demonstrating the many useful properties that plants have. It will also be looking at ways of growing plants that work in co-operation with nature, rather than in a state of constant conflict. See Appendix 2 for more details of our activities.

About This Book

The main intention of this book is to introduce you to some of the edible plants that have been forgotten, to see how they can fit into the ornamental and kitchen gardens, the allotment and the farm. I hope it will also show how to make growing food more enjoyable, more productive and more attractive visually whilst providing more habitats for our native wild life and some very tasty and health-promoting foods for us to eat. The book also promotes a way of gardening that does not depend on large inputs of fertilizers, pesticides, herbicides etc. and also requires far less hard work thus freeing us to enjoy the plants more instead of being their slaves.

The book also takes a brief look at plants that you can grow for non-food uses, including fibres, dyes, fuel, oil, crafts and perhaps one or two more esoteric uses! However it only mentions a few medicinal herbs. There are plenty of good herbals that can guide you here and I am certainly not a qualified herbalist

With almost 7,000 species to choose from it is only possible to list a selection of plants here. I have concentrated on perennial species (and especially trees and shrubs) but have also included a section on some of the more promising annuals. The choice of plants is very personal. I have grown, or at least eaten, most of those edible species included in this book but there are many other exciting species just waiting to be discovered, written about, grown and eaten. If I have left out any of your personal favourites then I apologise – maybe I'll have to write an even larger book one day!

There has been very little research into the cropping potential of many of the plants contained in this book. Some of the species discussed here have at times been grown as a commercial crop and so are known to yield well. Others I know from personal experience to be good yielders. There are many which I just cannot say for sure how well they will do here.

There are others that I know to be low yielding but they either have the potential of higher yields or produce such a nice crop that I do not mind the low yields. Very often these low yielding species can be grown in a mixed planting with other more productive plants without taking up any extra space. Whatever they yield in such a position can be viewed as a bonus on top of the main crop, and a way of increasing the overall productivity and diversity of the land. Wherever yields are known to be low I have noted it in the text.

My research into useful plants is an on-going process and one of my motives for writing this book has been to widen my own knowledge on useful plants and then make this available to others. Thus you will often see notes in the book requesting feedback from you, the reader. Even when I do not ask for this, it would be most valuable for me to hear from you about these plants and how well (or badly) you have got on with them. Where appropriate, this feedback will be added to the plant database, thus making it available to a very wide range of people.

I have used the botanical names of plants throughout this book, including a common name only when this is often used in Britain. Although this might seem more difficult for people who do not normally use botanical names, it does lead to less confusion and also to less potential problems. For example, the English call the plant *Campanula latifolia* a HAREBELL, whilst in Scotland they call it a BLUEBELL. The plant that the English call a BLUEBELL (*Hyacinthoides non-scriptus*) is called a HAREBELL in Scotland. Since the English BLUEBELL is a poisonous plant whilst the Scottish BLUEBELL is a very tasty edible plant, you can see the potential for disaster!

In all cases in this book you should use the botanical name for identification and not the common name, to ensure that potentially harmful mix-ups do not occur.

Botanical names notwithstanding, I hope you enjoy the book...

Chapter One

THE PRACTICE

This book is for people who would like to experiment with alternative food plants. It can be used by anyone, no matter what methods of gardening or farming they follow. Nor does it matter whether you live in a flat and only have a window box, or if you have a 1,000 acre farm – there are plants in this book that are suitable for all sizes and types of garden or farm. It is not primarily about growing methods, on which there are already many good books (see Appendix 1). But I would like to mention a few general principles before getting down to the plants.

I am an organic grower and by personal choice do not use manure from domesticated animals, which makes me vegan-organic. I am also a lazy gardener. I don't want to spend all my time growing plants, I want to be able to walk around and look at them, to sit back and enjoy them. Therefore I look for methods that will reduce my workload. The most obvious way to do this is to grow plants that can look after themselves so that you don't have to spend forever and a day weeding them and manicuring them. Trees are a very good example of this. Once planted, so long as they are given a good weed-excluding mulch, it is almost possible to walk away and forget them for a few years whilst they grow. I hope that when you read Chapter 2 it will convince you to plant more trees and shrubs.

Other perennial plants are also good for reducing the work load. If you want to eat good quality fresh lettuce from your garden all year round then you are going to have to prepare the ground, sow seeds, weed and thin them for up to 10 separate crops each year. By growing a mixture of perennials, however, you will be able to harvest a variety of tasty fresh salad leaves all year round with very little effort. You will find examples of perennial salad plants in most chapters of this book, but see Chapter 8 for details of some outdoor winter salads that you can grow.

The technique is to grow a wide variety of plants and also to plan out your garden so that complementary species are grown together. If you sow your row of lettuces and then the slugs come along and eat all the seedlings, or the summer is hot and dry and the lettuces all run to seed before hearting, then you have lost all your salad plants until the next sowing is ready to harvest. By growing a range of perennial plants, no matter what the season throws at you, there will always be some species that will thrive. Also, once the perennials are established, they will be much better able to take care of themselves when the weeds or slugs do arrive.

You have probably realised by now that I am not the world's number one fan of lettuces. In fact I often wonder just why people expend so much energy in growing them. There are many salad plants about with much more interesting flavours, and with careful selection of species you can harvest tasty salad leaves all year round for a fraction of the work. See ***Tilia cordata*** in Chapter 2, ***Campanula versicolor*** and ***Malva moschata*** in Chapter 4 and ***Reichardia picroides*** in Chapter 5 for a few examples of easily-grown delicious salad leaves.

Edible leaves are a very strong part of my argument about alternative plants for food, but this argument can also be developed to cover all other types of plant foods. It is important to remember that the human race has been selectively breeding food plants for well over 2,500 years and most of this energy has been expended on the annual crops. The reason is quite simple – it is far quicker to develop improved varieties from annuals because a new generation is bred every year. Perennials usually take much longer and with some trees it can be 40 years or more before they will even produce their first seeds, which makes selective breeding a very long-term proposition.

When you consider that the mild-flavoured lettuce was developed from a bitter-tasting poisonous plant and that our large and lush apples have been bred from small, acid and astringent crab apples, then you begin to understand the potential that exists for developing new and improved varieties of the plants contained in this book. See Chapter 13 for more details about this.

Companion Planting

As I mentioned a little earlier, one of the techniques involved in cultivating these plants is to grow them in complementary plantings or communities. Most gardeners are aware that the plants they grow have certain needs and it is easier to put plants with similar needs into the same area. Thus, if you want to grow healthy plants, all the shade-loving plants will be put in shady positions and acid-loving plants will be planted in acid soils. It is also important to look at how each plant interacts with its neighbouring plant. Gardeners with an aesthetic sense will also want to grow groupings of plants that are visually attractive, but whilst this is a valid point it is not what I really mean.

Going back to the woodland mentioned in the introduction, the wide diversity of plants growing there actually contributes to the well-being of the whole system. Whilst there is obviously competition for space, light and nutrients, there is also adaptation to the environment which allows different plants to occupy different niches within the woodland. Thus there will be both shallow rooted and deep rooted species, short plants and tall. The soil is teeming with life, both animal and plant.

The overall effect of this diversity is to create a relatively stable environment within the wood that is protected from the worst excesses of heat, cold, rain, wind and the predations of insect pests. Thus a very wide variety of plants adapted to these conditions can grow and thrive together. If you try to introduce a seashore plant into this system then it will not grow very well in the shady conditions and will probably die despite any attention you give it.

There are many subtle and also direct interactions between these various life-forms that promote the growth and health of the whole system. One of the clearest examples of this concerns many members of the pea and bean family, plus a number of other species that have a relationship with certain bacteria or algae in the soil, resulting in the formation of nitrogen nodules on the roots of the plants. This nitrogen benefits both the host plants and also neighbouring plants.

Many other activities are taking place both in the soil and above it which benefit both the plants and other creatures in the woodland. As a very simple illustration, a bird will eat a fruit from a tree. Some time later, and often at a considerable distance from the fruit tree, the bird will defecate. This defecation will contain some seeds that have passed through the gut unharmed. Not only are they unharmed by this experience, their ability to germinate is often enhanced because the digestive acids in the bird's stomach will have started to break down the seed casing, thus making it easier for the seeds to absorb water and commence the process of growth. In addition, these seeds have also been given a nice parcel of fertility in which to commence the process of germination and growth into a new fruit tree.

In a mature ecosystem each plant and animal has a vital role to play in the well-being and stability of the system. They are all interconnected in an intricate web of life that modern science is only slowly coming to understand. In my opinion, successful gardening is all about understanding these natural systems and endeavouring to set them up on one's own land.

When we took on our land in Cornwall at the end of 1989 it was mainly bare earth with lots of dead barley stubble and a few weeds, most of which were annuals. The following growing season saw a number of plants establishing themselves, mainly annual meadow grass, thistles, dock and buttercups. However, by the end of the year there were still large areas of bare soil. Towards the end of that first growing season we noticed a few small clumps of WHITE CLOVER, *Trifolium repens*, which is a member of the pea family.

In the second year these clumps burst into very vigorous growth and many more clumps appeared. White clover is a low-growing creeping plant and each clump formed a rapidly expanding circle that eventually grew into neighbouring circles to form a dense sward across much of the land. These circles of clover were green and lush, compared with the much less vigorous growth of other plants.

Where the clover was growing the other plants were also becoming much more lush. In particular we noticed that fine grasses were appearing in amongst the clover and these gradually became the dominant plants, with a much more subdued clover growing amongst this grass. We still have plenty of buttercups and clover, but the grass has remained dominant. Most of it gets mown at least once a year, and sometimes more often, which prevents it turning to scrub. In places it almost looks like a lawn! It is very clear that the other plants have benefited as a result of growing with the clover.

Many of the plants in this book have the same ability as clover to enrich the soil with nitrogen, these are indicated in the index of plant uses at the back of the book and sometimes also in the entry on the plant. It is a simple matter to introduce some of these species into your garden and let them share your burden of trying to build up soil fertility.

Recent research has shown that some members of the genus *Tagetes* secrete substances into the soil which can have an insecticidal effect. In particular this is effective against nematodes and to a much lesser degree against keeled slugs. The growing plants also have a repellent effect on insects and, if interplanted with susceptible plants, can help to keep them free of pests. Like most of the information contained in this book this is not new knowledge, merely something that has been rediscovered; Tagetes species were being grown as companion plants over 2,000 years ago by the ancient South American civilisations.

Most members of this genus are half-hardy annuals and need to be started off in a greenhouse and then planted out. Whilst some of you might not know the name *Tagetes*, it is quite possible that you are already growing some of these plants since they are commonly used in bedding schemes. The species most commonly used are *T. erecta*, (AFRICAN MARIGOLD), *T. lucida* (MEXICAN TARRAGON), *T. minuta* and *T. patula* (FRENCH MARIGOLD).

Of these, *T. lucida* is the only perennial, and it is not very cold-hardy. Thanks to some friends, I am growing a few plants of this species that come from a cool winter area in western North America. Before trying them outdoors, I made sure that I had divided them and kept some plants back in the greenhouse as reserves. The plants have now survived two winters outdoors, the second of which was particularly cold for Cornwall with a series of damaging frosts in late spring. All the plants survived without damage, though they were rather late coming into growth after the late spring frosts. So long as they are given a well-drained soil and a sunny sheltered position, it seems that they will tolerate temperatures down to at least -5°C. As the common name of the plant suggests, the dried leaves can be used as a tarragon substitute for flavouring cooked foods and they can also be brewed into an anise-flavoured tea.

T. minuta (minuta means small, but this refers to the size of the flowers since the plants can be more than a metre tall) has also been shown to inhibit the growth of many garden weeds such as couch grass and ground elder. This is not a very practical treatment on any scale in Britain because the plant has to be started off in a greenhouse and it needs to be growing in the soil for a few months before the root secretions become effective.

Many other plants can have a deterrent effect on insects. For example, if you grow very aromatic plants the scent of them can confuse insects who seek out a plant by smell. It won't be of much use if the insect is close enough to see its host plant.

Once more this is where growing a diversity of plants comes in. In modern intensive agriculture it is not uncommon to see a block of hundreds of acres of land all growing the same plant. Once an insect pest comes across one plant in this field then it is in paradise. Plenty of food to eat means that it is going to breed freely and its offspring will have to be pretty stupid if they can't find another host plant since there are going to be dozens of them just centimetres away. The result is a population explosion and all the poor grower can do is spray some chemical to kill the insects. Of course, this will often also kill the predators of the insect pest who were perhaps just arriving on the scene.

If you have a diversity of plants then any insect is going to have to look much harder in order to find a new host, it is going to take more time to do this, might quite possibly fail in the attempt and die of starvation and will also be at a much greater risk of being caught by a predator. Not only that, but the very diversity of plants you are growing offers more habitats to the predators and so ensures a higher population of them which is then more able to control insect pests.

Many plants can be grown in order to attract useful species of birds and insects to your land. For example, the flowers of most members of the parsnip family (Umbelliferae) are like a magnet to insects, including hoverflies and predatory wasps. Interspersing some members of this genus amongst your other plants will make a considerable contribution to balancing the population between insect pests and predators and thereby reduce any need you might feel to use pesticides.

Chamaemelum nobile, or CAMOMILE, grows about 15cm tall and 30cm wide. It is a member of the daisy (Compositae) family. This is another family that tends to attract useful insects onto your land. Camomile is an excellent companion plant to grow and seems to have a beneficial effect on plants growing nearby. It also has many other uses in the home and garden. I have found an infusion of the flowers to be particularly effective when sprayed on ailing plants as a general tonic and liquid feed, I normally use it in conjunction with garlic. An infusion of the flowers is used as a herb tea, this is a very good tonic for the stomach and is particularly effective for children. This infusion is also used in hair shampoos where it is especially good for fair hair.

When using the herb medicinally or as a tea, the cultivar 'Flore Pleno' is often recommended. This is the double flowered form which has more petals and less disk florets. It is these disk florets that are the most active part medicinally, but also the most bitter. The flowers are milder-flavoured and therefore more suitable for children or as a tea.

The flowers are an ingredient of 'Quick Return' herbal compost activator (see the section on 'Feeding the Soil' later in this chapter). The whole plant was formerly used as a strewing herb, it is insect repellent both when growing and when dried. An essential oil from the whole plant is used as a flavouring and in perfumery. Yellow to gold dyes are obtained from the flowers. The plant makes a good ground cover and can also be used as an edging plant, see page 142 for more details.

Another way of reducing predation on your food crops is to grow plants that are more attractive to the pest. For example, if your apples are being eaten by birds then try growing plants such as ELDERBERRY (*Sambucus nigra*) in the hedge by the apples or even amongst them. Not only will it draw the birds away from the apples but you will also be able to use the elderberry in various ways as described on page 183.

Other plants that have also worked in this way include various *Berberis* species (BARBERRIES), *Sorbus aucuparia* (ROWAN) and *Viburnum opulus* (GUELDER ROSE), see Chapters 2 and 9. Many other good companion plants will be mentioned in later chapters – see the Index of Plant Uses if you want to look them up.

The Value of Diversity

For so many people, growing plants is a constant battle against all the setbacks nature throws at us. It really need not be like this. Instead of fighting against her and always complaining about our lot we would do better by trying to work with her. Nature is self-regulating and, when left to her own devices, finds a balance between the various species of plants and animals. A natural woodland receives no artificial fertilisers, fungicides or herbicides yet its lush growth feeds a wide range of mammals, birds and insects. There are fluctuations in the populations of different species, but the overall picture is one of balance.

No matter what the situation, nature will always seek to find a balance. The greater the diversity of species in the environment then the more stable that balance becomes with only gentle oscillations from side to side. The fewer the species then the larger are the oscillations. In a very dry desert, for example, there may be virtually no plant life for most of the time, then after it rains there is a frantic rush of growth as dormant seeds burst into life to grow, flower, set seed and die before all the water has gone. Along with the sudden burst of plant life, many other creatures appear in order to take advantage of this bonanza of food, only to seemingly disappear when the drier conditions return.

This same pattern of population explosions and crashes is what happens when we cultivate large areas of annual crops. Thus we become locked into trying to stabilize an inherently unstable system. Little wonder it is so much hard work.

"Why is it that all around me the land is lush and green, vibrant with life and untouched by pests or diseases whilst just about every slug in the area seems hell-bent on making its way to my plot and eating every last seedling I've just planted out?" When we think like this it becomes all too easy to rush out with the slug pellets, beer traps or some other fiendish method of terminating the existence of as many slugs as possible in the shortest possible time.

There is another way, though. We can look at the life-cycle of the slug, see which habitats it enjoys, which it does not like. We can see what creatures eat slugs and what habitats they require. If we encourage the natural predators by providing a suitable habitat for them, then in time a balance of predator and prey will come about and we will be able to sit back and let nature take care of itself. Chapter 12 will give some ideas on this.

I must admit that we have yet to develop this natural balance for the slugs on our land. When we first moved here there were virtually no slugs about. Mind you, there was very little of anything about and even bees were a rarity. This was partly due to an extended period of hot dry weather that we were experiencing but it was also because the aggressive growing methods of the previous owner meant the destruction of large numbers of slugs and their predators annually.

Unfortunately, this destruction of the slugs was largely due to the degradation of the environment and not because of an inherent natural balance. Hence, as soon as we started treating the land with more respect, the slug population boomed because there were very few natural predators around. Within 4 years of moving to our land we had a real plague of the slimy creatures. I remember planting out 100 tomato plants in early June, only to come back the very next morning to find that they had all been eaten down to the ground. Every evening, as the dew fell, the grass would turn from green to black as hordes of slugs emerged from their resting places. It was like a scene from a horror movie! The little blighters even managed to climb up and eat all the leaves of a tree 1.5 metres tall, eventually killing it.

It is taking time, but by providing habitats for hedgehogs, slowworms, frogs and thrushes we are gradually achieving a balance. Certainly the frog spawn that we introduced to the land in 1993 has produced some very fat and healthy frogs. We must also have some of the fattest hedgehogs in Cornwall! Gradually the slug population has fallen to acceptable levels and in 1996 they were no longer considered to be a major problem on the land.

As an indication that natural methods work if you give them the time, I would like to relate another experience we have had since moving to Cornwall. The mouse population increased from virtually nil in the first year we were here to real pest proportions by the end of the second year. I would plant out some broad bean seeds (which had been soaked in paraffin) and the next morning every one of them would have been dug up and eaten. Then, in the third year, we noticed that there were quite a few birds of prey hovering over the land, including four species of owl – the Little, Tawny, Barn and Short-eared. We were also regularly visited by every cat in the area. By the end of that year the mouse population had reduced to acceptable levels and, with slight fluctuations, has stayed there since then.

As A Last Resort...

There are a few slug and snail deterrents that we have found effective. Firstly, they do not like travelling over copper. A friend gave us a roll of copper strip about 8cm wide and as thick as a sheet of paper. This has proved to be a very good (though not 100% effective) barrier to slugs and snails. We use it mainly to protect young seedlings that are grown in pots. The pots are on tables and the copper is placed around the table legs to prevent the slugs climbing up. You can also place the strips around the trunks of trees – which, had we known about it at the time, would have saved our tree that was killed by slugs.

Some people also use the copper as a low wall around susceptible plants, though I have found this to be fairly ineffective for two main reasons. Either rain splash will coat the copper with soil which the slugs will then use to cross over the barrier, or some plant material will fall over the barrier forming a bridge for the slugs.

A mulch of leafmould made from oak trees has very noticeably reduced slug damage – it is quite probable that other tannin-rich leafmoulds will also work. If you can afford it, shredded bark is also quite effective, though try to get oak bark if at all possible.

A mulch of seaweed has also proved effective. The salt on newly gathered seaweed is a toxin to slugs and snails. Although much of this will be washed into the soil after a few rainy days, the slugs still do not like living in or travelling over the seaweed. You have to be careful, though, if you use seaweed like this. Whilst a certain amount of salt added to most soils does no harm – and is even used as a fertilizer for some crops such as beetroot – the salt can be very damaging to the structure of heavier soils with a high proportion of clay in them.

Coarse gravel or sharp sand and hair trimmings have also proved useful in deterring slugs, but as soon as these mulches get wet the slugs happily travel over the film of water on top of the mulch. Unfortunately, it is often wet in Cornwall!

There are times when things are so out of balance that you feel a need to do something more immediate than waiting for a natural balance to develop on the land. Fortunately there are many biological controls becoming available to help contain even the mighty slug. These controls usually introduce a predator species that will parasitise and kill the pest.

In the case of slugs, this is a tiny nematode that is a native of Britain. By introducing a massive number of the nematodes to an area of land (about 300,000 to a square metre is the recommended figure!) most of the slugs will be parasitised within a very short time. The effect, however, is short-lived. Because they rapidly parasitise and kill all the slugs living in the immediate area, this high population of nematodes is soon reduced by a lack of food and other environmental factors. After a few months the slug population begins to return to normal. Thus using the nematodes will only give you and the plants a breathing space. If a treatment is applied in the spring, for example, it will give seedlings enough time to get established (and thus become much more slug-proof) before the slugs return.

I would regard these biological controls as weapons of last resort, just as I would all the many organic insecticides that can be bought or made from plants growing in your garden. This is because rapid crashes in the population of any creature will have repercussions on other species in the ecosystem. Wipe out the slugs for a few months and the hedgehogs will be in trouble. They will either have to move on to pastures new or they will go short of food and perhaps not breed successfully. Either way, when the slug population recovers there will be less hedgehogs around to keep them under control and hence all the more need to apply the nematodes in succeeding years.

Due to a rather stupid law it is actually illegal to make your own insecticide from plants that you grow, but there is nothing to stop you making up a liquid feed from these plants and if this also happens to kill a few insects then that is just an unfortunate side effect. Do be very careful with using any plant as a liquid feed that also has insecticidal properties, though, because they do tend to be pretty indiscriminate in their actions and will kill beneficial insects as well as pests. Personally I would rather tolerate the damage caused by insects and slugs than use any form of poison, whether made from plants or in the chemist's laboratory.

Making liquid feeds from plants is actually a very good way of boosting the health of plants. Virtually any plant material can be used but the best known are probably COMFREY (*Symphytum* species), see page 80, and STINGING NETTLES (*Urtica dioica*), see page 245. Lawn mowings are also good as is a mixed bag of hedgerow plants.

The easiest way of making the feed is to stuff as much plant material as you possibly can into a large container (a large dustbin is a good size), then add water until full. It is surprising how much water will go in. Leave it for at least a week (longer in cool weather) and then draw off some of the incredibly smelly dark liquid. Dilute this with water and apply it to your plants. Ratios are not that important since everybody's brew seems to differ in strength but about 10 to 1 is a good guide. Observe how the plants react to it and adjust accordingly.

Feeding the Soil

In chemical-based farming and gardening, the grower is adding substances to the soil that can be taken up directly by the plant without the soil or the organisms the soil contains having an active role in the process. The three nutrients most commonly used are nitrogen, potassium and phosphorus since these are the substances that produce the most noticeable effect on plant growth. In this method of growing, the soil is seen as little more than a medium to support the plant and very little attention is paid to maintaining its structure or bio-systems.

This can be likened to feeding a person entirely on white sugar. Whilst this is a rich source of energy, it is very unbalanced and cannot be properly utilized by the body unless other nutrients are also available. When fed on a diet like this it will not be long before the body becomes very unhealthy and prone to all sorts of diseases.

The chemically grown annuals are either out of the ground before this effect becomes too noticeable or they have to be kept looking healthy by the use of more fertilizers, insecticides, fungicides etc. It has been shown that chemically grown plants have thinner cell walls. Whilst this means that they seem more tender and succulent to our palates, they are also more tender and succulent to the palates of insect pests such as aphids and thus are more likely to be attacked.

Organic growers see things in quite a different light. The soil is a living organism which, when healthy, can provide a wide range of nutrients to the plant. The idea is to feed the soil and the creatures living in the soil and then the plant will be able to pick and choose which nutrients it needs from a very large menu. Plant growth might be slower but it is healthier and, when eaten, the plant will provide a much more nourishing food. The food that is used to feed the soil is organic matter in one form or another.

Shortage of organic matter is probably the biggest problem for the majority of organic growers (and for those people obsessed with chemical fertilisers, though they might not have realised it yet). The ground always seems so hungry for humus, especially if you are converting ground that has been cultivated inorganically for any length of time. Why is the ground so hungry? Simply because regular cultivation of the soil is the biggest single cause of humus loss. Firstly, cultivation greatly increases the amount of oxygen in the soil, this then reacts with the organic matter and rapidly breaks it down. Not only that, but cultivation will also kill many of the invertebrates and soil micro-organisms that are essential for the healthy functioning of the soil and the building-up of organic matter.

Just walk back into that mature woodland I keep mentioning. Pick up a handful of soil and what do you notice? It is incredibly rich in organic matter, in fact in some woodlands you have to dig down through quite a few centimetres of decaying leafmould before you even come to the soil layer. This is the natural tendency of a climax vegetation – there is a gradual building up of soil fertility until a peak is reached and this is then maintained. Remove the trees, cultivate the soil and within a short space of time the humus disappears. As the humus goes so the land gets harder to work. It bakes hard when it is dry and becomes sodden when it is wet.

This seems to make the answer obvious – plant more tree crops. But until we know enough about tree species that are suitable for eating, plus we also become willing to adapt our diets to include these foods, then we will continue with annual crops and the constant chase for organic matter.

The most effective way of maintaining humus-levels is to find methods of growing plants that reduce or eliminate the need for digging the soil. See below for more details of this. The next thing to do is to save all organic waste from the garden, farm and kitchen, but you will be doing exceptionally well if you can get anywhere near enough from this source. You can also chase about for organic matter from other sources such as the local greengrocer or a riding stable if you happen to have one at hand. Be very careful of any animal manures unless they come from an organic source since the chemical residues they might contain could outweigh the benefit of the manure.

If you have some mature woodland on your plot then it is possible to remove some of the leafmould each year and use it on the cultivated ground. So long as this is done in moderation, and a different area of the woodland is used each year, it is sustainable. If you are managing the woodland then you will probably also be able to shred the bark of felled trees and use this as a mulch. Another method of obtaining organic matter is to have a wildflower meadow, see Chapter 12 for more details.

One of the most abundant sources of organic matter in this country is sadly wasted. Every time we flush the toilet we are literally flushing away the fertility of our soils. Human faecal matter, when properly treated, is an excellent soil conditioner and plant food. When I was a child my next door neighbour used to work at the local sewage treatment plant. He used to bring home sack loads of treated and dried human effluent and applied this to his garden. He grew by far the best fruits and vegetables in the area in a soil that was rich, friable and easily worked. My father, on the other hand, did not believe in feeding the soil and the soil in our garden was much harder to work and less productive. It was also several centimetres lower than the neighbouring garden!

Of course, there are potential health risks in using human faeces that should not be overlooked. There has been much research in this area, however, and there are many safe and proven ways of treating our faecal matter, either on a household level or in larger communal treatment plants. See Appendix 1 for further reading.

Once you have obtained the organic matter, you then need to apply it to the soil. It is possible simply to lay it on the surface and, in time, it will break down to provide nutrients to the soil and plants. If the right sorts of material are applied in a thick layer (straw or well-rotted leaves for example) this can also serve as an effective weed-excluding mulch. There are drawbacks to this way of using the organic matter, especially if kitchen wastes are used since these might attract rats to the garden. A much more effective way of using most organic materials is to compost them. This will promote a more rapid breakdown into a usable material and will also act to conserve the valuable nutrients contained in the organic matter.

I do not want to talk about methods of making compost in this book. Every gardener seems to have their own method and if it works well for you then carry on with it. If you are not satisfied with your compost-making method, or maybe do not as yet make your own compost, then some of the books mentioned in Appendix 1 should be helpful.

There are a couple of very good methods that can be used to speed up the compost-making process. 'Quick Return' herbal compost activator is made from the flowers and sometimes the bark of a number of native species of plants. If it is added to a compost heap then it encourages bacterial activity in the heap which leads to the swifter breaking down of organic matter into compost. All the species used in making 'Quick Return' are mentioned in this book and will be found in the index of plant uses, for details of how to make it see the book titled 'Commonsense Compost Making' which is listed in Appendix 1.

Urine makes a very useful compost activator when applied neat to the heap. It can also be used as a liquid feed (diluted about 10 to 1 with water) and has proved to be an effective fungicide (diluted 3 to 1 with water). A lot of people have an objection to using this most natural of materials, yet this was not always the case. In early 1994 Radio 4 devoted an entire programme to the uses of urine, mentioning among other things how it has been used as a mordant to fix dyes, as an anti-dandruff shampoo and as a skin toner (apparently people used to bathe their faces with babies' wet nappies!).

Green Manures

Green manures are a good way of growing a bulk of organic matter. Most green manures, however, are fast-growing annual crops so some of the benefits of growing them are mitigated by the need to cultivate the soil. Also, whilst the annuals are able to conserve the nutrients in the soil, they do not usually get their roots down far enough to tap the nutrients that lie deeper in the soil. One solution is to grow deep rooted perennials that will occupy the ground for a number of years and provide a bulk of material that can be harvested on a number of occasions in the growing season.

ALFALFA, or LUCERNE (*Medicago sativa*) is a good example of this. A member of the pea and bean family, it fixes atmospheric nitrogen. It can also send its roots down 6 metres or more into the soil, tapping all those minerals that have long been out of the reach of other plants. By cutting the alfalfa two or three times a year and composting it, or using it as a mulch, you can retain these nutrients within your ecosystem. You will have to rotate the alfalfa bed every few years in order that the other parts of your land can have the same treatment.

We are intending to intercrop alfalfa with our gooseberries. The gooseberries will be well mulched around their roots to prevent too much competition for nutrients. The alfalfa will be grown between the rows and allowed to grow over the gooseberries as they are ripening their fruit. Hopefully this will serve to keep them hidden from the birds and allow us to find out what they taste like when fully ripe! In 1993, for example, our gooseberries were carrying a very good crop of fruit, yet we harvested just one fully ripe fruit from over 100 plants – the birds had the rest in a space of just a few days. Once we harvest the fruits the alfalfa will be cut down and used as a mulch around the gooseberries. It should be a fairly self-sustaining system.

By the way, the young shoots of alfalfa can be eaten and the seed is a very good source of protein. Best known as a sprouted seed perhaps, it can also be ground into a flour and mixed with wheat or other cereals to make a protein-rich bread.

COMFREY (*Symphytum* **species**) is another very good example of a perennial green manure. It also has very deep roots and the leaves can be cut several times a year to provide compost material and liquid feeds. See page 80 for more details.

Many other species can be grown for green manures and a number of them are included in this book, see the Index of Plant Uses for more details.

Cultivating the Soil

If I am ever asked for the best method of cultivating the soil, my answer is always to avoid doing so if at all possible. I have already discussed various ways in which cultivation is actually harmful to soil fertility and structure, I would also like to add a couple of additional reasons.

Whilst many people dig the soil in order to get rid of weeds, the effect can actually be the opposite. Digging the soil will bring buried weed seeds to the surface where they will quickly germinate and grow. Try an experiment – dig a small area of soil in the autumn or spring, and then leave it until mid-summer. What you will have is a veritable abundance of weed growth that really does not look very different to before you dug it.

Another myth is that digging is healthy exercise. On the contrary. If, like me, you have ever spent a day digging your garden, allotment or whatever, then I am sure you will have experienced the aches and pains of this 'healthy exercise'. Digging is actually a great strain to the back and often leads to damage.

So, what are the alternatives?

If your soil is fairly weed-free, it is possible to simply apply an annual mulch, preferably in late winter or early spring, of some organic matter such as compost. Apply this about 5cm deep all over the ground. If your soil is lacking in humus then you will find that this dressing of organic matter will rapidly be drawn into the soil in the course of the year. Apply more mulch each succeeding year, to make a total depth of mulch of about 5cm. As the fertility of the soil is built up, you will notice that less mulch material is required because more is left over from the previous dressing. This method of gardening, however, does require large initial inputs of organic matter.

Most organic gardeners, when confronted by a heavily weed-infested site, will reach immediately for the fork or spade and spend many hours laboriously digging out as many weeds as they can. Not only is this exceedingly hard work, but it is often far less than successful. Many of the weeds, such as couch grass or thistles, will soon regrow with renewed vigour if even small parts of the roots are left in the ground. There will also usually be an explosion of germination from literally millions of seeds that have been given ideal germination conditions. The newly-dug ground will very soon be covered in weeds again.

The alternative, once more, is to mulch. But this time there must be some organic barrier placed below the mulch to prevent all the weeds from growing through. We have found that cardboard boxes are an ideal barrier to use. They are usually freely

Mulching with newspaper and straw.

available in quantity from local shops etc., will form an excellent barrier for a year or so, in which time most of the persistent weeds will have died, and then will rot down nicely to add their own organic matter to the fertility of the soil. Other materials that can also be used include newspapers (but try to avoid too many with colour printing and do not use colour supplements on land where you intend to grow food) and carpets (but only those made of natural materials such as hessian – avoid foam-backed carpets).

It is very important to ensure that you apply a sufficient thickness of barrier mulch, otherwise the more vigorous weeds such as thistles and docks will push their way through it. A carpet that is not too worn is usually sufficient, cardboard boxes folded flat but not opened out are generally enough, and newspapers about 15 sheets thick are also adequate. **Make sure that the edges of boxes, paper or whatever overlap by at least 8cm, otherwise the weeds will soon find their way to the surface.**

Autumn and early winter is the ideal time to mulch weed-infested beds, though it can be done at any time of the year so long as the soil is not dry. As well as helping to retain moisture in the soil, a mulch can also prevent moisture from reaching the soil, so a mulched dry soil will remain dry until there has been sufficient rain to soak the mulch and then penetrate into the soil.

It is possible to plant into this mulched bed within three months of mulching. You simply use a trowel to make a hole into the cardboard and then plant into this hole. You may find that some weeds will start to grow out of this planting hole, but these are easily controlled by hand weeding. By using this method, it is actually possible to produce a semi-mature bed from weed-infested land by the middle of the first summer.

Garden Habitats

When planning a garden, we need to look at the types of habitat that the garden already offers and also at the potential habitats that can be created. The line of least resistance is just to accept the habitats that are already there. It is much more fun and challenging to introduce new habitats, especially if they are ones that would naturally establish themselves if given time or ones that can be easily maintained.

For example, if you have running water or a high water table, it is a relatively simple matter to put in a pond and wet area of ground. You will have no problems keeping the pond full of water. If you do not have water already in the garden, it is still possible to put in a pond. There are several methods of doing this, one of the easiest is to direct the rainfall from a building so that it flows into the pond. See Chapter 6 for more details of ponds and pond plants. Unless you want to spend all your time in the garden, it might be wise not to try and create too many artificial habitats since they will need much more work to maintain than natural habitats.

The natural habitat for most of Britain is woodland. About 97% of the country was covered in trees before people started clearing areas of ground for cultivation and grazing animals. If you leave almost any land in this country unworked for any period of time then it will start to move back towards woodland. So if you have an area of ground that was intensively cultivated for annual crops, for the first year or two there will be an abundance of annual weeds growing on the land and very little else. There will already be a few perennials about and these will rapidly increase in the second and subsequent years whilst the annuals are crowded out. Even as the perennials are establishing themselves, the first elements of the woodland will be appearing. Areas of bramble will appear, growing from seeds deposited in the excrement of birds and mammals. Wind-sown seedlings of many trees such as ash, willow and sycamore will sprout up. The land will begin to revert to scrub. As this scrub establishes itself other tree seeds will find their way to the land, these will germinate and flourish in the sheltered conditions provided by the scrub. Within 20 years the land will be starting to look like a woodland.

We can, of course, emulate and speed up this process, though we should not try to make the new system run before it can walk. Therefore we can plant out the main framework of the woodland and gradually add the other pieces of the jigsaw as appropriate. See Chapters 2 and 3 for more details of species and methods.

If you want to grow perennial plants, but either do not have the space for, or do not want to grow trees, it is still a good idea to grow plants in communities. Chapter 4 will give you some ideas on this if you want to grow ornamental plants whilst Chapter 5 will mention some of the less ornamental species.

In addition to all the annual vegetables that are likely to be found in our gardens, there are many other exciting annuals we might want to grow. Whilst these can often be intermingled with trees and perennials, this can be rather difficult if we want to grow a large quantity of any specific annual. Chapter 11 could give you some ideas here and also briefly mentions how to grow annuals without digging the soil each year.

All of these steps mean that you the grower will have less work to do and will have to pay out less money to do it (which will allow you to buy more plants!).

Once the system is up and running it will also mean higher and sustainable yields from the land with far less inputs of fertilizers etc.

Hardiness of Plants

Throughout this book, if a plant is unlikely to be hardy in all parts of Britain I have tried to give some indication of how cold-hardy it is likely to be. This is by no means an easy task because plants, gardens and gardeners are individuals. What might very well be the case for one species in one garden and with one gardener could very well be totally different even for the next door garden. There are so many factors to be taken into account.

In general terms, any figure for hardiness is based on a best case scenario and assumes that you have taken all the plant's requirements into account. For example, if a plant is said to be hardy to -10°C and also requires a well-drained soil, then it might very well be killed at a much lesser cold temperature if either the winter is excessively wet or if it is growing in a soil that is not very free-draining.

Conversely, if you select an especially appropriate site for a plant, then it might tolerate even colder conditions than the book says. Thus you might use the shelter of a tree to give just that little bit more frost protection to a plant, or perhaps grow it close to the base of a south-facing wall. It is these little skills that can make gardening so interesting.

Another point to remember is that cold winds will significantly reduce the cold-tolerance of a plant. There are many species we are unable to grow on our land in Cornwall even though the books claim they should thrive there. Because the site is so exposed the wind can have an effect of lowering the temperature by several degrees.

There is also the general climate to take into account. Britain has a maritime climate – it is a relatively small island and nowhere in the country is very far from the sea and thus the sea has a very strong influence on our weather. The sea warms up more slowly than the land, and so in the summer the sea tends to have a cooling influence on the weather. It also cools down more slowly than the land and is therefore warmer in winter. Thus the weather in winter will tend to be mild. In this way we have less extremes of temperatures.

Because Britain is at a relatively high latitude, there is always the risk of cold air plunging down from the Arctic Circle to bring freezing conditions in the winter or very cool conditions in the summer. Thus our weather is relatively unpredictable. In many parts of the world there is a very clear distinction between the seasons – winter moves to spring and thence to summer. In Britain, we might have spring-like weather in the middle of winter, then have another cold snap. Just as we think that spring is moving into summer we might have a spell of frosty nights and cold days.

This is very difficult for many plants. There are some species, for example, that will grow happily in the Arctic Circle without any damage from the cold even when temperatures drop below -40°C, but just try and grow them in Britain. They will be excited into growth by the very first spell of mild weather in the winter and then this young growth will be killed by the next spell of cold weather. Whilst the dormant plant is very cold tolerant, it does not expect our stop-start weather and has never adapted its young growth to survive in such conditions

There are many plants that will be much more cold-hardy if they have had a hot summer first. The summer heat ensures that the plant fully ripens its wood, bulbs or whatever. In a climate with cool summers, this ripening process is not completed and thus the plant is far less likely to withstand the cold. Central Europe, for example, experiences much colder winters than Britain, but it also has sunnier and hotter summers. There are many species of plants that will happily grow there but will not tolerate anything like the same degree of cold in Britain.

In the end it all comes down to the individual gardener trying to understand the plants she or he is growing, and siting them according to this understanding. A lot will still be based on trial and error, and I do not know of a single gardener who has never been overly optimistic about the chances of growing a particular species in their garden, but it is a very valuable learning process that helps us to develop our understanding of nature.

The Size of the Plants

Wherever possible, a figure for the **probable** height and spread of the plants has been given. I stress probable, because this is another area where plants refuse to be governed by the words of people who write books. There are many factors that determine whether a plant will grow to this mythical size, or be somewhat larger or smaller.

As an example, if the plant is on the edges of its climatic tolerance, it is unlikely to reach the stated size. If, on the other hand, it is in the ideal climatic zone and is very well placed by the gardener, it might very well grow considerably larger than this book suggests.

Similarly, if the plant is growing in very fertile soil it is likely to be larger than the same species growing in a poor soil. It will also probably grow smaller if it is growing in soil conditions that do not suit it. A plant growing in the shade will also have a different size to a plant growing in full sun.

Certain plants spread quite freely at the roots and the longer they grow in any position then the wider they become. If you plant one strawberry plant, for example, it will produce new runners each summer. On what do you base the figure for width? In such cases, I have tried to make it clear in the text that the plant will continue to spread almost indefinitely.

Therefore, by all means use the quoted figures as a guide, but do not treat them as gospel. Once more, try to understand the plant and its needs, then you will have more idea as to whether it will grow larger or smaller than the quoted figures.

Obtaining the Plants

Whilst many of the plants mentioned in this book can be obtained fairly easily from garden centres or nurseries, there are also many that are not readily available. Appendix 2 lists some addresses of specialist suppliers that I have dealt with in the past and have provided good service.

You could also try growing the plants from seed. This is a very satisfying and fun way of obtaining plants, it is also much cheaper than buying the plants from nurseries but it is also usually much slower. The seed of some of the plants mentioned in this book can take two years or more to germinate and then you might have to wait many years with some of the trees before you obtain the first harvest. However, we need to take a much longer view of things than we have become used to. We need to start taking future generations into account and growing trees from seed is one very good way to do this. There are several very good companies that supply seeds of unusual species and these are also listed in Appendix 2.

Experimenting With Alternative Foods

If you decide to try growing some of the plants contained in this book, then I wouldn't advise you immediately to run out into the garden, dig up everything that is already growing there and then plant it out completely with all these wonderful alternative foods. You are likely to be disappointed! It makes more sense to take things easier.

Before making any changes, look carefully around at what is already growing. If you grow lots of annual vegetables then don't give them all up at once. You have been eating foods like this all your life and your palate has become used to them. It makes more sense to introduce plants from this book a few at a time.

For example, I eat a very wide range of leaves from perennial plants in my salads. Many of these leaves are strongly flavoured and are added in small quantities, others are much milder and make a good replacement for lettuce. However a leaf that I like to eat in quantity might not be to everyone's taste. If you give up growing lettuces and then find out that you do not like the alternative salad plants that you are growing then, apart from probably feeling angry with me for depriving you of fresh salads, you are also likely to develop a negative attitude to other alternative foods. Instead, try growing a range of the lettuce substitutes whilst still growing the lettuces – compare them in taste and compare them in ease of growing. In this way you are likely to find that over a period of time you will introduce more and more of these alternative plants to your garden, both because they are easier to grow and also because they can taste at least as nice if not nicer than your annuals.

As you read this book it is quite likely that you will discover that many of the ornamental plants you are already growing are included here. Lilies and day lilies are just two examples of common garden plants that are edible; you will find many more in these pages. These are the obvious plants for you to try out first, if you like them then you can consider growing and trying some of the other plants in the book.

It is not possible to give full cultivation details for all the plants contained in this book. Most of them are quite easy to grow, though some are more difficult. General guidelines are given in each chapter and a list of further reading is provided if you do not already have the expertise in growing plants. If you would like more detailed information on any of the plants contained in this book then this can be obtained from Plants for a Future (see the address and notes in Appendix 2).

Chapter Two

TREES & SHRUBS

We hear lots of reports about the destruction of the tropical rainforests, yet few people seem to realise that huge areas of Britain were deprived of their tree cover many centuries ago. It seems difficult to imagine, but 97% of Britain used to be covered in forest!

Forest clearance began with the need for fuel coupled with the desire for grazing and arable land as humans turned from hunter/gatherers to farmers. It gradually gathered pace as the human population grew and the need for wood increased, firstly for construction, ship building etc. and later for fuelling the industrial revolution. Whilst many woodland trees can survive being cut down by resprouting from the base (a system known as coppicing), the increasing need for agricultural land made sure that in most instances the woodland was not given a chance to do this.

We are very lucky in this country that our soils are fairly stable and have stood up remarkably well to the harsh treatment we have metred out to them. There is plenty of evidence to show that this is not going to last. Over the centuries more soil has been lost due to our farming methods than the land has been able to replace. The time is coming when it will no longer tolerate the intensive farming methods now being employed. Already much of the fertility has been lost from our uplands and areas which once supported arable crops are now only considered to be suitable for low-density sheep grazing.

There are ways where we can manage the land productively and sustainably. To do so, we need to look more at the needs of the soil, rather than regarding it merely as a support for the plants whilst we feed them with various chemical concoctions. Indeed, organic farming and gardening has demonstrated quite clearly that you can build up the fertility of the soil annually whilst still obtaining good yields of food from it. The act of cultivation hastens the decomposition of organic matter in the soil. Therefore even the traditional methods of organic growing, which involve annual cultivation, still require large inputs of organic matter in order to maintain the fertility of the cultivated soil.

The problem is that most organic growers still stick to the same traditional crops, most of them annuals. This is a great shame since trees and shrubs are some of the most undervalued plants for food production. Whilst they have the potential to out-yield any annual crop, very few species are utilized by present day society in the western world. Yet trees can provide us with so many different and delicious foods as well as a whole host of other commodities, and they really are so little work – quite often all you have to do is come along at the right time of year and harvest the crop.

You don't even need a large area of land in order to grow trees and shrubs. Size can vary dramatically, with some shrubs only a centimetre or so tall whilst the tallest tree in the world is more than 110 metres tall. In an April 1994 programme of the BBC's 'Gardener's World' there was an item about a person who lived in a high-rise block of flats and was growing a number of shrubs on his balcony! It is also possible to grow small trees in pots.

Apples on dwarfing rootstocks are particularly suitable for this purpose – which brings me on to an important point. This book is looking mainly at the less well-known useful plants and so the following list does not include common tree crops such as apples, pears, plums and cob nuts. I would, however, strongly recommend that these traditional crops **are** included as a major part of any planting plan, if I only had space for one tree I would rather go for a good cultivar of apple than an unknown species that someone else was enthusing over. Mind you, I wonder which I would choose if it was a choice between an apple or *Crataegus arnoldiana*? (See the list of plants below for details of this delicious fruit.) It is easy enough to buy apples from the shops, but when did you last see North American hawthorn fruits for sale?

Trees and shrubs also have a very important role to play in the well-being of the earth. They are quite literally the lungs of the planet, helping to purify the air and locking up huge quantities of carbon in their wood, thereby reducing the 'greenhouse' effect of carbon dioxide in the atmosphere. They also protect the soil from erosion, encourage rainfall, prevent flooding and regulate the flow of groundwater throughout the year.

Many trees and shrubs yield foods, medicines, fibres, dyes and oils, and they also provide us with a valuable construction commodity – their wood. By growing different species we can produce woods with differing qualities of strength, elasticity, durability and so forth, suitable for a wide variety of uses. The wood can also be used as a fuel (preferably burnt in efficient closed stoves). The bark can be made into an effective weed-suppressing mulch, whilst the dead leaves can be turned into a marvellous soil conditioner. Trees are also the source of pitch and resins, products that have many applications such as water-proofing and preserving wood. Trees provide valuable habitats for our native wildlife and, as well as all this, they are also quite beautiful and add something very special to a garden.

When planting out trees and shrubs, many gardeners want to put in large specimens in order to give them an instant effect. In almost all instances, and especially in windy sites, this is a mistake. Not only are these trees more expensive to obtain, they are also more difficult to establish. A tree planted out when small will usually establish much more easily and grow away more rapidly. Within a few years it will have overtaken the larger tree. It will also prove to be much more wind-firm in later years.

Of course, planting out small trees does have its problems, the main one being that it is all too easy to lose the tree amongst the surrounding growth. We overcome this in two ways. Firstly, we make sure that we apply a good weed-excluding mulch in a circle about a metre wide around the tree. Many materials can be used for this, we favour old newspapers or cardboard boxes laid on the ground and covered in organic matter such as shredded bark.

The other thing we usually do is to place a plastic bottle over the young plant.

We have found that 2 litre mineral water bottles are ideal for this, we cut off the bottoms and tops of the bottles to make a tube and then push it lightly into the soil around the tree. The bottle will mark the tree and also give it just a little bit of protection from the elements.

As I have mentioned several times before, our site is very windy yet we always try not to stake our trees and never use any of the tree tubes that promote faster growth. This is because the wind serves a very important function for the young tree. The stimulus of being swayed by the wind will actually encourage the tree to develop a stronger trunk and a firmer root system – those trees that are given the support of stakes or the protection of a tube are much more likely to blow down in later years.

If a tree shows signs of excessive rock due to the wind then it will be necessary to give it the support of a stake. In this case use a stake that is no more than 50cm above soil level to ensure that the trunk still receives the stimulus of the wind. Make sure that you also fill in the soil around the roots of the tree and make it firm, otherwise it will fill with water in wet weather and cause further damage to the tree.

In general we have found that it pays to give the young tree a fairly hard time of it – not hard enough to damage it, but certainly hard enough to ensure that you are growing a tough tree that will be with you for many years to come. Such a tree will grow more slowly in its very early years but will more than catch up later.

As described in the introduction to this book, a woodland is an ecosystem where many different species of plants and animals can live together in a harmony that benefits the entire system. Since many of the plants listed below are not native species and will not therefore support as wide a range of other creatures, it is not really feasible to create as productive an ecosystem as a native woodland. Nevertheless, it is possible and desirable to arrange your plantings using the lessons that nature offers us. In this way, we will be able to design systems that are very productive in providing us with food, whilst greatly reducing our need to expend time, energy and money in maintaining the system. A well-planned system will also provide far more opportunities for our native flora and fauna to flourish than conventional agriculture or gardening can.

The following lists of species are just a small selection from a huge range of possibilities. Unless it says otherwise in the text, they will thrive in any reasonable well-drained soil and should be hardy in most parts of Britain.

If you want to try growing a plant that is not hardy in your area, you might want to consider growing it against the protection of a wall. Chapter 8 can advise you on this. Most of the species listed here are not native to Britain, see Chapter 12 for more details.

The trees and shrubs are listed below in several sections depending on their place in the woodland system – within each section they are placed in alphabetical order of their Latin name.

PIONEER SPECIES

In the winter of 1990/91 we planted out almost 15,000 native trees on a very windswept site in Cornwall. These trees in general have grown away satisfactorily, if rather slowly. By the end of 1996 they tended to average about 1.5 metres in height.

However, there were huge differences between the different species with some still less than 1 metre tall and, at the other end of the scale, others were more than 5 metres tall.

Seeing these huge differences set me thinking about the way we were attempting to restore the tree cover on this site. Talking it over with a visiting Australian who designs permaculture sites in Australia and South America, I came to understand a little more about putting permaculture ideas into practice.

In conventional gardening there are certain species of plants just sitting there waiting to invade our freshly turned soil. These plants are either aggressively self-sowing, or they have aggressive root systems, or even worse they have both attributes. We call them weeds, but these are nature's pioneers and some of her strongest survivors.

Similarly, there are various trees and shrubs that, given half a chance, will rapidly colonize even the most inhospitable of sites.

My Australian friend was taking advantage of this by deliberately introducing these species into his designs. For example, if he was taking over a barren site, he would immediately plant it out with fast-growing leguminous trees. In his part of the world, these trees could grow 6 metres or more tall within 3 years of sowing the seed! By planting them fairly densely (at about 5 metre spacing), by the end of the first growing season he would have a mini woodland already 1 metre or more tall. Then, amongst these legumes he would start to plant out those species he really wanted to grow on the site. These plants would immediately start to benefit from the protection and the nitrogen that the legumes were providing.

By the end of the third year the new plantings would be established and growing away nicely. The site would be getting rather crowded and so he would start to cut down some of the fast-growing legumes, using the wood for fuel, construction or whatever and shredding everything that was left to be used as a mulch.

This is a marvellous method of restoring land to tree cover, and it can also be used on a smaller scale to provide nourishment and protection for herbaceous plants. There are many species suitable for this in Britain, though don't expect the same rates of growth that can be achieved in warmer climates.

One added attraction of this method is that many of the trees and shrubs we can use as pioneers will be unable to maintain themselves as the woodland develops. This is because, in general, they tend to be short-lived and also sun-lovers. As the woodland develops and shade increases, their seed will be unable to germinate in the shady conditions and therefore they will not be able to reproduce themselves.

Acer pseudo-platanus. SYCAMORES are exceptionally good at invading deforested land and will make good pioneer trees in almost any soil or situation. They do not really know when enough is enough and will continue to reproduce successfully even as the woodland matures. For this reason I would not really recommend using this species. See also page 192.

Alnus species. Several species of ALDER are excellent pioneer plants. They establish rapidly, grow very quickly, add nitrogen to the soil and have a heavy leaf-fall which will enrich the soil with humus. There are three species that I would particularly recommend.

My first choice would be our native species, *A. glutinosa*. This has grown to more than 5 metres tall with us in just 6 years from seed.

Even faster is the North American RED ALDER, *A. rubra*. This has reached 6 metres in just 4 years and, even on our windy site with its salt-laden gales, it is perfectly upright.

Alders in general require a fairly moist soil, and will be even shorter-lived than normal in drier soils. The ITALIAN ALDER, *A. cordata*, is much more tolerant of drier conditions. It has reached about 5 metres in 4 years with us and now seems to be catching up with the red alder.

How I wish I had known about these species when we first moved on to our land. I would have planted them out in large quantities all over the land and by now we would have an established woodland and a sheltered site. See also page 193.

Betula pendula and **B. pubescens**. Our two native BIRCH trees are often the first trees to invade deforested land and make very good pioneer species in drier soils. Their main disadvantage is that their thin branches tend to blow about in the wind and these branches can quite literally whip nearby small trees to death. See also page 234.

Hippophae salicifolia. See Plate 13. The WILLOW-LEAVED BUCKTHORN is one of my favourite trees. I planted three of them when we first moved to Cornwall and they are now over 8 metres tall with absolutely no sign of wind damage. This is another species that enriches the soil with nitrogen, its main disadvantage is that it suckers freely and therefore needs a lot of space. It is used extensively in the Himalayas to re-afforest the mountain slopes. Its aggressive root system soon binds the soil together, preventing further erosion and creating suitable conditions for the other woodland trees to be planted. It demands a very sunny position and will soon start to die out if in the shade – in fact if allowed to develop into a thicket it will even shade out its lower branches and cause them to die. Plants can grow up to 15 metres tall and, apart from their desire for the sun, they are fairly unfussy as to soil and situation. They are not hardy in all parts of the country, however, tolerating temperatures down to about -10°C.

This species is attracting a lot of attention as a fruit crop. The fruits are quite small, about 6mm in diameter, and are difficult to pick because the tree is very spiny, but they are believed to be the most nutritious fruit that can be grown in the temperate zone. The flavour is rather like a sharp lemon, which is by no means to everyone's taste, but if you like sharp flavours then you will love this one. I have been surprised by the amount of visitors who really like eating the raw fruit – most of them would only eat small quantities at a time though there are some who eat it in quantity. I am sure that there are few people who would not like the cooked fruit, it makes excellent juice and preserves.

The fruit ripens in early autumn and will hang on the tree until mid-winter, by which time the acidity has been considerably ameliorated. The fruit is quite firm in the autumn, but by the beginning of winter it has become very soft and is then quite difficult to pick without squashing it.

Experiments have shown that regular consumption of the fruit prevents cancer and that eating large quantities can reverse the growth of tumours. The plant is extensively grown in China as a commercial fruit crop. It is usually grown as a hedge with the branches being trimmed off every other year to make harvesting the fruit easier. You need to grow one male plant for every 5 or 6 females in order to ensure maximum crops.

Lupinus arboreus. The TREE LUPIN comes from south-western North America and is a legume so it enriches the soil with nitrogen. An evergreen shrub, growing rapidly to about 1.5 metres tall and 1.2 metres wide, it flowers and sets seed freely in Britain. Usually rather short-lived in our climate, it will normally self-sow freely in a sunny position. It requires a well-drained soil and does well in dry situations. It is not hardy in the colder areas of the country, tolerating temperatures down to about − 10°C. A plant of coastal situations, it is very tolerant of maritime exposure.

Because it is a fairly small plant, this species can be used to rapidly create sheltered conditions in small gardens – it is a superb nurse crop for a bed of herbaceous perennials, for example.

Populus **species**. Several species of POPLARS are suitable for use as pioneer species in soils that do not lack moisture. They are very fast-growing trees, though they do have aggressive root systems and, especially in clay soils, are best not used near buildings. The two species I would most recommend are:

    P. alba. The WHITE POPLAR which can grow 20 metres tall with a spread of 12 metres. This is one of the few members of the genus that succeeds in maritime exposure.

    P. tremula. The ASPEN can grow 18 metres tall and 10 metres wide. This species also produces suckers freely. It does well in poor soils and has also succeeded with us in maritime exposure.

These species are discussed more fully on page 193.

Salix **species**. Many of the WILLOWS are very good pioneer species for moister soils. Like the poplars, they have aggressive root systems and are best not used near buildings. My favoured species include the following, they are all fast-growing and succeed in maritime exposure:

    S. alba. The WHITE WILLOW can grow 25 metres tall and 10 metres wide.

    S. daphnoides. The VIOLET WILLOW grows up to 10 metres tall and 8 metres wide.

    S. viminalis. The OSIER is the species most grown for basket making. It reaches a height of 6 metres with a spread of 4 metres.

    S. 'Bowles Hybrid'. Perhaps the fastest growing willow, it will form a good screen 4 metres tall within 3 years from cuttings. It will reach a final height of about 8 metres with a spread of 5 metres.

All these species are discussed in more detail on page 194.

Sambucus nigra. The fruit of the ELDERBERRY is adored by birds and so the seed is spread far and wide. Thus this plant will often be found colonising deforested land. Tolerant of almost any soil and situation, it makes an excellent nurse plant for establishing a woodland. Fairly tolerant of shade, it will continue to thrive as the woodland develops, which is by no means a bad thing since it is such a useful species. See page 183 for more details.

Ulex europaeus. GORSE can quite literally be a pain with its ferocious thorns. This evergreen native plant is a very tough creature, doing especially well near the coast, in poor or very acid soils and in dry situations. It provides excellent conditions in which to establish a woodland. Growing about 1.5 metres tall and wide, it is a member of the pea and bean family and therefore enriches the soil with nitrogen. It needs a sunny situation if it is to thrive and so will gradually die out as the woodland develops. It does not like chalky or wet soils, but is otherwise unfussy. Although a native species, it will often be badly damaged in a cold winter, though it will usually grow back all right in the spring.

Gorse does have a number of other uses, including a yellow to orange dye from the flowers and the wood, which burns very hot, is used as a fuel. It is also sometimes used as a hedge, its thorns being very effective in keeping out intruders, but it is a rather rough hedge and is perhaps best used in a rural situation.

TALL TREES

A mature woodland is made up of several layers. Working down from the top of the woodland, we start with the taller trees that form the canopy. These trees tend to be long-lived and they provide shelter from the elements for the other plants in the woodland. They also get the lion's share of the light, casting their shade on all the smaller plants below them.

The following list comprises those taller species that are suitable for forming a canopy in a woodland. However, it is not essential to grow them as part of a woodland garden. Providing you have enough room for them, they can be grown in other situations, including as single specimen trees if required. For convenience, the list is sub-divided into evergreen and deciduous species.

DECIDUOUS SPECIES

Castanea sativa. The SWEET CHESTNUT can eventually reach about 30 metres in height with a spread to match. It succeeds in maritime exposure, though it will grow slowly in such a position and is unlikely to fruit well. It grows best in a sandy soil and is an excellent companion for pine trees, helping to correct the acidity in the soil that is caused by the pine needles.

Although not a native plant, the sweet chestnut has been grown here for at least 2,000 years and has made itself very much at home. Indeed, it was only because

Castanea sativa 'Marron de Lyon'. Developing seeds of the SWEET CHESTNUT on a plant only six years old.

the rising sea-levels after the last ice age covered the land bridge between Britain and the rest of Europe that this species was prevented from coming here under its own steam (or seed to be more precise).

The seeds ripen in mid-autumn and can be eaten raw though they are somewhat astringent, especially if you do not remove all the pithy skin that is found on the surface of the seed. They are much nicer cooked, and when roasted they develop a sweet flavour and a floury texture. This is a food that can be eaten in quantity and can be used as a cereal substitute. Far easier to grow and harvest than any of the cereals, I'm just waiting for the day when our plants are mature enough to bear large crops.

There are many named varieties that have been developed for their larger seeds, a few of these are available in this country and the one most commonly grown is 'Marron de Lyon'. Whilst seedling trees might take 20 years or more to produce a crop, a grafted 'Marron de Lyon' will commence to yield within 5 years of planting it out. Chestnuts prefer a continental climate with hotter summers than we usually experience in Britain and the seed produced from trees grown in this country is usually quite a bit smaller than from trees in areas with hot summers.

The sweet chestnut is one of the very few trees that is still commercially coppiced in Britain. It responds very well to this system and produces good yields of timber approximately every ten years. This timber is very rot-resistant in the soil and so it is often used for fencing. A hair shampoo can be made from an infusion of the leaves and fruit skins.

Cornus **species**. This genus contains many interesting fruiting trees and shrubs. The nicest we have tried to date is *C. kousa*. Tolerant of most soils and conditions except chalky soils, this tree grows slowly to reach an eventual height of 10 metres and width of 6 metres.

It produces an absolutely delicious fruit about 2cm in diameter in late summer and early autumn. The texture of the fruit is somewhat like a tropical custard apple, its only drawback is the skin which is tough and slightly bitter. The easiest way to eat it is to bite out a small section of the skin and then suck the sweet pulp out.

The sub-species *C. kousa chinensis* is very similar but it grows better in Britain and also flowers and fruits more heavily here.

C. capitata. A somewhat similar plant, producing its fruit in late autumn and early winter. Most of the fruits of this species have a marked bitterness to them, though we have occasionally come across trees with sweet and delicious fruits. The texture has ben described as that of an over-ripe banana. This plant is only hardy in the mildest areas of Britain, where it usually retains its leaves all winter, and is fairly wind tolerant.

Diospyros lotus and *D. virginiana*. See Plate 9. These two trees produce some of the most delicious fruits I have ever eaten from plants growing in Britain. They are related to the PERSIMMON or SHARON FRUIT that is sometimes seen in greengrocers. Their fruits are very similar in shape but much smaller, ranging in size from a cherry to a small crab apple. The persimmon, *D. kaki*, can be grown outdoors in Britain but does not ripen its fruit very reliably. It is, perhaps worthwhile experimenting with, especially in the warmer parts of the country. Who knows, if global warming does give Britain a warmer climate, then the persimmon could become a commonly grown fruit here.

With all members of this genus, it is important that you only eat the fruit when it is absolutely ripe and squidgy soft, before that it will be astringent and have an extremely unpleasant effect on your mouth. Fully ripe, it tastes somewhat like a rich apricot jelly (my wife says that I should just call it ambrosia). Plants do require a good summer in order to ripen their fruit properly, so they grow better in the south-east of Britain. The yield is normally very good. The fruit is also nicer after a frost.

Much of the fruit will fall naturally from the tree before it is fully ripe. It is possible to leave it on the ground to continue ripening so long as the birds or other creatures don't start eating it. At the first sign of damage, however, collect it up and store it in a cool place until it is really soft, in fact almost at the point of going rotten. If you want to store the rest of the fruit, then you need to pick it as late in the season as possible but before it becomes too soft – this will normally be some time in late November. Kept in a cool place, it should slowly complete its ripening over the next couple of months. Any fruit left on the trees will still be hanging there at least until December. By this time it should be ripe, or virtually so. Harvest it to eat as required – you will not be able to pick it for storage at this stage because it will be too soft.

All members of this genus are dioecious – they produce male flowers on some plants and females on others. It is therefore necessary to grow at least one male tree for every 5- 6 females if you want fruit with seeds inside it. However, the female trees will still produce seedless fruits if they are not pollinated.

D. lotus. Sometimes called the DATE PLUM. It can grow to about 9 metres tall with a spread of 6 metres. The fruit is about 1cm in diameter and is usually borne abundantly. It ripens a few weeks earlier and more reliably than *D. virginiana*.

D. virginiana. The AMERICAN PERSIMMON can be much taller. It can reach 30 metres in height in America though is unlikely to exceed 10 metres in this country with a spread of perhaps 8 metres. This species also has larger fruit, which is up to 4cm in diameter. It usually crops very well, especially in the southeast of the country and, when fully ripe, is probably the best flavoured. Ripening later than *D. lotus*, it is not quite such a reliable crop. Named forms of this plant are available in America.

Fagus sylvatica. Our native BEECH TREE can grow up to 30 metres tall with a spread of 15 metres or more. A beech wood casts such a dense shade that very few plants will be able to grow under the canopy. Usually found wild on chalky soils, beech trees will tolerate most conditions, including windy sites, but they dislike very heavy clay soils.

The plant's edible leaves are mentioned on page 182, its other edible uses include the seed which, whilst small, can be produced in great abundance (if you can get there before the squirrels). The seed can be eaten raw or cooked. It is rich in oil and has a pleasant sweet flavour, though it is rather small and fiddly. It can also be dried and ground into a powder then used with cereals to enhance their protein value. The seed should not be eaten in large quantities, however, because it could cause stomach upsets. Good seed years usually occur once in every 3 - 4 years.

The seed contains 17 - 20% of an edible semi-drying oil. This stores well without going rancid and is said to be equal in delicacy to olive oil. It is used as a dressing for salads and also for cooking. The oil can also be used as a wood polish and lubricant. The fallen leaves have been collected and used for filling mattresses whilst the leaf buds have been harvested in the winter, dried and used as toothpicks.

Ginkgo biloba. See Plate 11. The GINKGO or MAIDENHAIR TREE has large pleasant-tasting edible seeds that are a little smaller than almonds. The tree can grow about 30 metres tall but it is much smaller in cultivation, seldom exceeding 20 metres with a spread of about 8 metres. Ginkgo belongs to a very ancient group of plants that are related to tree ferns and cycads and was believed to be long extinct in the wild until it was discovered fairly recently in China. Indeed, fossil evidence indicates that this species has been around for almost 200 million years and so it would have existed alongside the dinosaurs! It is also unique in being the only tree that has motile sperm, and that fertilization of the seed might not actually take place until after the fruit has fallen from the tree!

An easily grown plant, it seems to be resistant to most pests and diseases, probably having evolved this resistance over its long history. There are male and female trees, you need to grow both sexes if you want to obtain the seeds, but one male plant can pollinate about 5 females. When there is a male plant to fertilize the female, then yields can be very good. There are many named varieties that have been developed for their ornamental value. The sex of these varieties is usually known and so it is possible to obtain the right mix of male and females. One word of warning – the plum-like fruits that are produced on female trees have a rather obnoxious smell and when ripe in the autumn they fall to burst like little stink bombs onto the ground below – therefore choose your site with care! The beauty of these obnoxious fruits is that the squirrels seem to find them as offensive as we do and therefore do not try and eat through them to get at the seed. This species, therefore, is one of the few squirrel-proof seed crops we can grow in Britain.

The sweet-tasting seed is a good source of protein but should be cooked before use. Once cooked, it has a floury texture that is somewhat reminiscent of potatoes – this is a nut that can be eaten in quantity as a staple food. An edible oil can be extracted from the seed. Quite good yields are usually obtained in Britain if both male and female trees are grown. If you have only one tree then it is possible to obtain good crops of seed by grafting a branch (if your tree is female) or a number of branches (if your tree is male) onto your tree from a tree of the opposite sex.

Juglans regia. The WALNUT is a large, spreading tree that can reach 20 metres in height and in width. It requires a sunny, sheltered position to really thrive and succeeds in most soils. It should be well enough known for me not to talk about its edible seed in this book. However, since it is one of my favourite nuts I would like to mention some of its other uses.

The sap is tapped in spring and used to make a sugar. A wide range of dyes can be obtained from various parts of the plant. An edible oil from the seed can also be used in making soap, paints, etc. though it quickly goes rancid. The nuts can be used as a wood polish – simply crack open the shell and rub the kernel into the wood to release the oils then wipe off with a clean cloth. The husk that covers the shell is dried then ground up and used as a pigment to paint doors, window frames etc. (it probably protects the wood due to its tannin content). The crushed leaves are an insect repellent. The fresh or dried bark of the tree and the fruit rind are dried and used as a tooth cleaner. The wood is a very valuable timber and is used for furniture making, veneer etc.

Walnut trees take many years before coming into bearing, though a number of named very hardy forms from Poland are becoming available that are said to fruit within 5 - 8 years. Anyone with enough land should seriously consider planting out a number of walnuts, though there are some drawbacks to using this tree in an integrated woodland system. A substance called 'juglone' is secreted from the roots and has an inhibitory effect on the growth of many other plants. The leaves also contain a substance that can inhibit the growth of other plants, this is washed out of the leaves when it rains and falls onto the ground below. The trees also cast a dense shade which makes it more difficult for plants to grow under their canopy. When planting walnuts as part of a woodland, I would tend to plant a mixture of cultivars in groups of two or three and then space the groups quite widely with other trees between them in order to ensure that I did not end up with a monoculture of walnut trees.

All the other members of this genus have similar cultural requirements and the same antisocial behaviour to other plants. They all also produce edible seeds, though I have yet to be convinced that they will do so reliably in Britain.

We are growing *J. ailanthifolia cordiformis* (the HEARTSEED) and this produced its first few fruits for us in 1996 when only 6 years old from seed. Although somewhat smaller than the walnut, the seed has a delicious flavour and a thin, easily cracked shell. A mature tree can reach 20 metres in height with a spread of 15 metres.

It would also be worth trying the MANCHURIAN WALNUT, *J. mandschurica*. The tree is similar in size to the preceding species and is very cold-tolerant. The books say that the seed is a good size but the shell is thick and difficult to crack.

Morus nigra. The MULBERRY is a slow growing, very long lived tree eventually reaching 10 metres in height and often wider than it is tall. It makes a fine specimen tree in the lawn, and does better in the southern half of the country, preferring a light soil.

The fruit, looking somewhat like a large loganberry, ripens intermittently over a period of about four weeks towards the end of summer and, when fully ripe, is delicious though somewhat acid. It does need to be eaten immediately, however, because it is easily squashed and will then soon start to decay. This is probably the only reason that mulberries are not grown commercially. The fruit falls from the tree as soon as it is ripe so grow the plant in short grass or lay a sheet under the tree to make fruit collection easier. In cool wet summers the fruit is likely to go mouldy before it fully ripens.

The mulberry tree is said to make a very good companion for a grape vine – the vine is allowed to grow into a mature tree (don't plant it by a young tree or the mulberry will be swamped), giving two fruit crops for the space of one. There are a number of named varieties available, but I am told that 'Chelsea' comes into bearing quite early in its life.

Sorbus domestica. The SERVICE TREE is a large spreading tree reaching about 15 metres in height and width, growing best in the eastern half of the country. In the wetter west it can often suffer very badly from canker and we have been unable to grow it on our site. It has recently been discovered as a genuinely wild tree in two locations near Cardiff and so since 1994 it has become the newest addition to the list of native British species.

The fruit, which ripens from mid autumn to early winter, is up to 3cm across and can be eaten raw or cooked. It falls from the tree just before it is ripe and can either be left on the ground to continue ripening or, more safely, collected and stored in a cool, dry, mouse-free place. It is somewhat astringent unless allowed to blet (for details of this process, see *Mespilus germanica* in the section on small trees) and is then absolutely delicious. When ready for eating, the skin will have turned brown and the fruit will be very soft. The flesh will either be white, or it will have turned a light brown. A friend described the raw fruit as tasting like plum brandy, others have said that it is like sherry trifle whilst I feel it is more like a luscious tropical fruit. It can also be dried and used like prunes.

All members of this genus have potentially edible fruits that ripen in the autumn. They usually need to be bletted in order to develop their flavour and lose their astringency. The following are some of the better species:

S. aria. Our native WHITEBEAM, will grow up to 12 metres tall and 8 metres wide. It is a very tolerant tree that succeeds in heavy clays, shallow chalky soils and acid sands, as well as in very exposed positions. The fruit is up to 12mm across and is best bletted. It can also be dried, ground into a powder and then mixed with cereals such as wheat when making bread, cakes etc.

S. aucuparia. Our native ROWAN, is another tolerant tree that succeeds in very exposed positions. It grows up to 15 metres tall and 7 metres wide. The fruit, which is about the size of a blackcurrant and freely produced, is not that pleasant raw and can cause stomach upsets, though my small son eats and enjoys it. It is much nicer when cooked and it makes a reasonable preserve. The birds love the fruit, however, and if you plant a tree or two near your orchard then it can draw them away from the cultivated fruits.

There are some named forms that have been selected for larger and tastier fruits, these include 'Beissneri', 'Edulis' and 'Rossica Major'. I have only tried 'Edulis' so far, this fruit is well over twice the size of the species and much more acceptable. It is still on the acid side, but has lost that unpleasant bitterness. Children usually love this fruit raw, though adults are more reserved. It does, however, make excellent preserves.

S. devoniensis. Another native tree and is found only in the west country. It grows about 12 metres tall with a spread to match. The fruit is about 15mm in diameter, it has a mild flavour when raw and is very pleasant when bletted.

S. latifolia. Very closely related to *S. devoniensis* and has a similar tasting fruit.

S. thibetica 'John Mitchel'. This has fruits about 10 - 15mm in diameter which, when ripe, are quite pleasant to eat raw even before bletting them.

S. torminalis. The native WILD SERVICE TREE. It grows up to 20 metres tall and prefers clay or limestone soils. Its fruit is about 15mm in diameter.

Tilia cordata. Our native SMALL-LEAVED LIME can grow up to 30 metres tall with a spread of perhaps 12 metres. It is fairly tolerant of soils and conditions though it grows poorly in very wet or dry soils.

This plant produces the nicest edible leaves I have eaten from a tree. Mild tasting and somewhat mucilaginous, if eaten whilst young they make an excellent salad. Lime trees often produce a mass of young shoots at the base of the trunk and, especially if these shoots are cut down every other year, they can provide fresh young leaves from April until as late as September. This really has to be the easiest way of growing salads. The flowers, which are a magnet for bees, have a delicious smell and make a very nice herbal tea. I have read that a chocolate substitute can be made by grinding the flowers and immature fruit together, this has to be consumed straight away, though, because it is apt to decompose.

One of the best ways of growing this tree is to coppice it at intervals of about every ten years. This ensures that trees produce their young leaves for as long a season as possible and also provide the following commodities: a fibre from the inner bark that is used to make mats, shoes, baskets, ropes, and which is also suitable for making cloth and paper; a soft, white easily carved wood that is very suitable for carving domestic items and small non-durable items; a good quality charcoal that is used by artists.

T. platyphyllos and *T. x vulgaris.* Our other native limes, they have similar uses and usually produce young basal shoots more freely than *T. cordata.* The young leaves of all other members of this genus are also edible, though not always so nicely flavoured.

A few words of warning about this genus and especially *T. x vulgaris.* Whilst the flowers are very attractive to bees (and make a very good honey) there are occasional reports of toxicity to bees. This is because the sugar produced in the nectar cannot be digested by the bees and they literally starve to death with a full stomach. Bumble bees are much more likely to suffer. *T. x vulgaris* is said to be more prone to this than the other species mentioned here. Some species, especially *T. x vulgaris,* are often heavily infested with aphids. These aphids secrete honeydew which falls onto whatever is below the trees and can cause unsightly marks and sooty mould fungus.

Toona sinensis. The CHINESE CEDAR is a fast-growing ornamental tree that can reach 20 metres in height with a spread of about 8 metres, though it is usually smaller. Easily grown in most soils, it does well on chalk. It is said to be resistant to most pests and diseases.

This species is cultivated in China for its edible leaves and young shoots which are rich in vitamin A. These are usually boiled and are said to resemble onions in flavour. A highly esteemed food in China, where it is often sold in local markets.

EVERGREEN SPECIES

Araucaria araucana. The MONKEY PUZZLE TREE is quite slow-growing but can in time reach up to 30 metres in height with a spread of about 15 metres. It prefers a deep well-drained soil and is very tolerant of maritime exposure. It prefers growing in the milder, wetter western half of the country but good specimens can also be found in the east. Some people do not like the appearance of the tree but, with its fairly open canopy that does not cast too much shade, it makes a good top storey for a woodland or forest garden.

The monkey puzzle produces an almond-sized seed that can be eaten raw or cooked. This has a pleasant mild flavour and soft texture that is somewhat like a cross between a brazil nut and a sweet chestnut. It is a good source of fats and protein. The tree forms quite large stands in some areas of Chile and the seed is used as a staple food in these areas. Research in the 19th century showed that the monkey puzzle is a reliable cropper in Britain, at least in the west of the country, with the potential to out-yield our native hazel nut.

The seed is produced in a cone about the size of a person's head and each cone can contain up to 200 seeds. Some reports say that the cone breaks up on the tree whilst others say that the cone falls intact to the ground before ejecting its seed.

Araucaria araucana. Pictured here is a six year old MONKEY PUZZLE TREE with a mature cone shown at its base. In thirty years time this tree could be producing heavy crops of large nuts as shown in the inset above.

Either way (and both seem to be true at times) the seed can be picked up from under the tree quite easily. We have heard reports of people shovelling them up and putting them in the dustbin in some gardens, or of another garden where the owners hoe out the unwanted self-sown seedlings!

There are a number of problems connected with growing this tree. Firstly, there are male and female forms. At least one male is required to fertilize 5 females and the sex of a tree cannot be known until it flowers. To make matters worse, this can take 30 - 40 years from seed though the tree can then go on yielding for another hundred years or more. It is possible to take cuttings from trees of known sexes, so there is the potential of selecting superior fruiting cultivars. You need to take cuttings of epicormic side shoots – these are the young shoots that can sometimes be seen growing out of the main trunk of older trees. (It took three botanical dictionaries before I could find out what epicormic meant!) If you should notice such shoots growing on mature fruiting trees and do not want to propagate them yourself, then you could always send them to me with details of the tree. Indeed, I would be very grateful for any details you might have of monkey puzzles fruiting in this country.

One other quite surprising thing about this tree is that squirrels move through it with equanimity and are only too willing to eat the seeds before you get a chance to do so. If you have ever grasped a leafy branch of this tree then you will know just what a prickly character it is. Squirrels obviously have very tough feet!

Whilst this is not a tree to plant if you want immediate returns, it is an excellent food and has the potential to be a staple crop in this country. I am in my mid forties but have planted 15 on our land and it is a tree that I would strongly recommend to anyone who has the space for it.

Pinus **species**. PINE trees are in general very easy trees to grow. They should be planted out into their permanent positions as soon as possible because they have weak root systems and will not be very wind firm if planted out as larger specimens. We actually plant ours out when only a few centimetres tall, making sure that they are well mulched and protected – they usually thrive on this treatment. Pines prefer lighter soils, usually growing well on poor acid sands and tolerating drought and exposure. They do not usually like alkaline conditions. They can be fairly antisocial trees – a substance washed out from the leaves by rain can inhibit the germination of seeds in the ground beneath the tree.

All the species produce edible seeds, though these are often too small to be worthwhile. The seed is rich in oil and usually has a slightly resinous flavour. It has a soft texture and can be eaten raw or cooked. It is sold in health food shops in Britain and is seen as a great delicacy.

There are a number of species that produce quite good-sized seeds though there are also some potential problems with growing them in this country. Firstly, it is difficult to obtain details of their ability to set seed reliably here. I certainly have never seen heavy crops on any trees though this could be because very often single specimens of a species are grown. Pines are strongly out-breeding and, although they can hybridize with other species, it is quite possible that they might not be pollinated properly unless another tree of the same species is growing nearby. The next problem is that those species of pine with large seeds tend to be slow-growing and also to take 20 or more years to come into bearing. Therefore it is very difficult for me to recommend any species. However, if you have the space to spare, and the patience to wait, you could try the following:

P. albicaulis. The WHITE-BARK PINE can eventually reach 20 metres in height with a spread of perhaps 10 metres. The tree produces small numbers of cones every year in the wild and does not have years of higher crops. The cones fall from the tree with their seeds intact. This species cones regularly at Kew Gardens and in the colder and higher areas of Britain but does not do well in milder areas. The seeds are sweet and about 9 x 7mm.

P. armandii. The CHINESE WHITE PINE can reach 15 metres tall with a spread of 8 metres. It generally grows well in Britain, the best specimens being found in Sussex and Ireland. Its seed is esteemed as a great delicacy in China and is about 13 x 11mm.

P. cembra. The SWISS STONE PINE is a narrow tree up to 15 metres tall and 6 metres wide. It grows best in the cooler and wetter parts of Britain, it cones less well and appears to live less long in the south. The cones take 3 years to ripen and then fall to the ground with the seed still inside – which makes harvesting easier if the squirrels don't eat it first. The seed is about 10 x 8mm. The sub-species *P. cembra sibirica* is very similar but has a more northerly range and so would probably be best in Scotland.

P. cembroides. The MEXICAN PINE NUT is the smallest pine in this list, reaching a height of 8 metres with a spread of 5 metres. It is also less hardy, suffering damage at temperatures around -10°C. It grows well in hot dry positions and so is probably best in the south-east of the country. This is a major food plant in North America, the seeds are about 15mm long and have an excellent flavour. The cones open and shed their seeds whilst still attached to the tree.

The sub-species *P. cembroides orizabensis* is very similar but has larger seeds up to 20mm long.

P. edulis has seeds up to 25mm long. *P. monophylla* (20mm long) and *P. quadrifolia* (16mm long) are closely related species needing the same conditions.

P. coulteri. See Plate 12. The BIG-CONE PINE grows up to 18 metres tall and 7 metres wide. It is not hardy in the colder areas of the country, tolerating temperatures down to between -5 and -10°C. A specimen at Kew Gardens is about 40 years old and thriving. It has produced several cones on a number of occasions in the past few years.

The fresh cones can weigh 2.2 kilos and when dried in a warm room for a year or so still weigh 1/2 kilo. The cones can hang on the tree for a number of years before shedding their seed – they open and shed their seed whilst still attached to the tree. The seed is up to 15 x 8mm and used to be a staple food of the local Indian tribes.

P. koraiensis. The KOREAN NUT PINE can reach 20 metres in height,

I have no figures for how wide it can be. It prefers a cool moist climate and grows better in the west and north of the country. It does not do well in the south-east. Trees in Cornwall have produced cones when only 3.5 metres tall. The cones fall from the tree with their seeds intact. The seed, which is about 16mm x 12mm, is a major export crop in North China.

P. pinea. The ITALIAN STONE PINE can eventually reach 10 metres tall and wide. It grows best in southern England, though it can succeed as far north as south-east Scotland. It is one of the few species that does well on chalk. The cones take 3 years to ripen and can then hang on the tree for several years before falling with their seeds intact. The seed is 20 x 10mm.

This species can produce its first cones in just 10 years from seed, which is a very short time for a pine. Our trees produced one solitary female cone when 6 years old in 1995, but this was not fertilized. In 1996 they produced an abundance of male cones, but no females. Lets hope they get it right soon and produce males and females in the same year.

There is a cultivar called 'Fragilis' which has a thinner shell and this is the form that is usually grown for its seeds, but I do not know of a source in this country.

All species of pines are the source of many other products including a vanillin flavouring, dyes, turpentine and resins. Those plants mentioned above are fairly poor sources of resin and turpentine and I will not be dealing with the species that are utilized commercially for these substances in this book.

There is still much to be understood about the potential of this genus as a food crop in Britain. I would appreciate any information people might have on any large-seeded pine tree that is yielding well in Britain.

Quercus ilex. The HOLM OAK grows well in most parts of Britain. A slow-growing, large spreading evergreen tree, it can eventually reach a height of 25 metres with a spread of 20 metres. It can also be trimmed and used as a hedge though it is unlikely to produce many of its edible seeds when grown this way. Very resistant to maritime exposure, it is often used to provide shelter in the windy gardens of western Britain.

The seed, similar to but smaller than our native oak, is rich in carbohydrates. Trees are slow-growing and take many years to come into bearing, but then usually fruit abundantly and regularly. The quality of the seed varies from tree to tree, the best are free of any bitterness and can be eaten raw or cooked. When baked they develop a soft, floury texture and a sweet flavour that is rather like sweet chestnuts.

The sub-species *Q. ilex ballota* used to be cultivated as a food crop in Spain and Portugal, it is said to fruit less well in this country though I have seen good crops on a number of occasions.

The best way to obtain trees with good quality seeds is to eat seeds from the different trees until you find some that are sweet, then sow seeds from them. Make sure you obtain permission from the owners of the trees.

Many other species of oak also produce a relatively sweet edible seed, but I do not know of any that will do so reliably in Britain, most of them demanding much hotter summers than we usually experience here. If you want to try other species then you would be best advised to try those that come from Mediterranean-type climates since these in general seem to do better here. The eastern half of the country, and particularly the south-east, is where they are most likely to succeed.

SMALLER TREES

Beneath the canopy of tall trees, the second layer in a woodland is usually comprised of the smaller trees. Many of these will thrive in the shade and shelter provided by the canopy, but many others, whilst enjoying the protection of the canopy, are less happy with the shade. This second group, which includes some of the nicest woodland fruits, will usually be found growing towards the edges of the woodland, and most often along the sunnier edges. Thus, if you have the space and want to grow a forest or woodland garden, then it is a good idea to try and design it with as much edge as possible. The simplest way of doing this is to have a number of paths or rides running through the woodland – not only will this give you more edges, these paths will help to encourage plenty of wildlife into the woodland.

I mentioned the traditional tree crops of apples, pears etc. earlier in this chapter. If you are growing a forest garden with tall trees then it is in the sunnier but sheltered edges that your fruit trees will thrive. If your land is not large enough to allow you to grow the larger trees, then consider using these fruits as the canopy of a smaller forest garden.

There is no necessity to grow any of the trees in the following lists in woodland conditions. They are, in general, quite suitable for smaller gardens and can often be grown as specimen trees. If you want to develop a forest garden, but do not have enough space for the taller trees, then you can use the sun-lovers from this list as your canopy trees.

This list is again divided into evergreen and deciduous species. I had also considered further sub-dividing it into those species that want shade and those that want the sun, but there was so much over lap that I decided to stick with just two lists. Unless it says otherwise, all the plants listed below will do better in a sunny position.

DECIDUOUS SPECIES

Amelanchier **species**. JUNEBERRIES produce an abundance of blackcurrant-size juicy fruits in July (which is why we call them Juneberries!). If you can get there before the birds then you will find that the fruits have a pleasant apple-like flavour and can be eaten raw in quantity. This genus produces some of my favourite mid-summer fruits.

The main problem with juneberries is that birds like the fruits so much they will often eat them under-ripe and will not leave many for you to try. This can be turned to advantage because if you plant some near your soft fruit then the birds will leave the soft fruit alone whilst the juneberries are available. Alternatively, if you scatter individual plants along the sunnier edges of the woodland then the birds will have more difficulty in finding them all and you should at least be able to share this crop with them. The plants produce a mass of white blossom in early to mid spring before they come into leaf and they are exceedingly beautiful at this time.

All members of this genus produce edible fruits, though some are not very desirable, and the species range in size from small shrubs to tall trees. The following all have very nice fruits:

A. canadensis. A suckering tree growing about 6 metres tall and forming a gradually spreading thicket. It grows so well in Britain that it has become naturalized here. The fruit is usually sweet and juicy, though occasional plants have a distinct bitterness. This is due to the presence of prussic acid (the substance that gives bitter almonds their flavour) and if well cooked in puddings, tarts etc. the fruit will impart an almond flavour. See Appendix 4 for more information.

The cultivar 'Prince William' is a large multi-stemmed shrub that will only grow to 3 metres tall and 2 metres across. It crops heavily and its good quality fruit is about 12mm in diameter.

A. laevis. A somewhat taller tree, capable of reaching 9 metres in height with a spread of 6 metres. It also produces suckers. This is a very tasty fruit, it is said to be up to 18mm in diameter, though I have never seen it this large.

Asimina triloba. The PAPAW (often wrongly spelt pawpaw) is a small tree growing up to 4.5 metres tall with a spread to match.

This exquisite fruit from North America is closely related to the tropical 'custard apples' and there are some named varieties in America where it is being cultivated commercially on a small scale. The fruit is fairly large, about 16cm long. Although the tree should be hardy in most parts of Britain, and it grows well in light woodland shade, unfortunately our summers are usually not hot enough for it to produce fruit. It could be worthwhile trying it in a very sunny sheltered position, perhaps with the reflected heat of a south-facing wall behind it. A few words of caution though. Firstly, there are a number of basic forms of this tree, only those that produce fruits with orange skins will reliably produce good quality fruits. The large seed should not be eaten because it is poisonous and the fruit has been known to cause dermatitis in some people.

Broussonetia papyrifera. See Plate 2. The PAPER MULBERRY is a very adaptable tree, its natural range extending from the tropical South Sea Islands to northern China in the temperate zone. A mature specimen can be more than 10 metres tall and one specimen at Cambridge Botanic Gardens has a spread of 16 metres. However, it is very unlikely to achieve these dimensions and is generally best grown as a specimen tree or on the sunny edges of a woodland. It does well in southern Britain, though it is unlikely to be hardy in the colder parts of the country. A drought resistant plant, it also tolerates poor soils.

The paper mulberry is often cultivated for its bark in Asia where it is coppiced on a rotation of 1 - 5 years depending on the climate. This bark is used as a source of fibre for making paper, cloth, rope etc. The fibre can be extracted from the bark, but the traditional method of using it is by beating strips of bark on a flat surface with a wooden mallet. A very fine cloth can be made in this way, the more the bark is beaten the finer the cloth becomes. Larger sizes can be made by overlapping 2 pieces of bark and beating them together. A leather look-alike can also be made from the bark, though it does not have the same strength and flexibility as leather.

When male and female plants are grown, the females often produce a very unusual looking fruit. A number of insignificant flowers are produced in a green ball about 3cm in diameter – when fertilized a tiny fruit with a very pleasant sweet-tasting pulp grows out of each flower. The overall effect reminds me of a ball with lots of orange tongues sticking out of it. My wife, who is a botanist and therefore much more technical in her descriptions, says that it looks like a fig inside out. I adore eating this fruit, but it would probably take me a week to eat one meal's worth!

Cercis siliquastrum. The JUDAS TREE grows up to 10 metres tall and almost as wide. It requires a very warm sunny position in a well-drained soil if it is to grow and flower well. A member of the pea and bean family, it produces nitrogen nodules on its roots and grows well in poor soils. It is not hardy in the colder parts of the country, indeed the leaves will be killed off by the first real frosts of the autumn. The young growth in the spring can also be damaged by frost, so try and site the plant where it will be sheltered from the early morning sun as it is quick defrosting that kills plant cells.

The flowers, which open in April and May, have a sweetish-acid taste and make a nice ornamental and tasty addition to the salad bowl. The plant is unusual in producing its flowers along the main trunk and the branches before it comes into leaf in spring, it looks extremely pretty at this time.

Crataegus **species**. This genus of shrubs and small trees includes our native HAWTHORNS (see Chapter 12 on conservation gardening for more details). All members of the genus have edible fruits but, whilst the fruit of the native hawthorn is edible, it is far from being appetizing. There are, however, several species that produce absolutely delicious fruits in the autumn and I would highly recommend them as a fruit crop. The plants are very easy to grow, they tolerate most soils and situations including windy sites, drought and occasional water logging. They are highly ornamental when flowering in the spring and also when in fruit. Most *Crataegus* species can be grown as small specimen trees, though they generally have a tendency to form multi-stems. This genus is a very good example of where the distinction between trees and shrubs becomes very blurred.

Hawthorns are a perfect example of permaculture. All you have to do is plant the trees and make sure that you have given them a good weed-excluding mulch. You then go away for 2 - 3 years (if your plants are grafted) or 5 - 7 years (if they are seedlings) and then come along every autumn to eat and enjoy the fruits. It really is as simple as that. They make very good specimen trees and do very well on the sunnier edges of a woodland. They will also succeed in more shady positions, but will not fruit very well there.

Many of the species, including all those listed below, fruit abundantly in Britain. Their fruits can be up to the size of a large cherry and they usually have a group of five seeds in the centre. These seeds often stick together and so the effect is of eating a fruit with one large seed. The fruit also tends to fall to the ground when fully ripe and then needs to be eaten within a week. If picked from the tree and stored with care it will remain in good condition for up to a month.

This is a genus that is just crying out for development and has a huge potential as a commercial crop. The following is just a small selection of my favourites and there are many others that are worthy of inclusion on this list. Unless the description says otherwise, the fruit is sweet and juicy with a mealy texture that often has a hint of apple in its flavour and is about 15mm in diameter.

C. arnoldiana. Growing up to 6 metres tall and about 4 metres wide. The fruit ripens in September in southern Britain. This is one of the nicest fruits that I have eaten from plants that can be grown outdoors in Britain (a view echoed by all the people who accompanied me on a fruit-tasting trip in 1993). It certainly makes the cultivated strawberries seem boring! The sweet and juicy fruit is up to 20mm in diameter.

C. azarolus. The AZEROLE, which can grow about 10 metres tall and 6 metres wide, is sometimes cultivated for its fruit in the Mediterranean. It is rather variable in fruit but the best forms are up to 25mm in diameter. It usually ripens in October.

C. durobrivensis. More often a multi-stemmed shrub about 5 metres tall and wide. It ripens in September.

C. ellwangeriana. Another species with a strong tendency to becoming a multi-stemmed shrub up to 6 metres tall and wide. Very heavy yielding, the fruit ripens in September and usually falls to the ground just before it is fully ripe, so is easy to harvest.

C. missouriensis grows about 5 metres tall with a spread of 4 metres. Ripening in late September, the fruits can be up to 25mm in diameter. This is one of the very best fruits in the genus.

C. opaca. The MAYHAW can reach 9 metres tall with a spread of 6 metres or more. This species is being cultivated for its fruit on a small scale in North America and the fruit is also often harvested from wild trees there. The fruit is about 20mm in diameter and is usually cooked in pies, preserves etc., though it is very acceptable raw.

C. pedicellata. Eventually reaching about 6 metres tall and wide, this is one of the last hawthorns to ripen its fruit. We have picked them in mid-October and they have stored until late November. The best forms have fruits 20mm or more in diameter and they are very well-flavoured.

C. pensylvanica. See Plate 6. Sometimes reaching 9 metres in height, though is normally much smaller with a spread of perhaps 6 metres. I do not know how many favourites I am allowed to have in this genus, but this is another of them. Whilst most hawthorn fruits have a slight bitterness if they are not fully ripe, this species is deliciously sweet a good 2 weeks before it fully ripens, which means that it has a considerably longer period of usage. It is also one of the largest fruits in the genus and can be up to 3cm in diameter.

C. schraderiana. See Plate 7. Growing about 6 metres tall with a spread of perhaps 5 metres. This is probably my most favourite hawthorn fruit and it is certainly the one my wife likes best. It ripens towards the end of September and will hang on the tree for at least another 4 weeks. The best specimens will have fruits 20mm or more in diameter, the flesh is much softer and juicier than any of the other species that I have tried. An incredible taste sensation, this is a fruit that you can eat an entire meal of and still want more!

C. tanacetifolia. Growing up to 10 metres tall and nearly as wide. It has a yellow fruit with a much firmer flesh than the other species mentioned here and it is decidedly apple-like in its flavour. A very pleasant taste, it ripens in early October and is up to 25mm in diameter.

A number of *Crataegus* species are suitable for hedging, see page 181 for more details.

Cydonia oblonga. The QUINCE is sometimes cultivated for its edible fruit, especially in the Mediterranean region, though it has never been very common in Britain. A relatively small tree, growing up to 6 metres tall and wide, it needs a sunny position if it is to fruit well. Although fully hardy in Britain, it seldom ripens its fruit in the north of the country unless it is grown against a sunny wall.

This fruit is occasionally eaten raw, but it is very harsh and astringent unless the summer has been exceptionally good. The cooked fruit is strongly aromatic and adds a delicious flavour when used with apples to make pies etc. It can also be used on its own to make a very nice jelly or jam. The fruit is rich in pectin, which makes it useful for adding to other fruits when making jams – pectin has also been shown to protect the body from radiation. There is a report that a drink can be made by adding the dried crushed seed to water, simmering for 5 minutes and sweetening to taste, but some care should be exercised since the seed contains prussic acid and is mildly poisonous (see Appendix 4 for more details).

There are several named varieties of quince, 'Vranja' and 'Meech's Prolific' are the two most often offered and both are good. 'Maliformis' is said to ripen well even in cooler summers, but as far as I know this is not available in Britain at present.

Hovenia dulcis. The JAPANESE RAISIN TREE is one of those plants that should grow well in this country, though I have yet to see a good specimen. This tree grows about 9 metres tall and 6 metres wide in the wild and the books say that it is hardy to about -15°C in Britain, but that it really requires a continental climate with the extra summer heat that ripens wood so much better than our cool damp maritime summers. When well ripened the wood is said to be hardy to about -25°C. Most of the plants that I have observed have been of very poor quality, they suffer considerable die-back each winter and usually die after a few years. If anyone is successfully growing this tree and, even more important, has obtained its edible 'fruit' (more about that in a minute) then please let me know. If you want to grow it, then give the plant as sunny a position as possible, shelter from cold winds and a fertile well-drained sandy loam.

The Japanese cultivate this plant for its edible fruit which can be eaten raw or cooked. It is up to 3cm long, rather dry but sweet and fragrant with a pear-like flavour. The fruit is often dried when it is said to have the sweet flavour and texture of raisins and can be used similarly. Time to be technical now. For the botanists, this is not a true fruit but a swollen receptacle. Mind you, if you want to be pedantic about it, the part of the apple that we eat is also not a fruit but a swollen receptacle. The part of the apple that is botanically the fruit is the central core that most people throw away. However, since you eat swollen receptacles like fruits and they taste like fruits I will continue to call them fruits. A sweet extract of the seed, boughs and young leaves of the plant is used as a substitute for honey.

Malus species. All members of this genus, which includes the cultivated APPLE, produce edible fruits, though these can often be less than desirable. Personally, I am happy to stick with the cultivated apples most of the time, but one other species that I do rather like is *M. mandschurica*. I have seen a tree with this name in a number of arboreta and believe that it should more correctly be called *M. baccata mandschurica*. The tree is up to 7 metres tall and wide, its fruit is about crab apple size and when fully ripe it has a very pleasant taste somewhat like stewed apples. Cooked apples without the cooking!

Mespilus germanica. Plate 14. Sometimes it is hard to draw the line between what is a well-known food crop and what isn't. The MEDLAR falls into this twilight zone. This tree grows up to 8 metres tall, though it is usually much lower and it is also wider than it is tall. It has often been cultivated over the centuries for its edible fruit, though it has never quite made it to prominence. This is a pity because when properly prepared the fruit is exquisite. The trick is to harvest the fruit as late in the autumn as possible, preferably after a frost or two, and then blet it. This involves storing the fruit in a cool dry place until it is almost but not quite going rotten, a state that has been called 'incipient decay'. At this stage the flesh will have become very soft and turned brown in colour. It has a delicious taste, somewhat like a luscious tropical fruit. Don't overdo the bletting though, or the fruit will ferment inside your stomach. There are several named varieties of medlar, with larger fruits, that are often available from nurseries and garden centres.

Sassafras albidum. SASSAFRAS can grow up to 25 metres tall with a spread of 10 metres, though all the trees I've seen in this country have been much smaller. It produces suckers and can form thickets if allowed. Somewhat tender when young, the trees become fairly hardy in most parts of Britain as they get older. The young shoots even of older plants are susceptible to damage by frost in the spring. The best place to grow the tree is probably on the sheltered edge your garden, preferably with a west or southerly aspect.

The plant has a very wide range of uses. The leaves can be added to salads or used as a flavouring and as a thickening agent in soups etc. We use them like bay leaves and find they add a very nice flavour to the food. The leaves are often dried and ground into powder for later use. The dried root bark can be boiled with sugar and water until it forms a thick paste and is then used as a condiment. The root and the berries can be used as flavourings. A tea that is made from the root bark is very refreshing and is considered to be a good tonic, a tea can also be made by brewing the root in maple syrup and this can be concentrated into a jelly. An essential oil is obtained from the bark of the root, this is medicinal and is also used in soaps, perfumery, toothpaste, soft drinks etc. and as an antiseptic in dentistry. A yellow dye is obtained from the wood and the bark. The growing plant is said to repel mosquitoes and other insects. A very useful tree, it is occasionally cultivated for its many uses and is often harvested commercially from wild trees.

EVERGREEN SPECIES

Arbutus unedo. Whilst the STRAWBERRY TREE can grow up to 8 metres tall and wide, it is usually somewhat smaller and there are several smaller growing cultivars. The plant is tolerant of a wide range of soils and will also tolerate maritime exposure, though it does not like cold, drying winds.

The edible fruits are produced in late autumn and, since it has taken 12 months to mature these fruits, the plant is also flowering at the same time. This makes it look particularly beautiful. The Latin name '*unedo*' means 'I eat one' and is meant to refer to the fruits, implying that one is enough for anyone. This is rather an injustice to the fruit for, whilst not highly flavoured, it does have a nice, subtle sweet taste and the texture is lush and rather like that of a tropical fruit. The fruit falls from the tree when it is fully ripe and is best harvested daily and used the same day. I eat it in quantity when it is available. 'Elfin King' and 'Rubra' are particularly good varieties that make quite small plants 2 - 3 metres tall. I have seen a specimen of 'Rubra' that was only 1.2 metres tall but was laden down with fruit and flowers.

Gevuina avellana. The CHILEAN HAZEL NUT can grow up to 10 metres tall and wide, though it is usually much smaller in this country. It tolerates temperatures down to about -10°C and so only succeeds outdoors in the mildest areas of the country. It will not succeed in alkaline soils and grows best in the light shade of a woodland.

I have not eaten the seed yet, but it is said to taste like a hazel nut. The plants produce their fruit regularly in the gardens at Coleton Fishacre in south Devon, though I have never seen fruits in other gardens.

Laurus nobilis. BAY is a shrub or small tree growing up to 12 metres tall and 10 metres wide, though it seldom achieves this size in Britain. It is only reliably hardy in the milder areas of Britain, but is very amenable to pot culture and so can be kept in a sheltered position over the winter if necessary and be moved into the garden during the warmer months. It also grows surprisingly well in moderate shade, and so can be grown outdoors under the protection of a woodland canopy in areas that are often considered too cold for it. The plant is highly resistant to pests and diseases and is said to protect neighbouring plants from insect and health problems. There are suggestions, however, that it can also inhibit the germination of seeds and growth of nearby young plants. It tolerates clipping well so is often grown as an ornamental plant and as a hedge in the Mediterranean.

The leaves are well known as a flavouring in cooking but the tree also produces an essential oil from the fruit that is used in soap making, its highly aromatic leaves can be used as an insect repellent and the dried leaves are used to protect stored grain, beans etc. from weevils.

Taxus baccata. See Plate 16. YEW is a native evergreen tree that can grow up to 15 metres tall, but there are many named varieties available that are much smaller. This tree, though slow growing, is remarkably tolerant of clipping and makes a superb hedge, succeeding in most soils and situations from full sun to deep shade. The yew is also an exceedingly long-lived tree, it is believed to be second only to *Pinus longaeva* in longevity. There are specimens thought to be over 4,000 years old, whilst it is possible to grow and trim it as a hedge for at least a thousand years. This is most certainly a tree to plant for future generations.

All parts of this plant, except the fully-ripe fruit, are highly poisonous, but this fruit is completely toxin free, it is sweet and very tasty. The texture is somewhat gelatinous, however, which does put a number of people off. Should you accidentally swallow the seed whilst eating the flesh there is no cause for concern because it will pass quite safely through you without being digested and, indeed, will germinate all the better for its experience. Don't chew the bitter-tasting seed though, as this would release the toxins.

Those of you who bothered to read about the swollen receptacles of *Hovenia dulcis* (see earlier in this chapter) might like to know that the correct botanical term for this fruit is an aril, since strictly speaking conifers do not bear fruit.

The fruit is about the size of a small blackcurrant and we eat it in quantity whenever we come across a fruiting tree. I remember one particular instance when a friend and I were making a meal of the fruit from a tree in a park. We had been eating for 10 - 15 minutes and had noticed that a man was watching us and obviously talking to other people about what we were doing. Eventually he could stand it no more and came over to let us know we were poisoning ourselves. I think his warning would have come a bit too late if the fruit really had been poisonous! I tried to convince him to give the fruit a try but he wasn't interested – he'll never know what a treat he is missing.

Yew also has a number of other uses, its wood is very durable and elastic, highly esteemed by cabinet makers it is also used for bows, tool handles etc. The wood is very aromatic and has been burnt as an incense whilst a decoction of the leaves has been used as an insecticide. There is a lot of excitement about a substance found in yew trees that has potential as a treatment for cancer. One company is offering to buy the clippings from yew hedges – all you do is let them know when you will be trimming the hedge and they will arrange collection.

The yew tree is dioecious (male and female flowers are produced on different trees) so you will need at least one male with up to five female plants growing near each other to ensure fruiting. Some of the nicest tasting cultivars I have tried include: 'Dovastoniana' which has larger fruits than average and eventually makes a large tree; 'Fastigiata' is a tall, narrow columnar form that makes an excellent specimen plant;

'Fructu-luteo' is a wide-spreading bushy form with very nicely flavoured yellow fruit; 'Repandens' forms an excellent ground cover up to 1 metre tall and eventually about 4 metres wide. All other species in this genus have similar-tasting edible fruits, though once again their leaves, seeds etc. are poisonous.

Torreya nucifera. A slow-growing tree, it can eventually reach 20 metres in height and 10 metres wide, though it is unlikely to achieve this in Britain. It grows very well in southern Britain, though it is probably not hardy in the colder areas of the country. It prefers an acid soil but will tolerate some lime and grows best in light woodland shade.

The almond-sized seed can be eaten raw or cooked, it has an agreeable sweet slightly resinous flavour and is cultivated as a staple crop in Japan where there are some named varieties. An edible oil is obtained from the seed. The seed seems to be fairly free from the ravages of squirrels, I believe this is because they do not like biting through the resinous flesh that surrounds the seed. Certainly, the squirrels at Kew Gardens, who generally eat every edible seed going some time before it is fully ripe, rarely try to eat this seed. I am not certain how reliable a cropper this tree is in Britain but have seen some excellent crops produced on several occasions in the past few years at Kew and Cambridge Botanic Gardens. The trees are usually either male or female, at least one male is required to fertilize up to 6 females. There are some forms of the species that have both male and female flowers.

TALL SHRUBS

As we move further down into the woodland, we come to the shrub layer. There is a gradual change from trees to shrubs, and this change can be difficult to categorise. Many species of trees, for example, will form multiple stems in certain situations and are then more shrubs than trees. Similarly, a number of shrubby species can be encouraged to grow on single stems and are then much more tree-like.

Nevertheless, there is an overall distinction between trees and shrubs and so those species which usually form multi-trunks are included here.

As with the smaller trees, some of the species mentioned below prefer the deeper shade of the woodland, whilst others will only be really happy if they are growing on the sunnier edges. Given a suitable sunny or shady position, there is no necessity to grow these plants in a woodland and they could all be grown in a garden context.

This list comprises those shrubs that will usually grow more than 2 metres tall. Once again, it is sub-divided into deciduous and evergreen species.

DECIDUOUS SPECIES

Abutilon vitifolium. My wife and I only found out about this beautiful large shrub in June 1994 when we came across a specimen of the cultivar 'Album' that was literally covered in large white blossoms. I have not found any records of edibility for this species, but it belongs to a family in which all the species are likely to be edible and it is certainly safe to eat. The mild-tasting leaves have an unpleasant texture but the beautiful flowers have a delicious flavour and can be added in quantity to salads. Many people are still surprised about the possibilities of eating flowers, and they will be even more surprised when confronted with a salad containing a number of large white blooms 5cm or more across. Flowers often make very pleasant eating because they are sweetened by the nectar they contain, and their pollen makes them a reasonable source of a high-quality protein.

This plant grows best in a sunny position, it tolerates temperatures down to about -10°C and so is unlikely to be hardy in the colder areas of the country. When well grown it can be 6 metres or more tall and 5 metres wide. Plants often flower so freely that they literally die of exhaustion – one way of trying to prevent this is to remove all the flowers as they die (or eat them before they die) and thus prevent the formation of seed.

Amelanchier lamarckii. We have already discussed various members of this genus in the previous section. This species is quite clearly a shrub, growing about 6 metres tall and 4 metres wide, and so is best included here. It requires the same conditions as mentioned earlier. The fruit is about 10mm in diameter and has a juicy texture with an excellent flavour that has a hint of apples.

There are several named varieties with superior fruits in North America, the only one I know to be available in this country is 'Ballerina'. This plant has larger than average fruit with a pleasant sweet taste and it yields heavily in most years.

A. intermedia. This is a very similar and closely related species. The fruit, however, ripens about 2 - 3 weeks later than any other member of this genus that I have experience of, and is therefore very valuable for extending the season. The fruit also develops a delicious flavour before it is fully ripe, thus allowing you to pick it before the birds eat it all.

Calycanthus floridus. CAROLINA ALLSPICE is a very aromatic shrub growing about 2.5 metres tall and 2 metres wide. An easily grown plant, it usually does very well in Britain, especially when grown on the sunny edges of a woodland.

The dried bark makes a good cinnamon substitute and the leaves, which contain camphor, are used as an insect repellent and disinfectant.

C. occidentalis. This has similar uses but is somewhat larger, to 3 metres tall and wide. It is also less hardy and so will not succeed in the coldest parts of the country.

Slugs have been strongly attracted to my young plants of both species. They usually eat out all the buds and young leaves in the spring, and it is not until late summer that the plants show signs of recovery. After 5 years of growth they are still only 40cm tall!

Caragana arborescens. The SIBERIAN PEA SHRUB grows up to 6 metres tall and wide, though there are smaller forms such as 'Nana'. This species is wind-resistant and very hardy – in fact it prefers continental climates with much colder winters but hotter summers than we experience in Britain. It really demands a sunny position and a well-drained soil if it is to do well and does not like moist climates,

Plate 1. *Berberis georgii*. A highly productive fruit for the woodland edge. Its acid flavour being adored by children. See page 55.

Plate 2. *Broussonetia papyrifera*. These unusual orange fruit, sticking out like little tongues from the green core, are juicy with a sweet and rich flavour. See page 38.

Plate 3. *Cephalotaxus fortunei*. Although the fruit seldom ripens in Britain, the disgusting taste of the immature fruit protects the edible seed from squirrels. See page 54.

Plate 4. *Chaenomeles japonica*. Commonly grown as a garden ornamental for its early spring flowers, the cooked fruit also makes excellent jellies and pies. See page 56.

Plate 5. *Cornus mas.* Producing a spectacular mass of yellow flowers in late winter, the fully ripe fruit is delicious raw or cooked. See page 47.

Plate 6. *Crataegus pensylvanica.* One of the most reliable and heavy cropping HAWTHORNS, with a juicy fruit that has an exquisitely rich flavour. See page 40.

Plate 7. *Crataegus schraderiana*. One of the later ripening HAWTHORNS, when fully ripe the delicious fruit literally melts in your mouth. See page 41.

Plate 8. *Decaisnea fargesii*. More like a blue sausage than a fruit, when peeled it looks like a slug, but has a pleasantly sweet, mild flavour. See page 47.

Plate 9. *Diospyros virginiana*. Eaten when squidgy soft the fruit is like ambrosia, making even an apricot seem tasteless. See page 27.

Plate 10. *Gaultheria shallon*. Growing well in woodland shade, the mild flavoured fruit is produced in abundance and makes an excellent dessert. See page 59.

Plate 11. *Ginkgo biloba.* So long as male and female trees are grown together, you will be blessed with a huge crop of edible seeds. When baked, the seeds have a floury texture and taste somewhat like sweet chestnuts. Be warned though, the fruit surrounding the seed smells like a sewage works on a hot summer's day! See page 28.

Plate 12. *Pinus coulteri.* Weighing up to 2.2 kilos, the huge cones can contain well over a hundred tasty pine nuts. See page 35.

Plate 13. *Hippophae salicifolia*. Probably the most nutritious fruit that can be grown in a temperate climate, the sharply acid fruit makes an excellent drink. See page 23.

Plate 14. *Mespilus germanica*. Picked in late autumn and allowed to blet, this unusual fruit develops the flavour of a luscious tropical fruit. See page 42. Photo: Tim Harland.

Plate 15. *Ribes odoratum*. Growing well on the woodland edge, the fruit is somewhat like a whitecurrant but larger, juicier and with less seed. See page 57.

Plate 16. *Taxus baccata*. Although all other parts of the YEW are poisonous, including the seed, the fleshy fruit is pleasantly sweet and perfectly safe to eat. See page 44.

so it normally grows better in the eastern part of the country.

The edible fully-ripe seed is a little bit smaller than a lentil and is usually produced in abundance. Although it takes quite a time to harvest large quantities of the seed, this pales into insignificance when you realise that this is probably the only attention the plant needs during the year. A rich source of protein, the seed can be cooked and used in all the ways that you would use cooked beans. The young seed pods can also be used as a vegetable. Amongst the plant's other uses: a fibre obtained from the bark is used for cordage; a blue dye is obtained from the leaves. The plant's extensive root system make it useful for erosion control, especially on marginal land. Because the plant is a legume it also enriches the soil with nitrogen.

This plant has excellent potential as a staple food crop in temperate zones and through selective breeding it should be possible to produce cultivars with larger seeds. There are many other species in this genus, several of which are closely related to *C. arborescens*, and there is considerable scope for research into their food-producing potential. See also page 259.

Castanea pumila. We have already discussed *C. sativa* in the section on tall trees. This species, which has the same cultivation needs, is a much smaller suckering shrub that grows about 3.5 metres tall. It is an excellent under-storey shrub in pine woodlands, where its leaf fall helps to counteract the acid-forming tendency of pine needles. Whilst its seeds are only half the size of a British-grown *C. sativa*, they have a nicer flavour and are pleasant even when eaten raw. Many books say that this species does not fruit well in Britain, but a plant in the Royal Horticultural Society gardens at Wisley has borne good crops in most years.

Cornus mas. See Plate 5. The CORNELIAN CHERRY. A number of Cornus species have already been mentioned in the section on trees. This shrub, which is naturalized in Britain, grows up to 5 metres tall and wide though it is very amenable to trimming and can be kept smaller in cultivation. Formerly cultivated for its fruit, which can be 2cm or more long in some forms, it is now mainly grown as an ornamental, where it is valued for its yellow flowers in late winter and early spring. It prefers a chalky soil but tolerates most conditions and is wind tolerant.

The fruit ripens in late summer. It is juicy and very nice raw with a somewhat plum-like flavour, though it will be rather astringent unless it is fully ripe. An edible oil can be extracted from the seeds, and the wood, which is very tough, is much valued for making tools, cogs etc.

There are several named forms of this plant, selected for their superior fruits but I do not know of a source in this country. I have often seen the cultivar 'Variegata' fruiting prolifically here, even in years that the species does not do so well. It is said that seedling plants will take up to 20 years before they commence to bear fruit, though some of our seedlings produced a very small crop in their 6th year from seed.

Decaisnea fargesii. See Plate 8. This shrub eventually reaches a height and width of about 4 metres. In the autumn it produces an abundance of bright blue edible fruits that look rather like sausages or broad bean pods. Opening these 'pods' you will find a long line of seeds surrounded by a juicy flesh, when removed from the skin this flesh looks rather like a maggot. If you can manage to put it in your mouth (and a number of people cannot) then you will find that it has a pleasant though delicate flavour. It's great fun to see a person's face when you give them a dish of these fruits to eat.

An easily grown plant, it succeeds in most soils. Although very hardy when dormant, the young growth in the spring is damaged by late frosts, so it is best to site the plant in a position that is sheltered from the early morning sun. It also dislikes a windy position and will not normally fruit when growing there, thus the ideal site for it is in the dappled shade of deciduous trees.

Hydrangea **species**. There are three members of this genus that are supposed to have very sweet-flavoured leaves. The young leaves, when dried and rubbed between the hands, are said to become very sweet and are used to make a tea called 'tea of heaven' which is used in Buddhist ceremonies. The leaves contain phellodulcin, a very sweet substance that can be used as a sugar substitute. The older leaves can be dried, powdered and used as a flavouring on foods.

I am growing a couple of these plants but, as yet, have failed to detect this sweetness. Perhaps I am not following the method closely enough, certainly the fresh raw leaf has a bitterness in the flavour. The species in question are *H. macrophylla*, (which grows about 3 metres tall and wide) *H. serrata amagiana* and *H. serrata thunbergii* (both of which grow about 2 metres tall and 1 metre wide). The leaves of the third species need to be fermented before they become sweet.

The plants grow best in an acid soil with a pH around 4.5, though they will tolerate a slightly alkaline soil as long as it is not over chalk. They resent dryness at the roots and are best given some shelter from the midday sun in the hottest parts of the country. They grow very well in light woodland shade. The flowers are a good indicator of soil pH, in acid soils they are blue, but in more alkaline soils they turn pink.

Lonicera angustifolia. This species is a shrubby HONEYSUCKLE, but does not look at all like our native honeysuckle. It grows about 2.5 metres tall and produces a good crop of juicy sweet fruits a bit smaller than a blackcurrant in early summer. It often also produces a small second crop in late summer. The plant demands a sunny position if it is to do well, preferring a more continental climate with its hotter summers and colder winters, so it grows better in the eastern half of the country. I used to get reasonable crops when I was growing this plant in Surrey, but yields have been disappointing since moving to Cornwall.

There are also several other members of this genus with edible fruits, though I have yet to see a good crop on any of them. *L. villosa* is perhaps the one most often grown, the plants we have only crop lightly and they have a bitter flavour. If you know of a plant with sweet fruit that is yielding well then I'd love to hear about it.

L. involucrata is also said to have edible fruits but, although the plants we have grow and fruit extremely well, the fruit is much too bitter to eat. It is always possible that we have a poor form and that other forms will have a nicer fruit, so once again please let me know if you have a good form.

***Prunus* species**. This large genus includes the PLUMS, DAMSONS, CHERRIES, ALMONDS, PEACHES and APRICOTS. I list them here because I do not intend to cover them in this book, concentrating instead on some lesser-known members of the genus. That should not stop you growing them, of course, and the sunnier edges of a forest garden are an excellent site for them.

All members of the genus produce more or less edible fruits – though several are too small or too bitter for human palates. They also have edible seeds, though do not eat them if they are bitter since this would be due to the presence of hydrogen cyanide, the toxin that gives bitter almonds their flavour. Whilst this toxin can be eaten in small quantities (and is considered to be beneficial by many authorities) in larger doses it can cause illness and even death. See Appendix 4 for more details.

Many species are cultivated in other countries for their edible fruits, though they often do not yield well in Britain due mainly to our cooler summers and unpredictable springs. There are a couple of large shrubs that do have promise. They grow best in a sunny position.

P. brigantina. The BRIANÇON APRICOT, is a shrub or small tree growing to about 5 metres and almost as wide. The sweet-tasting fruit, which ripens in late summer, is about 3cm in diameter and has a pleasant mealy texture. It is often borne in abundance, even on small plants.

P. maritima. The BEACH PLUM, as its Latin name suggests, grows on or near beaches by the coast. A suckering shrub only 2.5 metres tall, it is resistant to maritime winds and should be adaptable to coastal conditions in Britain, though it is said to yield badly when grown inland in this country. I have not yet tried the fruit and do not know how well it will yield, but it is said to be of variable quality. There are several named forms in North America – these are not as yet available here though we are hoping to obtain them in 1997. 'Eastham' has large well-flavoured fruit and is a heavy cropper, 'Hancock' is an early ripening form with sweet juicy fruit whilst 'Squibnocket' is of high quality and is also a good sand binder. This species is certainly worthy of a trial in this country.

Rhus typhina. The STAG'S HORN SUMACH is a shrub that can grow up to 6 metres tall and suckers freely – too freely for many people since it can end up making a large thicket. However, this root behaviour can be a blessing when the right position is chosen for the plant. It can, for example, be very useful for stabilising banks and, because it soon forms thickets, it can also be used to provide shelter from the wind. A very easily grown plant, it succeeds in most situations and is tolerant of poor dry soils.

The plant is a striking sight in winter when its bare branches carry purple-red spikes of the small fruits at their tips. These spikes look rather like the flame of a candle and, when soaked for at least 10 minutes in cold or warm water, yield a very refreshing drink that is used in America as a lemonade substitute. The longer you soak it, the stronger the flavour, and so some people leave it in the water for 12 hours or more. Do not use hot water because the drink could then become astringent.

The leaves are rich in tannin and turn a beautiful colour in the autumn. If these leaves are gathered as they fall, they can be used as a brown dye or as a mordant to fix other dyes.

Many other members of this genus have fruits that can be used similarly, including:

R. aromatica. The LEMON SUMACH grows about 1.5 metres tall and wide. This species is very drought tolerant and grows well in poor soils. One additional use for this species is that an oil can be extracted from the seeds. This oil attains a tallow-like consistency on standing and is used to make candles. These burn brilliantly, though they emit a pungent smoke.

R. glabra. The SMOOTH SUMACH grows about 3 metres tall and wide. Some members of this genus are very poisonous but they are easily distinguished because the fruits of poisonous species are smooth whilst non-poisonous fruits are hairy. Some botanists separate these poisonous species off into a different genus called *Toxicodendron*.

Rosa **species**. ROSES are widely grown as ornamental plants in gardens. They grow well in full sun or light shade and do very well in the sunnier areas of a woodland.

All roses produce edible fruits and these are usually a very good source of vitamin C. However, the fruit is rather fiddly to eat, it normally has only a very thin layer of edible flesh and, to make things more difficult, just below this flesh the seeds are covered with fine hairs which can act as a gastric irritant if ingested in any quantity. Young children often put these hairs down people's backs as an itching powder. There are some species, however, with a much thicker layer of flesh and, indeed, some of these have at times been cultivated for their fruits.

It is best to wait until the fruit is just going soft before picking it (which is usually after a frost) and then it can be quite palatable raw – in some species it is sweet and absolutely delicious. The fruits can also be used to make conserves, jams etc. and a vitamin C rich drink. The flower petals can also be eaten, they often have a pleasant aromatic flavour but make sure that you remove the white base from the petals since this can be rather bitter. An essential oil that is very popular for perfumery can be extracted from the flowers. The dried leaves are a tea substitute. The seed can be ground into a flour and used as a vitamin E supplement but be careful to remove the seed hairs first. This can be done either by lightly scorching the seed or by abrading (by putting the seed into a drum and revolving it so that the hairs are rubbed off) and then winnowing it. Species worth trying include the following:

R. acicularis. The PRICKLY ROSE grows about 2.5 metres tall. This species fruits prolifically. The flesh is rather thin but is very sweet and pleasant.

R. canina. Our native DOG ROSE is a scrambling shrub that sends out new shoots up to 3 metres long and grows very well in hedgerows. Another high yielder, though once again with a rather thin flesh.

R. rugosa. The RAMANAS ROSE grows about 2 metres tall and can spread quite widely by means of suckers. This plant produces the nicest tasting rose hips I have tried to date. They are about 3cm in diameter and ripen in the summer – they do not need a frost to make them edible. This species makes an excellent hedge and so is dealt with more fully on page 178.

R. villosa. The APPLE ROSE grows about 1.8 metres tall and 1 metre wide. This species is said to have the largest fruit in the genus, and they can be up to 3cm in diameter. It has been cultivated in the past for this fruit which was used mainly for making preserves. The form that I am growing has disappointingly small fruits, so please let me know if you have a good form.

Rubus **species.** All members of this genus, which includes the cultivated RASPBERRIES and BLACKBERRIES, produce edible fruits, though these are often not very worthwhile. Many members of this genus, including the raspberries and blackberries, make ideal woodland edge plants in the sunnier areas of the woodland. They will also succeed in semi-shade, though will not fruit so well in such a position.

One of my favourite species is the JAPANESE WINEBERRY, *R. phoenicolasius.* This very attractive shrub produces its small raspberry-like fruits in abundance towards the end of summer. Apart from having a nice flavour, the fruit is also usually free of maggots because, after the plant flowers, it wraps the developing fruit up in the calyx, conveniently unwrapping it as the fruit ripens. The plant can grow 3 metres tall and perhaps 2 metres wide, though it is usually a bit smaller. Its reddish stems add interest to the garden in winter.

There are several species of North American raspberries that grow well in the light shade of a woodland. Some of these species are cultivated in America for their fruits and, though they grow very well here, they don't always fruit so well. In cool summers the fruits fail to develop their full flavour and will often be insipid. We grow them in sunny positions and they fruit quite well with us.

R. leucodermis. The WHITEBARK RASPBERRY grows about 2.5 metres tall and 1 metre wide. Like our cultivated raspberries, it produces many new stems each year. These stems flower and fruit in their second year and then die. The fruit ripens over a period of several weeks in July and August. Yields have proved to be good with us, the fruit being juicy and well-flavoured though not as nice as the cultivated raspberry. It is about half the size of a cultivated raspberry and much darker in colour.

R. occidentalis. The BLACK RASPBERRY is rather similar in fruit to the above but the plant is somewhat larger, growing to 3 metres tall.

R. odoratus. The THIMBLEBERRY is a vigorous suckering shrub with perennial stems. It grows about 2.5 metres tall and forms a gradually spreading clump. It has fruited well with us, the crop ripening in mid to late summer. The flavour is a pleasant blend of sweetness and acidity and we are very keen on it, though the flesh is frustratingly thin and rather seedy.

R. parviflorus. Another THIMBLEBERRY rather similar in habit and fruit to the above species.

R. spectabilis. The SALMONBERRY has a similar habit to the above but is a somewhat smaller plant growing to about 2 metres in height. The fruit, which is produced in early summer, varies in colour from yellow through orange to red. It is similar in size to the cultivated raspberry and is pleasantly juicy though it often has a distinct bitterness. It has a much better flavour when we have hot weather and so is probably better suited for the eastern half of the country.

See Chapters 10 and 12 for more members of this genus.

Sambucus species. This genus includes our native ELDER, *Sambucus nigra*, which is discussed on page 183. There are a number of other interesting species in the genus that have edible fruits and flowers, my favourites are *S. canadensis* and *S. racemosa*, which both grow from 3 - 4 metres tall and wide. Very adaptable and easily grown plants, they will succeed in almost any situation but do especially well in light shade in a woodland.

Individual fruits are very small, but they are produced in large bunches and are very easy to harvest in quantity. The raw fruit does not taste that wonderful, in fact many people feel sick after eating it, but it is much nicer when cooked and can be used in making jams etc. The flowers are the bit I like most, they make a very pleasant munch on a summers day, though look out for pollinating insects or else your munch might be more protein rich than you had anticipated! Both the flowers and the fruits are popularly used by home brewers for making wine. The rather smelly leaves of elders make an excellent insect repellent if rubbed on the skin, staying effective for 2 hours or more. I find them especially effective against midges and horseflies.

Vitex agnus-castus. The CHASTE TREE grows about 3 metres tall and wide. It requires a sunny position and is only hardy in the milder parts of the country, tolerating occasional lows to about -10°C.

The fruit can be used as a pepper substitute and the leaves are also used as a spice. For the gourmets amongst you, this plant forms one of the ingredients of the legendary Moroccan spice mixture 'ras el hanout'. The young stems are used in making baskets and a yellow dye can be obtained from the leaves, fruit and roots. However, the plant's most interesting feature, from my point of view, is the fact that the fruit contains a substance that is very similar to certain female hormones and it has been used with success to restore and normalise menstrual flow as well as improve female fertility. I know I said in the introduction that I wasn't going to talk about medicinal plants, but I couldn't resist this one because whilst writing the first draft of this book my wife gave birth to a beautiful baby boy due, at least in part, to this plant.

EVERGREEN SPECIES

Berberis species. This large genus contains both evergreen and deciduous species, though I will only mention some evergreen species here. BARBERRIES are amongst the most accommodating of shrubs, often succeeding despite total neglect and tolerant of most conditions. They grow exceedingly well in light woodland shade, though they will also tolerate deeper shade and full sun.

All members of the genus have edible fruits but many of them are dry and bitter. The best usually have an acid taste, which often resembles lemons. There are also, usually, rather a lot of seeds in the fruit. I find the taste very pleasant, and eat the fruit in large quantities either raw or cooked. If you are not used to the fruit then only eat small amounts at first because the large quantity of seeds make it act as a laxative. This is an effect that wears off as your body becomes used to the fruit.

Some of the nicest species include:

B. *aristata*. Growing about 3.5 metres tall and almost as wide, it usually fruits abundantly in this country. These fruits, which ripen in mid to late autumn, are about 10mm long and pleasantly juicy with a mild acidity. In the Himalayas the fruits are dried and used as raisins. Although hardy in most parts of Britain, it will often be defoliated in cold winters.

B. *asiatica*. This species is not hardy outside western and southern Britain. It is similar in size to the above and the fruit also ripens in mid to late autumn though our plants have not yielded as yet. The fruit is about 8mm long and is used like the species above.

B. *buxifolia*. Growing about 2.5 metres tall and wide. The fruits, which are produced abundantly, are juicy and very well flavoured, being less acid than most species. They ripen in mid-summer and are especially pleasant when mixed with muesli or porridge. It is quite difficult to get hold of this species in Britain, the form most often offered is a dwarf cultivar called 'Nana' and this very rarely sets fruit.

B. *darwinii*. This is my favourite barberry. When fully ripe in mid-summer, the juicy fruit has a pleasantly mild flavour, though it contains a lot of seeds. This is one of those fruits that you have to share with the birds because they absolutely adore it. See also page 185.

B. *lycium*. Growing up to 3 metres tall and wide with juicy fruit, about 8mm long, with a mild acid flavour ripening in late summer.

B. *x lologensis*. This is a hybrid species with *B. darwinii* as one of its parents. It grows about 2.5 metres tall and wide. The cultivar 'Mystery Fire' is an extremely productive plant, producing large crops even on small plants. Ripening in mid-summer, this fruit is very similar to *B. darwinii*.

Cephalotaxus harringtonia. The JAPANESE PLUM-YEW looks rather like our native yew tree and can grow about 5 metres tall and wide, though it is usually much smaller. It needs a shady position in southern Britain though it will also succeed in a sunny position in the cooler north of the country. A slow-growing shrub, you need to grow both male and female forms if you want its edible seed and fruit.

The fruit is about 20 - 30mm long and perhaps 15mm wide. When fully ripe in late autumn it has a pleasant sweet flavour, but before this it tastes totally disgusting. The flavour is so awful, and also clings to the tongue for hours afterwards no matter what else you might eat, that even the squirrels will not bite their way through it to get at the seed. This is really good news, because the seed is edible and therefore one of the very few squirrel-proof nuts that can be grown in Britain. The fairly large seed often has a bitterness and can need leaching (see notes on *Quercus petraea* on page 237 for more details of this), it is eaten raw or cooked. The seed is rich in oil and this can be extracted for edible use or for lighting etc. The tree usually crops very heavily and is easy to harvest.

Succeeding in the shade of other trees, this species is an ideal part of the forest garden. I believe that it has the potential to be a staple nut crop in this country, though more research is needed. The sub-species **C. harringtonia drupacea** and **C. harringtonia nana** (which is a dwarf, suckering form) produce the best tasting fruits. It is also worthwhile growing the similar **C. fortunei**, see Plate 3.

Elaeagnus species. The evergreen members of this genus are discussed in detail on page 185. I would like to point out here that they make excellent woodland plants, succeeding in full sun as well as deep shade. They provide a tasty fruit in early spring, weeks before any other fruit comes out of the garden. Species to consider include **E. macrophylla** and **E. x ebbingei**.

Juniperus communis. The fruit of our native JUNIPER is commonly used as a flavouring in cooking and is an essential ingredient of gin. It should be used with some discretion, however, since large doses can be harmful to the kidneys. It should not be used at all by pregnant women since it can induce menstrual flow. Amongst its other uses: a decoction of the branches is used as an anti-dandruff shampoo; it yields the resin 'Sandarac' which is used in the production of a white varnish; the stems can be used as a strewing herb or can be burnt as an incense and fumigant – it makes a good insect repellent.

The plant succeeds in most well-drained soils including nutrient-poor ones, tolerates a pH from 4 to 8 and also resists drought. It tolerates light shade but is really best in a sunny position. This is a very variable plant, there are many named varieties and they can vary in size from a few centimetres to 9 metres tall.

SMALL SHRUBS

This chapter ends with the lowest-growing woody plants in the woodland, the smaller shrubs that rarely exceed 2 metres in height. These shrubs will often be tolerant of quite deep shade (they need to be considering how many plants might be growing above them and shading them from the sun), though once again some of them will only thrive if they are growing on the sunnier edges of the woodland.

Most of the plants mentioned here will also thrive outside a woodland as long as their light requirements are taken into account. In general, these shrubs will all be suitable for the smaller garden.

DECIDUOUS SPECIES

Amelanchier alnifolia. The JUNEBERRIES have already been discussed in the section on small trees. This is one of the smaller-growing species, usually forming a suckering shrub about 2 metres tall and wide. Because the plant is quite small, it is a fairly simple matter to protect the fruit from the birds.

Probably the nicest tasting of the juneberries, the fruit is up to 15mm in diameter and is very juicy with a hint of apple in the flavour. This is a fruit that deserves to be far more widely grown. There are many named cultivars in North America where it is cultivated on a small scale as a fruit crop. These cultivars are not currently available in Britain, though we hope to be obtaining some of them soon.

***Berberis* species**. This genus includes some of the easiest to grow plants in the garden. Tolerant of most soils and conditions, they will succeed in heavy clay as well as in thin, dry and shallow soils, but do best in a good moist loam. They are ideal plants to grow on the sunny edges or in light shade of the woodland, also succeeding in deeper shade though not fruiting so well in such a situation. Many species fruit exceedingly well in this country, this fruit tends to have a sharp, lemon-like flavour and so is not to everyone's taste. However, most children adore it, as well as a good number of adults. It also makes an excellent cooked fruit in pies, jams, etc. Even if you do not like it, the birds adore it and will happily devour the lot whilst ignoring the fruits that you are growing for yourself. Any of the species can be tried, since none of them are poisonous, though many are dry and bitter. The following are some of my favourites:

B. aggregata. Growing about 1.5 metres tall and wide, this species fruits incredibly heavily in mid to late autumn. The fruit are a bit on the small side, about 7mm in diameter, and you have to be a bit careful when picking it because the stems are very prickly, but it does not take long to pick a large quantity.

The cultivar **'Buccaneer'** is closely related to this species and has similar tasting fruit. The fruit, however, is about twice the size of *B. aggregata* and so is much easier to pick and use.

B. georgii. See Plate 1. Growing to about 2 metres tall and wide. The fruit ripens in early autumn and is about 10mm long and 4mm wide. This is another species that really has no sense of proportion when fruiting – it often produces so much fruit that you can hardly see the leaves!

B. vulgaris. The common BARBERRY is another species for the woodland edge. It makes a good hedge and so is discussed in more detail on page 180.

Ceanothus americanus. NEW JERSEY TEA is a small but fast-growing shrub reaching a maximum height and spread of around 1.2 metres. It is tolerant of poor soils but will need a sunny position if it is to flower well. These flowers are produced for much of the summer and even young seedlings a year or so old will produce some blossom.

Rich in saponins, the flowers lather up like soap when they are crushed in water. This lather is a gentle and very effective cleaner of dirt, though it will not be very good at removing oil. This does mean that it is very good for the skin because it will not remove the natural oils and thus does not dry out the skin. It can also be used on clothes etc., leaving a pleasant scent after use. New Jersey Tea often grows along river banks in North America and the native Indians would pluck handfuls of the flowers and then bathe with them in the river. It was used especially by the women on the eve of their marriage so that they would smell nice for their husband. Presumably it did not matter what the men smelt like!

The plant has a number of other uses. The dried leaves, harvested when the plant is in flower, make a very acceptable tea substitute that is free from caffeine. A green dye is obtained from the flowers, a cinnamon-coloured dye from the whole plant and a red dye from the root.

Many species and cultivars of this genus are widely grown as ornamental plants. All of them have flowers that can be used as a soap. With a careful selection of plants it is possible to have flowers available from early spring until the autumn frosts.

Chaenomeles species. DWARF QUINCES. Not the true quince, which is *Cydonia oblonga*, but the fruits of these deciduous shrubs are so similar in taste that you would hardly notice the difference. The plants vary in height from about 60cm to 4 metres and are very easily grown, fruiting best when in a sunny position. The fruit ripens in late autumn and is best after a frost or two.

Harsh and astringent raw, the cooked fruit becomes very aromatic and can be added to other cooked fruit (they are especially good with apples) or used to make jams, jellies etc. There are three species in the genus:

C. cathayensis. Growing about 3 metres tall and wide, it has the largest fruits in the genus. These are usually the size of a large cooking apple though they do not always ripen fully in Britain. The best plants that I've seen have been grown on south or west facing walls, though our plant, which is growing in a very open position, successfully ripened its first crop with us in the fairly average summer of 1996.

C. japonica. See Plate 4. The most commonly grown species. It grows about 1 metre tall and will sucker to form a clump about 2 metres wide. The fruit can be up to 4cm in diameter.

C. speciosa. Growing up to 3 metres tall and 5 metres wide, though it is usually much smaller. The fruit is about 6cm in diameter and is normally produced abundantly.

C. x superba. A hybrid of garden origin involving the preceding two species. There are very many named forms and they range considerably in size from dwarf forms less than 1 metre tall to larger plants up to 3 metres tall. The fruit is about 5cm in diameter.

Crataegus baroussana. We have already discussed the hawthorns in the section dealing with small trees. This is a considerably smaller species, perhaps growing no more than 2 metres tall and wide. I have very little information on this plant, except that it comes from Mexico. I have seen it growing well in a couple of sites in southern England and it was fruiting heavily when only seven years old and 1 metre tall. The same plants, when nine years old, were still only 1.2 metres tall and forming neat bushes, which suggests that they are going to remain small shrubs.

The fruit ripens in early autumn and is about 15mm in diameter. It is very pleasant to eat raw, though is not of such a good quality as some of the other species mentioned earlier. It is not possible at present to determine how hardy this plant is going to be, but there must be some doubts about its ability to survive in the north of Britain.

Prunus tenella. This genus has already been discussed in the section on taller shrubs. The DWARF RUSSIAN ALMOND is an extremely cold-tolerant plant that only grows about 1.5 metres tall. The fruit ripens in late summer, it is about 25mm in diameter and looks rather like a sloe. Unlike that fruit, it has a reasonable flavour. The seed is rather bitter but an oil extracted from it is used as an almond flavouring. The plant is very frost-resistant and can be used as a dwarfing rootstock for other members of the genus.

Ribes **species**. This genus includes the cultivated RED, WHITE and BLACK-CURRANTS, GOOSEBERRIES, WORCESTERBERRY and JOSTABERRY. These are all excellent plants for the sunnier edges of the woodland and for positions in semi-shade. The gooseberries will also fruit well in deeper shade, ripening their fruit later than plants in a sunny position and thereby extending the fruiting season.

There are a number of other species that are worthy of consideration in the garden. They are very easily grown in most soils and prefer a sunny sheltered position. I particularly like **R. aureum** and **R. odoratum**, see Plate 15, the GOLDEN CURRANTS. These rather similar species, growing about 2.5 metres tall and producing suckers, are very ornamental with edible yellow flowers in early spring. Don't eat too many of the flowers, though, or you might miss out on the fruit. This is about the size of a blackcurrant and is pleasantly flavoured, it can be red, black, yellow or golden in colour. It ripens in mid-summer and can hang on the plants for several weeks. To date plants have not fruited heavily with me in Cornwall but I have seen reasonable to very good yields on plants away from the wetter western part of the country. There are some named varieties in North America where these species are occasionally cultivated for their fruit.

R. warszewiczii. A very nicely flavoured redcurrant that has fruited heavily with us in Cornwall. The fruit is a deeper red than other red currants and looks very attractive. I find it rather tastier than other redcurrants, though I do tend to be biased towards some of these alternative foods. It ripens in mid-summer. The plant grows about 1.5 metres tall and perhaps 1 metre wide.

Vaccinium **species**. This large genus, which includes the BLUEBERRIES, CRANBERRIES and BILBERRIES, contains both deciduous and evergreen species, but I will deal with them all here. Unless stated otherwise, they are deciduous. They all require a light loamy humus-rich acid soil and a sunny position, a pH around 4.5 to 6 suiting most of them. All members of the genus produce edible fruits, some of the nicest include:

V. corymbosum. A species of BLUEBERRY that can reach 3.5 metres in height, though it is usually much smaller in cultivation. It has proved the most productive species in Britain to date. It is widely cultivated in North America and there are many named varieties. The sweet-tasting fruit ripens in late summer and is up to 15mm in diameter.

V. deliciosum. Only growing 30cm tall but spreading freely by suckers, growing well in a rock garden. The fruit is only about 6mm in diameter but has a very nice sweet flavour. It ripens in late summer.

V. macrocarpon. The AMERICAN CRANBERRY is evergreen, growing only 20cm tall but spreading by means of its rooting branches. It requires a wetter soil than many of the species in this genus. The fruit, which ripens in late summer and early autumn, is up to 20cm in diameter. It has a rather acid flavour and is usually cooked or used in preserves. Cranberries are a cultivated crop in America, there are several named varieties.

V. myrtillus. Our native BILBERRY is a sub-evergreen plant, usually retaining at least some of its leaves over the winter. It grows about 45cm tall and spreads freely by means of suckers. It grows well in exposed positions, though it tends to be low yielding. The well-flavoured fruit ripens in the summer and is about 10mm in diameter.

V. oxycoccus. Our native CRANBERRY is a low-growing evergreen plant only about 10cm tall, though it spreads freely to form a clump 1 metre or more wide. It requires a wetter soil than most members of the genus, succeeding in boggy conditions. The fruit ripens in the autumn, it is about 6mm in diameter and rather sour.

V. praestans. Only 15cm tall and spreading slowly by suckers. The fruit is about 12mm in diameter and has a delicious strawberry-like flavour, it is ripe in mid to late summer. This species grows best in the northern half of the country, in the south it requires some protection from the sun.

V. vitis-idaea. Our native COWBERRY is an evergreen shrub about 30cm tall forming a clump about 1 metre wide. The fruit ripens in early to mid autumn, it is about 6mm in diameter and looks somewhat like a cranberry, though some people find it superior in flavour.

Zanthoxylum piperitum. The JAPANESE PEPPER TREE grows about 2 metres tall and perhaps 1 metre wide. Easily grown and very ornamental, it prefers growing in light shade. The only problem we have had with it is that the young plants are extremely attractive to slugs and, given half a chance, these can totally destroy plants that are up to 1 metre tall.

The bark and the leaves are used as a flavouring but the plant's main use is its seeds which are ground up and used as a pepper substitute. You will have to grow both male and female plants if you want the seed and unfortunately most nurseries will not be able to tell you the sex of their plants. The easiest way round this is to grow plants from seed (it germinates easily) and to grow on a number of the plants – you can then discard surplus males if you want to once the sex is determined. The plant is grown commercially for its seed in Japan and yields well in Britain.

Make sure you remove the seed case that covers the black seeds. This seed case (or the fruit to be more precise) has the interesting property of being able to numb the skin. It is especially effective when rubbed on the more sensitive and moist parts of the skin such as the lips and so can be rubbed on the gums as a temporary expedient to numb the pain of a toothache. Do not use it too often though, or it could cause irritation.

Other members of this genus have similar uses. They are all fairly small-growing and usually very ornamental woodland shrubs. Species worth trying include *Z. alatum*, *Z. americanum*, *Z. planispinum*, *Z. schinifolium* and *Z. simulans*.

EVERGREEN SPECIES

Gaultheria species. These shrubs require a moist but not boggy lime-free soil and some shade, growing very well under trees. They are drought tolerant once established. They vary in height from a few centimetres to 1.5 metres and all of them have edible fruits. Of those that I've tasted, the following are my favourites:

G. procumbens. WINTERGREEN only grows about 15cm tall but spreads freely by suckers and can become invasive when in suitable conditions. The fruit is up to 15mm in diameter and ripens in late summer, though it will hang on the plant for many weeks if not eaten by the birds. It is highly aromatic with a germolene flavour that reminds you of a hospital waiting room! Some people love them, others are less sure! The cultivar 'Dart's Red Giant' has specially large berries. The leaves can be used to make a refreshing tea.

G. shallon. See Plate 10. The SALAL grows up to 1.5 metres tall and forms a slowly spreading clump 1 metre or more wide. The fruit is about 10mm in diameter and is very freely produced over a period of several weeks from mid to late summer. It has a sweet and pleasant flavour and can be eaten raw in quantity. A number of species that were previously included in the genus *Pernettya* have recently been moved to this genus. Whilst they also have edible fruits, these are usually dry and uninteresting.

Mahonia species. This genus is closely related to the Berberis species that were mentioned earlier. Several species grow very well in a woodland and, with careful selection of the species, it is possible to have ripe fruit for about 8 moths of the year.

M. aquifolium. OREGON GRAPE grows about 1.2 metres tall, spreading by means of suckers and eventually forming a dense thicket. This really is one of the most tolerant of plants, succeeding in most situations, even in dense shade, and surviving almost total neglect. Strong winds, especially if they carry salt, are about the only thing that will finish it off. Fruit production will be greatly improved, though, if you give the plant just a little bit of attention. About 15mm in diameter, the fruit is on the acid side and can be eaten raw or used in jams, preserves etc. When it is fully ripe I find it delicious if mixed with muesli or porridge. There are rather a lot of seeds in the fruit unfortunately, and like the barberries it can be laxative if you are not used to it. The fruit ripens in late summer and will often hang on the plant until early winter if it is not eaten by birds. The longer it hangs, the nicer the flavour becomes, especially if there are some frosts.

M. japonica. Growing about 2 metres tall and perhaps 3 metres wide, this species does best in semi-shade, though it will also succeed in full sun as well as deep shade. Fruit yields will be rather low in deep shade, though. The plant flowers in the winter and its bright yellow flowers can really lighten a dark corner of the garden. The fruit, which is about 9mm long, is produced on quite long racemes and is easily harvested. It has a similar taste to the preceding species and ripens in mid spring – just after the *Elaeagnus* species mentioned earlier in this chapter and a few weeks before the first strawberries. Yields are not always very good, especially if the plant is in an open position. However, when given the protection of a woodland it usually produces good crops.

This species is not often seen in gardens, but the closely related **M. x media** is a commonly grown garden plant. We grow the cultivars 'Charity' and 'Lionel Fortescue', both of them fruit well in a sheltered position.

All other members of this genus also have edible fruits, see page 209 for other species that are used for ground cover.

Myrtus ugni. This plant is really begging to be cultivated in the milder parts of Britain. It is quite high yielding, giving a crop even when very small, and it has to be one of the most delicious fruits you can grow in this country. The fruit is about 15mm in diameter and is very aromatic. The flavour has been described as a cross between wild strawberries and guavas though personally I do not think there are words to describe their exquisite taste.

There was an attempt to bring the plant into commercial cultivation in the 19th century when orchards were established in Cornwall and good yields were obtained. In an attempt to promote the fruit, one enterprising grower sent a basket of it to Queen Victoria and she was so impressed that she used to send a train to Cornwall once a week when the fruit was in season in order to collect a basket of the fruit. For some reason, unfortunately, Cornish growers were unable to convince enough other people to give the fruit a try and the plant was lost to commercial cultivation.

The plant grows about 2.5 metres tall and wide, and is fairly resistant of drought and maritime exposure. It is only hardy in the milder parts of the country though I have seen it succeed on a sunny wall in the London area. In selected areas of Cornwall it would probably make a good edible hedge.

Rosmarinus officinalis. ROSEMARY is a well known herb that is up to 2 metres tall and wide. It grows best in a hot sunny position and is quite resistant to maritime winds. The leaves are sometimes used as an aromatic flavouring in cooked foods and a tea is also made from them.

The plant's other uses include: the growing plant is said to repel insects from neighbouring plants; branches or sachets of the dried leaves can be placed in clothes cupboards to keep moths away; an infusion of the leaves is used in shampoos and is effective against dandruff; the leaves are burnt as a fumigant and disinfectant; a yellow-green dye is obtained from the leaves and flowers; an essential oil from the leaves and flowering stems is used in perfumery, soaps etc.

Salvia officinalis. SAGE is another well-known herb, growing best in a sunny position and a well-drained soil. It is about 60cm tall and wide. It is used mainly as a food flavouring and for its medicinal virtues.

Its other uses include: the leaves have antiseptic qualities and can heal diseased gums, therefore they make excellent tooth cleaners that leave the mouth feeling clean and fresh – you simply rub the top side of the leaf over the teeth and gums; an essential oil from the leaves is used in perfumery, hair shampoos (it is good for dark hair) and as a food flavouring. The flowers are an alternative ingredient of 'Quick Return' herbal compost activator. The growing or dried plant is said to repel insects, it is especially useful when grown amongst cabbages and carrots and was formerly used as a strewing herb.

The cultivar 'Purpurea' has ornamental purple foliage and we have found the leaves of this cultivar to be thicker and better at cleaning the teeth than the type species.

Vaccinium **species**. The evergreen members of this genus are included with the deciduous species mentioned earlier in this section.

Chapter Three

WOODLAND PLANTS

Having looked at trees and shrubs in the previous chapter, now would be a good time to look at some of the other plants that can be grown with them. In general this means plants that are fairly tolerant of shade, though it also includes many that like growing along the edges of woodlands and therefore need reasonable amounts of sun. Several more species suitable for the woodland will be found in Chapter 8 which deals with many climbing plants, and in Chapter 10 which deals with ground cover plants.

Of course, you don't need to have a large forest or woodland garden in order to grow these plants, most of them will grow quite happily in the shade of shrubs or in other shady places that you may have on your land. Hedges, walls, buildings and other structures usually have shady and sunny sides, simply use the shadier aspects for some of your woodland plants. One of the joys of gardening is in creating habitats either by the careful selection of plants or by using existing features in the garden.

The subject of forest gardening has been receiving increasing attention in recent years thanks to the work of pioneers such as Robert Hart. However, all too often people plan out their forest garden still thinking that they will be able to grow many of the vegetables that they used to grow in a more conventional setting. In almost all cases they are disappointed because the majority of our traditional vegetables and herbs are sun-lovers and do not really fit into a forest garden.

What is needed, I believe, is a radically new approach to the plants we grow in a woodland or forest garden setting. You might not be able to grow carrots such a garden but you can grow some beautiful *Erythroniums* (see below for more details) and eat any of the surplus bulbs. Just as the previous chapter showed that a huge range of trees and shrubs can be grown to form the top and middle layers, so I hope to demonstrate that there is also a very wide range of useful plants to occupy the lower levels of the forest garden.

At this stage I should say that I have not as yet got a working forest garden. This is mainly because the piece of land that I work on had been used as a barley field until 1989. There were no trees or internal hedges anywhere on the land when we bought it, even the hedge around the perimeter was no more than about 1 metre high. It takes time to grow trees, and it takes even more time to create a woodland or forest garden. Therefore I cannot talk about my own experiences of growing the plants contained in the following list under woodland conditions. I have seen them growing successfully in a number of forest gardens and, as with all the edible plants that I talk about, if I have not actually tried them myself then I will let you know.

Many people are very impatient when it comes to creating a garden. They want an immediate effect and do not want to have to wait a number of years for the garden to gradually take shape. Every spring they troop down to the garden centre to buy in bedding plants so that they can have lots of flowers in the garden all summer long. It costs a fortune and has to be repeated every year since most of the plants are annuals. A forest garden is a labour of love and, especially if you are starting off without mature trees, it is a labour that will take many years to come to complete fruition.

When planting you need vision, and you also need to be thinking at least as much about the future generations as you are about yourself. There is very little point in trying to create an 'instant woodland' by planting out your trees and then planting out the other woodland plants at the same time. I have, for example, seen a recommendation to plant out a tree and a vigorous climbing plant into the same planting hole. What will normally happen is that the climber will smother the tree within a few years since the tree just will not be able to grow fast enough to compete.

Plant your trees first, along with any other woodlanders that will be happy with the lack of shade, will not out-compete the trees and will not be out-competed by the non-woodland plants that will find their way into your embryo woodland. Then give them some years to establish and begin to effect their environment before bringing in the other woodland plants. In the meantime you can, if you so desire, grow other plants amongst the trees that are more suited to the open conditions. At least in the earlier years, this can include many of the conventional annual vegetables and these will ensure a harvest whilst the trees are establishing.

CLIMBING PLANTS

In the previous chapter we looked at three of the layers in a woodland – the canopy trees, smaller trees and the shrub layer. The next layer we will look at is the climbing plants.

A well-balanced woodland will find plants taking advantage of every possible niche. Climbing plants exploit the woodland trees, using them as supports in order to climb up into the light. In general, this means that they like their roots growing in the cool moist shade of the woodland floor, but want their leaves to get up into the sunshine. Most of the flowering will take place towards the top of the plants, in the sunnier areas. Some of the species in this list will succeed in deep shade, but most will be at their best nearer the sunnier edges of the woodland. All of the plants will do best in a humus-rich soil. Unless it says otherwise in the text, all the plants will succeed in any reasonable well-drained soil.

WOODY CLIMBERS

Actinidia deliciosa. The KIWI FRUIT is becoming quite well known, but many people still do not realise that it can be grown successfully outdoors in Britain. A vigorous climbing plant, it supports itself by twining around the branches of trees and shrubs. I have seen it make its way to the top of a 20 metre tall tree and then produce a huge crop of fruit right at the top of the tree. Whilst this might be a very productive method of growing the plant, I'm not at all sure how you would harvest the fruit – hire a helicopter maybe! Plants can be kept much smaller in cultivation, however, by judicious pruning in the winter. Fruits are formed on second year wood and also on fruit spurs on older wood, so when pruning you need to ensure plenty of the previous year's growth is left, whilst also encouraging fresh growth.

Grow kiwi fruits on the sunny side of the woodland, preferably with a south-westerly aspect because, although the dormant plant is frost-hardy, the new growth in spring can be damaged by temperatures below zero. Plants dislike alkaline soils and are best grown in a soil with a pH below 6.

The fruit ripens in late autumn and, if stored in a cool frost-free place, will keep for at least a couple of months. It is about 8cm long and has a soft juicy texture and a pleasant flavour that reminds some people of very ripe gooseberries. The only drawback is the skin which is very hairy. I have known people who eat this skin though I find the texture very unpleasant and if I eat more than one fruit with its skin then my mouth becomes very sore.

You need one male plant to every five or six females in order to ensure fertilisation and thus a crop of fruit. There are several named varieties. The most commonly available female is 'Heywood' whilst 'Tomuri' is a free-flowering and disease-resistant male. 'Blake' produces hermaphrodite flowers and so does not need a male plant for fertilisation. I have read, though, that the fruit of this variety is not so well flavoured.

All members of this genus produce edible fruits and, like the kiwi, you normally need male and female plants. Other species worth trying include:

A. arguta. This has been receiving quite a bit of attention recently and a number of named varieties are now available in this country, though there is little experience of how well they will fruit here. At least one of these varieties, called 'Issai', is hermaphrodite and is therefore self-fertile. In general, however, you need to grow male and female plants if you want the fruit. The fruit has a very pleasant flavour and is said to be 5 times as rich in vitamin C as blackcurrants. It is rather smaller than the kiwi, averaging about 25mm in diameter, but it is smooth-skinned and so does not need to be peeled. This is another very vigorous plant and it can climb 15 metres or more into the trees, though judicious pruning will keep it much smaller. Dormant plants are hardy to about -50°C but, as with all the kiwi fruits, the young growth in spring is frost-tender.

A. kolomikta. Often grown as an ornamental plant in Britain, the male form especially often has a very attractive variegation. Given the chance, it will climb about 10 metres into the trees. The fruit is about 2cm in diameter and is said to be very well flavoured, though I have not tried it. It is very rare to see this species in fruit in Britain – this is probably because plants of just one sex are usually grown. However, if you grow both sexes then there is no reason I can think of why they should not crop well. There are some named varieties that have been selected for their superior fruits, but I do not know of a British source for them. This plant emits an odour that is very attractive to cats, who will sometimes claw a young plant to pieces if they are given the chance.

A. melanandra. Less vigorous than most other species, climbing perhaps 7 metres into the trees. In the autumn it produces a sweet-tasting fruit about 3cm in diameter. Although the books say that it crops well at Kew Gardens, I have yet to see any plants producing fruit.

A. purpurea. Closely related to *A. arguta*. It can grow about 10 metres tall. The sweet tasting fruit is about 25mm in diameter and ripens in late autumn.
Cultivation for all these species is the same as for *A. deliciosa* except that they are more tolerant of alkaline soils.

Akebia **species**. Members of this genus can produce a delicately flavoured edible fruit. The plants grow very well along the sunnier edges of a woodland. See also page 157.

Schisandra **species**. They grow very well on the shadier edges of a woodland and provide tasty edible fruits. See also page 159.

Smilax rotundifolia. HORSEBRIER is a deciduous woody climbing plant. A vigorous grower with prickly shoots up to 12 metres long, it occupies the same sort of niche in American woodlands that blackberries do in Britain. It is considered to be an obnoxious pest in America, but is not so vigorous in this country and does not spread itself around. This is a plant for the woodland edge, in a position that receives at least moderate amounts of sun.

We have only been growing this plant for 3 years and have yet to try out any of its uses but it certainly seems to be promising. The edible root is rich in starch, it can be dried and ground into a flour that is used in making cakes, puddings, sweet drinks etc. and can also be made into a jelly or eaten in soups. A beer resembling root beer or sarsaparilla is made from the roots. The young shoots can be added to salads or cooked like asparagus.

I have very little experience of growing or eating plants from this genus but all of the following grow well in this country and seem to be promising food plants. All are deciduous woody climbers unless stated otherwise:

S. aspera. SARSAPARILLA is evergreen and grows to about 3 metres tall, it only succeeds outdoors in the mildest parts of the country. Whilst it is not the true sarsaparilla (which is a tropical plant), its root is used in a similar way to make a drink and the young shoots are cooked like asparagus.

S. bona-nox. GREENBRIER grows about 6 metres tall. It has similar uses to *S. rotundifolia* with the addition that the root is rich in pectin and can be made into a gelatine substitute. A report on the fruit says that it has a rubbery texture and can be chewed. And chewed and chewed and chewed presumably!

S. china. CHINA ROOT grows about 4.5 metres tall. Its uses are similar to *S. bona-nox* except that the fruit sounds more interesting since it is eaten to quench the thirst.

S. hispida. HAG BRIER has shoots up to 15 metres long. It is used like *S. rotundifolia*.

Vitis **species**. I do not really want to discuss the GRAPE in detail since it is a well-known crop. This is just a reminder that selected cultivars should do well on the sunny edges of a woodland. See also Chapter 8 for some interesting cultivars that produce fruit reliably in this country.

HERBACEOUS CLIMBERS

Amphicarpaea bracteata. The HOG PEANUT is not a true peanut though the two plants are related and this species buries its edible seed in the soil in much the same way that peanuts do. The seed, which tastes more like a bean than a peanut, is about the size of a small pea. It is quite pleasant raw and can also be sprouted or cooked. Yields are not very high but hog peanut probably has the potential through selective breeding to become a very useful food crop. Smaller seeds are produced from flowers higher up the plant and these can be eaten cooked. The books say that the plant has a fleshy nutritious root, but those I've been growing only have thin roots that are not worthwhile trying to eat.

Hog peanuts send out new shoots up to 1.5 metres long each year. They can be left to their own devices to scramble about small shrubs in the sunnier areas of the woodland, or they can be supplied with thin supports for them to twine around.

Apios americana. The GROUND NUT is a vigorous perennial climber up to 1.5 metres tall and capable of becoming invasive when well sited. I am not certain that it would be that well-sited in a British woodland because although it is a woodland plant in its native North America it experiences much sunnier summers there than in our relatively sunless climate. It quite possibly needs a sunnier position in this country, especially in areas with cooler summers, because I have not yet seen it being grown in shade and I have no woodland of my own to experiment with. Perhaps a sunny woodland edge is the answer.

The tubers of this plant are absolutely delicious when cooked. The texture is soft and floury and the flavour is somewhat like roasted sweet potatoes. The tubers can also be dried and ground into a powder then used as a thickener in soups etc. or mixed with cereal flours to enhance their nutritional value. They contain 17% crude protein which is more than 3 times that found in potatoes. They can be harvested in their first year but take 2 - 3 years to become a sizeable crop.

The tubers are formed quite near the surface of the soil and sometimes at a considerable distance from the plant. The plant sends out a thin root which swells at intervals along its length to form the tubers. When harvested, these roots look somewhat like a necklace. Individual tubers are fairly small, perhaps 30mm long and 15mm wide, and yields do not compare with cultivated crops like potatoes, but there is some research taking place in America at present, selecting higher yielding cultivars with considerably larger roots for commercial cultivation. These cultivars have produced yields of up to 2.3 kilos per plant and will hopefully soon become available in Britain. The seed and the young seedpods can also be eaten when cooked.

Bomarea edulis. Some reports say that this beautiful plant is not hardy outdoors in Britain, whilst one says that it will tolerate temperatures down to about -10°C. It has been growing successfully in light shade in a woodland garden at Kew Botanical Gardens for at least the last 5 years, where it scrambles over other plants to reach a height of about 2 metres and produces its beautiful flowers in late summer. Make sure that the plant receives at least some sun during the day and also try and protect it from slugs since they adore the young spring growth. If leaving the plant in the ground over the winter, give it the extra protection of a mulch to protect the roots from the cold.

This species is cultivated as a root crop in South America. Although it is unlikely to yield heavily in this country, its small edible tubers have a mild starchy flavour and when boiled they make a light and delicate food.

Humulus lupulus. Our native HOP can climb up to 6 metres tall, supporting itself by twining around other plants. It usually goes sideways as much as it goes up. This is an easily grown plant that prefers a rich soil and a fairly sunny position on the woodland edge. Hops can also succeed in dry shade if plenty of humus is incorporated into the soil, once established they are also somewhat drought tolerant.

Hops are frequently cultivated, both commercially and on a domestic scale, for their seed heads which have many medicinal qualities and are also used as a flavouring and preservative in beer. There are many named varieties. If seed is required, you need to grow both male and female plants, one male being able to

Humulus lupulus. The female flowers of the HOP can be used medicinally and in the making of beer.

fertilize 5 - 6 females. Generally, when grown for beer making, the unfertilized seed heads are preferred and so most male plants are weeded out.

Hops are also sometimes cultivated in the garden for their edible young shoots. I find the shoots somewhat bitter but one report says that they are unique and, to many tastes, delicious. Amongst the plant's other uses, a brown dye is obtained from the leaves and flower heads plus a fibre obtained from the stems is similar to hemp but not as strong and is used to make cloth and paper.

BAMBOOS

I was not really sure where to place these plants. Although they are grasses, they do have persistent woody stems and could therefore be included with the shrubs. In the end, however, I decided to give them their own section.

Many bamboos are ideal woodland plants, they adore growing in dappled shade and look so natural in such a situation. They are all shallow rooted and so are best grown close to deeper-rooted plants. There are many different genera of bamboos, and there seem to be more new ones almost every day as taxonomists constantly review current names. I am only going to deal with the genus *Phyllostachys* in this chapter since this is probably the best all-rounder for British gardens. It produces the nicest and largest edible young shoots and its canes are usually of a very good quality. A number of other bamboo species are discussed in Chapter 9.

There are complete industries based around bamboos in China, Japan and the tropics where some incredibly tall species with stems like tree trunks grow. The canes are used in construction, a huge range of arts and crafts such as basket making, for making paper and are also harvested in the spring for their edible young shoots.

Bamboos do not have quite the same potential here, unfortunately, because our cool summers do not encourage them to put out lots of new canes each year or to grow so tall, but even so there are many ways in which we can use them. The size can vary tremendously from species to species in both thickness and strength and they are used for such things as plant supports, water pipes, minor construction and various handicrafts. The canes can also be pulped and the fibre obtained from them makes an excellent paper.

In a warmer climate the plants in this genus tend to spread widely and aggressively, but in Britain they are generally well-behaved and usually form a fairly compact clump. The plants produce less new shoots in spring than they would in their native Asia, and these young shoots are somewhat smaller than shop-bought edible bamboo shoots. Nevertheless, yields can be quite reasonable and there are some species that can produce shoots of 8cm or more in diameter in Britain. Most bamboo shoots are bitter and need to be cooked in one change of water in order to remove this bitterness. I have not as yet eaten young shoots from British plants but the species listed later all grow well in this country and are amongst the best to try.

A word or two about the growth habits of bamboos. Each year a healthy plant will produce a number of new canes. These canes generally start growing in late spring.

However tall each cane grows to in its first year will be the maximum height of that cane. In subsequent years it will produce side branches but will not grow any taller. Also, when the cane emerges from the ground it is already at its maximum diameter – it will not get any thicker. Growing bamboos in pots, or dividing them, has a dwarfing effect on the plants. When planted back into the open ground it will take them some years to recover. They will start off producing much shorter thinner canes in their first year, larger specimens will be produced in subsequent years until after 5 years or so they should be producing full-sized canes.

Most bamboos do not flower very often, in fact there can be gaps of a hundred years or more between periods of flowering. There is a common fallacy that bamboos always die after they have flowered, but this is not usually the case. What happens more frequently is that the plants put almost all their energies into flowering and this severely weakens the clumps. If you are patient, the plants will usually recover though they will look rather tatty for a few years. Whatever you do, do not be tempted to feed the plants with artificial fertilisers at this time, since this will almost certainly kill them. Well-rotted compost will do them a lot more good, or just leave things to nature. If your bamboos do flower, and if they also produce viable seed, then you could use this seed in all the same ways that wheat is used in making bread, cakes etc. However, unless you obtain huge quantities, you might find it more worthwhile to sow the seed and pass some of it on to other growers (including me!).

A word of warning: the bamboos listed here are generally well behaved in a cool temperate climate such as Britain's, but they can 'run' and become invasive in warmer climes.

Phyllostachys **species.** Ideal plants for the dappled shade of a woodland. They grow best in a rich damp soil in a sheltered position. Although the species listed here are quite cold-tolerant, with some of them surviving temperatures down to -20°C, they dislike prolonged exposure to hard frosts. This is another reason for siting them in a woodland because this will give them the protection from frosts they prefer.

I think that all bamboos are wonderful, but if you forced me to make a short-list from this genus then the following would be included:

P. aurea. The GOLDEN BAMBOO grows about 5 metres tall and wide. Established plants are said to be drought resistant. The young shoots are about 15mm in diameter, they have very little bitterness and so can also be eaten raw. The canes are very hard but also very flexible, they are used for plant supports, umbrella handles etc.

P. aureosulcata. The YELLOW-GROOVE BAMBOO grows up to 6 metres tall and wide. The young shoots are about 25mm in diameter and are not very bitter.

P. bambusoides. MADAKE can reach 8 metres in height and width. Its thick young shoots are rather bitter and need to be cooked in a couple of changes of water before being eaten. The cultivar 'Castillon' has smaller canes which are less bitter, so are more acceptable for food. Individual canes of this species are very long lived and can stay healthy for 20 years or more. These large canes are considered to be the most versatile of the genus for making furniture, scaffolding etc.

Phyllostachys nigra. A graceful woodland plant providing edible shoots and canes for plant supports and other uses (see overleaf).

P. dulcis. The SWEETSHOOT BAMBOO grows about 5 metres tall and wide. It strongly dislikes drought. There is some doubt over the hardiness of this species with some reports saying that it only succeeds outdoors in the milder areas of the country and others saying that it will tolerate occasional lows down to -20°C. The young shoots are entirely free of acridity and this species is considered to be the best edible species in China. The canes are rather weak and so are seldom used as plant supports or in construction etc.

P. edulis. MOSO-CHIKU can grow up to 6 metres tall and wide and prefers a position on the sunny edges of a woodland. It produces some of the largest young shoots in the genus – these are not of the best quality but are very acceptable when cooked in one change of water. The canes are much used in construction etc.

P. nidularia. The BIG-NODE BAMBOO grows 6 metres tall and wide. Its shoots are highly prized in China, both for their earliness and their delicate flavour that is completely free of bitterness.

P. nigra. The BLACK BAMBOO grows up to 7.5 metres tall and wide. This is one of the most beautiful bamboos that can be grown in Britain. The young shoots are somewhat acrid and need to be cooked in one change of water. The canes are thin-walled but durable, they make excellent plant supports and are also much used in making decorative panels and inlays.

P. nuda. Growing 5 metres tall and wide. This is one of the hardiest members of the genus and has withstood temperatures as low as -22°C. The young shoots are of good quality, being almost free of bitterness.

P. sulphurea viridis. KOU-CHIKU grows 4 metres tall and wide. A very hardy plant, tolerating temperatures down to about -20°C, though persistent cold springs make it very lazy in sending up new shoots. The shoots are almost free of any bitterness and can be finely sliced and eaten raw, though they are usually boiled for a short time first.

P. viridi-glaucescens. Growing up to 10 metres tall and wide. The new shoots can be 4cm or more in diameter, they are virtually free of bitterness and can be eaten raw.

HERBACEOUS PLANTS
(including bulbs)

We are now moving down to the woodland floor where light is at a premium. Here the plants employ various techniques in order to prosper. For example, they might come into leaf early in the year before the trees produce their leaves. Although the sun is less powerful at this time of year, there is still more light in the woodland than there will be in the summer. The plants grow away rapidly, flowering and setting seed in the spring and early summer before dying down as the shade from the trees increases. These plants will generally also do well outside of a woodland as long as the soil is rich in humus.

Other plants develop thick leaves that are more efficient at trapping the light. Being adapted to shady conditions, these plants will not be very adaptable to life in the sun and so if you want to grow them outside a woodland you will need to give then some other shade, such as the ground by a north-facing wall. Once again, they will normally require a humus-rich soil if they are to thrive.

Another group of plants will make full use of the protection that the woodland offers them, but will also want to find as much sun as possible. These plants will be found growing along the sunnier edges of the woodland. So long as your garden is sheltered you should have no trouble growing these plants in non-woodland conditions.

One of the main advantages of growing all these plants in a woodland situation if possible is that they are going to be a lot easier to maintain. Since they are adapted to life amongst the trees they will usually be vigorous enough to maintain themselves against weed competition. Indeed, weed competition will be less intense because only woodland plants will thrive in this habitat.

When well designed, the woodland or forest garden is self-fertilizing (see the Introduction for more details of this) and so there is little or no need to feed the plants growing in it. Moisture levels are also more constant and so there is no need to water, even in years of severe drought. Even in the driest of years the plants in a woodland will be able to grow longer than plants in the open ground and, if the drought really bites, they will merely become dormant and wait for next spring to start growing again.

The plants in the following lists will all succeed in any reasonable soil unless the text says otherwise. They also grow best in soils that are rich in organic matter and will be unhappy if the soil is low in organic matter, especially in dry weather.

PLANTS FOR SHADE – HERBACEOUS

Dentaria laciniata. TOOTHWORT grows about 30cm tall and forms a slowly spreading clump about 30cm wide. It flowers in the spring and has disappeared by early summer, so it does particularly well under deciduous trees.

The edible root can be harvested in the summer and autumn. It has a pleasant pungent peppery taste somewhat like watercress, it makes a nice flavouring in salads and can also be used as a relish. The leaves can be eaten either raw or cooked and have a peppery flavour. This plant is rather low-yielding but is a rather pleasant nibble and makes good utilization of the space under trees.

D. diphylla. A very similar plant and has the same uses.

Medeola virginica. INDIAN CUCUMBER ROOT grows about 25cm tall and is best in a slightly acid sandy soil. I have not eaten this one as yet but it grows well in the light shade of British woodlands.

The edible root, as the name suggests, tastes like cucumber. It is fairly thick, up to 8cm long and is said to be crisp and tender with a slight sweetness. It is not a very productive crop.

Montia perfoliata and *M. sibirica*. These species are marvellous plants for deep shade, and will even succeed under the dense canopy of beech trees. They make excellent salad plants and can be harvested all year round. See also page 207.

Oxalis acetosella. WOOD SORREL forms a gradually spreading clump about 8cm tall and 30cm wide. A very tolerant plant, it thrives in the deep shade of a woodland and will also succeed in sunnier positions.

Wood sorrel comes into leaf in early spring and provides a delicious salad leaf with a lemon-like flavour from then until well into the summer. The spring flowers can also be eaten. The plant contains oxalic acid and so the leaves should only be eaten in small quantities. If you suffer from rheumatism or arthritis, then you would be advised to give this one a miss completely. See Appendix 4 for more details.

Podophyllum peltatum. AMERICAN MANDRAKE grows about 30cm tall and wide. Although slow to establish, this species is very long-lived. It prefers dappled shade but can succeed even in quite dense shade – it has succeeded under the dense shade of beech trees for example.

The fruit is 5cm or more long, it ripens in early to mid summer and can be eaten raw or cooked. It is best peeled and when fully ripe has a pleasant flavour, though it contains a lot of seeds. Make sure that it is fully ripe because otherwise it is strongly laxative. This plant has been attracting quite a lot of attention from the drug companies because it contains substances that can be used in the treatment of cancer and AIDS.

P. hexandrum. A slightly larger Asian species with similar uses.

Pulmonaria officinalis. LUNGWORT grows about 30cm tall and wide and thrives in deep shade, though it will also tolerate full sun if the soil is rich in humus. Very easily grown, it will succeed in most soils though it dislikes dry conditions.

The leaves are rather bland, but make an acceptable addition to a mixed salad. Because the plant is evergreen, these leaves can be harvested at almost any time of the year, though care should be exercised not to overpick in the winter when there is little new growth taking place. The plant can also be used as a ground cover in the shadier aspects of a woodland or when grown by a north-facing wall. Lungwort is best known, however, as a medicinal herb with a specific effect upon the lungs.

Smilacena stellata. This species grows well in the darker areas of the woodland. About 60cm tall, it can be rather slow to get established but then spreads vigorously to form large clumps 60cm or more wide. It does not like alkaline or heavily acid soils.

The small fruits are often formed abundantly on racemes at the top of the plant. These fruits ripen in late summer to early autumn and, when fully ripe, have an unusual bitter-sweet flavour that reminds me of treacle. It is rather an acquired taste, though it can be acquired quite easily. Don't acquire it too easily, however,

Smilacena stellata. Showing the mature treacle flavoured fruits.

because until you get used to them the fruits can have a laxative effect on the body.

Other edible uses that I have not tried as yet are the young shoots that are said to be an asparagus substitute and the root which needs to be soaked first in order to get rid of a bitter flavour but is then used like potatoes.

S. racemosa. The FALSE SPIKENARD is a better known plant and easier to obtain. Somewhat larger than the previous species, it can be up to 1 metre tall and almost as wide. It can be used in the same ways as *S. stellata*, but to my mind does not taste quite so nice.

Streptopus amplexifolius. CUCUMBER ROOT grows about 1 metre tall with a spread of about 30cm. It grows well in the darker areas of the woodland and prefers lighter soils.

This is another plant that I have not yet tried. Its blackcurrant-sized fruit ripens in early autumn and can be eaten raw or be cooked in soups and stews. It is said to be juicy with a cucumber flavour, but don't eat too many of the fruits when you first try them because they can be laxative when eaten in large quantities by people who are not used to them. The young shoots are added to salads or can be cooked like asparagus, they also have a cucumber-like flavour. The root can be harvested in the autumn and eaten in salads. Guess what? It also tastes like cucumber.

Two other members of the genus have similar uses, the only difference being that their fruits are said to taste like watermelons. *S. roseus* is about 50cm tall and *S. streptopoides* is about 30cm tall, both grow about 30cm wide.

PLANTS FOR SHADE – BULBS

Allium **species**. All members of this genus have edible leaves and flowers – if they produce bulbs then these are edible too. Most of them require sunny conditions and are dealt with in Chapters 4 and 5, but there are a few that thrive in a woodland. These include:

A. ursinum. See Plate 17. Our native WILD GARLIC grows exceedingly well in a shady position, sometimes too well if you have a limited space in which to grow it since it easily becomes invasive. Reaching a height of 30cm, when well-sited it usually forms carpets of growth many yards wide. Wild garlic is often found growing in quite wet soils, though it is also found in drier parts of the woodland and in hedgerows.

This is a plant that we use a lot of, especially since it comes into growth so early in the year and is very productive. The leaves are produced from February, they can be eaten raw or cooked and have a strong garlic flavour. The flowers appear in mid to late spring, they have a slightly stronger flavour than the leaves and are a very decorative and tasty addition to the salad bowl. We continue eating these flowers as the seeds start to be formed, by which time the flavour has got even stronger. The bulbs can also be eaten, though they are rather small. The flavour is similar to the leaves and they can be harvested all year round if required. The leaves start to die down as the plant comes into flower and by the middle of summer wild garlic has disappeared completely from view.

A. triquetrum. The THREE CORNERED LEEK grows about 35cm tall and spreads to 10cm wide. It has a milder flavour than wild garlic and is excellent in salads. It is commonly naturalised in Cornish hedgerows and, whilst it will succeed in deep shade, grows best along the sunnier edges of the woodland.

The plant comes into growth in mid-autumn and the leaves can be harvested judiciously throughout the winter. The flowers are formed in mid spring, these are excellent decorative and tasty additions to a salad. The plant dies down in early summer and the small bulbs, which are about 2cm in diameter, can be harvested from then until the autumn. This species tolerates temperatures down to about –10°C and is not hardy in the colder areas of the country.

A. tricoccum is said to be one of the best North American wild species for sweetness, with a flavour that is rather like leeks. It grows about 30cm tall and perhaps 20cm wide. This is a plant that I have only just started to grow and have not as yet eaten. The leaves are available in the spring, the flowers in late spring to early summer and the bulb, which is about 5cm long by 1cm wide, can be harvested from the summer to early winter.

Erythronium dens-canis. DOG'S TOOTH VIOLET is a beautiful spring flowering bulb, growing about 15cm tall and 10cm wide. It comes into growth in early spring and has disappeared by the summer. It spreads freely by means of stolons when in a suitable position, though the flowers are often produced only sparsely.

The smallish bulb, which can be harvested from early summer until early winter, can be eaten raw or cooked and has a very acceptable taste. It is rich in starch and can also be dried then ground into a flour to be used in making vermicelli and cakes. The leaves can be eaten if they are cooked, but this would weaken the bulbs and is not really recommended.

All members of this genus produce edible bulbs. I have not eaten any of the following plants but they have the same uses and habit of growth as *E. dens-canis*. They grow well in this country and are at least as beautiful as that species:

E. albidum. This plant does not flower well in Britain, though it increases well by division. The bulb is only 25mm long but has a delicious flavour. The plant grows about 10cm tall and forms clumps about 25cm wide.

E. americanum. Another species that does not flower very well in Britain but spreads well by means of stolons. It grows about 20cm tall and forms a gradually spreading clump perhaps 25cm wide. The bulb is up to 25mm long and has a crisp, chewy, pleasant taste.

E. revolutum. Growing about 30cm tall and almost as wide. It does very well in Britain and flowers more freely than most species. The cultivars 'Pagoda' and 'White Beauty' have good sized bulbs, are some of the easiest *Erythroniums* to grow in Britain and usually increase freely when well-sited. When growing plants from this genus, these are the forms that I would be most inclined to try first.

PLANTS FOR THE WOODLAND EDGE – HERBACEOUS

Angelica archangelica. ANGELICA is a vigorous biennial growing about 1.5 metres tall and 1 metre wide. A very cold-hardy and easily grown plant, it does well in dappled shade or in full sun and tolerates very acid soils. Although a biennial, if it is prevented from flowering the plant will live for a number of years. This does leave you with a bit of a dilemma because the flowering plant attracts bees and hoverflies to the garden, helping to create a natural balance of insect pests and predators. Should you allow it to flower, then it should self-sow if in a suitable site. To be on the safe side, harvest some of the seed and sow it immediately in a cold frame because it only has a short period of viability.

Angelica is occasionally cultivated in the herb garden, mainly for its culinary uses. The plants have a pervading aromatic odour and are almost untroubled by pests and diseases. The leaves can be harvested from spring to early summer, and then again in late summer if the plant is cut back to prevent flowering. They are eaten raw or cooked and have a liquorice-like flavour, they are also added to tart fruits when cooking in order to sweeten them and reduce the need to add sugar. The peeled stalks and young shoots are also edible, the stems are used like celery.

Aquilegia vulgaris. COLUMBINE will look after itself very well along the sunnier edges of a woodland. It has delightfully sweet edible flowers that make a pleasant thirst-relieving munch on a summer's day or can be added to salads. See also page 89.

Aralia cordata. UDO grows about 1.8 metres tall and 1 metre wide. Commonly cultivated as a vegetable in Japan, there are conflicting reports as to its hardiness in Britain. One book suggests that it will only succeed in the mildest areas of the country whilst another says that it is hardy to about -25°C. It likes the dappled shade of a woodland edge and is probably hardier if the soil is not too fertile. I have lost this plant over winter on two occasions, but this was probably more due to slugs, wind and lack of woodland protection than the cold.

The Japanese eat the shoots either raw or cooked. These shoots are up to 1.5 metres long, so they can be a bit of a handful to bring back from the greengrocer! A mild and agreeable flavour, they are usually blanched by excluding light from the growing plant and are crisp and tender with a unique lemon-like flavour. The root is also edible and can be baked or boiled.

Asarum canadense. SNAKE ROOT grows about 10cm tall and forms a spreading clump perhaps 50cm wide. The roots are used as a ginger substitute in flavouring cooked foods. See also page 206.

Chrysosplenium alternifolium. GOLDEN SAXIFRAGE forms a slowly spreading carpet up to 30cm tall. It grows well in acid soils in wet woodlands. See page 136 for more details.

Conopodium majus. PIGNUT is a native plant growing about 30cm tall and 25cm wide in the dappled shade of the woodland edge. It dislikes alkaline soils but is otherwise not too fussy.

The tubers are rather small and fiddly to harvest, but they make very pleasant eating either raw or cooked, with a flavour somewhere between a sweet potato and hazel nuts. When eaten raw, some people detect a hot aftertaste of radish. The plant produces larger tubers in cultivation, and perhaps has the potential to become a productive root crop.

Cornus canadensis. Growing about 25cm tall and spreading slowly to form a patch perhaps 1 metre wide, this species grows well in acid soils. Its edible fruit ripens in late summer. See also page 206.

Cryptotaenia japonica. MITSUBA, or JAPANESE PARSLEY, is a short-lived perennial that is often cultivated in Japan and is sometimes also found in British seed catalogues. It grows up to 1 metre tall with a spread of 60cm. I'm not sure if this plant will be able to maintain itself in a woodland, but it certainly grows well there. I have found that it tends to die out over winter when grown in the open, but a friend who grows it in fairly deep shade has been growing the same plants for several years now. The leaves will turn yellow in hot weather if the plant is in full sun.

The leaves and stems can be used raw or cooked as a flavouring, they taste like parsley if you let your imagination run away with you. Do not add the leaves until a couple of minutes before the food is ready if you are using them as a flavouring in cooked foods, otherwise their flavour will be destroyed. Seedlings and young leaves are an acceptable addition to salads and the root is also edible though I haven't tried it yet. If the growing stem is blanched by excluding light, it can be used as a celery substitute whilst the seed is also used as a parsley-like flavouring.

C. canadensis. A very closely related plant from North America, it has similar uses.

Fagopyrum dibotrys. PERENNIAL BUCKWHEAT is a very vigorous plant that grows well on the edges of the woodland, and probably also in the shadier areas. It grows up to 1.5 metres tall and will spread very freely if given the chance. The leaves can be used in salads, but are better cooked. See also page 111.

Hemerocallis fulva. The DAY LILLIES are dealt with more fully on page 93. This species in particular will grow well on the woodland edge and will provide you with edible flowers, roots and young shoots.

Hosta species. These are dealt with on page 206. This is just a reminder that they make very good woodland plants and their leaf stems can be eaten raw or cooked.

Malva moschata. The MUSK MALLOW grows about 75cm tall and 50cm wide. One of the best summer salad plants, it thrives in light shade along the woodland edge. See also page 94.

Another member of this genus that I have seen growing well in a woodland is the annual *M. verticillata.* This plant can produce delicious but mild flavoured leaves 20cm or more across and is one of my very favourite leaves for using in quantity in salads. I have been growing it for a number of years in sunny positions and it has never thrived with me. However, it grows extremely well in Robert Hart's forest garden and self-sows freely there. See also page 217.

Melissa officinalis. LEMON BALM is often grown in the herb garden, but it can also succeed in light shade in a woodland. It grows about 70cm tall and 40cm wide. A very tolerant plant, succeeding in most soils and situations, it grows well in dry soils.

The lemon-scented leaves can be added to salads or cooked as a flavouring, they also make a very nice tea. The growing plant can help repel insects in the garden and you can also hang up bunches of it indoors to keep flies away.

Myrrhis odorata. SWEET CICELY is a very easily grown plant reaching about 1 metre tall and wide. It prefers a moist soil and a position in dappled shade, though it also succeeds in full sun.

Sweet Cicely was at one time commonly cultivated as a vegetable but has now fallen into virtual disuse. This is a great pity because it is a very tasty and productive plant. It comes into growth very early in the year and can provide its delicious aniseed-flavoured leaves from late January right round into December. I adore these leaves in mixed salads, they can also be cooked with acid fruits in order to reduce the need for sugar. The root and seed are also edible, with the same flavour of aniseed. The leaves and the seed make a good wood polish – you just rub them quite firmly over the wood and then polish the wood with a clean cloth to remove any greenness. They are particularly good on oak panels.

Peltaria alliacea. GARLIC CRESS is an evergreen plant growing about 30cm tall and spreading freely to form large clumps. The leaves have a flavour of garlic and cress combined (which explains the common name) and they can be harvested almost all year round, the plant dying down for just a few weeks in the summer after setting seed. See also page 203.

Rumex acetosa. SORREL is a native plant growing about 60cm tall and 30cm wide. A very tolerant and easily grown plant, it will succeed in most soils and situations.

The leaves have a delicious lemon-like flavour and are one of our favourite additions to salads, they can also be cooked though this does seem to be a waste of such a tasty leaf. Some years ago I obtained a superb large-leaved form of this species from a Polish gardener. This has hardly ever flowered since I obtained it and instead concentrates on growing leaves which means that it does not die down in the summer or the winter and so we can normally harvest it all 12 months of the year. Sorrel leaves contain oxalic acid and so should be used in moderation, and perhaps not at all if you suffer from rheumatism or arthritis. See Appendix 4 for more details. Nevertheless, in small quantities they are a delicious and nutritious addition to the diet.

All other parts of the plant are edible, though a lot less interesting than the leaves. Non-edible uses of the plant include an infusion of the stems that is used as a polish for bamboo, wicker furniture and silver. The juice of the plant removes stains from linen and also ink stains (but not ball-point ink) from white material. Dark green to brown and dark grey dyes can be obtained from the roots and a grey-blue dye is obtained from the leaves and stems.

Symphytum officinale. COMFREY is an easily grown plant reaching about 1.2 metres tall and 60cm wide. It does best in a moist soil on the sunnier edges of the woodland. This native woodland plant is quite well known, especially to organic growers, for its many uses in the garden and on the farm. It self-sows freely when in a suitable position and can become a bit of a nuisance at times. The hybrid **S. x uplandicum** is more often used by gardeners and, unlike our native plant, does not normally set viable seed so is less likely to become a nuisance. Both species have deep roots and are very difficult to eradicate once established. Even small sections of the root will regrow if they are left in the ground.

The young leaves can be cooked or eaten raw and are very nutritious. If you like hairy slimy leaves then you will love this one. If on the other hand that does not appeal, you can always chop a small amount very finely into a large bowl of mixed salad, then you will almost not know that it is there.

The blanched stems are said to be used as an asparagus substitute and the peeled roots can be added to soups but the leaves have put me off so completely that I have never got round to trying either of these uses. A tea made from the dried leaves is quite pleasant drinking though and the roasted roots have been used for making coffee. One word of warning – there have been some reports that prolonged heavy use of comfrey for food might cause liver damage. This applies most particularly to the older leaves. When used in moderation the health benefits should far outweigh any unhealthy effects.

Moving away from the plant's edible uses we come to the main reason that comfrey is grown so much by organic growers. It is very fast-growing and is tolerant of being cut to the ground a number of times each year and so can produce a large bulk of organic material for the garden. This is rich in minerals, especially nitrogen and potassium, and can be used in the compost heap to speed up fermentation though it is more often used to make a liquid feed (see Chapter 1 for details) or as an instant compost for crops such as potatoes or tomatoes. Cut the leaves, leave them to wilt and then simply layer the wilted leaves at the bottom of the potato trench or apply them as a mulch. For optimum production of the leaves it is best to grow the plant in a sunny position but even on the woodland edge this is a very productive plant.

Comfrey is also a famous medicinal herb, exceedingly useful for first aid in the treatment of cuts and burns. Simply chew up some of the leaves (this is the only time that they get into my mouth), apply the chewed leaves to the burn or cut and then wrap it up. You will be amazed how it will speed up the healing process. Some years ago I acquired my first scythe. Although I had no experience of using it, I felt like a true farmer and went out onto my plot of land to cut the grass. After a few ineffective sweeps (which did my back no good whatsoever), I decided it was time to sharpen the blade. Having no idea how to do this, I sat down on a chair, rested the blade against my leg and ran the sharpening stone up and down. Then the blade slipped from my grasp and slid down my thigh. At first I was annoyed because it cut a slice in my jeans, then I realised that it had also cut a slice into my thigh about 1.5cm deep and maybe 4cm long. Fortunately I was sitting very close to the comfrey patch and applied a poultice of the leaves to the cut. For a while I sat down feeling rather sorry for myself, but then got bored with this and carried on with my attempts to use the scythe. By the time evening came I was not much better with the scythe but the cut was looking clean and had already started to knit together. Within a few days it was healed.

Viola odorata. I am becoming more and more impressed with the SWEET VIOLET as a salad. Growing about 10cm tall and spreading quite freely to form clumps 1 metre or more wide, this native species succeeds in most soils in sun or shade and tolerates considerable neglect.

A very productive salad plant, it has a mild flavour (some would say bland) and can be used in quantity in the salad bowl. An evergreen plant, it is especially useful as a winter salad and has the added bonus of flowering in late winter and early spring. These flowers have a delightful fragrance and make a very pleasant addition to salads. The leaves can also be cooked and are sometimes used to thicken soups in much the same way that okra is used in America.

An essential oil from the flowers and leaves is used in perfumery, whilst a pigment extracted from the flowers is used as a litmus to test for acids and alkalines.

All other members of this genus of low-growing plants have edible leaves and flowers, though if the flowers are yellow the plant can be laxative when eaten in quantity. Many other species are suitable for the woodland edge, these include *V. canadensis*, *V. mirabilis*, *V. obliqua*, *V. palmata*, *V. riviniana* and *V. sororaria*.

PLANTS FOR THE WOODLAND EDGE – BULBS

Lilium **species**. Lilies are superb in the semi-shade of a woodland though you have to keep the slugs off them, especially in the spring. They like growing with their roots in the cool, moist, shady woodland floor but with their flowers reaching up into the light, thus they grow very well amongst shrubs.

These bulbous plants are well-known for their beautiful flowers. What is less well-known is that the bulbs are edible and several of the species are cultivated as root crops in the Orient. The bulbs are used in much the same way as potatoes, in some species there is a bitter taste but others are delicious. What you have to decide, of course, is whether you could ever bring yourself to eat the bulb of such a beautiful plant. Although I might try one bulb of a species, I wouldn't want to eat them in quantity unless they were increasing freely in my garden. Most species will not do this, unfortunately, but there are some that do and this varies greatly from garden to garden. Those that I would be most inclined to make a meal of include:

L. bulbiferum. The FIRE LILY grows about 1.2 metres tall and 20cm wide. The bulbs have a pleasant sweet and mealy taste.

L. lancifolium. The TIGER LILY grows about 1.2 metres tall and 25cm wide. The bulbs are slightly bitter, but are pleasant when cooked and have a flavour somewhat like parsley. This easily-grown species should be kept away from other members of the genus because, although it is tolerant of virus diseases, it is often infected by them and can pass them on to the other species.

L. superbum. Growing to 2.4 metres tall and about 30cm wide. It requires an acid soil. The bulb is about 5cm in diameter and has a starchy, slightly sweet flavour.

There are also numerous cultivars – if you ever find yourself in the fortunate position of having too many of any cultivar or species then you could try baking and eating a bulb. If it tastes nice, please send a few bulbs to me so that I can grow them too, then munch your way through the rest or spread them around to other gardeners.

Orchis mascula. See Plate 33. The native EARLY PURPLE ORCHID grows about 60cm tall and 15cm wide. It can form quite large colonies when grown in the dappled shade of trees. Its bulb, like those of any other member of the genus, can be eaten raw or cooked. I have not as yet eaten any orchid bulbs and would want to have an abundant supply growing on my own land before even considering it, but they were commonly used for food in the past.

The bulbs can be dried and ground into a flour which is called 'salep' and is said to be extremely nutritious. This flour can be made into a drink or it can be added to other cereals and used in making bread etc. One ounce of salep is said to be enough to sustain a person for a day though I'm not at all sure it would keep me going for that long and wonder how active the person would be!

Orchid seed is extremely simple, it consists of a minute embryo covered with a single layer of protective cells. It has almost no food reserves and depends upon a symbiotic relationship with a certain soil-dwelling fungus if it is to germinate and grow successfully. This fungus is fairly widespread, but if the germinating seed does not come into contact with it during the first few days then it is unlikely to survive. When sowing seed, it is best to use some of the soil that is growing around established plants in order to introduce the fungus. If you are growing orchids, then do not use any artificial fertilizers, since these can interfere with the plant/fungus relationship.

It can be very difficult to transplant orchids, autumn is probably the best time to move the dormant bulbs, but make sure you move some soil with them. Bulbs can also be moved with a large ball of soil around the roots when they are in leaf. Needless to say, do not dig them up from the wild – it is possible to buy plants of this and several other orchid species from specialist nurseries but only buy pot-grown plants to ensure that you also get the fungus.

Chapter Four

THE FLOWER GARDEN

I was visiting Kew Gardens a couple of years ago and, in the flower beds outside the palm house, there was a display of ornamental plants. Nothing unusual about that of course, except that the display consisted entirely of vegetables and edible fruits. There were runner beans, curly kale, ruby chard, globe artichokes, chives, tomatoes and a number of other plants. The overall effect was quite eye-catching and does go to show that we can be rather narrow-minded when we draw a dividing line between edible and ornamental.

Of course, it is not the intention of this book to look at the more traditional vegetable crops, but when you start to look at some of the alternative food plants that can be grown then you will find a great many that do not look at all out of place in a flower garden. Indeed, you might be surprised to find that you are already growing a number of the plants mentioned in this chapter for their ornamental value. One of my little eccentricities when visiting peoples' gardens is to start munching on their plants (with permission of course!). It certainly stimulates conversation when you start eating a person's day lily flowers or the leaves of their *Campanulas*!

Perhaps I should define the flower garden. I have already talked about trees and shrubs as well as some of the plants that can be grown under them, in this chapter I want to look at the herbaceous perennials and bulbs that people often grow in flower beds. The primary purpose of these beds is to produce a good display of flowers for as much of the year as possible and, in order to achieve this, the gardener often grows a great many annual bedding plants amongst the perennials. The beds are often devoid of any woody species, or might contain a few dwarf shrubs. They are often in a sunny position since this promotes a better flower display, though they can also be found in shadier aspects.

Chapters 2 and 3 dealt with plants that, in the main, could look after themselves. Whilst many of the plants mentioned in this chapter are very robust and can also be grown in other settings (see individual entries for more details) there are several species that really could not look after themselves on a long term basis in this country without some help from the gardener. This is still a lot less than the work involved in growing lettuces or bedding plants, but you should realise that if, for example, you do not keep the *Alliums* mentioned here reasonably weed-free then they will gradually weaken and disappear.

Whereas in most of the other chapters I have divided up the lists according to habitat, here they are divided according to usage. The reason is simple – they will all succeed in a similar situation and thus it should be more helpful for you to be able to sort the plant by usage.

As with all methods of trying to put plants into an order, there are always inconsistencies. Many of the plants listed below will have more than one use. The *Allium* species, for example, have edible leaves, flowers and bulbs. In cases such as this, I have placed the plant according to the main use we make of it. If the secondary use is also substantial I have then made a reference to the plant in the other list.

Unless mentioned otherwise, all the following plants are perennials, they require a sunny position and succeed in most well-drained soils. See Chapter 10 for ground cover plants that can also be grown here.

EDIBLE LEAVES & FLOWERS

Agastache foeniculum. ANISE HYSSOP is a herb from North America growing about 1 metre tall and 40cm wide. It grows best in drier soils. The plant flowers in mid-summer and is an absolute magnet for bees and butterflies at this time.

The leaves are available from the middle of spring until the end of summer or early autumn. They have a delicious, sweet, aniseed flavour and are excellent when added to a chopped salad or used as a flavouring in cooked foods. The shoot tips are the best part to eat, this slows down the plant's desire to flower and also encourages side shoots, and thus more shoot tips. Older leaves are rather tough, but can be used for cooking. Children especially love these leaves and adding some to salads can be a good way of getting them to eat more raw leaves. The texture is a bit dry and powdery, so we tend not to eat it in quantity. Protect the young shoots from slugs in early spring or you might end up losing even well-established plants.

Allium **species**. There are a great many ornamental ONIONS and they deserve to be widely grown in the garden both for their edible uses and also as a good companion for other plants. We find them to be some of the most valuable plants we grow. Not only are they very beneficial to human health when included in the diet, they also seem to have a beneficial effect on neighbouring plants in the garden. We spread them about in clumps all over the garden and, by growing a range of species, it is possible to have at least some of them in flower from March round to October.

The various onion species are all too little grown as ornamentals, which is a shame because they are excellent garden plants. Some people object to their smell, though this is usually not very apparent unless the plant is bruised or cut. Others say that onions can all too easily become weeds. Whilst there are some species with a propensity to do this, the vast majority of them are very well behaved.

All parts of the plants are edible. The leaves range in flavour from mild onion, through leek to strong garlic. They make a very tasty addition to salads, can be used as a flavouring in cooked foods and can also be cooked as greens. In general the leaves should be harvested in moderation otherwise the plant will be weakened, though a few species, such as chives, are so vigorous that they can be harvested quite heavily without detriment to the plants. With careful selection it is possible to obtain fresh leaves all the year round.

My favourite part of the plant is the flowers. These are often very beautiful and they generally have a slightly stronger flavour than the leaves. The flavour becomes even stronger as the seeds start to form. The flowers make an extremely attractive edible garnish to salads and are also a thirst-satisfying munch when working in the garden.

Most members of this genus form bulbs, though these are often on the small size. The bulbs can be used in all the ways conventional onion bulbs are used.

The species listed below make nice ornamental edgings to beds, though they will not prevent grass or other weeds growing into the beds. You could also try growing them dotted about the garden. They are good companion plants for most other species, growing especially well with roses. They do not seem to mix well with plants in the pea and bean family, however, having an inhibitory effect on their growth.

In general, members of this genus prefer soils on the light side. They do not grow so well in areas with high rainfall but, as is the case when dealing with plants, there are always exceptions. Most species are intolerant of weed competition and so, if you do not give them at least a little attention, they will gradually fade away.

The following species are just a few of my favourites, a number of other species are mentioned in Chapter 3 and Chapter 5:

A. cernuum. The NODDING ONION grows about 45cm tall and forms a slowly spreading clump about 20 - 30cm wide. It comes into growth in early spring and its leaves can be harvested from then until early in the autumn so long as this is done in moderation. This is just about my favourite member of the genus, though it was a very close contest. It is remarkably beautiful when it flowers in mid-summer and these flowers really add something special to a salad. Both the leaves and the flowers have a nice strong onion flavour. The bulb is rather fibrous and not very worthwhile.

A. moly. Growing to about 30cm tall and 10cm wide, it produces beautiful yellow flowers in early to mid summer. This is a commonly grown species, though most people do not realise its culinary properties. All parts of the plant have a very pleasant mild garlic flavour, we have found the bulb to be particularly tasty.

An easily grown plant, it is fairly drought tolerant, and will also succeed in wetter gardens. It has proved to be invasive in some gardens, though this is usually because the sub-species *A. moly bulbiferum* has been grown. This form produces bulbils in the flowering head and these will spread far and wide if given the chance. The plant is said to taint the milk of cows who eat it, so keep it away from pasture land if you want to stay friendly with the farmer. This species is useful for naturalising in fairly sunny positions between shrubs and has also been seen to grow well along the sunny base of a beech hedge in a wet garden.

A. neopolitanum. DAFFODIL GARLIC grows about 25cm tall and 10cm wide, it is one of my favourite members of the genus, both to look at and to eat. The plants come into growth in early autumn, they produce an abundance of white flowers in the spring and then die down in the summer.

The leaves can be harvested in moderation throughout the winter and make an excellent addition to mixed salads. When eating the leaf, the first taste is that of delicious sweetness, this is then followed by a mild garlic flavour. The flowers in spring can really bring a salad to life, both visually and gastronomically.

The bulbs can be harvested at any time when the plant is dormant. They are rather small but have an excellent mild garlic flavour.

This plant is not fully hardy in colder parts of the country, especially if the soil is on the wetter side. Try growing it by a sunny south-facing wall in such areas.

A. schoenoprasum. CHIVES are a well-known native herb producing their onion-flavoured leaves from late February right round to November with us in Cornwall. These leaves are excellent in salads or as a flavouring in cooked foods. The plants flower abundantly in the early summer and can be induced to repeat the performance later in the season if they are cut down to the ground after flowering and before the seed is formed. The flowers are very attractive to bees and butterflies, though they are drier and more fibrous than many other onion flowers and are not that nice for the human palate.

A. tuberosum. GARLIC CHIVES grows about 40cm tall and 30cm wide. It is much cultivated for its leaves and flowering stems in China and Japan. As the common name suggests, the plant has a flavour rather like a cross between garlic and chives. A very tolerant and easily grown plant, it produces its edible leaves in abundance for about 9 months of the year and its beautiful white flowers in late summer and early autumn. Garlic chives is able to continue in growth all year round if the temperature does not fall below about 5°C. This means that it is possible to dig up some plants in the autumn, pot them up and grow them in a reasonably warm place to provide small pickings of leaves all winter long.

Althaea officinalis. MARSH MALLOW grows about 1.2 metres tall and 60cm wide. A very tolerant and easily grown plant, and despite its common name it also does well on drier soils in the garden.

This plant has a wide range of uses. Its mild-flavoured leaves can be used from late spring until late summer. They make pleasant eating when raw, though they do have a rather hairy texture. We normally chop them into a mixed salad and then you don't really notice the hairiness. The leaves can also be cooked, but then have a rather slimy texture that we dislike. The flowers can be eaten raw or cooked and have a nice mild flavour with some sweetness.

The root is eaten either raw or cooked, though has a bland flavour and contains a lot of fibres. It used to be dried, ground into a powder and then sifted to remove the fibres. The powder was then moistened and roasted, when it would swell up considerably to make the sweet, 'marshmallow', but like many of our traditional sweets, this product is now synthesized in the chemist's lab. The water left over from cooking any part of the plant can be used as an egg-white substitute in making meringues etc., though the water from the root is most effective. You simply add a little sugar to the water and whisk vigorously. A tea is made from the flowers and another is made from the root.

Amongst the plant's non-edible uses, the dried root can be used as a toothbrush, it can also be chewed by teething children. A fibre from the stem and roots is used in paper-making. A glue can be made from the root and an oil from the seed can be used in making paints and varnishes.

Aquilegia vulgaris. COLUMBINE is a very easily grown native species that can reach 1 metre tall and 50cm wide. All parts of the plant are mildly poisonous except the flowers and these have a delightfully sweet flavour. I often pick and eat a flower or three when in the garden, or add them to salads. The crushed seeds have been used externally to rid the body of parasites and are particularly effective against lice, but you should not use them internally.

All other members of the genus have the same uses as this species, I have eaten the flowers of many of them and have yet to be disappointed. Columbine is a short-lived perennial, though it usually self-sows freely and once it is in your garden you are unlikely ever to be without it. It is said to be a bad companion plant, depleting the soil and inhibiting the growth of nearby plants, though I have not experienced this. This is a very promiscuous genus, the different species hybridizing freely with each other. *A. vulgaris* tends to be the dominant partner in any hybridization and if you grow it with other members of the genus, in time most of your seedlings will come to resemble it.

Asclepias **species**. The MILKWEEDS have a huge potential in a permaculture garden. These magnificent flowering plants have edible young shoots which are cooked and used as an asparagus substitute. The stem tips of older shoots can be cooked and used like spinach. The flower buds can also be cooked and have a pleasant pea-like flavour. The very young seed pods have a similar taste and are used like the flower buds, The flowers of some species (especially *A. tuberosa*) are so rich in nectar that in hot summers this crystallizes out and hangs in small lumps from the flowers. It is a really nice taste experience to place your mouth over these flowers and gently suck this nectar. Boiled sweets grown on a plant! The flowers can also be boiled down into a sweet syrup.

As if their edible uses were not enough, a fibre produced in the stems can be used for making cloth and ropes. You wait until the plant dies down in the autumn, leave the stems for a few weeks and then simply peel off the fibres. The seed floss is also a useful fibre, though it needs to be mixed with other, longer fibres if it is used in making clothes. The floss is water repellent and is also very buoyant so during the Second World War, when the British were busy harvesting rosehips for their vitamin C, the Americans were out harvesting the seed pods of milkweeds. The seed floss was then used as a stuffing material for life jackets and could keep a person afloat for at least 72 hours. Another property of the floss is that it soaks up oil and so it can be used to mop up oil spills at sea. As if all that is not enough, the plants also produce a latex in their stems. Although not produced in sufficient quantity to be used commercially, this latex makes a high quality rubber.

The plants are fairly easy to grow, most of them preferring a light soil and doing well in drier conditions. They flower less well in the wetter parts of the country, really preferring hot summers. The only problem we have had with them is that slugs absolutely adore the young growth in spring and will kill even large plants if given the opportunity.

The following species are most commonly grown in Britain:

A. incarnata. The SWAMP MILKWEED grows 1 metre or more tall, forming a clump about 50cm wide. Although it prefers a moister soil, it does well in dry conditions.

A. purpurascens. The PURPLE MILKWEED is a very vigorous plant, flowering well in its first year from seed. It grows about 75cm tall and 60cm wide.

A. speciosa. See Plate 18. The SHOWY MILKWEED is rather similar to the preceding species. It can spread quite freely when well sited, though it is unlikely to get out of control.

A. syriaca. The COMMON MILKWEED grows about 1 metre tall and usually spreads freely when in a suitable position. It has so far refused to flower with us in Cornwall, though it flowers well in the east of the country.

A. tuberosa. PLEURISY ROOT grows about 75cm tall and 40cm wide. It produces beautiful orange-yellow flowers in mid to late summer, but has yet to produce seed with us in Cornwall. This species is also said to have an edible root. Unlike other members of the genus, it does not produce latex.

Asphodeline lutea. See Plate 25. YELLOW ASPHODEL grows about 1 metre tall and forms a slowly spreading clump 1 metre or more wide. It starts its growth-cycle in early autumn, producing fountains of grass-like leaves which grow slowly through the autumn and winter then romp away in the spring. It produces a spike of yellow flowers from May to July and then dies down for a couple of months in late summer, leaving a rather bare space behind it.

The flowers have a delightful sweetness and are an excellent ornamental addition to the salad bowl. They are probably the most popular flower we are growing, even one of the dogs who lives with us goes round eating them. Individual flowers only live for one day, though the plants produce so many that there are always plenty open. We usually go round in the evening picking them, this way we can enjoy them visually during the day and then have a taste treat in the evening. Make sure that you do not pick them until shortly before you use them since they will start to decay within a few hours.

Yellow asphodel used to be cultivated in ancient Greece for its edible roots, these were baked with figs and used like potatoes. I have not baked them with figs as yet, but when boiled they do have a pleasant nutty flavour. The main drawback is their size, since the roots are no thicker than a child's finger. They are produced in quantity, however, and it does not take long to harvest a decent amount. See *Stachys affinis* on page 119 for details of a quick method of cleaning small and fiddly roots.

The young shoots can be harvested from mid autumn until the spring and used as an asparagus substitute. They smell disgusting whilst cooking but have a surprisingly mild and pleasant flavour.

Campanula species. This is a large genus of over 300 species, many of which are very ornamental with their bell-shaped flowers. It includes our native HAREBELLS – or BLUEBELLS if you live in Scotland. All the species have edible leaves and flowers which are often very well-flavoured with a delicate sweetness that makes them ideal in salads, though the leaf texture can be rather tough. To date I have eaten the leaves and flowers of more than 20 different species and only *C. alliariifolia* has disappointed me. This is a very exciting genus for the grower of perennial food crops and has great potential to develop several of these species as ornamental salad plants.

Many of the species are very easily grown, though they are all more or less susceptible to the ravages of slugs. The young growth in spring is most at risk, though the slugs will be happy to have a chew at them at almost any time of the year.

C. versicolor. See Plate 19. This is the Mediterranean species, possibly the nicest tasting and my personal favourite. This grows about 1.2 metres tall and 40cm wide, flowering over a very long period from mid summer until well into the autumn. Indeed, the plants flower so freely that they can exhaust themselves and die. If you want to ensure a good production of leaves then you will be well advised to cut down the flowering stems in September. This will ensure that the plants put more energy into leaf production.

The leaves make an excellent salad, they have a mild flavour with a delightful sweetness that reminds me of fresh garden peas. This has proved to be one of the most popular leaves in our taste trials and we would use them a lot more in salads if only we could keep the slugs off the plants. Slugs are one of the perennial problems of gardening in a wetter part of Britain, there is nowhere near as much damage to these plants when they are grown in the eastern side of the country.

C. versicolor produces an overwintering basal rosette of leaves, and these can be harvested in moderation throughout the winter without harm to the plant. It is only hardy in the milder parts of the country and requires a very sunny, sheltered position in a well-drained soil if it is to thrive. It does very well at the base of a south or west facing wall.

C. persicifolia. This grows to about 1.2 metres tall and spreads at the roots to form clumps 70cm or more wide. The leaves have a mild flavour and are pleasantly sweet, but they are very narrow and it is therefore quite time consuming to pick any quantity. Like the above species, the plants form overwintering rosettes of leaves and so can be harvested judiciously throughout the winter. I recently obtained the sub-species *C. persicifolia crystalocalyx*, this has rather larger leaves than the species and they also seem to be produced in greater abundance. It certainly looks more promising than the species, but time will tell.

The flowers are produced freely from early to mid summer and, if the plant is cut down immediately after flowering and before setting seed, it will produce a small crop of flowers in late summer and autumn.

This is an easily grown, long-lived and very tolerant plant. As well as growing in a sunny flower bed, it will thrive in light woodland shade.

C. rapunculoides. The CREEPING BELLFLOWER is another British native that will also succeed in the light shade of a woodland. A very vigorous and invasive plant, it grows about 1.2 metres tall and can form clumps 1 metre or more wide. Give it space to romp or it will smother its neighbouring plants.

The leaves have a mild flavour with a slight sweetness, though the texture is not that wonderful. Much nicer are the young roots. Although rather small, these have a sweet, nut-like flavour and are very palatable raw or cooked.

C. takesimana. This produces beautiful bell-shaped flowers in mid-summer. It grows about 50cm tall and spreads fairly freely at the roots to form clumps 60cm or more wide. This is a fairly new species to cultivation and I am not sure how hardy it will be, though it survives Cornish winters with no problems.

The leaves, and especially the leaf stems, taste almost exactly like lettuce and make a very acceptable salad. They can turn somewhat bitter in the summer, however, especially if the plant is growing in a very sunny position and the weather is dry.
See also Chapters 8 and 10 for details about more members of this genus.

Cynara scolymus. The GLOBE ARTICHOKE has very attractive leaves and is a good architectural plant, growing about 1.5 metres tall and 1 metre wide. It adds height and elegance to the flower border, especially when in flower in late summer.

The flower buds, eaten just before they open, are considered to be a gourmet vegetable. The flavour is mild and pleasant but this is a very fiddly food to eat. So fiddly, in fact, that I am happy to forego the pleasure of eating them, though they are a favourite food of my wife. The flowering heads are usually boiled before being eaten, only the base of each bract is eaten, plus the 'heart' or base that the florets grow from. Smaller artichokes are produced on lateral stems and these can be pickled or used in soups and stews. This is a low-yielding plant, producing about 5 to 6 main heads per year from the second year onwards.

The young leaf stems have been used as a celery substitute. They are normally blanched to remove the bitterness and then boiled or eaten raw. Blanching involves excluding the light from the leaf stems for at least a couple of weeks before harvesting them. It is most easily done by loosely tying the leaves to the stem so that the plant looks like a large wide post and then wrapping something like straw around it.

Cynara cardunculus. The flowerhead of the CARDOON pictured here is too late for eating, but will attract a multitude of butterflies, bees and other insects.

Cynara cardunculus. The CARDOON is a very similar-looking to the Globe Artichoke, but a slightly more vigorous plant growing up to 2 metres tall and 1 metre wide. Its flower heads are smaller and even more fiddly than the globe artichoke, though they can be used in the same way. My wife says that they have a more delicate flavour and are nicer than globe artichokes. The plant is more usually grown for its edible leaf-stems which are blanched and used as a rather bitter-tasting celery substitute.

Hemerocallis species. DAY LILIES are very common garden plants, and rightly so, being of very easy cultivation in most soils and situations though they prefer at least some sun. Many species spread freely at the root, though they are easy to control and are unlikely to become a nuisance. Some species are so tough that they can establish themselves in short grass and there are reports of them growing through tarmac.

The large lily-like flowers only live for one or two days but they are freely produced over a period of several weeks. These flowers have a delicious sweet flavour (especially at the base where the nectar is to be found) and make a very ornamental addition to salads. In the Orient, where several species are cultivated as food crops, the flowers are harvested at the end of the day as they begin to wither. They are then dried and used as a thickener and flavouring in soups and stews.

One word of warning: regarding any species or cultivars with yellow or scented flowers. Virtually every male I have given these flowers to has liked them, but about 50% of females have a violent reaction, saying that the flowers leave a distinct and unpleasant aftertaste which has been likened to sweaty armpits by some of them! The species *H. lilioasphodelus* is especially to blame here. The flowers of the other species are free of this aftertaste.

The young shoots in spring, which look something like leeks, can be eaten cooked and have a very pleasant sweet flavour, quite free from the flavour of sweaty armpits. Make sure that you only use very young shoots because they quickly become fibrous as they age. Some reports say that very large quantities of the leaves can be hallucinogenic, but normal quantities are perfectly safe to eat.

Many of the species have tuberous roots and these can also be eaten, they have a nice nutty flavour. Although these roots are rather on the small side, most species are rather vigorous and will need dividing from time to time. Then there should be a reasonable quantity of roots for you to try.

Any species in this genus can be tried as well as any of the countless cultivars. Which brings me back to something I have said on more than one occasion in this book – if you come across a cultivar with good eating qualities please let me know and also let me have a division if possible. We particularly like the following:

Hemerocallis dumortieri. This is a vigorous clump-forming species that grows about 50cm tall and 60cm wide. Each flowering stem carries up to eight trumpet-shaped flowers that are about 8cm long. This is one of the first species in the genus to come into flower, usually in May and June. Each flower lives for less than a day. It is also quite early coming into new growth and makes a good ground cover.

Hemerocallis fulva. This species is one of the most interesting for the gardener, as well as being perhaps the best one as an edible crop. A vigorous running species once established, it grows about 1 metre tall and will spread as far as you let it. It flowers from June to August. There are a number of named forms, most if not all of which are sterile triploids and will not produce seed. The pollen, however, is fertile and can be used to fertilize other plants.

There are a number of named forms of special interest as food plants. Their nomenclature is confusing, so I will describe them under the names I was given when I obtained them from the nursery. All of these have double flowers, so you get a lot more petals for your flower!

- 'Kwanso', see Front Cover photograph, is a variegated form with white stripes along the length of the leaves.
- 'Green Kwanso' is very similar to the above, except its leaves are not variegated. Its roots are larger than average.
- 'Flore Pleno' is rather similar to 'Green Kwanso'. The flowers are about 15cm long. This is the form that is most commonly cultivated as a food crop in China.

Hemerocallis middendorffii esculenta. A vigorous clumping plant growing about 60cm tall and wide. Another species that is cultivated in the Orient for its edible flowers, they are certainly one of the tastiest species. The flowers, which are produced in June and July, are up to 10cm long with 5 - 6 blooms carried on each flowering stem. This species does not have swollen roots.

Hemerocallis minor. See Plate 20. Growing to about 40cm tall and wide, and flowering in May and June. The flowers are about 5cm long with up to 5 being carried on each flowering stem. They open in the evening and are relatively long-lived, with individual blooms lasting up to 3 days. This species has small bulbous swellings at the ends of its roots, these have a mild radish-like flavour.

H. multiflora grows about 1 metre tall, forming a clump 60cm or more across. It has much smaller flowers than most species, though they are produced in greater abundance. It flowers for several weeks in late summer, each flowering stem can produce up to 100 flowers. The roots are rather small, they have a tender texture and a fairly bland flavour with a slight sweetness.

Malva **species**. Most, if not all, members of this genus have edible leaves. Two particularly ornamental and robust species are *M. alcea* and the similar *M. moschata* our native MUSK MALLOW, see Plate 21. These easily grown plants reach about 1 metre tall and 60cm wide. They flower very freely in mid-summer and again in late summer if the flowering stems are cut down before the plant sets seed. *M. moschata* especially will also succeed in grass and on the sunny sides of hedgerows.

We use their leaves as one of our main lettuce substitutes in salads, they have a very acceptable mild flavour with a mucilaginous texture. Most people who try them are impressed and want to grow the plants. The leaves can be harvested from mid spring until mid summer when the plants desire to flower will stop it producing new leaves. At this stage you simply switch from the leaves to the flowers. These have a similar pleasant mild flavour and make a decorative addition to the salad bowl.

If you cut the plants back to the ground when they are coming into flower then you will be rewarded by a fresh crop of succulent leaves – though you will miss out on the flowers of course. The other alternative is to wait until the plant has almost finished flowering and then cut it down, though if the weather is very dry then the plant might decide not to put on any fresh growth until the rain returns, or even until the following spring.

M. sylvestris, the COMMON MALLOW, is another native plant. Although the leaves and flowers of this species are very nice in salads, the plant is too straggly to be considered ornamental. There is a cultivar called 'Mauritiana', see Plate 22, that has much larger showy flowers. Both the flowers and the leaves of this cultivar have a superior flavour to the species. The common mallow is usually short-lived in cultivation and gets rather straggly after its second year so many gardeners grub it up and replace it every 2 years.

All members of this genus are rather prone to rust, unfortunately, and might need to be replaced every few years. Fortunately all the species mentioned here will usually arrange this for you, since they often self-sow freely if well sited.

Oxalis deppei. The IRON CROSS PLANT is a very pretty little bulb. It grows about 20cm tall and 15cm wide, producing a fountain of leaves that look rather like 4-leaved clovers with a darker marking at their base. It flowers from early summer until cut down by autumn frosts and makes a very decorative edging to a bed. About as hardy as the *Commelina* mentioned below under edible roots, and with the same requirements, this plant provides a succession of edible young leaves and flowers throughout the summer. Both leaves and flowers have a lovely acid-lemon flavour and are a delightful addition to the salad bowl. They should not be eaten in large quantities because they contain oxalic acid. See Appendix 4 for more details.

The plants have never set seed with us, but bulbs can be obtained quite cheaply and are best planted out in April. They die down in late autumn and, if dug up, each bulb will be found to have formed a tap root up to 7 - 10cm long and about 3cm in diameter with a clump of bulbs at the top. Keep the bulbs for next year and eat the tap root raw or cooked. It has the texture of a crisp juicy 'Golden Delicious' apple but, unfortunately, it also has the same lack of flavour. It does occasionally develop a lovely lemon flavour, we think this is either connected with climate or cultivation methods but it needs more research.

We have recently come across the plant *O. triangularis*. This is a little smaller than *O. deppei* and has lovely dark purple leaves that look rather like a butterfly. The leaves and flowers have a similar flavour to *O. deppei* and look lovely in a salad. We have yet to find out how hardy it is but believe that it should succeed outdoors in all but the colder areas of the country.

Tropaeolum majus. This is one of the few annuals that made it onto this list. NASTURTIUMS are very easily grown plants that succeed in sun or shade and flower from early summer until killed by the first hard frost of autumn. They usually self-sow in disturbed ground, thereby maintaining themselves with very little effort from the gardener, though if the spring is cold these self-sown seedlings might not appear until mid to late summer and will never put on much of a display.

A climbing plant, it will grow about 60cm tall and happily scrambles into neighbouring plants for support. There are many named forms and these vary widely in habit, many of them being low-growing non-climbing plants. Since these forms are widely available in seed catalogues, and have little if any, differences from the culinary point of view, I will not bother to describe any of them here.

All parts of the plants are edible and have a hot, pungent flavour very similar to watercress. The flowers make delightfully decorative additions to a salad, whilst the leaves and young seed pods can also be added to chopped salads. In order of hotness, the leaves are the mildest, then the flowers with the seedpods being the hottest.

T. minus. A very similar looking plant, but is much smaller and does not climb.

Viola **species**. This genus is dealt with more fully on page 81, but there are many very ornamental species that will thrive in the sunnier areas of the garden. The leaves, flowers and flower buds of all members of this genus are edible, but be careful of those with yellow flowers. I would strongly recommend *V. odorata* as one of the best to grow, providing salad leaves all year round and edible flowers in the winter and early spring. *V. mandschurica* and *V. tricolor* are the only others I have tried, but that should not stop you experimenting with other species.

EDIBLE ROOTS

Asphodeline lutea. YELLOW ASPHODEL has pleasant tasting roots. It was discussed earlier in the section on edible leaves and flowers.

Camassia quamash. QUAMASH produces a bulb about 25mm in diameter with a delicious chestnut-like flavour when baked. Growing about 50cm tall and 10cm wide, the plant succeeds in most soils and situations, tolerating light shade and flowering in early summer. Simple to grow from seed, it usually flowers in its third year and thereafter increases quite freely by division. When in flower in early summer, the plants look rather similar to bluebells – until you get close enough to spot the differences that is.

Quamash was a staple food of the North American Indians and, in the autumn, many tribes would move their entire village to the quamash fields. Whilst some people harvested the bulbs, others dug a large fire-pit. This pit was lined with boulders and then filled with wood. The wood was set alight and more was added until the boulders were hot enough. The ashes were then removed, the boulders lined with ferns and the bulbs placed on top. More ferns were added to cover the bulbs and then earth was heaped on top in order to keep the heat in. The pile was left for a couple of days for the bulbs to cook thoroughly, it was then opened up and the Indians started eating and eating and eating... Indeed, they continued eating the bulbs until they could fit no more into their stomachs and then slept it off for a day or two. After this they dried whatever was left and stored it for use in the winter. Whilst not expecting you to try out the Indian way of eating them, I do think you will find them a very acceptable potato substitute.

The related *C. leichtlinii* can also be used. See Plate 26.

Canna indica. INDIAN SHOT is commonly grown in summer tropical bedding displays in Britain. Looking like a banana plant about 1.5 metres tall and 60cm wide, it adds an exotic air to the garden, especially when flowering in late summer. Although native to the West Indies and tropical regions of south America, this is a surprisingly tough plant and it will often survive the winter outdoors in the milder areas of the country. The top growth will be killed by the first real frosts of the autumn, but the roots will survive temperatures down to about -5°C as long as the soil is free-draining. For added protection, give the plants a good mulch in the autumn.

In areas where the tubers will not survive the winter, they can be dug up in late autumn and stored in a cool but frost-free place until the early spring, making sure that they do not dry out. Pot them up around the time of the spring equinox and grow them on in a cool greenhouse, planting them out in late spring after the last expected frosts.

The root is a bit on the fibrous side, but it has a mild, slightly sweet flavour and is very nice cooked. In the West Indies it is dried and ground into flour to be used as an arrowroot. There are many named forms of this plant that have been selected for their ornamental value. I have only eaten the species but there is no reason why these named forms cannot also be used.

Chlorogalum pomeridianum. The SOAP LILY is a bulbous plant from California where it grows up to 1.5 metres tall and 50cm wide. It will generally be a bit smaller in Britain. The plant comes into growth in the late autumn and produces a tall, branching stem with masses of small white flowers in late spring. It dies down completely in the summer. Although not often seen in Britain, it grows quite well in the milder parts of the country if given a reasonably rich soil and a sheltered, warm sunny position. It prefers dry conditions when dormant in the summer and will do especially well if given the protection of a south or south-west facing wall. It is rather slow to increase, though, and would not yield heavily.

The bulb can be up to 15cm in diameter and is very rich in saponins. These substances will form a lather if agitated in water and so the bulb can be dried and then grated up as required to be used as soap flakes. This soap is a very effective though gentle cleaner for the skin, it also makes a very good anti-dandruff shampoo and can be used for washing clothes. It does not work very well on oils, which means that it will not dry out the skin and is therefore especially to be recommended for use by people with skin complaints.

Although saponins are poisonous they are destroyed by heat. Thus the bulb, if stripped of its fibrous outer covering, becomes edible after a long slow baking. I have not tried eating it as yet, but the bulb is said to become very sweet and pleasant when thoroughly cooked. The Indians would slow-bake it for 2 days in a fire-pit (see *Camassia quamash* above for more details), though as far as I know they did not binge on it! See Appendix 4 for more information on saponins.

A fibre on the outside of the bulb is used as a stuffing material for mattresses and also to make small brushes. The sap that exudes from a baking bulb can be used as a glue that is especially effective on paper.

Commelina coelestis. BLUE SPIDER WORT grows about 40cm tall and 30cm wide. It produces a succession of short-lived blue flowers for most of the summer. Very easily grown from seed, it prefers a light soil and, once established, is drought tolerant.

By the end of the first summer each plant should have produced a clump of tuberous roots up to 10cm long and about as thick as a baby's finger. These roots can be eaten cooked, they are rich in starch but have no pronounced flavour and are rather boring unless spiced up with herbs. Yields are also rather low, though perhaps there is a potential for improvement.

The plant is about as hardy as a dahlia and can survive mild winters outside, but is probably best dug up in the autumn after the frosts have killed off the top growth. It can be stored over winter in a frost-free place in the same way as dahlias and can then be planted out in the spring. The clump of roots can be divided before replanting in spring but each division must have a growth bud, which should be a clearly visible green swelling at the top of the root.

Tigridia pavonia. See Plate 23. The TIGER IRIS has the same cultivation requirements as the *Commelina* mentioned above, though it seems to be somewhat hardier. It has survived being left in the ground during cold winters both in Surrey and in Cornwall, though it will need a very well-drained soil if you are prepared to risk it. A mulch applied in the autumn once the top growth has died down will help to protect the bulb from cold. In a sandy soil in our Cornish garden, the tiger iris is self-sowing very freely.

An easy plant to grow from seed, it often flowers in its second year and has beautiful blooms 10cm or more across. These flowers are usually yellow-orange with dark red markings towards the middle, though there is considerable variation. Each flower only lasts one day but they are continually produced from July to October in a good year.

The bulbs divide freely and will soon form large clumps. To ensure good flowering, it is wise to divide these clumps every 3 years or so. Although they are rather small, any spare bulbs can be roasted and have a very pleasant floury texture with a sweet flavour that is similar to sweet chestnuts. Do not eat them raw, though, because they will then produce a very unpleasant burning sensation in the mouth and throat.

Tropaeolum tuberosum. MACHUA is a perennial climbing plant, growing about 2 metres tall and supporting itself by scrambling into neighbouring plants. It flowers freely in late summer and then dies down with the first hard frosts of the autumn. It requires a lime-free soil and prefers growing with its roots in the shade and its flowers reaching up into the sun. It dislikes dry conditions and can become dormant in hot dry weather.

Machua is a short-day plant, which means that in Britain it will not flower until September when there are less than 121/2 hours of daylight each day. This does mean that if you live in an area with early frosts you will not really have much opportunity to enjoy the flowers. However, the cultivar 'Ken Aslet' commences flowering much earlier and, since it also has larger tubers, this is the form I would recommend you to grow.

The plant produces a number of quite large edible tubers near the soil surface and can be fairly heavy-yielding. In mild winter areas the tubers can be left in the ground if required, though it would be a good idea to give them the protection of a mulch. In colder areas they should be harvested and stored in much the same way as dahlias. The tubers are quite popular in South America, but they are probably best described as an acquired taste. The rather peppery flavour is improved considerably if the tubers are cooked and then frozen before eating them. (You can warm them up again if you like!) We have also found that if the tubers are left in the ground and then harvested after being frosted the flavour is much nicer.

One word of warning – the tuber is considered by people in the Andes to lower the sex-drive and many men refuse to eat it, whilst recommending it for women! Clinical trials have indicated a reduction of up to 45% in some male hormones when the tuber forms a considerable part of the diet, but no loss in fertility has been observed.

The growing plant is very resistant to diseases and insects, it contains nematocidal, bactericidal and insecticidal compounds and so has lots of interesting potential as a companion plant.

EDIBLE FRUITS

Fragaria vesca '**Semperflorens**'. ALPINE STRAWBERRIES are almost unique amongst strawberries in that they do not form runners. This is good in as much as the plant stays where you put it, but it does mean that you have to sow fresh seed every 2 - 3 years in order to maintain a good stock. Otherwise the plants, which usually fruit so freely that they quickly wear themselves out, will degenerate after a few years or catch a virus disease. These compact plants, growing about 30cm tall and wide, make a very good edging for a garden border. This also makes them easier to harvest since then you can pick the fruit whilst standing on the lawn.

The small fruits are sweet and delicious – this is the real taste of strawberries and is vastly superior to the overblown and watery cultivated strawberries that are usually grown. Since the fruits are rather small, they are rather fiddly to harvest in quantity. Mind you, if you like strawberries and want to eat as you pick, then for much of the summer it is normally possible to pick quickly enough to keep up with your mouth!

The plants fruit most heavily in early summer but will go on yielding well until the autumn frosts put them to sleep for the winter. The flavour is also at its best in the summer, the cooler autumn weather means that less sugars are produced in the fruits.

We are also growing a white-fruited form which has even nicer fruits that are less attractive to the birds.

Fuchsia **species**. Although they are actually shrubs, most FUCHSIAS often die down to the ground in British winters and are effectively used as herbaceous perennials in the garden. They flower freely from mid-summer to early autumn and succeed in sun or light shade. The fruits of all species and cultivars are edible either raw or cooked, but many of these fruits are less than desirable and they are often not very freely produced. Unless fully ripe, even the nicer species will leave a slightly unpleasant sensation in the back of the throat if they are eaten on their own, though this does not happen when they are mixed with other fruits.

There is such a huge range of cultivars being grown in British gardens that there are probably many tasty and good yielding forms that I don't know about. Should you come across any particularly good fruiting forms then I would not be too upset if you sent me a cutting of the plant so that I can grow it as well!

F. megallanica. The hardiest species in the genus. It makes a good hedge in the mildest areas of the country, though its fruit is not very pleasant.

The cultivars 'Globosa' and 'Tresco', however, will normally yield heavily in late summer and have rather nicer fruits that are sweet and juicy but with a slightly peppery aftertaste.

F. splendens. This is only hardy in the milder parts of the country where it can be grown on north or south facing walls as well as in a more open position. In the very mildest areas of the country it forms a shrub 2 metres or more tall and 1 metre wide. If the stems are not killed back in the winter, it will flower very freely in early summer and then less freely until the autumn. If the stems are killed off, then flowering will be delayed until late summer. The cultivar 'Karl Hartweg' is said to be an improved form of this species, though it seems virtually identical to me.

The fruits, which are usually produced very freely a few weeks after flowering, are about the size and shape of a baby's finger. They are very juicy with a refreshing, slightly acid flavour.

This is a fruit that can be eaten and enjoyed in quantity. My little son first came across it in 1995 when just 14 months old. Until then he had always been very controlled in the way he ate food – he would put a bit in his mouth and chew (or gum!) it well before swallowing it. This time things were different. As soon as he tasted the first fruit, he went mad for it. He quite literally stuffed his mouth full, and was still trying to get more in. He would not stop eating them until he was satisfied that no more remained. Obviously he had read about the North American Indians and the way they eat quamash! (See *Camassia quamash* earlier in this chapter.)

Yucca **species**. This genus of desert plants is surprisingly hardy in Britain. They require a hot sunny position and a well-drained soil if they are to thrive, and are hardier when grown in poor sandy soils. Although the books say that they need a sheltered position, we have found that they generally tolerate the mild, though strong and salt laden maritime winds. What they do not like are the cold drying winds that normally come from the east and north in Britain.

Many of the species are monocarpic – they grow for a number of years without flowering and then die after flowering. However, they produce a number of offsets and these will continue to live for a number of years until they also produce offsets, flower and die. In general, they will only flower in hot summers.

Yuccas are excellent architectural plants and have a very tropical appearance. They add a very special quality to a garden, especially the tree-like forms and even more so when producing their long spikes of ivory-white flowers.

Although we are unlikely to get large crops in this country, these plants were an essential part of the desert economy for the indigenous native North American Indians. The fruit can be eaten raw or cooked, in some species it is said to taste like a date, though in other species it is dry and not very appetizing.

In the plant's natural habitat the flowers of most species can only be pollinated in a unique way by a moth. This moth eats a hole into the ovary beneath the flower and lays some eggs in there. It then plugs the hole by filling it with a ball of pollen from the flower – this pollen fertilizes the seeds in the ovary. When the moth larvae hatch they eat some of these developing seeds but leave enough for the yucca to be able to reproduce.

Unfortunately this moth cannot survive in Britain so, in order to obtain fruit, it is necessary to mimic the moth and hand pollinate the flowers. If you don't hand pollinate then you can always eat the young flowering stems as an asparagus substitute or eat the flowers in salads. If you do pollinate then, as well as the fruit, the seed can be ground into a flour and added to wheat when making bread.

Amongst the non-food uses, a fibre is obtained from the leaves which can be used to make ropes, cloth etc., whilst the leaves are also used in weaving baskets, mats and so on. A soap is obtained by boiling the roots – this soap is a gentle and effective cleanser and is a common ingredient of many hair shampoos as well as being used in soaps.

Some species to grow include:

Y. baccata. The books say that this species is only hardy in the milder parts of Britain, though it has been thriving outdoors at Kew Gardens since about 1990. It is said to have the nicest fruit in the genus. These fruits are said to be up to 17cm long and 7cm wide, though I have not yet seen them. The descriptions say that they are fleshy, sweet and palatable, the North American Indians would usually eat them baked. If you do obtain the fruits, then only try a few at first because they can cause diarrhoea if you are not used to them. The plant grows about 1 metre tall and does not form a trunk.

Y. brevifolia. This forms a woody trunk and branches. It can grow up to 9 metres tall and 1.5 metres wide in the wild but is usually much smaller in Britain.

Y. filamentosa. Probably the hardiest and most commonly grown yucca. About 75cm tall, it spreads freely by suckers and flowers regularly even in cooler summers. Unfortunately, its fruit is of the dry variety and I find its flowers a trifle bitter.

MISCELLANEOUS USES

Boehmeria nivea. RAMIE is a tall growing plant, reaching about 1.8 metres high in this country and forming a clump 1 metre or more wide. It is even larger when grown in hotter climates. It requires a very warm position in a fertile sandy soil to be at its best, and is only hardy in the southern part of the country, and perhaps along the western side if you can give it enough summer heat. The flowers are insignificant, but the plant is very striking with large attractive leaves and adds height to the flower border.

The root is edible cooked and is said to have a pleasant sweet taste. Our experience is that it is rather bland with a really strange mucilaginous texture that we find rather difficult to enjoy. It is one of those things that you put in your mouth and chew and keep chewing without really knowing what to do with it. What you do know is that you do not want to put any more in your mouth!

The main reason we grow this plant is that it produces an excellent quality fibre from the stems. This is used for textiles, linen etc. and is said to be moth-proof. The silky fibres are the longest known in the plant realm, they are 7 times stronger than silk and 8 times stronger than cotton. We have made thread with it that is no thicker than cotton thread and this is so strong that two strong men used it in a tug-of-war and were unable to break it! Ramie fibre is increasingly being used commercially, usually in mixtures with cotton where it gives the clothing more strength and durability as well as a softer texture.

Melianthus major. This is a plant that provided a pleasant surprise for me for the first time in the spring of 1993. An evergreen shrub in its native habitat, where it can grow 3 metres tall and wide, the top growth is not very winter-hardy in Britain. It is normally cut back to the ground if temperatures regularly fall to about -10°C or if the plant is not in a very sheltered site. However, the rootstock is considerably hardier and will tolerate temperatures down to at least -15°C, resprouting in the spring and growing rapidly to a metre or more in height and width.

Although in a very exposed position, our plants did not die down in the mild winter of 1992/3 and came into flower in the spring. Normally, when cut to the ground, plants will not flower until the late summer or autumn. In its native South Africa, the plants produce so much nectar that it drips out of the flowers. I had assumed that our climate would be too cool for the plant to do the same here but was mistaken.

Whilst showing a visitor around I noticed that the leaves of this plant were covered in a dark substance which at first glance looked like some kind of fungal infection. It was soon clear that this was actually the nectar dripping out of the flowers and staining the leaves. The visitor and I had a lovely time sucking out this nectar, we probably only got a couple of teaspoonfuls each but the flavour was so good that it seemed like a lot more. The plant continued to drip nectar for the next couple of weeks. This species will never be anything other than a curiosity in Britain, but what a delightful curiosity it is.

Tagetes species. MARIGOLDS are an essential companion plant for the flower garden. See page 3 for details of these annuals and perennials.

Chapter Five

PERENNIAL VEGETABLES & HERBS

I could perhaps sub-title this chapter 'The non-ornamental species' since most gardeners would not think many of the following plants to be particularly beautiful. Indeed, some of the plants contained in this chapter look remarkably like weeds. *Rumex alpinus*, for example, is a dock and therefore not the sort of plant most people would think of cultivating. Still, beauty is very much in the eye of the beholder and inside every ugly duckling there is a beautiful swan waiting to emerge. If any of these plants look a little coarse to you, then I hope that you will find their beauty when you taste them.

Just because they are not considered to be in the first rank for beauty, that is no reason to consign these species to some out of the way corner at the far end of the garden. A number of the plants in this list can be harvested for their edible leaves all through the winter – you will be far less inclined to do this if it means a long walk down the garden on a cold wet windy day. Find somewhere a bit nearer the kitchen door if possible.

This chapter is a collection of some very promising perennial vegetables and herbs. All of them should give good yields and a number of them crop exceedingly well. There are a number of very exciting root crops, for example.

It could be said that these plants are the perennial alternatives for the conventional kitchen garden. Many of them could easily be fitted into other parts of the garden, but they tend to do better when given more individual attention. For example, they might produce a much more worthwhile crop when taken away from the competition of other plants, or they might not be very vigorous in this country and so are easily out-competed if intermixed with other plants. Alternatively, some of them are very vigorous indeed and the problem is more one of containing them. One way to do this (and it works well with us) is to keep them in their own small beds and mow around then occasionally to stop them taking over the garden.

Incidentally, when planning out small beds for vegetables, don't become trapped by the idea that either the beds, or the crops, need to be based on straight lines. We are developing a perennial vegetable bed on our land that is based round a small circular central bed with other beds radiating out from it. The shape is very satisfying, it is possible to get access into the beds from all sides and it is nice to be able to show visitors a group of perennial vegetables growing together.

Where possible, we also try and grow the plants in mixtures, in much the same way as people grow a variety of plants in flower beds. This looks more attractive and also helps to reduce problems with pests and diseases in much the same way as a natural mixture of plants in a woodland. See the Introduction to this book for more details about this.

As in Chapter 4, the plants are listed here according to their main use.

Unless stated otherwise, all the following plants grow best in a sunny position and will succeed in most well-drained soils. Where appropriate, we have given ideas of any other places they can be grown in the garden.

EDIBLE LEAVES & FLOWERS

This list contains plants that produce edible leaves that can be eaten in quantity, either in salads or cooked. If the leaves are mainly used as a flavouring they will be found listed under herbs later in this chapter.

Allium **species**. This large genus contains many very valuable plants for the perennial garden. You will find several other species described in different chapters of this book, and with good reason. The ONIONS and GARLICS should be widely planted all over your land because, as well as being good food crops, they are excellent companion plants and will promote the health of other plants growing nearby. All the species in the genus provide edible leaves and flowers whilst many of them produce edible bulbs. The flowers of the following species, however, are not that wonderful to eat.

A number of books say that they also repel moles but either the moles on our land have no sense of smell or they have not read the same books that I read. They certainly dig up as many onions as they do any of the other plants.

The following species do not like wet conditions and would rather not grow in very heavy soils unless you are prepared to put some effort into lightening them or making raised beds. They will also be unhappy in overcrowded conditions or with strong competition from weeds and will just slowly fade away unless you give them at least a modicum of attention. It has also been our experience that when there are lots of slugs they will often totally destroy the onion-flavoured members of this genus. They do not, however, usually touch those species with more of a garlic flavour.

The following species are very worthy of being included in a bed of perennial vegetables:

A. canadense. The AMERICAN WILD GARLIC grows about 45cm tall, forming a clump about 20cm wide. It has a very pleasant mild garlic flavour. The leaves are available for about 9 months of the year, dying down for a short time in the winter. The bulbs are not that large, averaging about 3cm in diameter, but they are crisp and sweet with a nice mild garlic flavour.

A very easily grown plant, American wild garlic is more tolerant of adverse conditions than the other species in this list. The bulbs increase quite freely and so it is a good idea to lift and divide the plant every 3 years or so. This will give you a chance to get at the tasty bulbs.

Some care has to be taken when introducing this species to your land because there are some forms that produce bulbils instead of flowers and can become

A. canadense. The flowers make an attractive addition to salads.

invasive. You might not be too popular if this plant escapes from your garden and gets into pasture land since it can taint the milk of cows. ***A. canadense mobilense*** is the sub-species that we grow and this never produces bulbils.

***A. cepa* 'Perutile'**. The EVERLASTING ONION is an extremely useful plant and has a taste that is very similar to the cultivated onion. It grows more like chives quickly forming clumps 30cm or more tall and wide. It usually stays green all year round, even in quite severe winters, and so can be harvested all 12 months of the year. It does not flower every year, but in hot dry weather it will often decide that now is the time to concentrate on flowering and will then stop producing leaves for a few weeks. You can either cut the leaves off just above the tops of the bulbs and use them as flavourings in salads or cooked dishes, or you can break off bulbs from the outside of the clumps and use them like spring onions – the bulbs are a similar size.

This very productive plant was one of our staple salad leaves until the summer of 1993 when the slugs found out just how nice it is and reduced our stock from over 200 down to just 2 plants. Fortunately, with the increase in the populations of frogs, hedgehogs and slow-worms on the land the slug problem has been brought back to manageable levels and our stocks of the plant are increasing again. Because the bulbs increase freely, it is possible to divide the plant every year in order to get the maximum build up of stock. This incident with the slugs was yet one more reminder of the value of diversity. Because we grow such a wide range of plants the devastation of this species was not a complete disaster.

Allium cepa proliferum. The TREE ONION is not a very productive plant, but it is easy to grow and produces some very well-flavoured bulbs. Rather a novelty plant, instead of producing flowers at the end of the flowering stems, it produces a head of small bulbs that can each be 1cm or more in diameter. These bulbs themselves often come into growth whilst still attached to the parent plant and they can produce another small head of bulbs. Eventually the weight of bulbs weighs down the plant, the stem folds over and the head falls to the ground, thus allowing the bulbs to root and produce new plants.

The bulbs have a hot onion flavour and are excellent when chopped up in salads or used as a flavouring in cooked foods – their small size also makes them a very useful pickle. As well as the top bulbs, the plant also produces a number of bulbs underground – nothing to compare with the yields of shallots, but a useful little crop all the same. The leaves are also edible, and have a mild onion flavour, but it is our experience that harvesting the leaves makes the plant more prone to disease and so we let well enough alone.

It is best to plant out the bulbs in late autumn, the plants will come into growth during the winter and will mature their top bulbs by mid to late summer. They keep well in store for at least 9 months.

A. fistulosum. The WELSH ONION has the same uses and a very similar flavour to the everlasting onion (mentioned above). It grows about 50cm tall and 20cm wide. Not quite as hardy as that species, it will often die down for a short period in cold winters. It will also flower regularly in the summer and does not produce leaves at this time. Slugs love eating this plant just as much as the everlasting onion, unfortunately.

Incidentally, the name welsh onion has nothing to do with the country Wales, it is derived from the Germanic word 'welsche' meaning foreign.

A. sativum. Although usually grown as an annual, GARLIC is a perennial species and can be left in the ground for a number of years if required. Although you will end up with more cloves and higher overall yields this way, the size of individual cloves will be rather smaller. Garlic grows about 1 metre tall and 10cm wide, though it would form a clump 20cm or more wide if left in the ground.

I probably have no need to tell you about the flavour and uses of garlic bulbs in the kitchen, though I would remind you that the leaves are also edible and can be harvested in the winter if you allow the plants to grow as perennials. The flavour is distinctly garlic, though it is milder than the bulbs.

Garlic is an almost essential plant to grow in the perennial food garden. Not only does it confer its health-promoting benefits to us when it is part of our diet, it also helps to maintain the health of the plants it grows close to. It also has a very impressive range of non-food uses as listed below.

The juice from the bulb is used as an insect repellent – you simply spread it onto bare skin, or onto clothes that you are wearing. It has a very strong smell though and some people would prefer to be bitten. If you don't use it and do get bitten, then the juice can always be applied to the stings in order to ease the pain.

Three to four tablespoons of chopped garlic and 2 tablespoons of grated soap can be infused in 1 litre of boiling water, allowed to cool and this has been used as an insecticide. An extract of the plant has been used as a fungicide, it is said to be effective in the treatment of blight and mould or fungal diseases of tomatoes and potatoes but has not been effective against blight with us. An excellent glue made from the juice of the bulb is used in mending glass and china. The growing plant is said to repel insects, rabbits and moles but it hasn't worked against rabbits and moles with us.

A. sativum ophioscorodon. See Plate 24. SERPENT GARLIC is a very interesting and productive form of garlic. We grow this as a perennial, only lifting and dividing it every 3 - 4 years when the clumps are getting crowded. The bulbs are a bit smaller than garlic, especially if the clump gets crowded, but can be used in all the same ways and have the same flavour. The main reason we grow the plant is for the small bulbs that are formed on the flowering stalks instead of flowers. These have the same delicious garlic flavour as the underground bulbs and, although they are rather smaller, they are very easy to harvest without the need for digging up the plants.

One very interesting and amusing trait of this plant is that it seems to lose its sense of direction when forming the flowering stem. At first this grows upright, as you would expect. Then the top of the stem starts to perform acrobatics and quite literally loops the loop. As the small bulbs begin to form at the top of the stem the plant seems to regain its sense of propriety and gradually straightens itself back up. A great novelty to have in the garden, it always draws comments from visitors.

There are a number of named forms of this species, developed for greater productivity. Some of these should become available in Britain over the next few years.

Brassica oleracea **'Tree Collards'**. I obtained this plant in the spring of 1996 and, although it is early days as yet, it looks like it is going to be the best perennial cabbage we are growing. I am told that it can grow up to 2 metres tall and almost as wide. It should also be very cold hardy because it comes from an area of North America that experiences much colder winters than most of Britain.

The leaves are a lovely dark green and look very similar to the leaves of savoy cabbages, though the plant has shown no sign at all of forming a head. You wait until the plants are at least 30cm tall before harvesting the ends of the shoots in much the same way as with spring greens. The plant will then quickly form side shoots and, when these are long enough, you harvest the ends of these shoots. The plant then simply forms new side shoots and the process continues. Make sure you never remove all of a side shoot, you want to leave the plant plenty of opportunity to form new side growths.

After a few years the plant gets a bit leggy. Now is the time for courage. You cut it back quite severely to encourage new growth lower down the stems in much the same way as you would coppice a tree (but leave at least 30cm of trunk). I am told that the plant usually responds well to this, though it will sometimes die. However, this is a very easy plant to grow from cuttings (they form roots within a week in the summer and will also succeed, though more slowly, in the winter), so always make sure that you have reserve plants before doing anything drastic.

We find the flavour to be exceptionally good. It can be eaten raw, though I do not really like the flavour of raw cabbage and nor does my digestive system. Cooked, however, it is superb and tastes just like other good quality cabbages.

The only drawback we have found so far is that the plant is at least as attractive to cabbage white caterpillars as other cabbages and they will decimate a plant if given the chance.

Incidentally, our native WILD CABBAGE, **B. oleracea**, is very worthy of a place in the perennial vegetable garden. A short-lived perennial, it will normally live for about 2 - 5 years and grow about 1 metre tall and 60cm wide. The leaves are delicious cooked – there is a slight bitterness but this seems to enhance the overall flavour. It can be harvested all year round in much the same way as the tree collards. This is the only cabbage plant we are growing that was not attacked by the cabbage white butterfly in 1996.

Brassica oleracea acephala 'Daubenton'. I obtained this PERENNIAL KALE in 1994 from a friend who was very impressed with the yields and flavour. He says that this is the nicest kale he has eaten and it has grown very well with him, reaching almost 2 metres in height. Our plants have not as yet done very well, they seem to attract all the slugs and cabbage white butterflies from miles around. This just goes to show that what does well with one gardener will not necessarily succeed with another. Yet another reason for diversity.

The leaves are available all year round, but are most valuable in the winter. Like other kales, the flavour is somewhat stronger than cabbages but it makes an excellent cooked vegetable.

There is some dispute over whether this plant flowers. My friend is adamant that it does not, yet there are also reports that it does. Should you grow it and it does flower, then you could eat the young flowering stems in much the same way as sprouting broccoli, either before the flowers open or just as they are opening. I would feel much more inclined to let it flower, excluding insects from the flowers to prevent cross-pollination, and then hand fertilizing in order to get seed. It is quite likely that plants with greater vigour could be obtained this way. In the absence of seed, you propagate the plant by cuttings as for the perennial cabbage above.

Brassica oleracea botrytis aparagoides. NINE-STAR PERENNIAL BROCCOLI grows about 1.2 metres tall and wide. It produces a small white cauliflower head in about April of each year, and then another 5 - 10 still smaller heads from sideshoots. They are very well-flavoured, rather like white sprouting broccoli, and can be eaten raw or cooked. The leaves can also be eaten as greens, but don't overcrop the plant or you will reduce the size of the cauliflowers. The plants are only just perennial and will often die after 3 years. Cabbage white caterpillars really love the leaves of this plant and will strip it naked if given half a chance.

Bunias orientalis. TURKISH ROCKET is a very easily grown plant, reaching about 1 metre tall and 40cm wide in good soils. The plant comes into growth quite early in the year and its leaves are usually available from March onwards. It forms a fountain of leaves and, before flowering, looks more like a dandelion than a member of the cabbage family.

The leaves have a mild cabbage flavour in early spring but becoming hotter with a hint of radish in the flavour as the season progresses. The spring leaves go well in a mixed salad, we prefer cooking them like spinach later in the year. The young flower buds make very pleasant eating either raw or cooked.

We have found these plants to be very vigorous and tough creatures. They have a deep taproot and if you leave even a small part of this in the ground it will resprout and form a new plant. They have survived for four years in rank grass without any help from us and so we will give them a trial on a sunny woodland edge when we find the time. They will do much better and be more productive with a little bit of tender loving care.

Chenopodium bonus-henricus. A native perennial growing about 30cm tall and wide, GOOD KING HENRY is a very easily grown and long-lived plant. Whilst the quality and quantity of leaves will be considerably improved by growing it in a rich soil and with at least a little tender loving care, this is a plant that knows how to look after itself and will tolerate considerable neglect.

Good King Henry was often cultivated as a vegetable in the past. The young leaves are very nutritious and can be eaten raw or cooked. They are best used in spring and early summer since the older leaves soon become tough and bitter. I find the cooked leaves quite pleasant, but do not like them raw since there is a bitterness in their flavour. This is caused by saponins in the leaves – these are broken down when the leaves are cooked. The leaves also contain oxalic acid, which gives them a slightly sharp flavour. Although both saponins and oxalic acid can be harmful in the diet (see Appendix 4 for more information), this plant is generally a very healthy addition to the diet.

The young shoots can be cooked in the spring – you cut them just beneath the soil surface, peel them and use them like asparagus. They have a very nice flavour, but are rather small and fiddly. If you really have nothing better to do with your time then you could try collecting the young flower buds just before they open. These can also be cooked and eaten, and are considered to be a gourmet food, but you will be at it all day if you want enough to feed a family.

The seed is rather small but it is a simple matter to collect a reasonable quantity. Whilst it can be used whole as a sweet or savoury dish in much the same ways that you use rice, you will get more goodness out of it if you grind it into a powder and then mix it with flour when making bread etc. The seed should be soaked in water overnight and thoroughly rinsed before it is used in order to remove any saponins.

Cichorium intybus. CHICORY is dealt with more fully on page 143. There are some cultivars, however, that would be best grown in the perennial vegetable bed. These have been selectively bred as a winter salad crop and produce a head of leaves in much the same way as a lettuce. The plants are quite hardy and the heads are also much less bitter than the wild chicory – though they do remain distinctly bitter.

When grown in a sheltered position they will provide salad leaves throughout all but the coldest winters without the need for protection.

Our favourite cultivar is 'Rossa di Treviso' with long leaves that turn a very attractive red as the winter sets in. It is very productive and has been the hardiest of the many cultivars we have tried. 'Rossa di Verona' is similar, but with smaller, more rounded leaves and has a tendency to rot in wet weather. 'Grumelo Verde' is a smaller plant with green leaves and is very hardy but has a more bitter flavour.

When growing chicory as a winter salad, the seed will need to be sown annually in late spring or early summer. The plants will then grow without forming a flowering stem and will produce a lettuce-like head of leaves that can be used in the winter months. When harvesting the plant, you cut off all the leaves a little bit above the root. If the weather is not too cold the plant will then make some new growth and can supply a small second and sometimes even a third harvest. Make sure you do not sow the seed too early, or the plants will run to seed and there will be little or no winter harvest.

Unfortunately, the plants are rather reluctant to form a head of leaves in following years, being much more interested in flowering and setting seed. We are looking at ways of encouraging these older plants to form overwintering heads but without success as yet. Therefore they are used in spring and summer mixed salads, disguising the bitterness by adding sweeter tasting leaves to the mix. Thus you get the health-promoting properties of the leaves in an enjoyable form. The plants will continue to provide leaves for some years before gradually dying out.

The roots of chicory are also edible, but are very bitter. They can be dried, roasted and ground into a powder to make a coffee substitute. The roots also have the potential to be used for the commercial production of biomass for industrial use because they are rich in the starch 'inulin' which can easily be converted to alcohol.

Crambe maritima. SEAKALE. This native seashore plant grows about 60cm tall and wide. It is sometimes cultivated for its edible shoots and there are some named varieties that are available from most vegetable seed catalogues. The plants dislike very heavy soils and acid conditions, otherwise they are easily grown and tolerate both drought and poor soils.

The young leaves can be eaten raw or cooked like spinach. They have a pleasant almost nutty flavour with a slight bitterness. They go well in a mixed salad and also make a very pleasant cooked vegetable. Older leaves develop a stronger bitterness and are not so pleasant.

The young shoots can also be eaten raw or cooked. They have a crisp texture and a similar flavour to the leaves. The shoots are usually blanched before being used, this involves excluding the light from the shoots for at least two weeks prior to harvesting. This greatly reduces the bitterness and they are then considered to be a gourmet food. Unfortunately, the blanching also reduces the nutrient value of the shoots.

The young flowering shoots are my favourite part of this plant. They are produced in early to mid summer and are harvested when about 10 - 15cm long and before the flowers have opened. Used like sprouting broccoli, they are quite nice raw and delicious when lightly steamed.

Plate 17. *Allium ursinum*. An excellent woodland ground cover. The leaves and flowers make a good flavouring in salads and cooked foods. See page 76. Photo: Tim Harland.

Plate 18. *Asclepias speciosa*. A multi-use plant, with edible leaves, flowers and young seed pods. It also provides fibre and a latex for making rubber. See page 90.

Plate 19. *Campanula versicolor*. A superb winter salad plant with leaves tasting like garden peas. The flowers in summer are also edible. See page 91.

Plate 20. *Hemerocallis minor*. DAY LILY flowers make an attractive and succulent addition to salads. The roots and the young shoots in spring are also edible. See page 94.

Plate 21. *Malva moschata*. The leaves have a mild flavour and make a very good alternative to lettuce in salads. The flowers are also edible. See page 94.

Plate 22. *Malva sylvestris 'Mauritiana'*. A very attractive form of our wild MALLOW with the same uses as *M. moschata*, above. See page 95.

Plate 23. *Tigridia pavonia*. This striking flower has a small bulb that when roasted is sweet and floury with a flavour like sweet potatoes. See page 98.

Plate 24. *Allium sativum ophioscorodon*. Tasting identical to common garlic, the curious growth habit of serpent garlic makes it a talking point in the garden. See page 107.

Plate 25. *Asphodeline lutea*. The yellow flowers have a deliciously sweet flavour and are produced in abundance in early to mid summer. See page 90.

Plate 26. *Camassia leichtlinii*. When allowed to naturalize, the plant can form carpets of growth like bluebells. The bulbs are an excellent potato substitute. See page 97.

Plate 27. *Polymnia edulis.* Closely related to the sunflower and Jerusalem artichoke, the YACON produces an edible root (see below). See page 118.

Plate 28. *Polymnia edulis.* The YACON root is crisp, sweet and juicy raw or cooked. It is eaten more as a fruit than a root. See page 118.

Plate 29. *Oxalis tuberosa*. When first harvested, the roots have a lemon-like flavour. Left in the light for a few days they become sweet and are delicious raw. See page 117.

Plate 30. *Butomus umbellatus*. A pretty waterside plant, the FLOWERING RUSH also has an edible root. See page 132.

Plate 31. *Nymphaea alba*. A beautiful pond plant with edible seeds that can be roasted like sweetcorn. It also has an edible root. See page 130.

Plate 32. *Typha latifolia*. A very invasive plant, but with a huge variety of edible and non-edible uses. It is also a superb plant for wildlife. See page 134.

Fagopyrum dibotrys. PERENNIAL BUCKWHEAT is a very vigorous plant, growing 1.5 metres tall and spreading freely by suckers. It looks a little like Japanese knotweed, but is not as invasive as that plant and can be contained without fear of it taking over the garden. If growing it where space is at a premium, either put it in an island bed on its own so that you can mow down any suckers that try to escape, or place it in a deep bottomless container that is buried in the ground. This plant is very tolerant of soil conditions and can even succeed in sub-soils, it should also succeed on the sunny edges of a woodland garden. The top growth of the plant is very frost sensitive. The plant will often come into growth in early spring and then be cut back by the frosts. Don't worry, the roots are very hardy and the plant will soon be back again.

The leaves can be eaten raw or cooked. I find the flavour unpleasant and have yet to meet anyone who really likes it raw, though many find that it makes an excellent spinach. To my mind the main reason for eating the leaves is that they are rich in rutin. This substance is a very good blood tonic and purifier, it is used in the treatment of high blood pressure and arthritic diseases.

The seed is a bit smaller than the annual buckwheat but can be used in all the same ways. It is usually either sprouted or used as a cereal. Dried and ground into a flour, it can serve as a thickening agent in soups etc. Our plants flower regularly in late summer but have never set seed. This is possibly because all our plants come originally from just one seedling and they need a pollen partner. If you have any plants of this species (that you did not get from us or from anyone who got it from us) then our lonely buckwheat would love to hear from you. The flowers attract all sorts of beneficial insects to the garden, especially hoverflies whose larvae will eat aphids.

Foeniculum vulgare. A native plant, FENNEL grows about 1.8 metres tall and 80cm wide. A very easily grown plant, it prefers lighter soils and is drought tolerant. It is relatively short-lived but usually self-sows very freely and so you are never without it. In our Cornish garden it self-sows so freely that we have to pull lots of it out as a weed. Fennel is a very ornamental plant with its feathery leaves and does not look at all out of place in the flower garden. However, it does have a reputation of not being a good companion for other plants.

Fennel leaves have a delicious aniseed flavour and are very nice when added in moderation to the salad bowl. They can also be cooked as greens or can be added to soups etc. This is one of those leaves that you can give to young children who do not like eating leaves! In our mild Cornish climate we can harvest the leaves virtually all year round. Even in colder parts of the country it comes into new growth fairly early in the year.

The time you are most likely to be without fennel is in late summer when the plant is concentrating on producing seed. If you cut some of the plants down to ground level before they set seed then you should get plenty of fresh growth for late summer and autumn use. You might need to water the plants if the soil is very dry at this time or the plants will become dormant until the autumn.

All other parts of the plant are edible, the leaf stalks and flower heads being used raw or cooked, the aromatic seeds as a flavouring in cakes, bread, stuffings etc. and the root cooked – they all have an aniseed flavour. A herbal tea is made from the leaves or the seeds and an essential oil from the seed is used as a food flavouring and an additive to soaps and perfumery.

The dried plant is an insect repellent. The crushed leaves are effective for keeping dogs free of fleas, you can either put them into the dogs bedding or crush them and rub them into the dogs coats. The plant was formerly used as a strewing herb in order to keep houses smelling nice and free from insects.

Lactuca perennis. The PERENNIAL LETTUCE looks somewhat like a chicory/ dandelion cross and grows about 60cm tall and 25cm wide. It prefers growing in a light sandy loam. Like chicory, it has beautiful blue flowers and does not look at all out of place in an ornamental garden when it is in bloom in mid-summer. At other times, however, it looks rather weedy.

The raw leaves have a fairly acceptable mild flavour, especially in early spring, though they can develop a slight bitterness when the plant flowers in late spring and summer, especially if the weather is hot, and so they are best eaten with some caution at this time. It is possible to grow this plant on a cut and come again basis, to ensure the production of tender young leaves.

Phytolacca americana. POKEWEED is a vigorous plant growing 2 metres or more tall and perhaps 1.5 metres wide. Very easily grown in a sheltered position, an established plant will succeed even in coarse grass or do well in open woodland.

Pokeweed has occasionally been cultivated for its edible young shoots in America, these are used like asparagus and are said to be a gourmet's food. The young leaves can also be cooked and used like spinach, making a very tasty green. Some caution is advised in the use of this plant because the older leaves are poisonous and can cause severe diarrhoea and vomiting. Even the younger leaves are best cooked in one change of water.

There are reports that the fruit is cooked and used in pies but this is probably unwise since other reports say that even when cooked the fruit can cause diarrhoea. A much better use of this fruit is as a red dye and an ink, though it is water soluble and not very permanent. It also makes a very good body paint that is easily washed off in cold water, but make sure that young children do not apply it and then lick it off since this just might give them a tummy upset. A soap can be obtained by cutting the root into small pieces and simmering it in water.

Reichardia picroides. Looking somewhat like a dandelion and growing about 30cm tall and 25cm wide, when properly grown this plant can provide mild-flavoured salad leaves all the year round. For summer production, the plant will produce much better quality leaves if grown with some shade, at other times of the year a warm sheltered sunny position is required. The plant is also tolerant of poor soils, in such a position it will be somewhat more cold-tolerant, though the quality and quantity of the leaves will be reduced. It is not very hardy outside the milder areas of the country, but when well sited in a well-drained soil it has survived temperatures down to about -10°C. The plant has also successfully self-sown with us, usually quite freely in fact.

One of its attributes that most excites us is that it seems to be almost completely slug-proof. When we first obtained the plant in 1993 we were being totally overrun by our slimy friends and were losing plants hand over fist. This species was almost totally undamaged amongst all the carnage.

As mentioned earlier, the plant grows very much like a dandelion. The best way of harvesting the leaves is on a cut and come again basis. The plant has to be well established before you do this. The technique is to cut all the top growth off on a regular basis, making sure that you do not damage the root. In this way it is possible to obtain perhaps 6 - 8 harvests a year. The leaves are tender and have a mild flavour. They are the sort of leaf that you can use in quantity in a salad and then add some herbs or other more highly flavoured leaves to spice things up a bit.

The main drawback to this plant is that it really wants to flower – and it wants to do so from about April until the end of the summer. Whilst I find that the leaves produced on flowering stems are actually sweeter than the basal leaves, the stems themselves are very woody and harvesting leaves individually from a flowering plant is a very time-consuming business.

The root is also edible and is said to have a mild flavour with a mucilaginous texture, though I have yet to try it.

Reichardia was occasionally cultivated as a salad plant in Britain in the 19th century but modern books never mention it.

Rumex alpinus. MONK'S RHUBARB looks very much like a dock, which is no surprise really because that is exactly what it is. On more than one occasion helpful friends and relatives have triumphantly weeded this plant out for me. Fortunately it is a very tough creature and survived being put back in the ground! It grows up to a metre tall and forms a slowly spreading clump 40cm or more wide.

Most docks are very bitter and don't make at all nice eating, though their leaves are very nutritious. This species, however, has occasionally been cultivated for its leaves. These have a fairly mild flavour in the autumn and early spring, though they are rather bitter at other times. They make a very good spinach and can also be added in moderation to salads. They are quite a popular leaf with us. The plants are very productive, producing fresh leaves from about February to December. They also form a very dense ground cover that excludes weeds, and so are very easy to grow.

Another species of dock worth trying is **R. patienta**, HERB PATIENCE. This also produces fairly mild leaves and is easy to grow.

Taraxacum officinale. The DANDELION is discussed more fully on page 145, but there are some named cultivars of this plant, however, that will do much better in a perennial vegetable bed. We grow the cultivar 'Broad Leaved'. This has large broad dark green leaves that are more deeply lobed along the axis of the leaf than the wild form. The leaves are thick and tender and can be 30cm or more long when growing in a rich soil. The plants are semi-erect in habit and do not go to seed as quickly as French types.

We have found, though, that the cultivated dandelion is more likely to suffer from mildew than the wild form. This is most apparent in dry years. Urine, diluted 3 to 1 with water is quite a good treatment for mildew, but would you eat the leaves once you had sprayed them with urine?

The leaves are still rather bitter, but they are an exceedingly healthy food. If you chop them up quite small and add them to a mixed salad that contains milder flavoured leaves and also some of the many sweet-tasting leaves that are discussed in this book, then you will get their health benefits without really noticing the bitterness.

This is an extremely vigorous and productive plant. Spring is the best time for harvesting the leaves, though the plant can grow all year round and, if given a very sheltered warm position, can provide a few leaves even in the winter.

The only problem we have encountered with dandelions is that slugs seem to be particularly attracted to them as a resting place during the day. They do little if any damage to the plants, using them as a base from which to attack all the nicer tasting salads we are growing. I suppose that this could be seen as an advantage, all you have to do is go round the dandelion plants each day and collect up all the slugs resting there. The trouble with this is that we grow so many dandelions that a day would probably not be long enough to get round to them all!

EDIBLE ROOTS

Most of the species listed here have excellent potential as cultivated crops, indeed a number of them already yield very well in this country and offer a real alternative to potatoes as a staple food.

Allium **species**. These are discussed above in the section on edible leaves. They produce small but tasty bulbs.

Cyperus esculentus. TIGER NUTS are occasionally available in health food shops in Britain. The plant grows about 75cm tall and 25cm wide in its first year and spreads slowly if left in the ground for a number of years. This species is a pernicious weed in the tropics. It is surprisingly hardy and can be successfully grown outdoors at least in the south of this country. It prefers a moist sandy loam. We have only grown it in well-drained soils so far, but it should also do well in a fairly wet soil and so could be trialled in a bog garden.

The common name of this plant is rather misleading since it does not produce nuts but small edible tubers. These do have a delicious nut-like flavour and can be eaten raw, cooked or dried and ground into a flour. They are rather tough and you will need a good set of teeth if you want to eat them raw. Cooking does not soften them much either, though they make a delicious addition to stews. The tubers are surprisingly rich in oil; this is edible, stores well without going rancid and is considered to compare favourably with olive oil.

We have been getting reasonable yields but are having trouble getting the tubers to sprout in the spring and we do not yet know why this should be. Quite often they will not come into growth until the middle of the summer and so do not have enough growing time to do really well.

Dioscorea batatas. This is a hardy YAM from Japan. (*See photograph overleaf.*) The edible root can be up to 1 metre long and weigh 2 kilos or more if it is grown in a good deep soil. It is the shape of a club, about as thick as an adult's finger at its top and thickens to be the size of an arm at its base. The main problem with this plant is harvesting it, you have to dig deep! Once you get it out, the root has a very nice floury flavour when baked, it is not as tasty as a sweet potato but is better than most yams. We use it in all the ways that potatoes are used, and find it to have a superior flavour. It makes an excellent staple food and, since yams are now becoming a more common food in Britain, it has a very good potential as a commercial crop here. What is needed is a simple method of harvesting the root.

The plant is a vigorous twining herbaceous climber. It can send out shoots up to 3 metres long each year and these will need supporting. Probably the easiest way of doing this is to grow it up a frame or bamboo sticks in much the same way as you grow runner beans. It is also possible that this plant will do well on a sunny woodland edge, allowing its shoots to scramble into the branches of shrubs. The main problem here is that harvesting the root is going to cause a lot of disturbance to the other plant roots.

Because the plant produces a vertical root, it is possible to grow a number of plants very close to each other, perhaps at 20 - 30cm spacings. You also get a better overall yield if you leave the plants in the ground for two years. Exceedingly high yields are possible, certainly quite a bit higher than potatoes and with none of the associated disease problems.

Propagation is a simple matter. Cut off the top 15cm of the root (this is the thin bit, so it is less useful for eating), store it cool and dry for the winter and then replant it in early spring. Do not remove this top portion until you want to eat the yam, though, because it will store much better in one piece.

Yams also form tubercles in late summer and early autumn. These are pea-size swellings in the leaf axils which fall off the plant when they are ripe. These tubercles are actually baby tubers and are an excellent way of propagating a quantity of the plants. Try and harvest them just before they are ready to fall from the plant and store them in a cool, frost-free place over the winter. Make sure they do not dry out. Pot them up into individual pots in early spring and plant them out when in active growth. They will form tubers about 500 grams in weight their first year, if left in the ground this can increase to 2 kilos or more in their second year.

There are many named varieties in China and Japan, though these are not yet available in this country.

Helianthus tuberosus. JERUSALEM ARTICHOKES should be too well known to be included here, but they are one of the relatively few cultivated perennial vegetables. Well-grown plants can be more than 3 metres tall and are sometimes

Dioscorea batatas. The YAM is an exceedingly vigorous and productive root crop that can be planted as closely as 15cm apart. When baked, the root (see inset) tastes like a floury potato.

used to provide a screen or shelter for the summer. This will not work in a very windy garden, however, because the plants will be blown over! In such a site it is better to try and dwarf the plants by pinching out the growing tips when about 60cm tall to encourage more bushy growth.

I prefer leaving the tubers in the ground all winter, they are very cold-hardy and will not suffer unless the slugs take a liking to them. This way, the tubers become sweet tasting and are then quite acceptable raw. Like *Polymnia edulis* (see below) the tubers are rich in inulin, a carbohydrate that is not absorbed by the body.

The plants are a good source of biomass, the starchy tubers in particular can be fermented to produce alcohol for fuel.

Lathyrus tuberosus. The EARTH-NUT PEA is a herbaceous climbing plant, sending out new stems each year 1 metre or so long. The stems will tend to straggle over the ground unless they have some support to scramble over – small shrubs make an excellent climbing frame for it. In return for being given a helping hand, the earth-nut pea will repay the shrub by providing nitrogen from the nodules produced on is roots. Unfortunately, slugs are very keen on this plant and, given half a chance, they will soon destroy it. One report says that the plant can be invasive, spreading by new shoots from its roots, but this won't happen if you have many slugs.

This is one of the nicest tubers I have ever eaten, it has also proved very popular with all those people I've asked to try it. The tubers are about 3 - 8cm in diameter. They are rich in starch and can be eaten raw, though they are rather a chew and have a bland flavour. When cooked, though, it is a different matter. They become sweet and develop a floury texture. The flavour is then excellent, resembling roasted sweet chestnuts. Unfortunately the plant has never been selectively bred for yields and so the harvests are disappointingly small. There is potential for selective breeding, though, and so one day this root crop might just make it to eminence.

Oxalis tuberosa. See Plate 29. OCA is one of the more promising root crops for this country. It can be grown and used like the potato but, unlike that species, it is almost untroubled by pests or diseases. It has been cultivated in South America for thousands of years and has given good yields when grown in Britain. The plant is slightly more cold-hardy than the potato, it will tolerate light frosts but top growth is killed by heavy frosts. The tubers will be killed by soil temperatures below about -5°C. Well-grown plants are about 45cm tall and 60cm wide.

The main problem with growing this plant is that it does not start to form tubers until the shorter days of late summer and autumn and so, if there is an early hard frost, yields are likely to be low. Leave the plants in the ground until the tops have been killed by frosts, since every day in the autumn will mean larger yields. The tubers are somewhat smaller than potatoes but can be 8cm or more long and 3cm wide. They have a waxy skin and are very easy to clean. They store really well with very little attention so long as they are not wet. I left some tubers sitting on the shelf in the kitchen one winter and they were still firm and starting to sprout in April.

When first harvested, the tubers have a pleasant lemony flavour due to the presence of oxalic acid, so should not be eaten in large quantities. See Appendix 4 for more details. However, if they are left in a sunny position for a week or so, the acid breaks down and the tubers become quite sweet. Some cultivars in South America become so sweet that they are eaten raw like a fruit – we are still trying to get hold of these forms.

Earthing up the growing stems as the tubers begin to form can significantly increase the crop. Yields of 40 tonnes per hectare have been obtained in experimental plantings in South America, this compares very favourably with potatoes especially when you consider all the disease problems associated with our humble spud. Yields of 7 - 10 tonnes are more the average in South America at present.

Polymnia edulis. See Plates 27 and 28. YACON is often cultivated for its edible root in South America, where yields of 38 tonnes per hectare have been achieved. This frost-tender plant grows about 1 metre or more tall and 60cm wide. It can be cultivated in much the same way as potatoes, though it requires a 6 - 7 month growing season and so is best started off in pots in a greenhouse in early spring and then planted out after the last expected frosts. It will probably not succeed in the colder parts of the country. A fast-growing and tolerant plant, it succeeds in poor soils though it yields much better in soils of at least reasonable quality.

Individual roots can weigh up to 500 grams and be 30cm or more long. Well-grown plants can produce a number of these roots and individual yields with me have been as good if not better than potatoes. The root is crisp and juicy and in some cultivars is also incredibly sweet, though the skin usually has a resinous flavour and is removed. In taste and texture yacon is more like a fruit than a root, it is a real taste treat and has become one of our favourite foods. The nutritional value is low, however, because much of the carbohydrate in the root is in the form of inulin. The human gut is unable to assimilate inulin and so it passes straight through the digestive system. This makes it an ideal food if you are on a diet to lose weight and want to eat enough to fill yourself up, but it is not a root that could be used as a staple food.

A gentle warning is appropriate here. Inulin can cause fermentation in the gut of some people, leading to the expulsion of gases through the rear passage (I've tried to phrase this as delicately as possible!).

Inulin can be easily converted to fructose, a sugar that is safe for diabetics to use, and so it is sometimes used to make a sweetener.

Yacon is a very easy plant to propagate in that it forms two types of tuber. The large ones I have been discussing are for eating and will not produce new growth if you plant them. They are merely used as storage organs by the plant. At the base of the stems, just below soil level, a number of smaller, knobbly tubers are formed. These look like small Jerusalem artichokes, which is not surprising since the two plants are related. Store these tubers, preferably still attached to the stems, in a cool frost-free place for the winter and use these to propagate the plants in spring. You can cut them up into pieces so long as there is a growth bud on each piece.

Potentilla anserina. SILVERWEED is a common weed in Britain and can be grown in lawns, hedgerows and other habitats. Tolerant of most soils and conditions, once in your garden it will be quite a job to get rid of it. A low-growing plant no more than 30cm tall, it spreads very freely at the roots and is more than a little invasive.

I've included it here because, whilst in the wild its root is rather small and fiddly to use, in cultivation it can become much larger. It was at one time cultivated in the Scottish Highlands as a root crop. The root has a nice taste, crisp and nutty with a somewhat starchy flavour, it can be eaten raw or cooked, or can be dried and ground into a flour that can be used with cereals when making bread, biscuits etc. It is quite low-yielding, but has potential for selective breeding.

Reichardia picroides. This species is discussed above in the section on edible leaves. It also produces an edible root.

Stachys affinis. The CHINESE ARTICHOKE grows about 45cm tall and 25cm wide. An easily grown plant, it will yield best in a fairly rich soil and dislikes dry conditions.

This species is occasionally cultivated for its edible tubers. These are rather on the small size. Well-grown plants will produce some that are up to 8cm long and 2cm wide, but expect most of them to be rather smaller. The tubers look somewhat like knobbly maggots, and are fiddly to use but they have a pleasant mild flavour and can be eaten raw or cooked. The knobbly nature of the tuber means that plenty of soil will be stuck to it. This makes them rather a hassle to clean. There is, however, a simple and effective method of cleaning this and other fiddly small tubers. You half-fill a bucket with water and add a few handfuls of soil or sand so that you have a nice runny muddy mixture. Add your dirty roots and stir vigorously for a few minutes. Now tip out the roots and rinse thoroughly. Even the most awkward of roots are quickly and easily cleaned by this method.

EDIBLE SEEDS & SEEDPODS

A rather small list, this is an area where more research needs to be carried out in order to obtain and develop a wider range of seed crops. See Chapter 13 for more details.

Phaseolus coccineus. Most people don't realize that RUNNER BEANS are perennials. I won't go into details of the plant's uses here, since this is such a well-known vegetable, but I would like to speak a little about how to grow this plant without having to sow seeds every year.

Runner beans form small tubers which are about as hardy as dahlias and will tolerate soil temperatures down to about -5°C. It is possible to dig up these tubers in the autumn, store them in a cool but frost free place in much the same way as dahlias and then replant them in the spring. If, however, the plants are grown in the milder areas of the country, or in carefully selected positions in colder areas, and are given a good mulch in the autumn they will survive most winters. They will then provide an earlier though lighter crop of edible young pods and mature seeds in following years. Look out for slugs in the spring, though, because they will eat out most of the young shoots if you are not vigilant.

Runner bean plants can be quite long-lived, I have read of plants 20 years old in Cornish gardens that are still cropping well. When the plants were first introduced into this country, it was for the ornamental value of their flowers and it was some years before people realized that the seeds and pods were edible.

Secale montana. PERENNIAL RYE grows about 1.2 metres tall, forming slowly spreading clumps 30cm or more wide. It grows best in lighter soils.

This is one of the most promising perennial cereals that we have come across to date. The plant is an ancestor of the cultivated cereal rye, its seed is considerably smaller but it is borne quite heavily and plants that are five years old are still growing well with us, producing over 100 flowering stems each year. The seed is simple enough to harvest, but removing the husk from the seed is more of a problem. Still, this is exactly the same problem that confronts a person who grows small amounts of any of the cultivated cereals. The seed can be used in all the ways that rye is used.

Triticum turgidum. Most cultivars of WHEAT are annual but there is one cultivar from North America, called 'Perennial' appropriately enough, where a proportion of the plants live on for a second or third year. I have not grown this cultivar yet but seed can be obtained from North America (don't forget to send me a few seeds if you do obtain it!).

EDIBLE STEMS

A bit of a miscellaneous list really, it contains plants that are already fairly well known.

Asparagus officinalis. ASPARAGUS is a fairly well-known vegetable so perhaps I shouldn't have included it in this book, but it is nice to remind you that at least some of our cultivated vegetables are perennials.

In addition to its edible stems, asparagus has had a reputation as a good companion plant for tomatoes, the theory being that it repelled nematodes. Recent research has borne this out, the whole plant containing asparagusic acid, which has been shown to have nematocidal properties.

Rheum x cultorum. RHUBARB is another well-known perennial vegetable that I will just mention in passing. Most cultivars produce their edible leaf stems in late winter and early spring, though there are some, such as 'Glaskin's Perpetual' that are low in oxalic acid and can be harvested all through the summer.

The leaves have at times been simmered in hot water to make an insecticide, though be careful with this because it can kill friendly as well as pest species. See also page 8.

HERBS

A few plants that are used more as flavourings than major items in the diet. Most herbs are considered to be ornamental, and so are included in other chapters of the book.

Artemisia dracunculus. FRENCH TARRAGON only just got into this book because it is already quite well known. But since this is one of my favourite salad flavourings I bent the rules slightly. A drought-tolerant plant, it grows about 60cm tall and spreads slowly to form a clump 30cm or more wide. It dislikes wet or heavy soils. The leaves have a somewhat liquorice-like flavour. As well as being excellent in salads they can also be cooked and used as a potherb. The growing and the dried plant is said to repel insects, it is however very attractive to slugs and they will totally decimate a plant if given half a chance.

Glycyrrhiza glabra. LIQUORICE grows about 1.2 metres tall and 80cm wide. It prefers a deep fertile soil that is not too heavy.

Liquorice is sometimes cultivated for its root which is frequently used as a pleasant flavouring for nasty tasting medicines (to which it also adds its own medicinal virtues) and also as a food. The root contains glycyrrhizin, a substance that is 50 times sweeter than sugar, and is used in making sweets, as a food flavouring and as a sweetener for herb teas. The dried root is sometimes eaten raw, it has a delicious flavour but is very fibrous – it is this fibrous quality that makes it useful as a tooth brush substitute and also for teething children to chew on.

There are a number of named varieties. 'Pontefract' is perhaps the hardiest form, it succeeds in northern England though is unlikely to thrive in the colder areas of Scotland. The roots are less sweet than many other cultivars.

'Poznan' is the most commonly grown cultivar. The roots have a very high sugar content, though the plant is less hardy than 'Pontefract' and will need winter protection in the colder areas of the country.

Levisticum officinale. LOVAGE is a vigorous plant growing up to 1.8 metres tall and 1 metre wide. A good companion plant, it is said to improve the health and flavour of other plants growing nearby. The flowers are very attractive to bees and also draw insect predators such as hoverflies into the garden.

Lovage comes into new growth early in the spring. The leaves, which have a yeasty/celery taste, can be used raw or cooked as a savoury flavouring in salads, soups etc. They are also used to make a herb tea that tastes more like a broth.

All other parts of the plant have a similar flavour and are used for food. The stems can be blanched and used like celery. The seed can be used, either whole or ground into a flour, as a flavouring in cakes, soups and salads. The root can also be used as a flavouring or cooked as a vegetable and is best when 2 - 3 years old.

Rumex scutatus. FRENCH SORREL grows about 60cm tall and wide. It prefers growing in the lighter soils and is drought tolerant once established. Plants will often self-sow quite freely if they are growing in a suitable position.

French sorrel has delicious lemon-flavoured leaves that are produced from early spring to early winter, especially if you cut the plant down to ground level occasionally during the summer. The leaves are a very nice flavouring in salads and are also used as a pot-herb. They should not be eaten in quantity, however, because they contain oxalic acid and this can prevent the body absorbing many of the minerals from the food. See Appendix 4 for more details.

Chapter Six

THE POND
& BOG GARDEN

There is something very satisfying about a pond. I wonder how many times I have been walking past one of our ponds on my way to do some job or other, only to find myself drawn to all the activity taking place there? An hour later I will probably still be watching the dragonflies darting about, a whirly-gig beetle skittering around the pond or a swallow flying low to catch insects or take a drink from the water – all thought of work has vanished.

Quite apart from stopping me doing my work, ponds can also provide a habitat for a wide range of native wildlife, a place to grow some absolutely beautiful plants and a surprising amount of food. They have a moderating effect on the temperature and, if large enough, can reduce occurrences of frost close to them. They reflect light and so can be used to increase light levels in houses, on walls, special plants etc. They increase air humidity, can be used to store water for irrigation purposes and, if you are willing to make them large enough, they can also be used for swimming!

Ponds have been disappearing from the British countryside at an alarming rate this century. Either they dry up because of the falling water table (caused by us draining the land or taking too much water from underground reserves), they gradually fill up with organic matter as reeds and other wetland plants encroach, or they are filled in by people in order to provide more land for crops, buildings or whatever.

One of the results of this has been an enormous decline in the number of frogs, toads and newts in Britain. These creatures, of course, are some of the gardener's best friends, eating large quantities of slugs and other unwelcome visitors.

It is not only ponds that are disappearing, about 97% of our natural wetlands have been drained for agriculture this century. One of the saddest things about this is that these wetlands have a huge potential for providing food crops for people whilst remaining an absolute haven for wild life (see the entry for *Typha angustifolia* on page 134).

A pond does not have to be very large in order to be able to grow plants and attract wildlife. I have seen a successful pond made in an old kitchen sink! This idea has an added benefit in that there is no need to dig a hole, you merely make a ladder of some sort so that creatures can get in and out.

Many other waste products of society can also be used to make a pond. We use old baths, for example, and find them to be excellent. It is also amazing just how quickly creatures can find their way to a new pond, within a day or two of filling it with water you will find various insects swimming about in it.

MAKING A POND

Not many gardens or farms are lucky enough to have naturally occurring ponds. Sometimes, if the water table is high, it is possible simply to dig a hole which will then fill with water. If you are lucky enough to have a stream flowing through the land then it might be possible to divert some of the water into a pond, allowing an overflow back into the stream. If you are not blessed with any of these circumstances then it is still relatively easy to put a pond into your garden, though you will probably have to top up the water level from time to time in dry summers. This can be done by diverting rainfall from the gutters of your house to a reservoir and then feeding this into the pond in dry weather.

Any of the following methods of making a pond are suitable:

1. **Plastic pond liners** are the most versatile method of making a pond because you can make it almost any shape and size you like. They are also a relatively cheap method, especially if you use the lower grades of plastic.

   The trouble with these lower grades is that they break down relatively quickly, with some types only lasting for 5 - 10 years. The best grades, such as butyl rubber, have a guaranteed life of 20 years or more. All of them, but especially the cheaper grades, can be punctured by sharp stones, dogs claws etc. There are special repair patches that can be used if this does happen. The main drawback of plastic liners is that they will have to be disposed of at some indeterminate time in the future.

   Having dug the hole, it is important to line it with materials to prevent the liner being punctured by stones in the soil. A layer of about 5cm of sand, preferably covered by old carpets, is ideal.

2. **Pre-formed glass-fibre ponds** are very simple to put in. Simply dig a hole that approximately resembles the shape of the pond, then line it in the same way as for the plastic pond liners mentioned above. With care, such a pond should last for at least 20 years and perhaps considerably longer. You are rather restricted to the sizes and shapes that the manufacturers supply though, and this sort of pond is always rather small and relatively expensive. A well-made glass fibre pond does not easily get punctured, but should a leak occur, then this is relatively easy to fix with a glass fibre patch.

3. **Concrete** can be used as a liner, though it is a lot of work to put it in and it then needs to be treated to neutralize the lime. It is also rather difficult to have anything other than straight sides. Concrete ponds can be very strong and durable, but even well-made ones have been known to crack after 20 years or so. These cracks, of course, can be fixed relatively simply by the application of more concrete.

4. **Natural liners**. On sites where sub-soil with a sufficient clay content is present,

this can be used in compacted layers to form a water-retaining lining to make a natural pond. Alternatively a powdered clay called 'bentonite' can be spread over the newly excavated site and then mixed into the top 5cm of soil. It swells up and binds together as the pond fills with water and thus forms a natural lining.

One great advantage of a natural liner over the previous three options is that it can be self-sealing. Put a fork through one of the previous linings and the water will leak away. With a clay lining the hole will fill in naturally.

The main drawback with clay linings is that, when the water level falls in dry weather, the exposed clay can develop wide cracks. These are too wide to enable the clay to reseal when the levels rise again. Over a period of years, therefore, you will gradually lose more and more of your pond. This makes it particularly unsuitable for very small ponds since the water-level rises and falls more rapidly. Burying the clay below a layer of soil can help to prevent the cracking. Clay-lined ponds can last for many centuries, making them the best natural option for medium to large ponds.

It is not intended to go into much detail here of making ponds and establishing a water garden, for more information on this please refer to the book list contained in Appendix 1. There are a few basic points that are worth mentioning:

1. Make sure that your pond has at least one shallow side to enable creatures, especially amphibians, to get in and out easily. This will also make sure that any cats, dogs, hedgehogs etc. that fall in will be able to get out!

2. Make sure that it has several different levels (preferably with at least one area more than 50cm deep) to enable you to grow a variety of plants and to make sure that even in severe weather some of the water at the bottom of the pond is not frozen.

3. When siting the pond it is important to give it as sunny a position as possible since most pond plants do not like shade. It is also important to choose a site that is sheltered from cold winds.

4. Try to choose a position with no overhanging trees. The leaves that fall in during the autumn will disturb the balance of the pond as they rot and, unless you are prepared to remove the leaves, they can destroy the life of the pond. If you do place a pond where tree leaves fall into it, then a net placed over the pond in autumn will protect it from the majority of the leaves.

5. Fish and amphibians do not really mix that well because many species of fish are likely to eat the spawn or the young tadpoles. If you want fish and amphibians, then either select your species carefully or consider putting in at least 2 ponds, one for the fish and one for the amphibians.

6. To ensure a healthy pond, make sure it contains creatures that can clean up the mess of plants decaying, defecations etc. Water snails are ideal for this.

7. Although not mentioned in the lists of plants later in this chapter, it is a good idea to grow some submerged plants such as ***Elodea canadensis***, the CANADIAN POND WEED. These plants will help to oxygenate the water, and will provide cover and food for many of the creatures living in the pond.

8. When filling the pond, try and obtain a bucket or so of water and mud from an established and healthy pond. This will introduce many creatures into your pond and help to establish a healthy and thriving ecosystem.

MAKING A BOG GARDEN

When planning the pond, it is nice also to have an area of very wet soil for those plants that might not like immersion in water but do demand very wet conditions. Natural ponds are often already surrounded by marshy land and on a garden scale it is possible to create this. Perhaps the simplest methods are:

1. If you have an old garden pond that keeps leaking then just fill it up with earth and use it as a bog garden. If it only leaks a little then you might have to put a few more holes in it first or you could end up with a quagmire.

2. Excavate an area of soil to about 50cm, line it with plastic, puncture it in a few places and then replace the soil.

3. Put a layer of gravel at the bottom of an old bath (with the plug left out) and then fill it to within 10cm of the top with soil.

4. Fill in the shallow edges of your pond with earth. This is by far the most natural looking of the options.

The first three options will need watering in dry weather, though it is possible to use waste 'grey' water from your bath or shower, or from any other relatively clean source, by plumbing in drain pipes. Do not use this waste water in the pond, though. The reason for this is that the waste water will contain a certain amount of nutrients and soil – the water from washing vegetables for example, or the soapy water from washing your hands. In reasonable quantities, the plants in a bog garden will grow all the better for these extra nutrients. In a pond, however, these nutrients will cause too much growth in the algae and this can actually lead to an imbalance and shortage of oxygen in the water with the resultant death of much of the pond life.

GROWING THE PLANTS

When growing plants in a pond you have to decide whether to grow them in pots or in a layer of soil in the pond. There are, as you might expect, advantages and disadvantages to each method.

In very small ponds it will generally be best to grow plants in pots if possible. This will contain them and help you keep at least some semblance of control. Otherwise you will find that you are constantly disturbing the pond by pulling out excessive growth.

In larger ponds, especially those made from natural materials such as clay, it is possible to put in a layer of soil 30cm or more deep on top of the pond lining. You will find that plants grown in this soil will be far more vigorous and healthy. You will have to be careful not to grow any plants that might grow into and damage the pond lining (this will be much more of a problem if you are using cheap plastic linings). You will also have to be careful not to puncture a plastic lining if you are digging out any plant roots.

Growing the plants in pots means that you are able to remove them from the water more easily if you want to propagate them or whatever. However, it will also mean that you need to give the plants more attention because they will need to be divided at regular intervals as they outgrow their pots. They will also need to be fed because the soil in the pot will not contain enough reserves of food to sustain them.

Growing the plants in soil in the pond will mean less work in large ponds because the plants will be able to look after themselves and obtain their nutrients from the soil around them. It will also mean that it will be very difficult if not impossible to remove a plant if you no longer want it there.

There are a number of plants that are just too vigorous to be grown in pots. These, obviously, are also too vigorous to be grown in the smaller ponds.

Most of the plants listed in this chapter are very easy to cultivate. Indeed, with some of them the problem will be more one of trying to contain them since they are so vigorous. However, much of this luxuriant growth can be used to good effect in the compost heap. You should find that your pond, once established, will require very little attention.

Water and bog plants are a very under-exploited resource for food and a wide range of other useful products. There has been very little research into their potential and even less to produce improved cultivars. Many of the species listed here are rather marginal as food crops at the present – they might be low-yielding, for example, or their flavour is not very acceptable to the average human palate. Nevertheless, almost all the species mentioned here have a good potential and some of them could rank amongst the most productive crops in the world if only we put a little effort into developing them.

The plants are divided into five groups according to their habitat. Unless stated otherwise, they are all perennials and require a sunny position.

FLOATING PLANTS

These species do not need to be grown in the soil or in pots. They float on the surface of the water and can extract their nutrients from the water.

Trapa natans. The WATER CHESTNUT is often cultivated for its edible seed. Although it is a perennial and is said to be hardy in all but the coldest areas of the country, the books say that it is best grown as an annual in Britain. It prefers a slightly acid water and dislikes lime. It will also succeed in slowly flowing water.

I have grown this plant on a number of occasions and, although it seems to do well, it does not flower and dies out in the winter. This has happened both outdoors and in a pond in a polytunnel. I do not know if I am doing something wrong, if I am getting hold of a tender form of the plant, or if it just is not suitable for Britain.

There are a number of very closely related species (so closely related in fact that many botanists say that they are all forms of one variable species) and at least one of these is said to have been cultivated as a food crop in Neolithic Britain. This species, *T. bicornis*, is also said by some books to be frost tender! All in all a very confusing situation. I would appreciate feedback from anyone who is successfully growing this plant and producing seeds and also if they just happen to have some seed or a plant or three to spare...

If you can obtain a yield from it, then this is a very tasty crop to grow. The seed is 2cm or more across. It has a sweet flavour and a floury texture, when roasted it tastes like sweet chestnuts. It can also be dried and ground into a powder then used with wheat in making biscuits etc. Most reports say that the seed can be eaten raw, but there is one report that says it needs to be cooked in order to destroy a toxic principle. Always one for erring on the side of caution, I have only eaten it cooked.

Wolffia arrhiza. The LEAST DUCKWEED is one of the smallest flowering plants in the world. It is cultivated as a vegetable in Burma, Laos and Thailand, and has been recommended for commercial cultivation, especially in tropical areas, because of its rapid multiplication and high nutritional value. It requires a sunny position in still water that is rich in nitrates and lime.

This species is at the limit of its climatic range in Britain and so is unlikely to succeed outdoors over the winter in any but the mildest areas of the country. It overwinters in temperate areas by means of resting buds which sink to the bottom of the pond in the late autumn and rise again in the spring. It is possible, therefore, to grow it outdoors as a summer crop and store some of the plants in a cold water aquarium or something similar for the winter.

I have not yet grown or eaten this plant, though it is on my short-list of plants to obtain. The leaves are said to have an excellent flavour when cooked, somewhat like a sweet cabbage. As mentioned earlier, they are very nutritious and contain about 20% protein, 44% carbohydrate, 5% fat and are rich in vitamins A, B2, B6, C and nicotinic acid.

DEEP WATER PLANTS

These are plants that grow best in the deeper water of the pond, usually requiring at least 30cm of water.

Aponogeton distachyos. WATER HAWTHORN grows best in water 15 - 60cm deep, the leaves floating on the water surface. It grows very well with us, but there is some confusion as to how hardy it is in all parts of Britain. One report says it is widely grown in ponds in Britain and is often more or less naturalised, another says it is not very hardy, being killed in areas where winter temperatures fall to about -5°C. The starchy tuber is harvested in the autumn and winter and eaten cooked. It is said to be a great luxury, though I have not tried it. The plant can flower from April to October, the immature flowering spikes and young shoots which can be used as a spinach or asparagus substitute. The flowers are used as a flavouring.

Nelumbo lutea. The AMERICAN WATER LOTUS grows in water up to 2 metres deep in the wild but in cool temperate zones is best in water no more than 60cm deep. This beautiful plant produces its flowers in early to mid summer. Unfortunately it is not fully hardy in colder areas of the country, but can be grown in large pots in an outdoor pond in the summer and then be removed to a cold greenhouse or shed when it dies down in the autumn. Make sure that you keep it in shallow water and that it does not freeze, then plant it out again in April.

I have not yet grown or eaten this plant, but it has been proposed for commercial cultivation in much the same way as the Chinese grow water lilies for food. It is very unlikely to be a commercial proposition in this country, though.

The baked root is sweet and mealy, somewhat like a sweet potato, though it is usually cut up and steeped in one or two changes of water beforehand in order to remove any bitterness. The seed can be eaten raw or cooked, when half-ripe it is said to be delicious with a taste like sweet chestnuts. The seed can also be dried, ground into a flour and used for making bread, thickening soups etc. or eaten dry. It does have a bitter embryo and this is often removed before the seed is eaten. An edible oil can be extracted from the seed whilst the leaves and young stems can be eaten cooked.

Nuphar lutea. Our native YELLOW WATER LILY grows in water up to 2.5 metres deep and will succeed in slow-flowing water as well as in ponds.

The root has a bitter taste but can be eaten cooked and an edible starch can be extracted from it. The seed can be ground into a flour and used with cereals in making bread and porridge, or as a thickener for soups etc. It can also be roasted like popcorn, when it swells considerably but does not burst. It is then normally eaten dry. In order to save the seed it is best to wrap the developing seed head in a muslin bag, the seed can then be harvested either when it goes below the surface of the water, or when it reappears 10 days or so later. A refreshing drink is said to be made from the flowers, though we have no details of how this is made. The leaves and leaf stalks can be eaten cooked, but are not that pleasant.

Two other members of this genus, *N. advena* and *N. polysepala*, have similar uses.

Nymphaea alba. See Plate 31. The WHITE WATER LILY is another native plant and grows in the deeper parts of the pond, 1.5 to 2.5 metres of water should suit it well, though you can also grow it in less deep ponds.

This is another of the many water plants that I have not yet eaten, the following are its lists of uses. The roots are cooked and eaten when several years old, they contain about 40% starch and 6% protein. The seed can also be cooked and eaten, it contains about 47% starch, and when roasted it can be used as a coffee substitute. Some caution should be applied with this species, however, because there are also reports that it could be toxic. There are several other members of this genus and they should all have similar uses.

SHALLOW WATER PLANTS

The plants in this list generally grow best in water from 5 - 30cm deep.

Nasturtium officinale. WATERCRESS is a native plant and is the familiar salading for sale in greengrocers. The plant prefers growing in slow-flowing very shallow water but it can also be found in ponds and marshy soils. The best way of obtaining this plant is to buy a bunch of the shoots from a greengrocer and then put it in a bowl of water. Roots will be formed within a few days. Pot up the shoots, standing the pots in shallow water. One the plants are well rooted they can be planted out in the pond.

The leaves are exceedingly nutritious, being a good source of many vitamins and minerals. They have a pungent, hot flavour and are often cooked as well as being used in salads. The plant will continue to grow in mild winters and so the leaves can often be harvested all 12 months of the year.

This plant can often be found growing wild in Britain, but be very careful if gathering leaves from the wild. Any plants growing in water that drains from fields where animals, particularly sheep, graze should not be used because of the risk that it could be infested with the liver fluke parasite. When grown in clean water there is no risk of this happening.

The seed can be sprouted and eaten in much the same way as mustard and cress, it can also be ground up into a powder and used as a mustard.

Nymphoides peltata. Our native WATER FRINGE grows freely in the shallow edges of the pond, too freely if the soil is rich. The leaves and stems float on the water and look rather like a small water lily. The stems will often grow 1.5 metres or more long. Roots will form at intervals along this stem, thus enabling the plant to propagate itself. Although it is rather vigorous, it is easily controlled by simply pulling the stems out of the water and makes good compost material.

Assuming you don't need the compost, then the leaves and leaf stems can be cooked like spinach. Books say that the interior of the stem is also eaten and has a nicer flavour, but the stem is rather thin and I'm not sure that I would want to spend my time peeling it! The flower buds are also said to be cooked like spinach.

***Sagittaria* species**. Most if not all members of this genus produce edible tubers and a number of them are cultivated for this purpose, especially in the Orient. They succeed in wet soils but are best in water 30 - 60cm deep. They need a fairly long growing season of around 6 months and do best in hot summers.

    S. sagittifolia. The ARROW HEAD is a native species growing about 1 metre tall and spreading freely at the roots. This is the species that is most frequently cultivated as a food crop. There are many named varieties developed for their edible qualities and larger tubers, though I do not know of a source for these in Britain. The tubers can often be purchased as a food in Chinese shops in this country and this is one of the best ways of obtaining plants for growing. The tubers need to be fresh if they are to grow away before rotting.

    According to the books, the tubers can be 15cm or more in diameter, though I have scarcely been able to grow them to half that size. They are starchy with a distinct flavour that people have likened to potatoes, though I'm not sure that I agree. There is a slight bitterness, but this is mainly in the skin which is best removed after cooking. They make a very acceptable 'stodge' part of the meal. The tubers can also be dried and ground into a flour which can then be used as a gruel or added to cereal flours and used in making bread, biscuits or cakes. The tubers, which can be produced up to 1 metre from the plant, are best harvested in the autumn as the leaves die down, they should not be eaten raw.

    Any other members of the genus can be used, though their tubers will not be so large. Some of the best are: ***S. cuneata***, the WAPATO; ***S. graminea***; and ***S. latifolia***, the DUCK POTATO.

Zizania aquatica. This is the WILD RICE plant whose horrendously expensive edible seeds can be seen for sale in health food shops. An annual growing about 3 metres tall and 20cm wide in slow-flowing water, the plant grows quite successfully in Britain but has to be started off in a greenhouse in order to give the plants a sufficiently long growing season to ripen their seed. They do self-sow in this country, but unfortunately the plants often germinate too late in the season for them to produce a worthwhile crop and so they die out after a few years. The seed must be kept moist if it is to retain its viability and I know of no source of viable seed in this country (the seed in health food shops has been dried and will not germinate) though there are sources in America. If you can get hold of some viable seed then (apart from letting us have some!) you could give it a try in shallow pond and lake margins or the sheltered edges of slow-moving streams.

    The black seed is about twice the length of rice, but rather thinner. It was a staple food of the North American Indians and nowadays this delicious grain is eaten as an expensive gourmet meal. It is used in the same ways that rice is used and is sometimes added to rice dishes to impart its subtle flavour. The seed can also be ground into a meal and used in making bread, thickening soups etc.

MARGINAL PLANTS

The following plants prefer to grow in the shallow edges of the pond and will also succeed in boggy soil by the side of a pond.

Acorus calamus. SWEET FLAG grows about 1 metre tall and wide. A very easily grown plant, it prefers growing in the shallow edges of ponds and in wet soils by the pond. It rarely flowers in Britain and never flowers unless it is growing in water.

I have not eaten this plant yet but its list of uses is impressive. The rhizome is candied and made into a sweetmeat. It can also be peeled and washed to remove the bitterness and then eaten raw like a fruit. An essential oil from the root is used as a food flavouring and in perfumery. The root can also be used as a substitute for ginger, cinnamon or nutmeg, depending on the condition of your palate or which report you want to believe! The inner portion of young stems can be eaten raw and makes a very palatable salad.

Other virtues of this plant include: the leaves are used in basket making or woven into mats; all parts of plant can be dried and used to repel insects or to scent linen cupboards; the whole plant can be burnt as an incense and was formerly used as a strewing herb; the growing plant is said to repel mosquitoes, whilst an essential oil from the roots is used as an insect repellent and as an insecticide.

Some caution should be exercised when using this plant for food. There is a report that the fresh root can be poisonous. Other reports say that the essential oil, when extracted from the plant, can cause problems if used medicinally. It seems that some forms of the plant from Asia are to blame here, plants from North America and Siberia being safe to use.

Butomus umbellatus. See Plate 30. FLOWERING RUSH is a native plant growing about 1 metre tall and 50cm wide. It is found in moist soil or in water up to 30cm deep. As the common name suggests, the plant looks like a rush but produces flowers. The plant is in flower from mid summer until early autumn and I find it to be exceptionally beautiful. This is a plant I would want to grow even if it had no edible uses.

The tuber is cooked after peeling and removing the rootlets. It can also be dried and ground into a meal to be used as a thickener in soups or added to flour when making bread. It contains more than 50% starch. The seed is said to be edible but it is very small and would be very fiddly to use.

Cyperus longus. GALINGALE grows about 1.2 metres tall and spreads rampantly at the roots to form large clumps. A very easily grown plant, it succeeds in moist or wet soils as well as in water up to 30cm deep.

The tuber has the scent of violets and is used as a spice in soups, pies and sweets. It was one of the favourite spices of the medieval kitchen and was an ingredient of 'pokerounce', a kind of medieval cinnamon toast. It has also been used in perfumery. The leaves are used in basket making and for weaving hats and matting whilst a fibre obtained from the plant is used in paper making.

Darmera peltata. The UMBRELLA PLANT can be up to 1.5 metres tall and 60cm wide, though the cultivar 'Nana' is only 30cm tall. The plant flowers in early spring, before the leaves appear. These leaves can be 30cm or more across and are produced on stems in a rather similar manner to rhubarb. The plant succeeds in wet soil or in shallow water.

The leafstalk can be peeled and eaten raw or cooked like asparagus, though this is another plant that I have yet to try.

The plant can be used as a ground cover in a sunny position and is also useful as a soil stabilizer for marshy land or muddy banks.

Glyceria fluitans. Our native FLOAT GRASS grows about 45cm tall and wide in wet soils or in shallow water.

The plant has an edible seed, though this is rather small and would be fiddly to use. I only obtained the plant in 1994 and have not eaten the seed yet, but it is said to have a sweetish taste and is considered a delicacy in some parts of Europe. The plant is occasionally cultivated for its seed and this was an article of commerce until well into the 20th century. A flour from the seed is said to make bread a little inferior to wheat bread. This flour can also be used as a thickener in soups to impart a sweet delicate flavour. Any other members of this genus could also be tried for their seeds.

Houttuynia cordata. This vigorous plant grows about 60cm tall, it spreads rapidly by its rhizomes and succeeds in wet soils as well as in shallow water. The leaves have a strong scent and flavour of orange peel and are one of our favourite flavourings in salads. See also page 201.

Menyanthes trifoliata. BOGBEAN is a native plant growing about 30cm tall and 60cm wide in wet soils or in shallow water to 30cm deep. The flowers, though small, are incredibly beautiful.

The root has an acrid taste, it has been dried and ground into a flour and used for making 'missen bread' (famine bread). This is very much an emergency food, only to be used in times of dire need! The bitter leaves are used as a substitute for hops in making beer.

The main reason for including this species here, apart from the fact that the flowers are very beautiful, is that the leaves are an extremely effective bitter tonic for the digestive system and so are often used in herbal medicine. They have proved to be of benefit in the treatment of muscular weakness in M.E..

Peltandra sagittifolia and ***P. virginica***. The WHITE ARROW ARUM and the GREEN ARROW ARUM grow in shallow water near the pond edges. They require lime-free conditions.

Their rhizomes are said to be edible and are rich in starch, apparently they can weigh up to 2.5 kilos, but they must be well cooked since they both contain calcium oxalate crystals and are poisonous raw. See Appendix 4 for details of this toxin.

The seed of *P. virginica* is said to be edible and to have a slightly sweetish flavour, resembling parched corn. A bread made from it tastes like corncake with a strong flavour of cocoa. Yields are likely to be low. The flowering stem and berries of *P. virginica* is said to be a great delicacy when cooked. Once again, it must be thoroughly cooked or it will be poisonous – the North American Indians would boil them for nine hours!

It is quite probable that the seed and flowering stems of *P. sagittifolia* could be used in the same way.

Phragmites australis. COMMON REED is a native grass growing in shallow waters and wet soils where it forms an excellent habitat for birds and other creatures. Plants can be up to 3.5 metres tall, so this is a species that is not really suitable for the smaller garden, particularly as it is very invasive. It is said to be tolerant of saline water.

The common reed more than makes up for its antisocial tendencies with its quite impressive list of uses. The roots, which contain 5% sugar, are edible and can be cooked like potatoes or dried, ground coarsely and used as a porridge. They are best when still young and growing, though they are not very large. The young shoots can be eaten raw or cooked and are best before the leaves form, when they can be used like rather thin bamboo shoots. The seed is also edible but this is small and very fiddly to use. If the stem is wounded it exudes a sugary substance which hardens upon exposure to the air. This has a sweet liquorice-like flavour and can be eaten raw or roasted. The dried and powdered inner stem can be moistened and then roasted to make a marshmallow substitute.

The non-edible virtues of this plant are also extensive. The stems have a multitude of uses, they are used for a high grade thatching that can last for 100 years, basket making, weaving into mats etc., insulation, fuel and as a cork substitute. A fibre from the leaves and stems is used for making paper. The leaves are used in basket making and for weaving mats etc. A light green dye is obtained from the flowers. The inflorescences are used as brooms. The plant has a very vigorous and running rootstock which makes it useful for binding the soil along the sides of streams. Plants have also been used in sewage and grey-water treatment in order to remove excess nutrients from the water – the plant growth can then be cut down at intervals and used to make compost. If that list does not convince you to grow the plant then nothing will.

Scirpus lacustris. Our native BULRUSH grows about 2.5 metres tall and succeeds in wet soils and shallow pond margins, it is also sometimes found in deeper water.

The starchy root is eaten raw or cooked and can be dried and ground into a flour or boiled and made into a syrup. The buds at the end of the rhizomes are crisp and sweet, making excellent eating raw. The seed is rather small and fiddly but has been ground into a flour and mixed with cereals for use in making cakes. The pollen has also been mixed with flour and used in making cakes etc. It is collected by tapping the flowering stems over a wide bowl and it takes ages to collect any reasonable quantity. It is a very good source of a high-quality protein, though, and has a pleasant flavour. The stems can be woven into mats and chair seats and are used for thatching.

Typha angustifolia and *T. latifolia*. See Plate 32. The SMALL REEDMACE and the REEDMACE grow in wet soil and pond margins up to 15cm deep. In the wild these native plants often cover extensive areas of wet ground and are a haven for wildlife, especially pond and river birds. These are very vigorous and invasive plants that grow up to 3 metres tall and will spread far and wide given the chance. Make sure that you've got room for them because they will soon overrun most of your other plants and start filling in your pond if you don't keep an eye on them.

However, their vigour is what makes them such an exciting prospect for food (they have the potential to be an exceedingly productive root crop for example) and a whole range of other uses. Why these plants are not exploited more is just beyond me. Instead of letting them grow in natural wetland and then just harvesting them as required, we waste lots of resources in draining the land to make it 'more productive' and thus destroy a valuable wildlife area. We then grow wheat or some other annual crop on the land which consumes more energy than the crop itself produces. It is a very perverse form of reasoning.

The roots of reedmace can be eaten raw or cooked like potatoes, they can also be macerated and boiled to yield a sweet syrup or can be dried, ground into a flour and then used as a thickener in soups or mixed with cereals. Yields of 8 tonnes of flour per hectare have been recorded. The young shoots can be eaten as an asparagus substitute in spring. The peeled base of mature stems can be eaten raw or cooked. The immature flowering stems can be eaten raw or cooked and taste like sweet corn. The seed has a pleasant nutty taste when roasted though it is very small and fiddly to harvest. An edible oil is obtained from the seed but it would probably take far too long to collect a reasonable quantity of the seed to make it worthwhile. The pollen is used as a protein rich additive to flour for making bread and porridge. It can also be eaten with the young flowers, which makes it considerably easier to use.

As if the list of edible uses is not impressive enough, how about this for the non-edible uses: the stems and leaves are gathered in the autumn and used for thatching and can also be woven into mats, chairs and hats; the stems are a good source of biomass, making an excellent addition to the compost heap or used as a source of fuel; the stems can be harvested in late summer and used to make rush lights – the outer stem is removed except for a small strip about 10mm wide which acts as a spine to keep the stem erect. The stem is then soaked in oil and can be lit and used like a candle; a fibre obtained from the leaves can be used for making paper; the hairs of the fruits are used for stuffing pillows; they have good insulating and buoyancy properties and have also been used as a wound dressing and a lining for babies' nappies; the flowering stems can also be dried and used for insulation; plants have also been used in sewage and grey-water treatment in order to remove excess nutrients from the water – the plant growth can then be cut down at intervals and used to make compost. As if all that isn't enough, the pollen is highly inflammable and can be used in making fireworks. Why aren't you growing this plant?

Zizania latifolia. MANCHURIAN WILD RICE is quite closely related to *Z. aquatica*, which was described in the previous section. It differs mainly in being a perennial, having smaller seed and preferring pond edges. It grows about 3.5 metres tall, I do not know how wide it will grow. It prefers a slightly acidic clay-loam soil.

This is another of those species where there is a dispute over its hardiness.

I have a report from Kew Gardens, dated 1909, saying it is an easily grown plant that grows well at Kew. More recent literature suggests that it is either not hardy, or only marginally so, in this country. Whichever report is true, it does seem that the plant requires hot summers with temperatures between 20 - 30°C if it is to do well.

It is often cultivated as a food crop in East Asia and makes an excellent cover for wild fowl along the sides of lakes. The swollen stem bases, deliberately infected with the smut fungus *Ustilago esculenta*, are eaten as a vegetable by the Chinese. They must be harvested before the fungus starts to produce spores since the flesh of the fungus deteriorates at this time. They are parboiled then sautéd with other vegetables and have a nutty flavour reminiscent of coconut. It is quite interesting that the wild forms of this species have developed resistance to the smut, so specially disease-susceptible cultivars are grown.

The young shoots can be eaten raw or cooked and are said to have a pleasant sweet taste.

BOG PLANTS

These plants like to grow in very wet soil around the pond, they do not usually grow into the water.

Beckmannia eruciformis. This is a grass that can grow up to 1.5 metres tall, though it has been quite a bit smaller with me. It is often a short-lived perennial and sometimes dies after the first year, especially when growing in drier soils. At its best in wet soils, it can also succeed in shallow water and is tolerant of saline conditions.

The seed is edible and can be ground into a flour then used as a cereal in making bread and biscuits. It has a mild flavour. Although the seed is easy to harvest, it is very small and fiddly to use.

Chrysosplenium alternifolium. GOLDEN SAXIFRAGE is a low-growing creeping native plant about 20cm tall and 50cm or more wide. It makes a good weed-excluding ground cover plant for the bog garden. Unlike most of the plants in this chapter, it prefers a shady position, so grow it amongst taller bog plants such as *Myrica gale*. It also grows well in woodland conditions.

In early spring the leaves have a reasonable flavour with a slight bitterness and are acceptable as an ingredient in mixed salads. They become rather more bitter from mid spring until mid summer when the plant is flowering and are then a bit milder again as the temperatures fall in the autumn.

C. oppositifolium is a very similar plant with the same use.

Gunnera tinctoria. This plant looks like a greatly overgrown rhubarb and, in sheltered positions and moist soils, the stem can be 2 metres tall and the leaf a metre or more across. The sheer size of the leaves means that the plants need to be grown in sheltered positions otherwise the wind will blow them to pieces. They spread slowly to form large clumps eventually and grow best close to the edges of streams, preferably in sheltered valleys. Walking amongst a planting of gunnera is quite an experience, somewhat like being in a primeval forest with the leaf stems looking like small tree trunks. The plant is not tremendously cold-hardy in Britain, the rootstock will survive temperatures down to about -10°C though the plants can be grown in colder areas if you give them a good protective mulch of bracken or some similar material.

Although they don't look tremendously appetizing, the leaf stalks are said to be peeled and eaten raw or cooked, the flavour is meant to be acid and refreshing but I have yet to feel a desire to try it. The root contains 9% tannin and is the source of a black dye. The leaves are used as a roof covering.

Hierochloe odorata. HOLY GRASS can be grown on the drier edges of the bog garden, it also succeeds in fairly dry soils. This rare native grass grows about 60cm tall and can spread aggressively, indeed it has such a vigorous root system that it has been planted to stabilize wet banks.

The seed is edible, but it is much too small and fiddly to be worthwhile unless you are really desperate. An essential oil from the leaves can be used as a vanilla-like flavouring. The plant contains coumarin (see Appendix 4 for details of this potentially toxic substance) and, when dried, it develops a delicious aroma. It has been used as an incense and also as a stewing herb or in the linen cupboard in order to keep moths away. The leaves are also used to make aromatic baskets.

Myrica gale. BOG MYRTLE is a native deciduous shrub that can grow about 2 metres tall, though it is usually smaller. Most reports say that it requires an acid soil but plants are also sometimes found wild in alkaline fens with a pH of 7.5. Plants are usually either male or female, but sometimes they change sex and they also sometimes carry flowers of both sexes.

The aromatic fruits and leaves are used to flavour soups and stews and are sometimes put in beer and ale to improve the flavour and increase foaming. The dried leaves make a delicate and palatable tea.

A wax covering on the fruit and leaves is extracted by simmering them in hot water and skimming off the wax as it melts and comes to the surface. The wax can be used to make aromatic candles but, unfortunately, this species does not produce enough wax to make it commercially viable. See Chapter 9 for some other members of this genus that produce much more wax. A yellow dye is obtained from the stem tips. The whole plant, and especially the leaves, repels moths and insects in general. A strong decoction of the leaves can be used as a parasiticide to kill external body parasites. A fragrant essential oil is obtained from the fruits.

Pontederia cordata. PICKEREL WEED grows about 75cm tall and 50cm wide. It succeeds in pond margins and marshy soils, though it is happiest in water about 15 - 30cm deep. The seeds can be eaten raw, cooked like rice or ground up and used as a flour substitute. They have an excellent nutty flavour but have not been freely produced with me to date. The young leaves and leafstalks can be added to salads or eaten cooked.

Rhexia virginica. DEER GRASS is not a grass and nor does it look like one. The common name arises from the fact that deer love to graze on it. The plant grows about 30cm tall. I do not know yet how wide it will grow because I had only been growing it for a couple of years when this book was written. It succeeds in wet soils but not in the pond. The main problem with this plant seems to be that slugs like eating it even more than I do and can find their way to it no matter how I try to stop them.

This is a great pity because the leaves have a very pleasant acid flavour and go well in salads. The root also has this acid flavour and can be chopped up then added to salads.

Chapter Seven

THE EDIBLE LAWN

Most gardens contain a lawn – it is an area where we can walk, play and relax, our own little area of relative privacy. The lawn is especially important for children, giving them space to run about and play without constantly being told to keep off the plants. In this chapter I would like to look at a few plants that can be grown in a lawn in order to improve its overall health and reduce the amount of work needed to maintain it – with the added bonus of providing a few food crops and some other useful commodities.

For some reason, many people feel that a lawn needs to be made up entirely of grasses and that any other plant species must be ruthlessly eliminated. They invest a considerable amount of money and time in getting rid of these plants, keeping the grass cut very short, raking out moss and fertilising the lawn in order to maintain the vigour of the grass. If they could only relax a little, let some of the non-grass plants establish themselves in the lawn, allow the grass to grow a little longer, then they would find that the lawn would become healthier, it would require less or no inputs of fertilizer whilst also becoming more interesting to look at and taking a lot less work to maintain.

For example, if you allow creeping clover to grow in the lawn, this plant will repay you by feeding the grass with nitrogen. Thus the grass will grow more strongly and will be a deeper green and you will not need to apply nitrogen fertilisers to the lawn.

Another example is yarrow. This plant grows superbly well in a lawn and in times of drought will stay green and lush when all around it is turning brown. Daisies are another good lawn plant and what can be nicer than daisy flowers in a lawn – even in the winter you will often find a few flowers opening to brighten your day. All of these plants will grow quite happily even if you keep the lawn cut very short. If you allow the grass to grow a bit longer, at least for part of the year, there are many other plants that can be grown there.

Of course, apart from improving the look and general health of a lawn, many of the plants that can be grown there also have other uses. They can provide habitats for many insects, butterflies, birds and small mammals, and they can also supply us with at least some of our saladings throughout the year. In the main, plants grown in the lawn will need to be tougher than many of our conventional crops since they need to be able to compete with the grasses and the trample of feet. Do not expect the most delicious salad leaves to come from this part of your land. The leaves that do come, however, will often be richer in vitamins and minerals, and thereby more nutritious.

An edible lawn is managed differently to a conventional lawn. The major differences are that you do not mow so often nor do you mow so short. The edible lawn remains at least as hard-wearing as the conventional lawn and, as mentioned earlier, is a lot less work. Mowing ensures a continuous supply of fresh young leaves, working on the same principle as growing salad plants on a cut-and-come-again basis.

If it is possible, leave the lawn uncut for a few weeks in mid-summer to allow the taller plants to flower and set seed. This will ensure that these plants have the opportunity to maintain themselves in the lawn and you will be surprised just how many butterflies, bees and other insects will come along to thank you.

It is also rather nice to allow some areas of the lawn to remain uncut for longer periods of the year to form a wildflower meadow. See Chapter 12 for more details.

When you do mow your edible lawn you can normally remove the mowings and either compost them (they make a very good activator if spread in thin layers through the heap) or use them to make a liquid feed (see Chapter 1 for more details). Alternatively, if you do not have a slug problem, the mowings can be used as a mulch around taller plants. If you do use it as a mulch, then make sure that the mowings do not contain seeds otherwise you might be creating a weed problem. It is a good idea to leave the mowings in situ for at least a couple of the cuttings each year to ensure that you do not reduce the overall fertility of the lawn.

If you have dogs, then these should not be allowed to defecate on areas of the lawn where you might be picking leaves to eat. This is especially important if you have children – in fact always be very careful to keep dog poos and children apart since children's fingers go everywhere and always return to their mouths. A parasite called 'Toxicara' that is found in dog poos can cause blindness in children,

Specimen trees with trunks 1.5 metres or more long are often grown in lawns to serve as a focal point and to provide welcome shade in the summer. So long as they do not have a dense canopy and are not planted too closely together, they will not usually adversely affect the growth of most of the lawn.

When planting a tree, it is important to bear in mind its final size. It can be hard to imagine that the small twig you are planting today might eventually end up being a massive tree 15 or more metres tall and wide. Whilst your small twig will have very little effect upon the lawn, the large tree will provide a great deal of shade and its falling leaves will act as a blanket to suppress the grass. Your lawn will be turning into a woodland garden!

If planting more than one tree, make sure you give each one the space to develop fully without eventually growing so close to each other that they will once more be turning your lawn into a woodland garden. A tree in a woodland will usually be less wide than an isolated specimen in a lawn. This is because competition for light from the other trees encourages upward growth rather than side growth. A specimen tree is able to develop a much wider branching system because there is little or no light competition. When selecting trees to grow in a lawn, you will in general be best off choosing smaller-growing trees such as the *Amelanchier* species (Juneberries) and *Crataegus* species (Hawthorns) mentioned in Chapter 2. A lawn is also a very good place to grow conventional fruit trees such as apples or pears.

Growth of grass around the tree will be somewhat inhibited due to competition with the tree roots and this can provide an opportunity for several species of bulbs. Daffodils and crocuses are often planted in drifts in a lawn, especially around trees.

Whilst these are not edible, several other species of bulbs are. If the right species are chosen, these will increase naturally and will have to be dug up and divided from time to time – any surplus bulbs can then be eaten. You will not get the heavy yields of a potato field, but don't forget that these bulbs will be a surplus food in addition to any crops you obtain from the trees, and you will still be able to use the area as a lawn for most months of the year. You will not be able to mow the area of the lawn where these bulbs are growing until they have finished flowering and the leaves have died down. Therefore by siting them around the tree this should not really interfere with activities on most of the lawn.

Apart from the bulbs, all the plants mentioned in the following lists are natives of Britain. If you garden in another country then I would recommend that you choose plants from this list that are also native to your country and then perhaps look for other native possibilities. This will ensure that you have the plants best adapted to your region and you are also growing a lawn with a high value to the local wildlife.

I have divided the plants into two lists as detailed below.

HERBACEOUS PERENNIALS

These are in general the plants that will grow in the main areas of the lawn and will tolerate at least some walking. Once established, all will survive quite happily in the lawn without the need for maintenance and will tolerate being mown on a fairly regular basis. Most of them grow best in a sunny position, though they should all succeed under the occasional small specimen tree since there should still be plenty of light available for them. Unless the text says otherwise, they all succeed in most well-drained soils.

Achillea millefolium. YARROW is a common 'weed' in lawns and succeeds even when the grass is cut very short. It grows up to 60cm tall when in flower and will spread to form large clumps. It grows very well in poor soils and, when established, is very drought tolerant. In times of severe drought, when the grass in the lawn turns brown, yarrow will still be green.

The young leaves make an acceptable though bitter addition to salads. You will probably only want to add small quantities of the leaves, but they make a very healthy addition to the diet being very rich in minerals and having many beneficial medicinal properties.

Yarrow is a very good companion plant for grass, increasing its vigour and resistance to disease. Any lawn mowings that include yarrow will greatly enrich the compost heap and help to speed up the composting process. If left uncut for a month at any time during the summer, the plant will quickly produce some lovely flowers. These flowers are one of the essential ingredients of 'Quick Return' herbal compost activator. Both the growing and the dried plant are said to repel beetles, ants and flies. A good liquid plant feed can be made from the leaves, either on their own or mixed in with other lawn mowings. See page 8 for more details.

Ajuga reptans. BUGLE is an evergreen plant that grows up to 30cm tall and will form a spreading clump 60cm or more wide. For it to succeed in a lawn, the grass would have to be allowed to grow a bit longer than usual. It does well in damp, slightly shaded areas of the lawn, though it also tolerates dry shade and so should do well under trees. If left uncut the plant will flower from May to July, these flowers are very attractive to bees.

Bugle is mainly known as a medicinal herb and can also be grown as a weed-excluding ground cover plant in the ornamental garden. The young shoots are slightly bitter but can be eaten in salads.

Alchemilla vulgaris. LADY'S MANTLE grows up to 30cm tall and wide. A tolerant and easily grown plant, it does very well in heavy clay soils. This is another species that requires a slightly longer grass than usual and, if allowed, it will flower from April to June.

The young leaves are nutritious but are by no means the most wonderful leaf you could eat. They can be eaten raw or cooked and in the north of Britain they are traditionally mixed with the leaves of two other native species, *Polygonum bistorta* and *Polygonum persicaria*, then used in making a bitter herb pudding called 'Easter ledger'. This is eaten during Lent. The root is also said to be edible but is rather astringent. Lady's mantle has a wide range of medicinal virtues. It is highly regarded as a treatment for a wide range of feminine problems and is a good blood purifier. It was used as a spring tonic after a winter of eating stored and preserved foods.

Bellis perennis. The DAISY is a common 'weed' in the lawn, able to tolerate constant cutting and still thrive. It grows about 15cm tall and forms spreading clumps 15cm or more across. The flowers are produced virtually all year round, the peak time is in spring but there will still be a few flowers about even in the middle of winter if the weather is mild.

The young leaves are eaten raw or cooked, they have a reasonably mild flavour but are often a bit tough and are far from my favourite leaf. A much better use for the leaves is that in the past an insect repellent spray has been made by infusing them in water. The flower buds and petals can also be eaten in salads, they are very decorative but look much nicer than they taste.

Chamaemelum nobile. CAMOMILE grows about 15cm tall and forms a spreading clump 30cm or more wide. It does very well in a lawn and flowers even if cut regularly.

Young sprigs can be used as a seasoning or as a flavouring in herb beers, but they are too aromatic for me to enjoy.

The cultivar 'Treneague' is a low-growing but spreading form about 2cm tall and forming clumps 30cm or more wide. It will succeed in a lawn so long as the grass is cut regularly and quite low. Alternatively, it can be grown on its own as a lawn. It will not take as much hard wear as grass, however, and will also need to be weeded fairly regularly, which can be very time consuming.

This cultivar does not flower so does not have some of the useful properties of the species. It will make a delightfully aromatic lawn that is a joy to sit and walk on. Laying down to sunbathe on a camomile lawn is quite an experience for the senses and the delicious aroma will also help to keep away most biting insects. See also page 5.

Cichorium intybus. CHICORY can grow up to 1.5 metres tall when in flower and is about 30cm wide. A very easily grown plant, it does especially well on chalky soils. This is a marvellous companion plant with a deep taproot that brings up minerals from deep in the subsoil. It will, therefore, help to fertilise the lawn. Whilst it will tolerate quite regular cutting, it will not survive long if the grass is cut very short. There are many cultivars of this plant that have been developed as salad crops. However, when growing it in a lawn, either grow the wild form or the cultivar 'Brussels Whitloof'.

The leaves are an extremely valuable source of nutrients and can be eaten in salads. They are somewhat bitter, though a taste for them can be acquired. Chicory leaves are a very valuable tonic, especially for the kidneys and liver.

Chicory is sometimes grown commercially to produce 'chicons'. These are the blanched (grown in the dark) young shoots of roots that are dug up in the autumn or winter and grown in a greenhouse. This produces a salad that is almost completely free of bitterness, but unfortunately it also drastically reduces the nutritional value of the leaves. If you want to try it, then it is a simple matter to dig up a few roots from the lawn, or perhaps just cover the plants with a pot – this will take longer but is much less work and produces a more nutritious product.

If allowed, the plant produces beautiful blue flowers between July and October but, as it is then likely to grow up to 1.5 metres tall, you may decide to keep it cut short. The flowers make a decorative addition to the salad bowl, they are also an alternative ingredient of 'Quick Return' herbal compost activator. See Chapter 5 for details of cultivars that can be grown for winter salads.

Hypochoeris radicata. CAT'S EAR grows about 30cm tall and forms spreading clumps 30cm or more wide. It is often found growing as a weed in lawns and will flower all summer if allowed. It does well in dry soils.

Its nutritious leaves are produced all year round and can be used in salads. One report says that the young leaves have a mild and agreeable flavour, but any leaves that I have tried have been rather bitter and very much an acquired taste. They are also rather hairy. The only time I am likely to eat these leaves is if there is a shortage of better leaves in the winter.

Leontodon hispidus. ROUGH HAWKBIT looks somewhat like a dandelion and is often found growing wild in the lawn and garden. It grows up to 45cm tall and 30cm wide, flowering all summer if allowed. It prefers a chalky soil but is by no means fussy. The young leaves can be eaten raw or cooked and, whilst they could hardly be described as wonderful, they are often available in late winter and make an acceptable addition to mixed salads. The flowering plant is very attractive to bees and butterflies.

Melilotus officinalis. MELILOT grows about 1.2 metres tall and 70cm wide when in flower. It succeeds in most soils, though it dislikes acid conditions. It does well in dry soils and is drought tolerant. This species is a biennial and therefore must be allowed to flower if you wish to keep it in the lawn. It can be cut regularly until early summer but would then have to be left uncut until it had set seed.

The young shoots can be cooked and used like asparagus. The young leaves are also eaten in salads whilst the leaves and seedpods are cooked as a vegetable. It is best to use only fresh leaves for food, since they contain coumarin which, when dried, can have an anti-clotting effect on the blood. See Appendix 4 for more details. There are, however, reports that the crushed dried leaves can be used as a vanilla flavouring in puddings, pastries etc.

The dried leaves become very aromatic and can be used as an insect repellent, they are especially good for repelling moths from clothing and can also be put in pillows and mattresses.

Plantago **species**. PLANTAINS are very common 'weeds' in lawns and will succeed in most soils. The lawn can be cut as often as you like and as short as you like without causing them any inconvenience at all, and they'll still send up a flowering stem that is almost immune to the cutting abilities of many lawn-mowers!

The young leaves have a slightly bitter flavour and can be eaten in salads or cooked like spinach, though they are quite tough and very quickly become bitter and fibrous as they grow older. The seeds, if you have the patience to collect them, can be eaten raw or cooked. They are very rich in vitamin B1. The seed can be ground into a meal and mixed with flour for making bread, or the whole seeds can be boiled and used like sago, they have a pleasant mild flavour.

The seed husks are very absorbent and swell up considerably when soaked in water. They can be used as a source of dietary fibre in order to treat constipation and other digestive disorders. A mucilage obtained from the seed coat is used as a starch for stiffening clothes. I have got unpleasant memories of sore necks caused by rubbing on stiff shirt collars when I was a child, so I will give this use a miss.

The species to try in the lawn are:

P. lanceolata. RIBWORT PLANTAIN grows up to 45cm tall and 20cm wide, flowering from mid spring to mid summer. It does well in poor soils.

P. major. COMMON PLANTAIN grows about 12cm tall and 10cm wide, flowering from late spring until the end of summer.

P. media. HOARY PLANTAIN grows about 10cm tall and wide, flowering from late spring to mid summer.

Prunella vulgaris. SELF-HEAL is able to tolerate regular cutting and still flower. In fact I have seen it no more than 1cm tall and flowering in lawns that are regularly shaved. If you do not cut it, the plant can grow 15cm tall and will form a spreading clump 30cm or more wide. The flowers are produced from mid to late summer and are very attractive to bees. Plants are fairly shade-tolerant and could be grown under trees in the lawn. They require moist conditions if they are to thrive.

The young leaves have a mild flavour with a slight bitterness and make a very acceptable addition to mixed salads, they can also be eaten cooked. A cold water infusion of the freshly chopped or dried and powdered leaves is used as a refreshing beverage and is said to be very tasty. An olive-green dye is obtained from the flowers and stems. As the common name suggests, the leaves of this plant have been widely used in the past for healing wounds.

Sanguisorba minor. SALAD BURNET grows about 60cm tall and 30cm wide. It prefers a light, dry calcareous soil, but will tolerate most conditions. It flowers from May to August.

Salad burnet is occasionally cultivated in the herb garden but it also grows very well in the lawn, especially if the grass is allowed to get a little bit longer than usual. The young leaves can be harvested all year round and are eaten in salads. The flavour is usually quite mild and many people say that they detect a cucumber-like flavour. When I grew this plant in Surrey, on a chalky soil, I found the leaves quite acceptable and often used them in salads. I now garden on a more acid soil and the plants I grow have a distinct and unpleasant bitterness, though this is greatly reduced in the winter. Whether this is due to the acid soil I cannot be sure, but my plants are descendants of those I grew in Surrey.

Taraxacum officinale. DANDELIONS grow up to 45cm tall and 30cm wide, though are usually smaller than this in a lawn. They are very easily grown in most soils and will self-sow very freely into the lawn and the surrounding garden.

These are superb plants for growing in the lawn, able to tolerate regular cutting and constant trampling – though constantly trampled plants will not produce much in the way of edible leaves. The quality of the leaves will be better if the grass is allowed to grow a little longer than usual, but this is not essential. Plants manage to flower even if they are cut regularly, merely reducing the length of the flowering stem. If you can manage to leave the mower alone for a couple of weeks in April without suffering withdrawal symptoms, the lawn can become a glorious sea of yellow. A few flowers will also be produced at other times of the year.

The rather bitter leaves are extremely nutritious and are best eaten raw though they can also be cooked. If you can tolerate them as a small part of a mixed salad then you will gain from all the ways they benefit the body, especially as a tonic for the liver and kidneys. If you allow the grass to be a bit longer in the winter this will usually give enough protection to allow the dandelions to produce a few fresh leaves for winter salads in all but the coldest weather. The leaves will be a lot less bitter at this time of year. The roasted roots, like chicory roots, are a coffee substitute should you ever find that you have got too many plants in the lawn.

Dandelions also have a very wide range of non-food uses. The old and mown leaves are an excellent addition to the compost heap, whilst the flowers are an ingredient of 'Quick Return' herbal compost activator. A liquid plant feed can be made from an infusion of the root and leaves. The growing plant releases ethylene gas, this stunts the growth of nearby plants and causes premature ripening of fruits. This can be a disadvantage if the dandelion is growing under fruit trees, but it can be used to advantage if you want to speed the ripening process of fruit. You simply put the fruit in a closed container for a few hours along with a dandelion plant.

Thymus serpyllum. WILD THYME is an evergreen shrub that grows about 10cm tall and forms a spreading clump 30cm or more wide. It can succeed in a fairly short regularly mown lawn and provides an aromatic flavouring for salads or cooked foods. See also page 168.

Trifolium repens. WHITE CLOVER is another common 'weed' of the lawn. It grows up to 10cm tall and forms an ever-increasing clump that can be more than 1 metre across. It flowers and flourishes even when cut regularly and short, and the grass will grow amongst it very happily, benefiting from the nitrogen formed on nodules on the clover roots. If you want to reduce the cost and work-load of maintaining a lawn, then let this plant grow there and do the nitrogen fertilising for you. The plant is very tolerant of soil conditions, though it prefers alkaline conditions in a clay soil.

White clover is an important food source for many caterpillars, whilst the flowers are very attractive to bees and butterflies.

The leaves, flowers and young seedpods can be eaten raw or cooked. I find that the leaves taste just like grass and are rather boring to eat, though my wife really enjoys them as part of a mixed salad. They are said to have all sorts of benefits to the health. The flowers taste a bit more interesting, with a delicate sweetness. The dried leaves are said to impart a vanilla flavouring to cakes. White clover is an excellent companion plant in the lawn, it is very tolerant of poor soils and can supply nitrogen to other plants growing nearby due to the presence of nitrogen-fixing bacteria that live on its roots.

Tussilago farfara. COLTSFOOT grows about 25cm tall and spreads forever. This is a very invasive plant so think very carefully before introducing it anywhere in your garden. It succeeds in almost any soil and will do well in light shade.

It sends up its flowering stems in March or April and these are a very welcome sign that spring is returning. The flowers are edible but it was not until spring 1994 that I was persuaded to try them. I had always assumed that they would be as bitter as the supposedly edible leaves but was pleasantly surprised to find out that they have a nice aniseed flavour. The leaves appear after the flowers in April and May, indeed people used to think that the flowers and the leaves were from different plants. An aromatic tea is made from the fresh or dried leaves and flowers.

Like all supposed problems, coltsfoot's invasive roots can be turned to advantage in the right situation. It has been planted on moist banks, where erosion is a problem. Within a year or two the roots have spread widely and hold the soil together, protecting it from erosion. The dried and burnt leaves are said to be used as a salt substitute. The soft down on the underside of the leaves is used as a stuffing material and as a tinder.

BULBS

Many bulb-forming plants will grow very well in grass, though there are very few that would be happy to be mown on anything like a regular basis. In general, it is best to grow bulbs in areas of the lawn that can be left uncut whilst the bulbs are growing. This means that you would be well advised to group the bulbs according to flowering time. Do not grow those that flower in the spring with those that flower in the summer or you will hardly ever be able to cut the grass and you will end up with a meadow rather than a lawn.

The species listed below can all be treated as spring-flowering plants, and it will be possible to mow them down in July, just in time for the children to be able to play on the lawn during the school holidays. They should all succeed in the light shade of trees and this is often the best place to grow them.

Allium oleraceum, FIELD GARLIC and *A. vineale*, CROW GARLIC. These two rather similar species both grow about 60cm tall and 5cm wide. They do well in grass but can be invasive, spreading freely by means of the small bulbils that are produced instead of flowers. If you live in an area with lots of dairy herds, the local farmers might get rather upset if they see you growing these plants since they taint the milk of cows that eat them. These are the latest-flowering of the plants in this list, with the field garlic not producing its bulbils until July or August. However, both species are very tolerant of being mown, so it is possible to cut them down before flowering. This will placate any local dairy farmers, since the plants will have no bulbils by which to spread.

The leaves can be used as a garlic substitute and are available from late autumn until early summer. They have a pleasant though strong flavour, and make a very nice cooked vegetable in the winter. They do become rather tough with a somewhat stringy texture as they get older. The bulbils are formed in early to mid summer and give a nice garlic flavour to stews etc. They are rather small and fiddly though. The bulbs are also rather small but can be used like garlic if you have nothing better available.

Camassia quamash. QUAMASH grows about 50cm tall and 10cm wide. It has an edible bulb that makes very pleasant eating when cooked. This bulb grows well in short grass and does particularly well in the light shade of trees so long as the soil is not dry. It grows well under apple trees for example. It flowers in late spring and early summer and then disappears completely until the following spring. See also page 96.

Erythronium species. DOG'S TOOTH VIOLETS are low-growing bulbous plants that have been discussed on page 76. They produce very tasty edible bulbs. Many of these species can be grown in the light shade of a tree and will normally increase quite freely. They are amongst the earliest flowering bulbs, with some species flowering in March. By June or early July they will completely disappeared until the next spring.

Muscari botryoides. TASSEL HYACINTH grows up to 40cm tall and divides freely to form clumps 20cm or more wide. A very easily grown plant, it can succeed in almost any soil or situation. This is a bulb that grows very well in short grass, almost too well because it can become invasive. It flowers in May. The bulb, which is about 3.5 cm in diameter, can be eaten cooked and has a slightly bitter taste that is said to be appreciated by certain ethnic groups, especially Greeks and Italians. I don't come from the Mediterranean and have eaten much nicer bulbs! Best used in spring, the bulbs can also be cooked then preserved in oil and used as a relish.

   M. neglectum. The GRAPE HYACINTH grows 30cm tall and spreads freely, forming clumps 15cm or more wide. It does especially well in dry sandy soils, flowering in early to mid spring. This species also has an edible bulb, in this case it is about 2.5cm in diameter. There is, however, one report that says the bulb contains saponin-like substances and is therefore poisonous. Many of our conventional foods, however, also contain saponins. See Appendix 4 for more details of this toxin.

Ophrys species and *Orchis* species. There are many species of ORCHID that can be grown around trees or in the lawn itself. The species mentioned below all flower in the spring and very early summer. See the notes on page 82 under *Orchis mascula* for details of their edible bulbs and for other comments.

   In general, alkaline soils are the most appropriate for growing orchids in short grass and *Ophrys apifera*, which grows about 50cm tall and 10cm wide, is one of the better species to try. *Orchis mascula*, growing 60cm tall and 10cm wide, and *Orchis morio*, about 30cm tall and 5cm wide, should also do well. *O. mascula* should also succeed in longer grass and in more acid soils. For wetter areas in neutral to acid soils try *Orchis laxiflora* which grows about 75cm tall and 10cm wide.

   There are many other species in these two genera that could also be tried, it is a matter of seeing which species are to be found in your own area and then trying to recreate suitable growing conditions for them.

   One word of warning – do not be tempted to dig up orchids from the wild, instead obtain them from a reputable nursery that propagates from its own stocks.

Chapter Eight

WALLS & FENCES

Most gardeners and growers will have at least one wall or solid fence that could be used for growing plants and providing a different habitat in the garden. Depending on the aspect of this wall, and the amount of shade it receives from other structures, there is quite a wide range of plants that can be grown against it. Also, depending on the structure of the wall, it is often possible to grow plants that actually root into the wall as well as lower-growing plants at the foot of the wall that would benefit from the local microclimate. This chapter is going to look at some of the plants that can be grown in these situations and to begin with we need to examine the habitats that walls can offer.

Most people will have noticed how much warmer it can feel when in front of a south-facing wall on a sunny day. The temperature is often several degrees higher than the surrounding garden. What is less well recognised is that this area will also be noticeably warmer during the night. This is partly due to the wall being heated up by the sun during the day and releasing the warmth overnight. The actual difference in temperature by early morning might only be a few degrees but this can make all the difference between survival and death for some plants. Very often there can be a frost in all parts of the garden but in the area close to the wall there is no frost. Be careful if the wall is at the bottom of a slope as it might act as a frost-trap which could make it colder overnight than the surrounding area.

The extra warmth is also due to the physical shelter from the wind that the wall can provide. Do not be misled into believing that walls are good windbreaks. Since they are solid structures the wind can be channelled along them or be forced to go over them, both of which can increase total wind speed and lead to extra turbulence. If you live in a windy site and want to provide effective wind shelter then you are much better off planting hedges and shelterbelts – see Chapter 9 for more details.

Sunny walls will also be much warmer during the day than the open garden. This will mean that many trees and shrubs that do not fully ripen their wood in a cool summer in the open garden will be able to do so if grown against the wall. Well-ripened wood is much more resistant to damage by wind or frost, so this effectively makes the plant more hardy.

The aspect of the wall makes quite a difference to the types of plant that will grow successfully against it. Assuming it is not shaded by other structures, a south-facing wall will receive the most sun, though the soil at its base will often be quite dry, especially in the summer. This makes it a good site for sun-lovers and also for those plants normally a bit too tender for the area where you live. However, it will receive sunlight quite early in the morning and, if this follows a frosty night, the rapid warming-up can cause damage to frost-sensitive plants.

For this same reason, an **east-facing wall** can often prove unsuitable for many plants. Unless shaded by other structures or plants, it will receive sunlight from the moment the sun rises and this will greatly increase any frost-damage to the plants growing there. In other respects, an easterly aspect can be very suitable for growing a wide range of plants. Those species that like a warm position but also like shade for part of the day will often do well here because they will be in shade during the hottest part of the day. This aspect is also likely to be quite dry though, because most rain in this country comes from the west and the wall creates a rain-shadow.

A **westerly aspect** is ideal for many plants. Sheltered from the sun until about midday, it will remain fairly cool for much of the morning. If the temperature has dipped below freezing overnight then any frost will disappear slowly and cause much less damage to the plants than a sudden warming. The west-facing wall will receive warmth from the sun all afternoon, when the effect of the sun is greater than in the morning, and it also usually receives more rain than other aspects since it faces the direction of the prevailing wind and rain in Britain. This and a south-west aspect are generally considered to be the most valuable wall spaces and will grow a wider range of plants than any of the other aspects.

A **northerly aspect** receives no direct sunlight in the winter, and only early morning and late afternoon sun in the summer, so far fewer plants can succeed in this position. Because of the lack of sunlight, a northerly aspect is also more humid than the other aspects and the soil is often moister. A north wall is ideal for growing plants that demand a lot of shade, it is also a very good site for growing some of our traditional fruits. Gooseberries and redcurrants, for example, do well on a north wall and will ripen their fruit later than plants grown in the open – thereby extending the fruiting season into late August or even September. Do not try to grow the more choice dessert fruits such as apples or pears, or you are likely to be disappointed.

The type of wall or fence is also important. A house wall, for example, should have a damp-proof course to prevent it soaking up moisture from the soil and making the house damp. A garden wall will not normally have a damp-proof course, so this wall will act as a wick, drawing up moisture from the soil which will then be evaporated by the sun or drawn off by the wind. Thus the soil by a garden wall will usually be drier than soil by a house wall.

A brick wall will retain quite a lot of the sun's heat from the day and will release it slowly overnight. Thus it will offer quite a lot of protection from frost. A wooden fence, on the other hand, does not store much of the sun's warmth and so offers much less extra protection from frosts.

PLANTS TO GROW AT THE BASE OF WALLS

The ground at the base of a wall offers plenty of opportunities for growing plants with special needs. For example, so long as you make sure that there is plenty of humus in the soil a north-facing wall will provide the shade that will allow you to grow many woodland perennials. See Chapter 3 for some ideas on species to grow here. Sunnier aspects offer a very select location for plants and will allow you to grow many of the species that are not very hardy in the open garden. This will obviously vary from area to area since what grows happily outdoors in Cornwall, for example, might need the extra protection of a wall in areas with colder winters. It is a matter for the individual gardener to decide what they would like to grow in such a position and you should find plenty of species to choose from in this book.

The soil at the base of a sunny wall is often quite dry, either because it is in a rain shadow or because the wall acts as a wick to draw moisture out of the soil. In such a site the soil is often fairly moist in the winter but becomes bone dry in the summer unless you are prepared to spend hours watering it. This is an ideal place for a range of bulbs and desert plants that can take all the cold weather that Britain can offer them but cannot accept all the rain and the cool summers that are also our lot. I am going to mention just a few species here but many other suitable species are mentioned in other chapters of this book. For more ideas look at Appendix 3 for species that succeed in dry soils and are drought tolerant.

Calochortus **species**. This genus contains some absolutely beautiful flowering bulbs, but they are very difficult to grow successfully in this country. They are tolerant of very cold weather but the small bulbs will quickly rot in wet soils, indeed they really need to be kept very dry whilst dormant, which is usually from some time in the summer until new root growth takes place in late autumn or winter. They are best grown in a deep sandy fertile soil in the company of shrubs that like dry conditions. These shrubs will help to keep the soil drier in late summer and autumn, which is crucial if you are to succeed in growing these bulbs.

Should you succeed with them and even manage to get them to increase, then the bulbs of all members of this genus can be eaten raw or cooked and are indeed very pleasant eating with a sweet flavour. The species I would recommend include:

C. gunnisonii. The MARIPOSA LILY grows about 30cm tall and 10cm wide. The bulb has a crisp nut-like texture and a pleasant flavour when cooked – one report likens it to new potatoes. The bulb can also be dried and ground into a powder for mixing with cereal flours when making foods such as porridge.

C. luteus. The YELLOW MARIPOSA grows about 30cm tall and 10cm wide. The bulb is about the size of a walnut and is very palatable and nutritious.

C. nuttallii. The SEGO LILY grows about 15cm tall and 8cm wide. The cooked bulb has a crisp nut-like texture.

Eremurus spectabilis. This perennial plant grows about 80cm tall and 60cm wide. It likes similar conditions to the *Calochortus* species mentioned above so should grow well with them. I have not tried this species yet, but the young shoots are eaten cooked and are considered a delicacy in Siberia, where they are sold in local markets. The flavour is said to be intermediate between spinach and purslane. The root contains about 30% starch and this makes a good quality glue. The root can be dried and powdered and then used for bookbinding and sizing cloth.

Opuntia compressa. INDIAN FIG is one of the hardiest species of cacti. It only grows about 20cm tall but, given time, can spread 1 metre or more. A native of North America, it grows in arid areas as far north as Canada, where it can be covered in a metre or more of snow during the winter. However, the soil will still be dry when the plant is covered in snow and it will also quickly drain as the snow melts so the plant still demands dry conditions in this country.

Related to the prickly pear cactus, like that species the fruit can be eaten raw, cooked or dried for later use and is sweet and gelatinous. The unripe fruits can be added to soups, imparting an okra-like mucilaginous quality. The leaf pads can also be eaten cooked or raw. They are watery and very mucilaginous and not to my taste. The seed can be briefly roasted then ground into a flour to be used as a thickener in soups.

Be very careful when handling any part of this plant because it has numerous minutely barbed glochids (hairs). These are easily dislodged when the plant is touched and they then become stuck to the skin where they are difficult to see and to remove. As I have found out to my cost, they itch like mad and can cause considerable discomfort. When harvesting the fruit or the pads these hairs can be easily destroyed by singeing the surface with a flame. Obviously, it is best not to grow the plant within reach of children or along the sides of paths.

There are many other members of this genus that will also succeed outdoors in Britain. In theory at least they all have edible fruits, though in practice they might be less than desirable.

Triteleia grandiflora. This bulb grows about 70cm tall and in a suitable position it will divide quite freely to form clumps 30cm or more in diameter. It likes moist growing conditions in the spring followed by dry conditions from late summer to the winter when it is dormant.

The bulb is rather small and is not produced very freely here unless you can give the plant its ideal habitat. It can be eaten raw or cooked and is considered by some people to be the tastiest of all the North American edible bulbs. It is nicest when slow roasted for an hour since then it becomes rather sweet and has a nut-like flavour. All other members of this genus can be grown and used in the same way.

WINTER SALADS

One other use of a sunny wall is to provide shelter in the winter which will enable plants to continue in growth and thereby extend their harvesting season. In this case the ground should not be too dry, but it must be well drained.

In 1994 we planted out the ground at the base of a south-facing wooden wall with perennial plants to provide us with fresh salads all through the winter. The extra protection of the wall is all that the plants will need to encourage earlier growth or to protect established growth. This is far easier than trying to grow lettuces and the like in greenhouses or frames and is also more productive since many of the plants will also provide fresh leaves at other times of the year. Many of the plants are also very attractive and are not at all out of place in the flower garden. The ideal place for this garden is near the kitchen door so that on cold wet winter days you do not have to travel far to get your salad.

In addition to a sunny, sheltered site, there are a few other factors to take into account when growing a winter salad garden. The first is that the ground must be free-draining. Excess water at the roots will actually cause more problems for the plants than cold weather.

In order to ensure that the plants produce strong, hardy growth that will stand up to winter cold it is important to ensure that the ground is not too fertile. You do not want to encourage the soft, sappy growth that occurs in very rich soils. On the other hand, you do not want a poor soil since, although the plants will tend to be more cold-tolerant, the leaves will be tougher and less freely produced. Therefore it is a matter of striking a balance. Feed the plants, but only in the spring and only with compost. Do not apply fertilizers, especially those rich in nitrogen. If the plant growth does not look vigorous enough in the summer then you can supplement the compost by giving the plants a liquid feed as described in Chapter 1.

When harvesting the leaves, it is especially important to take into account the plant's growth habit. Winter is a time when little new growth is made and so you cannot harvest the plants in the same way that is possible in the warmer months of the year. In general, this means harvesting just a few leaves from a plant at a time and allowing it to recover before picking again. There are several exceptions to this and these will be noted in the text.

Most of the plants in this winter salad garden are included in other chapters of the book, but I will also quickly run through them all here.

Allium **species**. Few salads are complete without an ONION to flavour them. The following species will enable you to harvest fresh leaves all through the winter.

    A. neapolitanum. DAFFODIL GARLIC leaves are sweet with a delicate garlic flavour and are available from November to April. See also page 87.

    A. schoenoprasum. CHIVES come into growth very early in the year and will provide pickings from late winter. See also page 88.

    A. cepa **'Perutile'**. The EVERLASTING ONION can be harvested all 12 months of the year. The leaves have a strong onion flavour and are used like spring onions. It is possible to cut off all the leaves of a plant (being careful not to damage the bulbs) at one time. New growth will be slow in the winter, but the plant will grow back satisfactorily. See also page 105.

    A. fistulosum. The WELSH ONION has onion-flavoured leaves which are often available all year round and can be harvested like the everlasting onion above. See also page 106.

Atriplex halimus. The SALT BUSH. The leaves of this evergreen shrub have a salty flavour that almost all our visitors like. See also page 178.

Barbarea vulgaris. This plant is our native YELLOW ROCKET. A short-lived perennial growing about 35cm tall and 25cm wide. The leaves have a hot watercress-like flavour and can be freely available – if you like eating lots of hot leaves! The plant might die down in colder winters but will be back again in the spring. It usually self-sows very freely when happy.

B. verna. AMERICAN LAND CRESS is related to this plant and has a similar flavour. It is a more reliable winter crop though is not reliably perennial. It is normally sown in late summer or early autumn in order to provide winter leaves and, left to its own devices, will self-sow freely.

Both of these species can be used to provide edible leaves all year round. Grow them by a sunny wall for winter crops, and by a shady wall for summer leaves.

Beta vulgaris cicla. The cultivated SPINACH BEET grows up to 1 metre tall and 60cm wide. Although it is a biennial, this plant usually self-sows freely in cultivated soils and provides fresh leaves all year round with very little effort from the grower. The much more ornamental cultivar 'Ruby Chard' can also be used but it does not self-sow as freely, nor is it so hardy, often dying down in cold winters. Not my favourite salad leaf, but some people like its raw beetroot-like flavour. I find it much nicer cooked when it makes a very acceptable spinach.

Campanula portenschlagiana and *C. poscharskyana*. These evergreen HAREBELLS form a very effective ground cover. The leaves have a mild but sweet flavour, though they are rather on the tough side. See also page 203.

Campanula versicolor. This really is the salad plant par excellence, though it is not very productive. The leaves have a delicious flavour rather like fresh garden peas. See also page 91.

Cardamine hirsuta. BITTER CRESS is a common garden weed that spreads its seeds around freely. This seed can germinate at any time of the year, though the autumn is the most common time. There are nearly always plenty of young plants about to provide their pungent watercress flavoured leaves, and winter is a time of particular abundance. Pull out whole young plants when harvesting this one, then you will be weeding at the same time as harvesting.

Cichorium intybus. CHICORY is one of the most productive winter salads. A lettuce-like head is produced in the autumn and will stand well throughout most winters. To harvest, you cut off the entire head, making sure that you do not damage the growing point of the plant, which is just above the root. The plant will grow back slowly to provide smaller harvests later in the winter. See also page 109.

Foeniculum vulgare. FENNEL can provide its aniseed-flavoured leaves all winter if the weather is not too severe, especially if it is allowed to self-sow. See also page 111.

Montia perfoliata and *M. sibirica*. These are ideal winter salads and can be picked in quantity. Although they are woodland plants by nature, they grow very well in the winter salad garden. They will tend to look rather sorry for themselves in the summer, though, especially if it is hot and dry. To provide salad leaves at this time of the year you either grow more of the plants in a woodland garden or by the side of a shady wall. See also page 207.

Myrrhis odorata. When grown in a winter salad garden, SWEET CICELY will provide small crops of its delicious aniseed-flavoured leaves for all but a few weeks in the depths of the winter. This is really a plant that likes some shade, so for summer harvesting grow some plants in the woodland garden. See also page 79.

Peltaria alliacea. GARLIC CRESS makes an excellent evergreen ground cover and can be harvested in quantity. Mind you, it has a very strong flavour and, whilst very acceptable in small quantities in a salad, it is rather overpowering if you put a lot in. See also page 203.

Reichardia picroides The mild-flavoured leaves are an excellent salad. See also page 112.

Rumex acetosa. Certain cultivars of SORREL will provide a small picking of the lemon-flavoured leaves all through any but the coldest winters. See also page 80.

Sanguisorba minor. SALAD BURNET can be harvested in quantity for winter salads. Cut the plants down to ground level in the autumn to encourage the growth of fresh young leaves and then harvest them as required during the winter. See also page 145.

Taraxacum officinale. DANDELIONS are rather bitter but make an excellent salad, especially in the winter when their bitterness is somewhat reduced. See also pages 113 and 145.

Thymus **species**. The THYMES are low-growing evergreen shrubs with aromatic leaves that add a lovely flavour to salads. They are dealt with below in the section dealing with plants that can be grown on walls.

Valerianella locusta. CORN SALAD is a native annual growing 30cm tall and 20cm wide. It is sometimes cultivated for its mild-tasting leaves and can be harvested in quantity. Like the lettuce, it quickly runs to seed in warm or dry weather and so is best given some shade in the summer. It needs to be sown at regular intervals of every few weeks in the spring and summer to provide a succession of fresh leaves. If allowed to flower it will usually self-sow and can then be available most of the year. If you want to make sure of a winter crop then it is necessary to sow the seed in early to mid autumn.

Viola odorata. SWEET VIOLET is a woodland plant, but it is growing very well in our sunny winter salad garden. It forms an effective ground cover and the mild-flavoured leaves can be harvested in quantity. An added bonus is that it flowers in winter and early spring, these flowers have a delicious scent of violets and can also be used in salads. See also page 81.

PLANTS TO GROW AGAINST WALLS

Many trees, shrubs and woody climbing plants can be trained to grow against a wall and I want to look at a few of these here. I will not be looking at those species of trees and shrubs that are hardy enough to be grown successfully in the open in most parts of Britain since this would often be rather a waste of valuable wall space. However, many of those species mentioned in Chapter 2 could also be grown against a wall if you so wished. Do not forget, either, that you can use a shady wall to extend the cropping season of some traditional fruits such as gooseberries.

What I want to concentrate on here is those plants that are either too tender to succeed outdoors in this country unless given the protection of a wall, or those climbing plants that can be allowed to grow against the wall with the minimum of effort on behalf of the grower.

CLIMBING PLANTS

This section will look at a number of climbing species and it is important to understand the tactics these plants employ in order to climb so as to know what support, if any, we need to give them. There are four main strategies for climbing plants as listed below. Some species adopt a belts and braces approach and use more than one method:

- **Twining** plants. Many species, such as the honeysuckle, support themselves by twining around the trunks and branches of other plants. They need a framework against the wall for them to twine around. This can be a trellis, attached to the wall so that it is a few centimetres away from the wall. Alternatively, wires can be trained horizontally along the wall at spaces of perhaps every 30cm and the plants can be tied in to these wires at intervals. Twining plants will often require some assistance from the grower, especially in the first few years after planting, in order to make sure that they use the provided supports.

- **Tendrils**. Some species, such as grapes, produce tendrils that coil themselves around any support they come into contact with and these can also be trained into a trellis or wires on the wall. The plants might need some encouragement at first but once established will normally look after themselves quite happily.

- **Aerial** roots. Ivy, and a number of other plants, produce aerial roots and these can attach themselves to many walls without the need for any supports. Plants might need some encouragement when they are first planted out, but should then look after themselves with very few problems.

- **Scramblers**. Roses, blackberries and some other species have sharp prickles and clamber over other plants, the prickles helping to keep the shoots in place.

The new growth of this type of climber will need to be tied in to a trellis or wires and are consequently a lot more work. They can also be rather antisocial when planted close to a path if any of the branches are allowed to dangle and attack unwary passers-by. A slight modification on this tactic is that some plants produce leaves on stalks that bend downwards from the stems. These leaf-stalks then act as a hook to support the plant.

***Actinidia* species**. KIWI FRUITS. You might want to try these twining plants on south and west facing walls because they can be extremely productive in such a situation. Yields of 20 kilos or more have been obtained by some growers. See also page 64.

Akebia quinata. AKEBIAS are very ornamental vigorous twining plants with shoots up to 12 metres long. Normally deciduous, though they often retain their leaves in mild winters.

The plants are hardy to about -20°C but they do not normally produce their edible fruit in this country. This is possibly due to a lack of pollinating insects if the weather is cold when the plants flower in early April, or it could be caused by frost damage to the pollen. Hand pollination of the flowers might be helpful. There is also a report that the plants might be self sterile. Since it is probable that most of the plants in this country have all been propagated by cuttings and layerings from one original plant, there is a lack of suitable pollen for fertilization.

What is needed is a supply of seed-grown plants but seed is often hard to get hold of and even harder to germinate. If you can overcome the problems associated with this plant, you will end up with a large crop of a fruit that is up to 10cm long and is said to be sweet but insipid! The description makes you wonder if it is all worthwhile, but it has been my experience that what most people term insipid so often turns out to mean a delicate pleasant flavour. I am working to produce fruit on this plant and would welcome feedback from anyone who has successfully produced fruit (especially if they can also send me some cuttings of the plant and a ripe fruit so that I can sow the fresh seed).

If you grow the plant but cannot get it to fruit, then all is not totally lost. You can always use the peeled stems in basket making!

A. trifoliata has a similar habit of growth, differing mainly in having three leaflets instead of five. It has the same problems and uses.

Both of these plants like some shelter from the sun and grow well on east and west facing walls, though of course, if you grow them on an east wall you will need to give the flowers extra protection from frosts.

Billardiera longiflora. The APPLEBERRY is an evergreen climbing plant for south, east or west-facing walls, growing up to 2.5 metres tall. It requires a cool root run if it is to be fully happy and this can be provided by growing a low ground cover plant around the roots. It also needs a lime-free soil.

A very ornamental edible blue fruit is produced in late summer, my experience is that this is a dry capsule full of seeds but the books say that it is aromatic, mealy and pleasant. Perhaps I just have a poor form – if you have a plant with nicer fruit then please let me know. This plant is not very hardy and is unlikely to succeed outside the milder areas of the country, even when grown against a wall.

Hedera helix. IVY is a superb climber for a north-facing wall. It has aerial roots and needs no support. When grown against a building it acts as an insulation to keep the wall drier and the inside of the building warmer and it can protect the wall from the elements. You have to be a bit careful with it since it can root strongly into moist or damaged walls which can cause problems as the stem and roots grow thicker over the years.

Passiflora **species**. PASSION FRUITS are evergreen and herbaceous plants that grow well on sunny walls, supporting themselves by means of tendrils. The hardiest evergreen member of the genus is *P. caerulea* which can tolerate occasional low temperatures down to about –15°C. In colder areas of the country the top growth is likely to be killed in the winter, but providing the roots are well-mulched it will resprout from the base in the late spring and can still flower and produce a crop of fruit. The books say that the fruit is only formed after long hot summers in Britain, but in our local village there is a plant that has reasonable crops most years. A very vigorous plant, it can climb to a height of 10 metres or more.

Unfortunately this species has one of the least interesting fruits of the genus. It is about 6cm in diameter, but most of the space within the skin is hollow. There is a small portion of edible flesh in the centre, but even this is mainly seeds. The flavour is rather nice, though, and it makes a pleasant drink. I was given a number of fruits from a garden in Eastbourne in the early autumn of 1996. These were a bit larger than average, about 8cm in diameter, and also had a nicer tasting flesh. Apparently this plant fruits very heavily every year so, needless to say, I now have a packet of seeds waiting to be sown in the late winter.

P. incarnata. MAYPOPS has a much more interesting fruit and is a little bit hardier. This species is truly herbaceous, but produces vigorous new growth each year and can climb 6 metres or more high. The fruit is up to 5cm in diameter and it can be eaten raw or cooked in jellies, jams, etc. The leaves are said to be delicious as a cooked vegetable and can also be eaten in salads whilst the flowers can be cooked as a vegetable or made into syrup. This plant is also a famous medicinal herb that is used in the treatment of complaints such as insomnia, nervous tension, irritable bowel syndrome and premenstrual tension. Large quantities of the leaves and stems are gathered from the wild each year and much of the crop is exported to Europe.

P. edulis and *P. mollisima*. These are much less hardy and are some of the tropical species that provide the passion fruits you will find in supermarkets and greengrocers. They will be cut to the ground in most winters but, if the ground is well mulched and prevented from freezing, the roots will usually survive to produce new shoots the following year. In hot summers these shoots can produce quite heavy crops of fruit in their first year of growth and I have heard of one person who harvests ripe fruits in most years.

The roots of all the above species should be restricted, perhaps by planting into a large container in the ground, in order to encourage fruiting. It is also best to hand pollinate using pollen from a flower that has been open for 12 hours to pollinate a newly opened flower before midday.

Schisandra grandiflora. This is a slow-growing deciduous climber that can reach 6 metres in height. It twines round supports but is not very good at supporting itself and usually needs to be tied in. A plant for shady conditions, it can fruit well on a north or east-facing wall. The fruits are about 6mm in diameter, they are borne in bunches about 12cm long and look rather like a very lax bunch of bright red grapes. The flavour is sweet and very pleasant.

    S. grandiflora rubriflora. This has red flowers and is perhaps more ornamental. I have seen this species carrying a good crop of fruit on several occasions. It is the form that I am growing and have eaten.

    One species that I have only recently obtained is **S. chinensis**. This is a more vigorous species and can climb 9 metres or more. It sounds very interesting and I am looking forward to trying it. The fruit is rich in sugars, it is said to have a sweet/sour flavour and also to be very sustaining, for which reason it is usually dried and used on journeys. The dried fruits are also used medicinally in the same way as ginseng (**Panax ginseng**). Ginseng can be grown outdoors in British woodlands, but is not included in this book since it is primarily a medicinal plant.

    Going back to *S. chinensis*, the young leaves can be cooked and used as a vegetable. A viscid mucoid material (don't blame me, that is what it says in the book!) obtained from the fruit and the branches is used as a size for paper and as a hair dressing. You need both male and female plants if fruit is required, which leaves me with a problem – I only have one plant of *S. chinensis* and do not know its sex yet. Looks like I still have quite a wait before I can try its fruit.

Vitis **species**. GRAPES are well enough known not to be included in this book, but they are one of my favourite fruits so I thought I would remind you to put some on your sunny walls. These are vigorous climbing plants, supporting themselves very well by means of tendrils. When well sited, they can produce quite heavy crops on a regular basis.

    If you live in a colder part of the country then try the cultivar 'Brandt'. The fruit is a bit small and not as nice as some of the choice cultivars that can be grown in this country, but it still makes very good eating and is a very reliable cropper even in less than ideal circumstances.

    Another cultivar that is doing very well with me is 'Isabella'. I am not certain to which species this cultivar belongs, it is either the CULTIVATED GRAPE, **V. vinifera**, or the NORTHERN FOX GRAPE, **V. labrusca**. Either way, it is a very vigorous plant and looks like it is going to climb 10 metres or more. It can crop very heavily, the dark fruit is a bit on the small size but hangs well on the plant if it is in a sheltered position. I know of one garden in Gloucestershire where they pick the last ripe bunches in December. The fruit is well-flavoured, and this flavour is improved by exposure to frosts.

SHRUBS AND TREES

The plants mentioned here are, in general, either too tender to be grown in the open garden or will fruit more reliably when grown against a wall. This list is very far from exhaustive and every gardener will have their own ideas on what plants they might like to grow against a wall.

There are a number of factors to take into account when deciding what plants to use:

- This point may sound too obvious, but make sure that you grow a sun-lover by a sunny wall and a shade-lover by a shady wall.

- Trees and shrubs do not naturally form the shape that you are going to want them to have when growing by a wall. Thus you should choose species that are amenable to any formative pruning you might want to give them. This applies particularly if the bed by the wall is narrow, or if you want to train the plant in some ornamental shape such as a fan. Smaller plants, or those growing in wider beds, do not necessarily need formative pruning.

- Try to choose plants appropriate to the size of wall you want to grow them by.

There are a number of well known fruiting trees and shrubs that are not included in the list below but that you might want to consider for planting against a wall. These include: APRICOTS, NECTARINES, PEACHES, PEARS and PLUMS for south and west aspects; REDCURRANTS and GOOSEBERRIES on all four aspects (though they are most valuable on the north side since this will extend their fruiting season); MORELLO CHERRIES for the east and north sides.

Aloysia triphylla. LEMON VERBENA is a shrub growing about 3 metres tall and wide. Even on a wall it will only succeed in the south and in the milder areas of western Britain where it will often still be cut back to the ground in winter, though it normally resprouts from the base. Very amenable to trimming, it is easily kept within bounds when grown on a wall.

The delicious lemon-scented leaves can be used in salads but they are more often employed to make a herb tea. An essential oil from the leaves is used in perfumery whilst the growing plant is said to repel midges, flies and other insects. This makes it an excellent plant to grow near the kitchen window.

Aristotelia chilensis. MACQUI is an evergreen shrub growing 3 metres tall and up to 5 metres wide. It succeeds outdoors in the mildest areas of the country but is best on a south or west-facing wall even there. You need to grow at least one male plant for every five females if you want to obtain the fruit.

This edible fruit is only about 6mm in diameter but it can be produced very freely and has a pleasant taste like bilberries. Macqui generally grows and fruits very well in the milder counties of Britain, but different plants can vary greatly in hardiness.

All our plants came from seed and, without exception, are cut back to the ground even in fairly mild winters. Therefore I would advise you to obtain plants from nurseries that can give you an indication of how hardy their particular stock is.

Citrus limon. Most people are surprised to learn that there are forms of the LEMON and some other citrus fruits that can be grown outdoors in Britain. 'Meyer's Lemon' is a cultivar that can tolerate occasional drops in temperature to about -6°C, so long as this is preceded by a period of cool weather that allows the plant to adjust. It cannot be grown permanently outdoors in any but the mildest areas of the country, but can be grown in a large pot that is kept outdoors in the summer and brought into a conservatory or cool greenhouse in the winter. It will eventually reach about 3 metres tall and wide, though it can be kept smaller by pruning.

We had our first crop of fruits in the autumn of 1993 when we harvested about a dozen full-sized and very tasty fruits from a plant growing in a polyhouse. This plant will eventually be going outdoors on a south-facing wall, though we will take cuttings first so that we have reserves in case of a very bad winter.

As well as eating the fruit, the peel can be used as a flavouring in cakes and other dishes. The flowers are also edible, though eating them will, of course, reduce the amount of fruit the plant can produce. If trying the plant outdoors, put it on a south or west-facing wall and be prepared to give it extra protection if there is a sudden cold snap.

A number of fairly hardy hybrids between other citrus fruits are slowly becoming available in Britain. These are normally crosses between the very hardy *Poncirus trifoliata* (see also page 177) and various cultivated citrus fruits.

The 'Citrange', is a cross with the orange and is hardy in south west England, where it bears somewhat nicer fruits than *Poncirus trifoliata*. This does not make them choice desert fruits but they do make a nice drink. Hardiness is a relative term with these hybrids since none of them are likely to tolerate more than a few degrees of frost, but they might be worth trying by the more adventurous among you. See Appendix 2 for details of suppliers.

Another plant worth trying on the south wall is *Citrofortunella microcarpa*, the CALAMONDIN ORANGE. This is a popular house plant and I have seen specimens less than 30cm tall with a dozen or more fruits on them. It is a fairly hardy plant, however, and can tolerate a few degrees of frost. The fruit is about 25 - 35mm in diameter and has a very acid flavour, though the skin is sweet and eating the two together is a pleasant taste sensation. The fruit is more often used in drinks, teas, marmalades, chutneys and so forth, and can be used in all the ways that lemons or limes are used.

You might also consider trying the KUMQUATS, *Fortunella* species, which are probably as hardy as 'Meyer's Lemon' and perhaps even a little bit hardier. The fruit is up to 4cm in diameter, the flesh has an acid flavour whilst the thin skin is sweet. You eat the lot, skin and all. It is very pleasant raw and also makes refreshing drinks and preserves. Some people gently massage or bruise the fruit just before eating it in order to mix the two flavours, I just pop the fruits into my mouth and chew well.

Eriobotrya japonica. LOQUATS are fairly hardy evergreen trees and can succeed in an open position outdoors in the south and milder western parts of Britain. You need to give them extra protection even in the milder areas though, because they flower in the winter and produce their edible fruits in the spring. If the winters are too cold then the fruit will not develop properly and will be inedible. Grow a plant on a south, east or west-facing wall in order to give the fruit a good chance of being produced – the westerly is probably best. The trees can grow up to 9 metres tall and 5 metres wide, though they can be kept smaller by pruning. They are often cultivated in warm temperate areas and there are many named varieties.

There is a tree in Northamptonshire that is said to fruit regularly, but most trees in this country only produce occasional light crops. The ripe fruit is up to 4cm in diameter, it has a slightly acid, sweet aromatic flavour and can be eaten raw or cooked. If it is cooked before it is fully ripe the flavour is said to be like cherries.

Feijoa sellowiana. FEIJOA is an evergreen shrub that can grow up to 6 metres tall and wide but is usually half that size in Britain. It requires a south or west facing wall if it is to succeed here and even then is only hardy in the south and milder western parts of the country. It is very tolerant of salt-laden maritime winds which makes it an excellent plant for seaside gardens. Very tolerant of pruning, it is grown as a hedge in warmer climates than Britain.

The fruit is up to 75mm long and can sometimes be found on sale in specialist greengrocers. It is pleasantly aromatic, the flavour has been likened to a cross between a pineapple and a strawberry. Unfortunately the fruit does not often ripen properly in our cool summers but don't let that put you off growing this plant. The beautiful flowers are often produced in abundance and are some of the nicest tasting I have eaten. The petals are sweet and crisp, in fact they taste more like a fruit than many fruits.

There are many named varieties of this plant, developed for their superior fruits. Some of these cultivars are now available in Britain, though I do not know if they will fruit here.

Ficus carica. The FIG is relatively well-known as a fruit crop in this country. This is just a reminder that a south or west-facing wall is an ideal site for it and that you need to contain the roots in order to prevent excessive vegetative growth at the expense of fruiting.

Fortunella **species**. The KUMQUAT has been discussed earlier in this section with Citrus limon.

Fuchsia splendens. This species produces an abundance of delicious fruits in mid summer. It is very tolerant of pruning and can be grown against walls with any aspect, though it prefers at least some shade and the foliage suffers somewhat when it is grown on a very sunny wall. See also page 100.

Laurus nobilis. BAY. This is a superb shrub for a west-facing wall, it responds very well to pruning and so can be kept within the available space on the wall.

Bay's culinary uses and insect-repelling qualities make it extra useful for growing on a wall of the house near the kitchen window or door. See also page 43.

Physalis peruviana. See Plate 35. The GOLDENBERRY is a shrubby plant growing up to 2 metres tall and 3 metres wide in British gardens. It is not very frost-tolerant and will normally be killed back to ground level even in mild winters. The roots, however, should survive temperatures down to at least -5°C so long as they are well mulched – our plants come from the seed of a plant whose roots have survived -12°C. The roots will send up vigorous new growth in late spring.

A plant for the south or west facing wall, it grows most vigorously in rich soils but will flower and fruit better if the soil is on the poor side. The plant produces straggly growth and, whilst this can be trimmed if necessary to keep the plant within bounds, for the highest yields of fruit it is better to tie the branches back. The goldenberry is closely related to tomatoes and can also be grown as an annual crop in much the same way as that species.

This is a fruit with a distinctive flavour that you will either love or hate. About the size of a cherry, it is enclosed in a papery husk and, if left in the husk, the ripe fruit will store for several weeks in good condition. The flavour is hard to describe, fruits have a very sweet taste but with an underlying acidity that I think enhances the flavour. The cultivar 'Edulis' has larger fruits, though the plant is not as robust and most people find that the flavour is not quite so good.

Because I have a very windy garden, I grow my plants in a polyhouse and they produce a heavy crop from early August until cut back by hard frosts in the late autumn. Stored fruit will then keep until about February or even later. Once our hedges are effective in reducing the wind, we will be putting some of these plants against a south or west facing wall; they will be a bit later coming into fruit but should still provide a fruit for almost 6 months of the year.

PLANTS TO GROW IN WALLS

Walls are not only useful for providing a habitat for plants to grow against, there are also some plants that grow very well in or on the walls. These plants in general require very well-drained conditions and can tolerate low nutrient levels. Traditional drystone walls are ideal for this, especially if they are the type that have a sandwich of soil between the two sides. Many other walls are also suitable, even old (and I stress **old**) brick and mortar walls can have many plants growing out of them.

I am not talking here about walls, particularly drystone walls, that are used to retain or terrace soil on a slope. In cases such as this, the wall is more effectively a bank and the plants will usually be able to root through into the soil behind. Very often this soil will be quite moist and so plant growth on a wall such as this can be very lush. This type of wall can provide a very useful habitat and grow a wide range of plants.

The types of walls this section is looking at can be pretty difficult environments for plants. You won't get the lush growth of plants growing in fertile soils so don't expect lots of wonderful salads and fruits from your wall. You will, however, be able to grow a number of interesting species as I hope the list of suggestions below will demonstrate. They will make your wall look much more interesting as well as providing a small amount of food.

It can be difficult to establish plants on the wall. This is not such a problem on drystone walls because there are often pockets of soil to plant into – but how do you plant into mortar? The answer is that you don't. On a wall such as this you will only succeed if you can induce seed to germinate in situ in the cracks on the wall. This will seem to happen quite easily without your help, but the plants that arrive by themselves are often not the ones you might choose to have there.

In order to grow the species of your choice, you need to get the seeds to stay on the wall and then get them to germinate and establish. I have no personal experience of this but one method that I have heard of is to mix up a fairly thick paste of well rotted compost (it should be free from weed seeds) and water, then add your seeds to the paste and paint it onto the wall. This should provide the seedling with sufficient nutrients to get it started on its rather difficult life, the paste should also help to hold a little moisture for the developing seedling. Sow fairly thickly because success rates are normally low.

There are many species of ferns that grow well on walls, particularly on the more shaded and moister aspects. There are, however, some potential health problems associated with eating many ferns so I have in general omitted this group of plants from the book.

Those species listed below are herbaceous perennials unless stated otherwise and all are drought tolerant. They are not really suitable for old bricks and mortar walls unless the text recommends them for this purpose.

Anthemis tinctoria. YELLOW CAMOMILE is a lovely little plant growing about 60cm tall and wide. It likes alkaline soils so is ideal for a sunny position on a limestone wall. It also does very well in maritime situations.

This species has formerly been cultivated as a dye plant, providing a good quality yellow from the flowers. The variety 'Kelawayi' is said to be the best form. The plants are apt to overflower and exhaust themselves, so it is best to remove the flowering stems as soon as they stop flowering in order to stimulate the production of basal shoots for the following year.

Aphanes arvensis. PARSLEY PIERT is a native annual growing about 10cm tall and 20cm wide. It succeeds in a sunny position in acid and alkaline soils. The leaves can be eaten in salads.

Arabis caucasica. ROCK CRESS is an evergreen perennial, it grows about 15cm tall and in rich soils can spread freely. It needs a sunny position.

The leaves have a cress-like flavour and can be used as a garnish in salads or as a pot herb. The texture is not of the most desirable, though.

A. hirsuta. A native species that is a short-lived perennial. It prefers alkaline conditions. The leaves can be used as above.

Buddleia davidii. The BUTTERFLY BUSH is a deciduous shrub growing about 3 metres tall and wide. It can often be found self-sown on old brick walls in towns. It requires a sunny position and is a superb plant for attracting bees and butterflies to the garden. Black or green dyes can be obtained from the flowers, leaves and stems combined whilst an orange-gold to brown dye can be obtained from the flowers.

***Campanula* species**. All the HAREBELLS have more or less edible leaves and flowers and these usually have a pleasant mild flavour with a hint of sweetness. Any of the smaller rock garden species are worthy of a try on a sunny or lightly shaded wall, those that I have seen doing well are **C. cochleariifolia**, **C. portenschlagiana** and **C. poscharskyana**. They are all vigorous plants, growing about 15cm tall and spreading freely, even when growing on a wall. The latter two species are evergreen and have been seen growing very well on old brick walls. They can provide salad leaves all year round, these have a pleasant enough flavour though they are a bit chewy. See also page 203.

Carpobrotus edulis. The HOTTENTOT FIG has established itself along much of the southern coast of Britain where it will often be seen growing on steep inhospitable cliffs. A sunny drystone wall is luxury for this creature. A low-growing plant, it can spread quite freely and forms dense carpets of vegetation on the ground. It is not very hardy, though, so only try it in the milder areas of the country.

The large beautiful flowers are followed by small edible fruits which, as the common name suggests, are said to taste like figs. Maybe I am unlucky, but I have yet to find one that wasn't rather astringent. Perhaps I am trying them before they are fully ripe. The leaves are also edible but I find them too slimy to really enjoy. In warmer zones such as California the plant is much used as a fire break. The plant covers the ground with such a thick mat of vegetation that it excludes almost all other plants, the leaves are so succulent that they do not burn and can therefore prevent the fire from spreading.

Other members of the genus that have similar uses include **C. acinaciformis**, **C. aequilaterus** and **C. deliciosus**. They are all very similar to look at, but hopefully they have nicer fruits.

***Ephedra* species**. This genus of evergreen shrubs supplies the drug 'ephedrine' that is often prescribed by doctors and herbalists alike for a range of problems including asthma, hay fever and certain heart diseases. Most species also produce a small edible fruit which, whilst not highly flavoured, makes acceptable eating. You will need to grow a male plant along with a number of females if you want to obtain the fruit. Since few if any nurseries supply plants of known sex, this means that growing the plants from seed is your best bet. About 50% of the plants should be female, you can discard any surplus males if necessary once the sexes have been determined.

I love growing these plants simply because they look so strange. The green leafless stems are reminiscent of our native horsetails (***Equisetum* species**) but the plants have a much more shrubby habit. They come from arid regions of the world and most will succeed on a sunny wall. Not all of them are hardy but the following should do well in all but the coldest or wettest parts of the country:

E. americana andina. This is one of the easiest species to grow. It can be up to 1.8 metres tall and wide and has fruited well with me. The fruit is about 8mm in diameter and is slightly sweet but a bit on the boring side.

E. distachya. The SEA GRAPE grows about 1 metre tall and wide and has been used as an effective weed-excluding ground cover. All our plants are one sex and so we have yet to see it fruit, but this is said to be about 6mm in diameter and have a sweet flavour.

E. gerardiana. Known as MA HUANG, a famous Chinese medicinal herb. It grows about 60cm tall and spreads to form a clump 2 metres or more wide.

E. nevadensis. MORMON TEA grows about 1.2 metres tall and wide. In addition to the edible fruit, the stems of this plant are used to make a tea. Not a great drinker of teas, I have not yet tried it, but it is said to be delicious.

Ferula communis. GIANT FENNEL might be a giant, but it is no fennel, as anyone who tries the leaves will soon find out. Another plant for sunny walls, this perennial grows about 1 metre tall and 40cm wide. It takes a few years of growth before the plant will flower, but it then sends up a stem which can be 4 metres tall and looks most impressive at this time. Plants will normally die after flowering though they usually set a large amount of seed which can be used to maintain a stock.

A gum from the root is used as an incense. The stems are used in making furniture, though I am not sure how. These hollow stems were also used in the days before matches and cigarette lighters for transporting fire. The dried pith inside the stem would smoulder very slowly for several hours whilst the stem was being moved from site to site.

***Fragaria* species**. So long as there are small pockets of soil to root into, many species of STRAWBERRY will grow well on a sunny or partly shaded wall and spread freely with their runners. These are all low-growing plants between 15 and 25cm tall.

I personally would go for our native wild strawberry, *F. vesca* as my first choice. Although its fruits are very small they have an exquisite flavour and are produced for much of the summer. The plants can be left entirely to their own devices.

If you want vigorous plants with larger highly flavoured fruits, and don't mind that yields are low, then try either *F. moschata*, the MUSK STRAWBERRY, or *F. viridis*, the GREEN STRAWBERRY. These rather similar plants produce the nicest strawberry fruits I have eaten, though you will spend ages finding enough for a meal. The fruit ripens in late June and July.

The cultivated forms of strawberry, *F. x ananassa*, should also succeed on a wall though they would appreciate some extra water especially in dry weather and some help in placing their runners in suitable pockets of soil on the wall. By choosing a range of cultivars, you could be harvesting fruit from June until the autumn.

Hyssopus officinalis. HYSSOP is a fairly well-known evergreen shrub growing up to 60cm tall and wide. It grows well in a sunny position on old limestone dry walls, enjoying the alkaline conditions.

The leaves and the flowers can be used as a food flavouring or added in moderation to salads. They have a strong, aromatic flavour like a cross between sage and mint. A tea made from the leaves is said to be useful in controlling bacterial plant diseases.

There are conflicting reports about the value of this plant as a companion to cabbages. Most reports agree that the plant attracts the cabbage white butterfly, some say this is good since it draws the butterflies away from the cabbages whilst others say that it simply attracts more butterflies to the garden. The plant does have insect-repellent properties, though, and has been used as a strewing herb and as an ingredient in incense.

Lavandula **species**. LAVENDERS are also low-growing evergreen shrubs for sunny walls. The leaves can be used as a food flavouring or to make a tea, but these are too aromatic for me. I prefer the plant's other uses. These include: an essential oil from the flowers is used in soap making, perfumery and as an insect repellent; the dried leaves and flowers can be placed in the linen cupboard where they will not only help to keep moths away but will also impart a nice smell to your clothes and sheets; the leaves are also said to repel mice. The following species can be tried:

L. angustifolia. COMMON LAVENDER grows about 1.2 metres tall and 1 metre wide. The hardiest member of the genus, it should succeed in most parts of the country.

L. latifolia. SPIKE LAVENDER is very closely related to the above species, but is not so hardy and is best grown in the milder areas of the country. It grows about 50cm tall and wide.

Rumex scutatus. FRENCH SORREL provides an abundance of acid-flavoured leaves for salads all through the spring and summer. This species has been mentioned on page 121, it grows well on a moderately sunny wall.

Ruta graveolens. RUE is an evergreen shrub growing about 50cm tall and wide, and thriving on a sunny wall.

There are many reports of the bitter leaves being used as a food flavouring, but there are also reports of toxicity so I for one am going to give them a miss. Apart from its many medicinal virtues, rue does have a number of other uses including: the growing or the dried plant can be used to repel insects and is said to be most useful when the plant is grown near roses and raspberries; the dried herb can be put in the linen cupboard to repel moths, though they won't impart the nice smell that lavender does; the growing plant is also said to repel cats though our feline monsters have not read this report; a red dye is obtained from the plant.

Satureia montana. WINTER SAVORY is another evergreen shrub for sunny positions on walls, where it grows up to 40cm tall and wide. It prefers a calcareous soil and will do well on an old brick wall if you can manage to get it established.

The leaves have a slight pepperiness and are an excellent flavouring for cooked beans. They are said to prevent the flatulence that is so often associated with eating this food. The growing plant is said to repel insects which makes it a good companion for the beans in more than one way.

My favourite use of this plant is as an antidote to bee, wasp and nettle stings. Simply chew up a few leaves and then rub them onto the sting. Relief is almost immediate.

Saxifraga stolonifera. I have only recently obtained this perennial plant, it is already spreading quite well and looks as though it might make a good ground cover. It prefers an acid soil, grows about 40cm tall and succeeds on shadier walls.

The leaves are said to be edible raw or cooked and to be relished in Japan when parboiled or fried and used in salads but those that I have tried so far have a decided bitterness. The flowering stem is said to be tasty when salted.

Sempervivum tectorum. Growing to about 15cm tall and forming slowly spreading clumps 20cm or more wide. Usually called the HOUSELEEK, the main reason I wanted to include it in this book was so that I could use another of its common names which is 'WELCOME HOME HUSBAND, HOWEVER DRUNK YOU MAY BE'.

Names aside, this plant does have a number of uses. The fleshy leaves are edible and a few of our visitors have almost liked them. The juice of the leaves is said to make a refreshing drink. The most useful attribute of the leaves, in my opinion, is that the pulp can be applied to the skin as a treatment for burns and stings. It is very effective, though not as good as *Aloe vera*. However, since *Aloe vera* is not hardy in Britain and this plant is, the houseleek will play an important role in my medicinal herb garden.

When planted into thatched roofs the houseleek is said to preserve the building from lightning strikes. This has nothing to do with acting as a lightning conductor as one book would have me believe. Rather, if you have a roof filled with this plant the very succulent leaves act as a fire-retardant (in much the same way as *Carpobrotus edulis* above) if the roof is set alight.

***Thymus* species**. These dwarf, spreading evergreen shrubs require a sunny position. When in flower during the summer they will be absolutely covered in bees and butterflies.

THYMES have edible leaves that can be added to salads but are more often used as a garnish or as a flavouring in cooked foods. The leaves retain their flavour very well, even if cooked for a long time.

If you are tired of life then this plant is not for you since medical evidence suggests that regular use of thyme in the diet can prolong a person's life by 10% or more. This is due to the presence of antioxidants which promote the health of individual cells in the body, thus leading to an overall improvement in the general health of the body. An essential oil from the leaves is used in perfumery, soaps etc. and has fungicidal properties. The dried flowers are used to repel moths from clothing whilst the growing plants are said to repel cabbage root fly.

The following are a selection of the species worth trying:

T. x citriodorus. LEMON THYME has, as the name suggests, lemon-flavoured leaves. These are delightful in salads and are my personal favourite in the genus. The plants grow about 10cm tall, forming a spreading clump 30cm or more wide. The leaves turn golden-yellow in the winter making the plant extra ornamental at that time. Unfortunately, the plant does not enjoy winters in my windy garden and is often defoliated by the time spring comes round, so I miss out rather on the yellow leaves. It normally recovers very well and by mid-summer is looking none the worse for its experience.

T. herba-barona. CARAWAY THYME has a deliciously strong scent of caraway. I find it too strong for culinary use but love running my hand through the plant to release the scent. Plants grow about 5cm tall and form clumps 30cm or more wide.

T. praecox arcticus. One of our native WILD THYMES growing to 5cm tall and 30cm or more wide.

T. serpyllum. See Plate 36. Our other native THYME. Slightly more vigorous, it grows 10cm tall and 30cm wide.

T. vulgaris. The COMMON or LARGE-LEAVED THYME of gardens, with its many named varieties. It grows 20cm or so tall and 30cm or more wide. The leaves vary greatly in flavour according to the variety you are growing, but most of them are very good flavourings for salads and cooked foods.

Chapter Nine

HEDGES, SCREENS & SHELTERBELTS

My wife and I moved to Cornwall at the end of 1989, onto an open and windswept field of 36 acres with no internal hedges. Some years earlier the previous owner had grubbed out about 3 kilometres of hedges to make a field that the locals had nicknamed 'The Prairie'. What was originally 13 small and fairly sheltered fields was now one large wind-blasted monstrosity.

Although Cornwall is one of the mildest areas in Britain, capable of growing a very wide range of plants, the effect of strong winds can drastically reduce growth or even kill plants. Winds of 80 kilometres per hour occur fairly regularly on our land, whilst in one exceptional period we had gusts in excess of 150 kilometres per hour. This greatly affects the numbers of plants that we can grow successfully. It takes a bulldozer just a few hours to smash down a hedge, but it takes many years to grow a new one. Even with the most wind-resistant and fast-growing plants, it can be 10 years before any real degree of shelter is re-established.

Hedges also act to prevent soil erosion, both from the wind and from the rain. Once the hedges were removed from the land, the farmer was able to plough a straight line for well over half a kilometre before having to turn around and start another furrow. The land is on a gentle to moderate south-facing slope and, in the spring following the removal of the hedges, the farmer ploughed up and down the hill before planting out some potatoes. The potato furrows were also aligned up and down the hill since it is safer for the farmer to plough this way than to plough along the contour.

The day after the potatoes were planted it started to rain, and rain and rain and rain... The furrows became channels to direct the water down the slope, these channels soon became tiny streams which grew larger and eventually started to wash soil and potatoes down the hill. The outcome was one very unhappy neighbour with a house and garden flooded with soil and potatoes, plus potatoes found in the stream half a mile from the land. Had the hedges remained, there could have been no such long furrows, not only that but the hedges would have acted as barriers to prevent the soil being washed away.

One of our major tasks, therefore, has been to plant lots of hedges and windbreaks in order to provide more shelter. Because of our interest in the multiple uses of plants, we have mainly used those species that can provide us with more than just shelter and we have been particularly interested in obtaining fruits, seeds and other foods from them. However, don't become obsessed with finding more than one use for a plant – better a species with only one specific use that it does very well than one that has a number of uses but does not fulfil its main criterion properly.

HEDGE & SHELTERBELT DESIGN

When planting a hedge or screen for protection from the wind, it is important to bear a few points in mind.

- Firstly, the most effective shelter from wind must be about 30 - 40% permeable. This has been shown to be the most effective at reducing wind speeds and also allows some of the wind to filter through the hedge or shelterbelt. This prevents the eddying and accompanying stronger winds that you get around solid structures such as walls. It also gives shelter downwind for a greater distance than does a solid barrier.

- A hedge can provide effective reductions of wind speed for a distance that is 10 times the height of the hedge. This is only the case if the wind is at right angles to the hedge, the more it moves away from a right angle then the less effective the protection that is provided. If the wind does hit a straight hedge at right angles, there is a tremendous pressure on the hedge. When living in a very windy area you need to be sure that the plants have strong roots and branches to take the strain.

- Since you cannot guarantee that the strongest winds will always come from exactly the same direction, it can be beneficial to plant the hedge in an arc or a v-shape in order to give more protection.

- Evergreen species provide effective wind protection all year round whilst the effectiveness of deciduous species is greatly reduced when they are not in leaf.

Of course, it isn't only food and shelter plus protection from erosion by wind or rain that hedges and shelterbelts can give us. Some of their other benefits include:

- They can be planted to provide privacy or screen out unwanted views.

- They can help to filter out noise from roads etc. The bamboos are very good at this, as are several evergreen conifers.

- The deep rooted species will bring up nutrients from deep in the soil, depositing them on the ground in the autumn as their leaves fall. By choosing species with heavy leaf-fall, such as alders, a shelterbelt can become the source of organic matter for other parts of the land.

- Certain species have nitrogen nodules on their roots and thereby enrich the soil, producing greater yields from the land with less need to apply fertilizers.

- An area can be made to look far more interesting by the careful siting of hedges and even fairly small sites can seem much larger when divided into separate areas by the hedge.

- Some thorny species are ideal for keeping out unwanted guests of both the two and four legged kind.

- Properly sited hedges can provide us with suitable microclimates for growing a wider range of plants. By reducing the wind speed they will provide warmer growing conditions for the plants (and for us of course). They can be sited so as to form sun-traps for growing some of the more tender plants in your area, or for you to sun-bathe.

- Hedges have sunny and shady sides, thus providing habitats for different types of plants. They can also provide both habitats and food for wildlife, thus leading to more balanced populations of predators and prey with a subsequent reduction in pest damage to our crops.

HEDGES

In this chapter I want to look at some of the plants we can use to provide shelter in the garden and on the farm. First of all I will look at some hedge plants and then at some shelterbelt trees.

When deciding on which species to use, you need to be clear in your mind on a number of points:

- Why do you want the hedge?
- How tall and wide do you want it to grow?
- Do you want deciduous or evergreen species?
- Do you want a formal (trimmed) or informal (untrimmed) hedge?
- Do you want to grow a single species or a mixture? If you want a mixture, then have you chosen plants that grow and look well together?
- How much work are you willing to put in to maintaining it?

All too frequently people choose unsuitable species and then some years later are faced with the choice of either grubbing it all out and starting again or tolerating what can quite literally become an increasingly large thorn in their side.

How often is Leyland cypress planted as a hedge in a small garden? It looks good for a few years as it quickly grows to fill the space, the trouble is that it carries on growing for the sky – and can reach 60 or more metres tall. Only major work each year can contain it and the ever longer shadow it casts. Each plant has its place and Leyland cypress is magnificent as a shelterbelt for large areas of land. It has, for example, put on 2.5 metres in height with us in the 3 years and this has been achieved despite all our winds. But in a small garden where space and light are at a premium...

If you are planting a mixed hedge then it is important to group together compatible plants. Apart from not making a very pleasing combination, if you planted a mixed hedge of BEECH (*Fagus sylvatica*) and BARBERRY (***Berberis darwinii***) then you would be left with a constant dilemma – the beech needs to be trimmed annually if it is to remain a hedge and retain its dead leaves in the winter whilst the barberry needs to be left untrimmed if it is to fruit well.

It can sometimes be difficult to reconcile the needs of a hedge with the desire to obtain some other use from the plants. For example, if you want to grow a fruiting hedge, unless the plants fruit on the current year's growth of wood you are going to have to leave the hedge untrimmed if you want to obtain a reasonable crop of fruit. This is no problem if you wanted an untrimmed hedge, but if you have sited the hedge in a very formal part of the garden then it could look out of place. An untrimmed hedge, of course, also takes up much more room than a trimmed hedge, so you have to make sure that you leave sufficient space for it.

Many hedges look much better if they are left untrimmed, but there are also many hedges that need to be trimmed in order to keep them as a hedge, otherwise after a few years they will start to lose their bottom branches and become more tree-like in appearance. One good compromise that often works is to trim a hedge every 3 - 4 years. This allows the plants to yield fruit in their untrimmed years whilst keeping them as hedges.

This treatment will also be very beneficial for birds that might want to nest in the hedge (and also share the fruit with you). By leaving the hedge untrimmed for a number of years, the hedge will be considerably wider and will offer more privacy for nesting birds. The occasional trimming might stop the birds nesting in the hedge for a year, but will ensure a thick mat of branches is produced that will soon be providing privacy again. If using this system, try to make sure that you do not trim all your hedges in the same year. If you try to trim a quarter of the hedges each year, not only will you be spreading your workload out more evenly, but you will be ensuring that there are always some areas of hedge suitable for the birds.

A wide variety of plants can be grown as hedges, providing us with small hedges suitable for even the tiniest gardens, rampant growing trees and shrubs for larger areas and all shades in between. There are evergreen or deciduous species to choose from, species that are best left untrimmed or others that are very amenable to cutting and, within reason, can be cut back to whatever size is required.

When planting the hedge you have to decide how close to space each plant. This varies widely from species to species, and also according to your budget. For faster establishment it makes sense to put the plants closer together, whilst if you are not in a hurry you can save money by extending the space between each plant. For the smaller hedges a spacing of 25 - 45cm is about right, whilst with some of the larger-growing species spaces of 2 metres are sometimes suitable. A figure for the planting distance will be given with each species – this will be an average figure and you can adjust it according to your own needs.

The list of hedging plants that follows has been divided into sections depending on the size of the hedge that it will make and whether it is deciduous or evergreen. Any references to the height of a hedge in the following lists can only be a guide since very often it depends upon your treatment of the plants. The YEW TREE (***Taxus baccata***), for example, is very amenable to trimming and can be kept very small or can be allowed to develop into a large hedge. I have therefore placed each species according to the most appropriate size of hedge I feel it would make and have mentioned in the text that it could also be kept small/allowed to grow larger. To try and make things clearer, I have also included the potential size of each species if allowed to grow without being trimmed.

Unless stated otherwise, the following species are best grown in a sunny position and succeed in most well-drained soils.

See also Chapter 12 for some more native species that are suitable for hedging.

SMALL HEDGES

The plants in this list can be used to make hedges less than 1.2 metres tall. This is obviously too low for use as a screen or barrier, but these small hedges can be very useful for marking out areas, especially in small gardens, without being imposing. A hedge this small is generally trimmed to keep it within the chosen size.

DECIDUOUS SPECIES

Ribes alpinum. The ALPINE CURRANT grows about 1.2 metres tall and 80cm wide. The cultivars 'Aureum', 'Green Mound' and 'Pumilum' grow about 1 metre tall and wide, making good dwarf hedges. An easily grown plant, it will form a better shape when grown in poorer soils. It also succeeds in shade, though is unlikely to fruit well in such a position. Space the plants about 50cm apart.

This species can harbour a stage of white pine blister rust, so should not be grown in the vicinity of pine trees.

The fruit, which is about 5mm in diameter, is a type of redcurrant and can be eaten raw or cooked. It is sweet and not very acid but is less palatable than the redcurrant. Plants produce either male or female flowers and so you need to grow at least 1 male plant with every 5 females if you want fruit. 'Aureum' and 'Pumilum' are females, I do not know which sex 'Green Mound' is. To try and ensure fruit is produced, it would be wise to have a known male plant growing near the hedge.

EVERGREEN SPECIES

Artemisia abrotanum. SOUTHERNWOOD grows about 1.2 metres tall and 1 metre wide. It is tolerant of quite hard trimming and so can be used as a small hedge. It grows well in maritime gardens and in dry soils, when established it is very drought tolerant. Space the plants about 50cm apart.

A good companion plant for cabbages, it is also a good plant to grow in the orchard, where it can help to reduce insect pests. The whole plant is insect repellent, the dried leaves remain effective for 6 - 12 months and can be used in the linen cupboard etc. The shoots can be burnt as an incense in the fireplace to mask cooking odours from the house. An infusion of the plant is used as a hair tonic or conditioner. Although some reports say that the bitter shoots can be used as a flavouring, I would rather give this a miss because of potential toxicity.

Buxus sempervirens. BOX is a slow-growing plant that can grow up to 5 metres tall and wide, though it is very amenable to trimming and can be kept much smaller if required. The cultivar 'Suffruticosa' in particular is used as a dwarf hedge and can be kept as small as 10cm if required. Space the plants about 30 cm apart.

This is the species that is widely used in topiary, where it is trimmed into all sorts of ornamental shapes. Box prefers light shade and chalky soils and also succeeds in dry shade.

Calluna vulgaris. HEATHER grows up to 60cm tall and 50cm wide. It requires a light acid soil and does well in poor peats. It is tolerant of fairly dry soils but dislikes prolonged drought. The flowers are rich in nectar and are very attractive to bees, butterflies and moths. It makes a useful edging to beds and is fairly amenable to trimming. Space the plants about 30cm apart.

The branches have many uses: in thatching, as a bedding, for insulation, basketry, rope making and for making brooms.

Helichrysum italicum. The CURRY PLANT can grow 60cm tall and 1 metre wide. It requires a very well-drained soil, being quite intolerant of wet soils, especially in the winter. It is not hardy in the colder areas of the country, tolerating temperatures down to about -10°C. The cultivar 'Serotinum' is very suitable as a low hedge and responds well to trimming, even when this is into the old wood. Space the plants about 40cm apart. The leaves are sometimes used as a flavouring, they have a slight flavour of curry, though they do not impart this very well to other foods.

Hyssopus officinalis. HYSSOP grows about 60cm tall and wide. It responds well to trimming in the spring and makes a neat dwarf hedge. Space the plants about 30cm apart. See also page 167.

Lavandula angustifolia. LAVENDER grows about 1.2 metres tall and 1 metre wide. It responds well to trimming after flowering and is a useful insect-repellent low hedge. Space the plants about 40cm apart. See also page 167.

Rosmarinus officinalis. ROSEMARY grows about 1.5 metres tall and wide. It is very tolerant of pruning and can regenerate from old wood, though any trimming is best carried out after the plant has flowered. It is fairly resistant to maritime exposure, though when this is coupled with very cold weather the plants can suffer severely. The cultivars 'Miss Jessopp's Upright' and 'Fastigiatus' are particularly suitable for hedging. Space the plants about 40cm apart. See also page 60.

Santolina chamaecyparissus. COTTON LAVENDER grows about 60cm tall and 1 metre wide. An easy and undemanding plant to grow, though it strongly dislikes wet conditions around the roots. It prefers a light sandy fairly poor soil on a sunny slope and does well on chalk. It grows well in a hot dry position and is drought and wind tolerant. The plants can be cut back hard in spring to maintain their form, though this will prevent them flowering. Space the plants about 50cm apart.

The aromatic leaves are used as a flavouring for broths, sauces and grain dishes.

The growing plant repels various insect pests, especially cabbage moths, whilst the leaves can be dried and strewn amongst clothes to repel moths. The dried leaves are also used in pot-pourri.

MEDIUM HEDGES

The following plants are used to make hedges 1.2 - 2 metres tall. This is the size of hedge that is usually most appropriate to the scale of the garden – large enough to give privacy without dominating the garden and excluding too much light. A hedge this size will often have to be kept in bounds by trimming, though there are several species that can be left untrimmed and will not outgrow their welcome.

DECIDUOUS SPECIES

Lycium barbarum. BOX THORN grows about 2.5 metres tall and forms suckers, spreading to a width of 4 metres or more if allowed. Choose a position where it does not matter if the suckers spread, or grow it alongside a lawn where unwanted suckers can simply be mown out. Very tolerant of maritime exposure, box thorn succeeds on poor sandy soils but will produce better quality shoots when grown in a richer soil. Although it can be trimmed if required, it is best left untrimmed. Slugs are very fond of the new growth of this plant and can cause quite a lot of damage both to new leaves and also to new suckers. Space the plants about 60cm apart.

Cultivated in China for its edible young shoots, these are used mainly as a flavouring though they can also be lightly cooked for 3 - 4 minutes and then used as a vegetable. The flavour has been described as somewhat cress-like or as peppermint-like. The plant belongs to the potato family, which is renowned for having poisonous leaves, so I have some reservations about eating it and have yet to give it a try. None the less, it does seem to be a popular crop in China. The leaves are also used as a tea substitute, which gives the plant another of its common names, the DUKE OF ARGYLE'S TEA PLANT.

An edible fruit, which has a mild sweet flavour, is produced in late summer though yields are usually small. The books say that the fruit is about 2cm in diameter, though the largest I have ever seen were less than 1cm.

Poncirus trifoliata. The BITTER ORANGE grows about 3 metres tall and wide, making an open hedge that is best left untrimmed. A sparsely leaved shrub with green stems, it has very large thorns which make it both attractive and a very effective barrier against all sorts of potential intruders. Much of the photosynthesis takes place in the young stems. An easily grown plant, it succeeds in most soils including poor acid ones, though it prefers a light sandy soil. It can fruit quite well in light shade, though it prefers full sun. Space the plants about 60cm apart.

This is the only fruit-bearing shrub of the orange family that is genuinely hardy in Britain. The fruit is about 3cm in diameter, though unfortunately it is much more peel than it is flesh and is also quite bitter. It ripens in mid to late autumn. Whilst almost inedible raw, it can be used in conserves especially for marmalade.

Rosa rugosa. See Plate 40. RAMANAS ROSE is a vigorous suckering shrub that grows up to 2 metres tall. It makes an excellent untrimmed hedge, though it is rather gaunt in winter. Unless you want to be forever pulling out the suckers, make sure that you grow it in a position where they can be easily controlled. The stems are very prickly and will serve as a barrier against unwanted visitors. A very tough and easily grown plant, it succeeds in most soils, is very tolerant of maritime exposure, resists most diseases and fruits abundantly. Space the plants about 60cm apart.

All species of rose produce edible fruits that are rich in vitamin C, though many are far less than desirable to eat. Ramanas rose has the largest and the nicest fruits that I have tried to date, averaging 30mm in diameter. They ripen over a period of several weeks in mid to late summer, are sweet with a delicious rich flavour and are very pleasant to eat either raw or cooked. It does, unfortunately, take quite a bit of patience to eat any quantity of them since they have a relatively thin layer of edible flesh. Below this flesh is a layer of irritant hairs that can inflame the digestive tract – these hairs are a traditional 'itching powder' of school children. I like munching on the occasional fruit in the summer whenever I pass a hedge, but my wife is much more patient and will sometimes spend an hour or more eating them for breakfast.

The petals can be eaten raw or cooked. They are somewhat variable in quality, the best are sweet and aromatic, others are quite bitter. Make sure you remove the white base of the petal since this is the most bitter part. The seed is a good source of vitamin E and can be ground and mixed with flour or added to other foods as a supplement. In this case you must make sure you remove the hairs first. This can be done by abrading the seeds in a large drum in much the same way as stones are polished, or by passing the seeds fairly quickly over a flame in order to burn off the hairs. A pleasant tasting sweet-flavoured tea can be made from the fresh or dried fruit.

EVERGREEN SPECIES

Atriplex halimus. SALT BUSH grows about 2 metres tall and 3 metres wide and has become naturalised by the coast in Britain. A very wind resistant plant, it succeeds even in the most exposed maritime areas where it will make a medium sized hedge and require very little trimming. This species succeeds in sandy and saline soils but does not like heavy soils or shade. Space the plants about 50cm apart.

The leaves and shoot tips have a salty tang and can be added to salads or cooked as a spinach. The steamed leaves make a delicious dish and are a great favourite with us. We pick this plant so frequently that we never have to come along with the shears to trim it! When harvesting the plant we either pick the top 5cm of the young shoots for use in salads, or we pick the younger stems 15 - 25cm long for cooking. Do not strip off the leaves and leave behind any bare stems. Apart from looking unsightly, they usually do not regrow and then rot on the plant bringing the added risk of disease. The leaves can be harvested all year round, though the plants virtually cease growing in the winter and should not be harvested heavily at this time.

Also well worth trying is the North American *A. canescens*, a very similar shrub with perhaps even nicer tasting leaves.

Baccharis patagonica. A very easily grown plant, reaching about 3 metres tall and wide if not trimmed. It succeeds in most soils from pure sand to heavy clays so long as it is in a sunny position. Space the plants about 50cm apart.

Apart from its wood being used for fuel (simply because it is about the only woody species that will grow in its very windy native environment) this lovely aromatic shrub has no other recorded uses. Although seldom offered by plant nurseries, this is one of the most frequently admired plants we grow on our land. It is slow growing but exceedingly resistant of maritime exposure and in time makes a hedge that is wider than it is tall. It does not need trimming unless you need to contain it and is not hardy in the colder areas of Britain.

Escallonia **species**. This is a group of evergreen plants for milder maritime gardens. Very fast growing, it is possible to have a good 2 metre high hedge within 4 - 5 years from planting unrooted cuttings in situ during the winter. A cheap and very effective hedge, it has a mass of lovely smelling flowers in early summer. Apart from all the exercise you will get from having to trim it at least twice a year, I have yet to find any other use for it, though it is possibly a source of essential oils. Space the plants about 50cm apart.

E. rubra macrantha. Try this species or any of the many hybrids that abound such as 'Apple Blossom' or 'Red Hedger'. One word of warning though – some of the cultivars grow too fast for their own good and can outgrow their roots. On our windy land this means that they can then suffer from wind-rock. To prevent this it is necessary to trim them back hard in their formative years, ensuring that they do not increase in height by more than 30cm each year. Some forms also have brittle wood and their branches get broken off in winter gales. 'Crimson Spire' is the one we have had most problems with, the others seem to be fine.

MEDIUM TO LARGE HEDGES

These species can be grown either as medium hedges or as tall ones depending on how much or little you want to trim them. This is by far the largest group of plants and the species listed here are suitable for small and large gardens.

DECIDUOUS SPECIES

Acer campestre. The FIELD MAPLE is a native deciduous tree that can grow up to 15 metres tall. It responds well to trimming and makes an excellent hedge in a fairly short time. It is fairly undemanding of soil or site though it prefers a neutral to alkaline soil. It does well on chalky soils, though it grows more slowly and never becomes more than a shrub. Space the plants about 60cm apart. The fallen leaves in autumn make an excellent packing material in which to store fruit or root crops.

Alnus glutinosa. The ALDER is another native deciduous tree. A fast-growing plant, it can be 25 metres tall in the wild with a spread of 10 metres or more. It will need quite a lot of trimming to keep it as a hedge. This is a plant for moist or wet soils, it is very wind resistant and will start to provide reasonable wind-shelter within 3 years. It produces nitrogen nodules at its roots, thereby helping to feed neighbouring plants. Space the plants about 60cm apart.

The alder is a very good source of dyes – yellow, green, pink and red being produced from the young shoots, catkins, greenwood and bark respectively. An ink can also be made from the bark.

Berberis vulgaris. The COMMON BARBERRY grows up to 3 metres tall and 2 metres wide. A very easily grown plant, it succeeds in sun or moderate shade and is very unfussy as to soil. It responds well to trimming, though I feel it looks better untrimmed in a mixed hedge. The prickly stems help to deter unwelcome visitors. Space the plants about 75cm apart.

The barberry produces an edible fruit about 10mm long and 3mm wide in the autumn. This is rather seedy, but has a pleasant sharp flavour which children seem to love. Most adults will probably prefer to cook it for preserves etc. It used to be cultivated for its edible fruit and a number of named varieties were grown. One of these had no seeds and so was especially useful, but I have been unable to find anyone growing it at present.

B. vulgaris should not be grown in cereal producing areas since it harbours the disease 'black stem rust' of wheat.

Cornus sanguinea. DOGWOOD is a native shrub growing up to 3 metres tall and suckering freely once established. Whilst it can be trimmed, it is probably best left to its own devices as an informal hedge and grows well in a mixed native hedge. Very tolerant of soil conditions, it succeeds in acid sands as well as on shallow chalk. It does not like strong winds and will be most unhappy in maritime exposure. Space the plants about 60cm apart.

A good quality oil is obtained from the fruit and the seed which is edible if refined but is more suitable for lighting and soap-making. The young branches can be used in basket making, the plant is best cut back to the ground each year for this purpose to ensure that long, straight branches are produced. The fruit is edible according to some reports, but it is very bitter and has an emetic effect on the body so is not likely to see the inside of my mouth.

One species with a very edible fruit is the related **Cornus mas** or CORNELIAN CHERRY. Left to its own devices it can grow 5 metres tall and wide, though it responds well to trimming. See also page 47.

Crataegus species. All members of this genus of deciduous trees and shrubs, which has been dealt with in more detail in Chapter 2, have more or less edible fruits. Many of the species also make good hedges and are very tolerant of trimming. The problem, though, is that if you trim a hedge regularly you will be cutting off most of its potential for fruiting. The genus as a whole is very easy to cultivate, being tolerant of most soil conditions and situations. A sunny position is best for good fruit production but plants also succeed in semi-shade. Space the plants about 60cm apart.

Probably the best choices for hedges in Britain are our native HAWTHORNS, *C. laevigata* and *C. monogyna*, which are dealt with more fully on page 240. Although edible, their fruit is hardly appetizing. If quality of fruit is a factor then you could try growing the following species:

C. mollis. The RED HAW can grow up to 9 metres tall and 12 metres wide. The fruit is up to 25mm in diameter and has a thick flesh covering the seeds. It is sub-acid, rather on the dry side and has a mealy texture. The flavour is pleasant, though this is not one of the best fruits in the genus.

C. submollis. A small tree or a shrub up to 8 metres tall and wide. The fruit is about 20mm in diameter and is sweet and juicy with a somewhat mealy texture. It makes a very acceptable dessert fruit.

Elaeagnus species. Virtually all the species in this genus make excellent hedging plants. The evergreen species will be dealt with in the next section.

The deciduous species are best left untrimmed. They all succeed in the windiest of sites and generally prefer well-drained soils that are not too rich, requiring a sunny position if they are to prosper. They produce nitrogen nodules on their roots and experiments in North America have shown that by putting some of these plants in an orchard you can increase the fruit yield of the orchard trees by 10%. This is especially effective with nut trees and plums since these respond well to the extra nitrogen.

All members of the genus produce edible fruits and seeds. The fruit must be fully ripe before it is eaten, otherwise it will be very astringent. Colour is **not** a reliable guide, the fruit looking very appetizing some weeks before it is ready. Wait until it is very soft before eating it. The best guide is the mouth – this will soon pucker up if the fruit is not ready. If you have picked a quantity of unripe fruit then leave it in a fairly warm room for a few days and it will probably ripen. The fruit is extremely attractive to birds. Fortunately it is often produced in such abundance that you will be able to afford to share it.

The species most worth growing are listed below. Space the plants about 75cm apart. There are some named varieties of each species that have been bred for improved fruits. These are not generally available in Britain at present, though a number of them will be grown here in the next few years.

E. angustifolia. The OLEASTER can grow 7 metres tall and wide. It forms a very open hedge. A very hardy plant, tolerating temperatures down to -40°C in its native range, though the young wood is sometimes damaged by much less cold conditions in Britain simply because our summers can be too cool to fully ripen the wood. The oval fruit is about 10mm long and is very sweet, though it is rather dry and mealy. It ripens in early autumn. This species has flowered very freely with us in Cornwall, though it has refused to produce more than the very occasional fruit. It seems to be much better suited to the eastern half of the country where it often fruits heavily.

E. multiflora. The GOUMI grows about 3 metres tall and 2 metres wide. It has a very dense habit of growth and its branches form a reasonable screen even in the winter. The fruit ripens in mid summer. It is up to 15mm long and 8mm wide. When fully ripe it is soft and juicy with a very nice flavour, though a hint of astringency remains. This is probably the best of the deciduous species for fruit. It usually crops well in all parts of the country.

E. parvifolia. See Plate 38. Growing to about 4.5 metres tall and 3 metres wide. This is possibly the most productive member of the genus. The fruit is almost round and about 8mm in diameter. It ripens towards the end of the summer and will hang on the bush for 8 weeks or more if the birds leave it alone. When fully ripe it is pleasantly juicy and is adored by our young son (who loves all the fruits in this genus), though we find it a bit astringent to eat raw in large quantities.

E. umbellata. The AUTUMN OLIVE grows up to 4.5 metres tall and 4 metres wide. Although it flowers very freely, we have yet to see fruit on this plant, though the books say that it fruits well in Britain. The fruit is very similar to the species above.

Eleutherococcus sieboldianus. Growing to about 3 metres tall and 2.5 metres wide. It is reasonably shade tolerant, grows well in the urban pollution of towns and also succeeds in very poor soils. It does not like windy positions. Space the plants about 60cm apart.

The edible leaves are said to have a delicious somewhat fragrant flavour when cooked. I have not yet tried cooking them because I only have one small plant, but the raw leaf is bitter and rather less than pleasant. The dried leaves are a tea substitute.

Fagus sylvatica. If left to its own devices our native BEECH will grow into a deciduous tree up to 30 metres tall and 15 metres wide. It is very tolerant of clipping and makes a splendid formal hedge. So long as it is trimmed in late summer it will retain its dead leaves throughout the winter, so providing an effective screen all year round. There is a hedge of this species in Scotland that is over 20 metres tall and has still retained its lower branches. A very impressive sight, though I would not like to be the person who has to trim it! Space the plants about 60cm apart.

Beech produces new shoots in April and usually another burst of growth about three months later. The young leaves make a very nice addition to salads, though I do stress that they must be young since the leaves quickly become tough and unpleasant. See also page 28.

Myrica pensylvanica. NORTHERN BAYBERRY is a deciduous shrub growing up to 3 metres tall and suckering to form small thickets. When grown as a hedge it is best left untrimmed. The plant prefers acid conditions and is tolerant of maritime winds and of dry soils. Space the plants about 75cm apart.

The leaves can be used as a food flavouring in much the same way as bay leaves.

The most interesting use of this plant is for making candles. As a protection against salt-laden maritime winds, the plants produce a layer of wax on their leaves and fruit – the fruits are a particularly good source of this wax. If you boil up the fruits in water, the wax will melt and float to the surface. This can then be skimmed off and used to make very aromatic candles that burn cleanly. Apparently there is a small industry in western North America making and selling candles from these plants. The fruits are often produced in abundance in this country. Unfortunately we don't get as much wax on the fruits in Britain as they do in America because our summers are not so hot, but even so there should be enough to play with. Plants are often either male or female, so you will need at least one male plant to every 5 - 6 females in order to ensure they produce fruit.

There are a number of other species in this genus with similar uses. The one most worth trying in Britain is probably **M. cerifera**. The WAX MYRTLE is closely related to the above species. It grows up to 9 metres tall and 3 metres wide in the wild, though it is usually much smaller in Britain. It is also less hardy – though it should succeed in all but the coldest parts of the country.

This species is probably more productive of wax than the northern bayberry. There is also a report that the fruit can hang on the plant for several years and so if you do not get enough in one year to make candles, you could always try leaving it on until the following year's crop is ready.

Sambucus nigra. ELDERBERRY is a native deciduous shrub that can grow up to 6 metres tall and wide. A very tolerant and easily grown plant, it is capable of growing in almost any soil or situation in sun or shade and is a very valuable ingredient of informal wildlife hedges. Like many deciduous hedges it offers little wind protection or screening when not in leaf. It looks nicer when untrimmed, but can be cut right back into very old wood if required and will soon be growing back as if nothing has happened. The flowers and fruit are formed on the current year's growth, so any trimming is best done in the winter months. This will encourage fresh growth and actually increase fruit yields. Space the plants about 75cm apart.

The fruit is fairly small, usually less than 8mm in diameter, but is produced in large clusters and is easily harvested. It ripens in late summer and early autumn, and can be eaten raw or cooked. It is fairly nice in preserves and makes an excellent wine or cordial, but I find the raw fruit less than pleasant. Some people have a very negative reaction to this raw fruit and get stomach upsets, but they are usually tolerant of the cooked fruit. Birds have no problems with it though, so plant some near your orchard trees in order to keep the birds happy and away from your apples and pears.

Some named forms have been selected for their fruit, but I have yet to find one I could classify as nice. The sub-species *S. nigra alba*, however, has white/green fruits that are nicer than the type species and were considered to be quite acceptable when eaten raw by a group of 7 people on a fruit-tasting trip.

Elder flowers make a very pleasant munch on a summers day. They have a somewhat unusual flavour which is liked by most people I have given them to, and have a very refreshing effect on the mouth and the body. Look out for the pollinating insects in them, however, or you will be eating more than you had bargained for.

I am one of those people who, if there is only one midge about, then it is me that will be eaten. Various plants are said to repel insects but this is the one that works for me. Simply rub the leaves firmly over the skin. You will end up with a slight green tinge to the skin and a rather unique aroma, but you won't be bothered by many biting insects for the next couple of hours. An insecticide has been made in the past by boiling 3 - 4 handfuls of leaves in 1 litre of water, this is also said to be effective against various fungal infections such as leaf rot and powdery mildew. The plant is a valuable addition to the compost heap and its flowers are an alternative ingredient of 'Quick Return' herbal compost activator.

EVERGREEN SPECIES

Berberis **species**. This genus contains some of the most tolerant and easily grown of garden plants. Many of them are suitable for hedging, most being very undemanding of soil or situation. They produce edible, though acid fruits and a good yellow dye from the roots. The genus is dealt with in more detail in Chapter 2, the following species are especially suitable for hedging. Both are tolerant of maritime exposure.

Berberis darwinii. The acid flavoured fruit ripens in mid summer and makes a tasty addition to mueslis and porridge.

B. darwinii. Growing up to 3 metres tall and 3.5 metres wide. It is very tolerant of trimming though it looks much better if left untrimmed. A fairly slow-growing plant, though it can in time make a fairly large hedge. Space the plants about 75cm apart.

This hedge will delight you in the spring with its racemes of yellow flowers and then again in mid-summer with its fruit. This looks rather like a small blackcurrant about 7mm in diameter and is usually produced in great abundance. When fully ripe it has a mildly acid flavour and is quite juicy. I find it very refreshing and like to eat it in quantity. It is best raw, though it goes very well in porridge and makes excellent preserves. Its main drawback is that there are rather a lot of seeds in the fruit and can have a laxative effect if you are not used to it.

This is a plant with an excellent potential to be a commercial crop. It fruits regularly and abundantly, is virtually untroubled by pests or diseases and needs very little attention from the grower. It is, however, a fruit that the birds will not leave alone and you will need to net it or find some means of deterring the birds.

B. x stenophylla. Growing to about 2.5 metres tall and wide, usually producing suckers. This is a hybrid species with *B. darwinii* as one of its parents. It is a bit faster growing than *B. darwinii* and makes a better formal hedge if you decide to trim it. Space the plants about 75cm apart.

The fruit is about the same size as the preceding species and ripens a few weeks later, though it is not produced so freely.

Ceanothus thyrsiflorus. BLUE BRUSH grows up to 4.5 metres tall and wide. This species is only for the milder areas of the country, it tolerates occasional temperatures down to about -10°C and does very well in maritime areas, tolerating salt-laden winds. Although not a legume, it has nitrogen-forming nodules on its roots and thereby helps to provide this element to neighbouring plants. Space the plants about 75cm apart.

The flowers, which are produced in late spring, make a pleasantly scented soap that is a safe and effective cleaner. To wash the hands simply pick a couple of bunches of blossom, wet your hands and then rub the flowers between the hands. You will be surprised just how much lather will be produced. This soap will not remove grease (so it is not much help if you have been working on the car), but neither will it remove the skin's natural oil and so it does not dry out the hands.

The flowers of any other members of this genus can also be used as a soap and, by careful selection of species, it is possible to have plants in flower from the spring until the autumn. The flowers can also be dried for later use.

Elaeagnus **species**. This genus contains some of the most exciting plants we have come across, and I hope that by the time you finish reading about them that you will want to rush down to your local plant nursery and buy at least a dozen plants.

The deciduous species have been dealt with in the previous section. The evergreen species are perhaps the more exciting. They make superb untrimmed screens but can also be trimmed regularly and heavily if required to form a very dense screen. As discussed in the section dealing with the deciduous species, these are ideal companion plants in the orchard where they can help to increase fruit yields.

These are very easy plants to grow, tolerant of most soils and situations. They actually grow and fruit better in poor soils and will succeed in full sun or in deep shade. They grow well in dry soils and are very drought-tolerant once established. The only condition that is an absolute no-no for them is wet soils. They are very wind-tolerant plants, growing well even in severe maritime exposure. Indeed, if you have an old windbreak of pine trees that are losing their bottom branches and the wind is being funnelled through these gaps, then these species can be planted under the pine trees and will in time climb into the lower branches and close the gaps. Space the plants about 75cm apart.

This genus as a whole has excellent potential for fruit production, and those species listed below each produce their edible fruits over a period of about 6 weeks in April and May. This is long before any of our traditional garden fruits come into bearing. This fruit is red in colour with a very attractive silvery marbling and, when fully ripe, is soft and juicy with a pleasant rich flavour. It is a fruit that can easily be eaten in quantity. Make sure the fruit is fully ripe before you eat it, or it will be astringent and rather unpleasant. It needs to be very soft and the colour will have turned to a dark red. If picked a bit under-ripe, it will usually ripen off if kept in a warm room for a couple of days.

The fruit contains one large seed and this is also edible. The flavour is mild and I can detect a hint of peanut, though my friends say that I am deluding myself because I like peanuts so much!

I find that it is best to eat the fruit and the seed at the same time because the two flavours go together very well. The seed is covered by a fibrous coat so you will end up with a small amount of fibre in your mouth which you will have to spit out. Alternatively, you can eat the fruit, remove the seed from your mouth, peel off the coat and then eat the seed separately.

The species I would most recommend are:

E. cordifolia. See Plate 37. I only came across this plant in the spring of 1996 when I visited two Cornish gardens in the space of a week and both were growing it. As yet I have been unable to find any record of the species in any book on the genus. I have been told by Alistair Rivers, the curator of the County Demonstration Gardens at Probus in Cornwall that it was introduced into this country probably around 1900 from seed collected in China. Incidentally, if you are in Cornwall at any time then this is a very good garden to visit. It has a good collection of the evergreen *Elaeagnus* and April is a very good time to go there and see the plants in fruit.

This plant grows about 4 metres tall and wide. The hardiness has yet to be established, it certainly is perfectly hardy in Cornwall but I do not know of any other sites in the country where it is being grown. It is close to *E. glabra* (mentioned below) but has a greatly superior fruit that is usually borne in great abundance.

The fruit ripens perhaps a week earlier than any other species, usually from around the second week of April in Cornwall. It is about 20mm long and 14mm wide.

E. glabra. Growing to about 6 metres tall and wide. It does not like cold winters and can be badly damaged if temperatures drop below about -10°C. It is quite difficult to get hold of the true species in this country, plants given this name in nurseries more often being the hybrid *E. x reflexa*. The fruit is not always produced, but I have seen plants with good crops on a number of occasions. It is about 15mm long and 8mm wide, ripening about 3 weeks later than *E. cordifolia*.

E. macrophylla. This species grows about 3 metres tall and wide. The fruit seems to be rather variable in size and quality, though I have seen one plant with very good quality fruit about 18mm long and 12mm wide. It ripens perhaps a week or so after *E. cordifolia*.

E. pungens. Growing to about 4 metres tall and wide. The true species is rarely seen in cultivation, though there are many cultivars with variegated leaves that are widely grown. In general these do not fruit well, if at all, though 'Variegata' usually produces good crops, especially if grown with *E. x ebbingei*. It is probably a good pollinator for that species, though there needs to be more research into this. The fruit of this cultivar, unfortunately, is rather small and of poor quality.

E. x ebbingei. A hybrid species of garden origin, its parents are *E. macrophylla* and *E. pungens*. There is a hedge of this hybrid at Heathrow airport in the middle of the dual carriageway just after you come out of the tunnel that leads into the central area of the airport. I have been observing this hedge from time to time since 1989 and if you go to Heathrow in early April you will probably find it weighed down with fruit. The fruit is about 20mm long and perhaps 10mm wide, it contains one large seed. When fully ripe (about the middle of April at Heathrow) the fruit has a very pleasant rich flavour, though before this there is an astringency in the taste.

In April of 1994 I picked about 300 fruits in 5 minutes from the hedge at Heathrow (enough for a good sized meal, though I would not want to eat many of them from this site due to pollution) before being asked to leave the central reservation by a policeman who thought I might be a member of the IRA planting a bomb. I did offer him a fruit but he was not very interested.

Seriously, though, can you think of any other fresh fruit you could harvest outdoors in Britain at this time of year? It is also worth remembering that this species has only ever been developed for its ornamental value, fruit size or flavour has never been a consideration. There is a huge potential here for a new commercial fruit crop – not only that but you could grow it between trees in existing orchards so that it does not take up any extra space and the trees in the orchard will benefit as a result and give higher yields. Permaculture in a Nutshell! (to quote the title of an excellent little book of the same name by Patrick Whitefield).

There still needs to be a lot of research into this genus, I have seen plants giving reasonable crops in many sites, though never as good as *E. x ebbingei* at Heathrow or *E. cordifolia* in Cornwall. I believe that better crops can be obtained when there is cross pollination. The cultivar 'Gilt Edge', for example, seems to increase the crop on *E. x ebbingei*. It is quite clear that the plants must not be mollycoddled. They fruit much better when growing in poor soils and will scarcely flower at all if you feed them.

All these species flower mainly on wood of the current years growth and so can be successfully grown as a trimmed hedge as well as untrimmed. You simply trim at any time between harvesting the fruit and early July in order to encourage lots of fresh growth.

Ligustrum vulgare. PRIVET grows up to 3 metres tall and wide. This used to be **the** hedge plant, though it is used far less nowadays. A native semi-evergreen shrub, it is very amenable to trimming – indeed you will be trimming it very frequently if you do grow it. A very easily grown plant, it will succeed almost anywhere, though its greedy surface roots will impoverish the soil and retard the growth of nearby plants. It will make a medium to tall hedge depending on how much you want to cut it back. Space the plants about 60cm apart.

A poisonous plant, you can get a yellow dye from the leaves or bark, a bluish-green dye from the berries whilst a black dye that can also be obtained from the fruit is used as an ink. The young twigs are used in basketry and also in making hurdles (which can be used as temporary fences or screens).

A number of other species in this genus are grown for hedging. The following are more reliably evergreen, are quite fast-growing and have the same cultivation needs as *L. vulgare*:

L. ovalifolium. This can grow up to 10 metres tall and 3 metres wide.

L. lucidum. Growing to 4 metres tall and 3 metres wide.

Phormium tenax. NEW ZEALAND FLAX grows up to 3 metres tall and 2 metres wide. It has very long sword-shaped leaves growing in a fountain from the base and makes a good untrimmed hedge. It is tolerant of most soil conditions including boggy moorland and is able to withstand severe maritime conditions, though in windy weather its long leaves tend to bang together and can get quite noisy. Space the plants about 90cm apart.

The plant has a number of uses. It is probably best known for the very high quality pliable fibre obtained from the leaves, which is used in the manufacture of ropes, twine, fine cloth and paper. A thin strip of leaf is an excellent string substitute for tying up plants in the garden, it is so pliable and strong that it can be tied into a knot without breaking, though it won't be very permanent unless treated beforehand with tannin or some other preservative. The split leaves can be woven to make nets, cloaks, sandals and straps and are also used in basket making. A gum found in the leaves is used as a paper glue and a good light-fast brown dye that is obtained from the flowers does not require a mordant in order to fix it.

Taxus baccata. The YEW tree is extremely tolerant of trimming and makes an excellent if slow-growing hedge. The plants are often used in topiary and even when fairly old, the trees can be cut back into old wood and will resprout. One report says that trees up to 1,000 years old respond well to trimming so this is a hedge that you are planting for the generations to come. Space the plants about 60cm apart. See also page 44.

LARGE HEDGES

The following plants can be used to make hedges more than 2 metres tall. These species are often too large for the smaller gardens, though they might still be usefully employed there as a screen or noise barrier, especially at the northern end of the garden where they will not rob the garden of light.

In general, though, most of the species listed here are more appropriate for larger areas, where their size will not be overly dominant.

DECIDUOUS SPECIES

Corylus avellana. Our native HAZEL grows up to 6 metres tall and 3 metres wide. It succeeds in most soils and situations, doing well on chalk, and is less productive of nuts if grown in very rich or in poor soils. Nut production is best when the plant is in a fairly sunny, sheltered position, though it also does well in light shade and fairly windy sites. When grown as a hedge it is best left untrimmed if its edible seeds are to be produced in any quantity. It could then prove to be too big for many gardens. Space the plants about 75cm apart, though perhaps 1 - 1.5 metres apart if you are using cultivars and are not trimming.

Apart from being one of my favourite nuts, the seed is also a source of an edible oil and a wood polish whilst the wood is excellent for hurdles, wattle fencing and basketry. The named cultivars with their larger seeds can also be grown as hedges, though they are considerably more expensive to buy.

Hibiscus syriacus. See Plate 39. The ROSE OF SHARON grows up to 3 metres tall and 2 metres wide. This is a very ornamental shrub with beautiful large flowers that are not produced until well into the autumn. It grows best in a sunny position in a well-drained soil, though it likes its roots to be in the shade. Although hardy to about -20°C, it is not very suitable for the colder areas of the country because it rarely flowers there. Although it can be trimmed into a formal hedge it is best to leave it alone if you want to enjoy the flowers. Space the plants about 75cm apart.

These flowers make a delightful ornamental addition to salads and have a pleasant mild flavour with a hint of sweetness. The young leaves are also edible, they have a delicate nutty flavour though most people say they are rather bland. You do need to eat them young, though, because they soon become tough and fibrous. They make a very acceptable addition to mixed salads. An edible oil can be extracted from the seed, the leaves are used in making a hair shampoo and a blue dye is obtained from the flowers.

Prunus cerasifera. The CHERRY PLUM is a wind-resistant shrub or small tree growing up to 10 metres tall and wide. Whilst it can be trimmed, it is much better left to itself and so is really only suitable for larger plots of land. An easily grown plant, it will succeed in most soils, though it requires a sunny position if you want to obtain the fruit. Space the plants about 1 - 1.5 metres apart.

As the common name suggests, the fruit looks something like a cross between a cherry and a plum. It is about 3cm in diameter and has a very nice plum-like flavour, ripening in late summer and early autumn. It occasionally fruits abundantly in this country but is more often a disappointment.

EVERGREEN SPECIES

Pleioblastus simonii. MEDAKE is a very tough bamboo that will take all that the elements can throw at it. Established plants can be up to 6 metres tall and will spread freely at the roots if given the chance. They can be controlled fairly easily, however, by simply breaking off unwanted shoots whilst they are still small. Tolerant of maritime exposure, this bamboo can be grown as a tall hedge or screen. The growth habit of bamboos is such that the plants are very unsuitable for being trimmed. If you want to grow this plant, then you do have to accept is final height. Space the plants about 1 metre apart.

Unfortunately, whilst they are edible, the shoots are too bitter to be enjoyed. The canes are very strong, they make good plant supports and can also be used in various handicrafts. Unlike most bamboos, this species often flowers in Britain and sets viable seed.

Pseudosasa japonica. METAKE is another tough and vigorous bamboo that makes an excellent tall hedge or screen up to 4.5 metres tall even in exposed conditions. It can be a bit invasive with new canes popping up a metre or more away from the clump. Like the previous species, these can easily be broken off when still small to prevent the plant taking over the garden. Also like the previous species, it is unsuitable for trimming. Space the plants about 1 metre apart.

The young shoots are bitter but can be eaten when cooked, especially if you change the cooking water once or twice. The main drawback with this, though, is that along with the bitterness you are also pouring away many of the minerals and vitamins. The stems are fairly thick and strong so make good plant supports.

Semiarundinaria fastuosa. NARIHIRADAKE is a beautiful bamboo from Japan growing up to 7.5 metres tall. It makes an excellent tall hedge or screen, though it is rather slow to spread, and will need to be planted fairly close together (about 75 - 100cm should be all right) to ensure that it does not take too long to form a screen. This is one of the very few bamboos that will tolerate maritime exposure. I have seen it growing well on the north coast of Cornwall where it frequently experiences salt-laden winds, though it dislikes cold north or east winds.

The young shoots are quite small but they are almost free of any acridity and are very nice when cooked. Harvest them in April or May as they poke through the soil surface, but don't take too many as this would weaken the clump. Canes two years or more old can be used as plant supports.

SHELTERBELTS

If you live in a very windy site, and you have the space, than a shelterbelt will prove more effective than single lines of hedges. The main differences between a hedge and a shelterbelt are that shelterbelts take up much more space and are much taller. The idea is to plant out a fairly wide belt of 3 or more rows of trees and shrubs on the side of your land that faces the strongest winds. You start by planting smaller trees and shrubs on the windward side of the shelter, then planting larger species towards the centre and perhaps smaller ones again on the sheltered side. The taller trees will help to give some protection to the smaller plants on the windy side of the shelterbelt. These smaller plants will also be giving protection to the taller trees. Thus the structure is more wind-tolerant than a single line of hedging and is less likely to be damaged in strong winds.

Because a shelterbelt does not allow as much air to flow through it as a well-designed hedge, it does not reduce the overall windspeed as effectively or for such a distance as a hedge. Thus it is a very good idea to have the shelterbelt as your first line of defence, but to then have hedges strategically placed on the land to provide additional protection.

This shelterbelt can be used as a woodland garden as it matures (see Chapter 3 for some ideas on what you could plant in it and on the sheltered side of it) so it is not wasted land. Many of the trees used in the shelterbelt can also have other uses as will be shown below.

Don't be tempted to plant large trees in a windy site in the belief that it will take less time to produce a good shelterbelt. You will be wasting your money. As an example of this, when we moved onto our windy site we planted out a number of sweet chestnut trees (*Castanea sativa*). Most of these were small seedlings, but we also had two specimens of the cultivar 'Marron de Lyon' that were 2 metres tall. Over the next 4 years the seedlings grew away strongly, but the 'Marron de Lyon' actually got smaller as their root systems failed to keep up with the extra demands of the top growth in a windy site. Eventually these cultivars had so much die-back that they were only 1 - 1.5 metres tall. Then they started to produce new growth from lower down the trunk and, in the last 3 years have started to grow away well. They are smaller than our seedling trees now, but are looking healthy and actually bore a small crop of seeds in 1996.

It is far better to plant out very small trees, preferably only one year old, than to plant out large specimens. As well as being a good deal cheaper, they will establish themselves much more rapidly, will develop a better root system, will not need staking and after a few years will actually be taller and better shaped than the other trees. Just make sure that you plant them well and give them a really good mulch to keep down the weeds, plus protection from rabbits, mice etc. See page 20 for more details.

If possible, do not use a tree shelter since this encourages too rapid a growth from the stems which will be out of balance with the roots. The stems will also be too thin since they would not have had the stimulus of the wind rocking them (which encourages them to thicken) and these two factors combined will lead to a relatively high percentage of the trees being wind-blown before they reach maturity. On top of all that, as soon as the shoots stick their tops out of the tree shelters they will be cut to pieces by the wind. Save your money and give the trees a relatively hard time, they will grow all the better for it.

When planting the shelterbelt, space the rows 2 - 4 metres apart with the smaller trees and shrubs 70 - 150cm apart in the rows and the taller trees about 2 metres apart. As the trees grow larger you will probably need to thin them – do not leave this too late or you will encourage too much height growth and not enough side branching lower down.

A number of the hedge plants mentioned earlier in this chapter are suitable for planting on the windward side of the shelterbelt (look for comments on wind-resistance), the following are some of the trees you could grow in it.

DECIDUOUS SPECIES

Acer pseudo-platanus. SYCAMORE is a fast-growing tree capable of reaching 30 metres in height with a spread of 15 metres. It is very wind resistant, tolerating maritime exposure, but will often be wind-pruned when growing in severely exposed sites.

You can tap the sap in a similar way to sugar maples though there is considerably less sugar in the sap and so if you want to concentrate it into a syrup the yields are much lower. If you bake foods in sycamore leaves than the leaves will impart a sweet flavour to the food. The fallen leaves can be used as a packing material for storing apples, rootcrops etc., helping to reduce rotting.

Whilst sycamore is one of the toughest trees going, and is certainly worthy of inclusion in planting schemes for difficult sites, there are a number of negative factors to take into account. It is a tree that likes to be in control of the land and therefore secretes chemicals that inhibit the growth of other species. It has a very dense canopy and heavy autumn leaf-fall, which also tends to discourage other plants from growing with it. It also produces seeds very freely and the seedlings will grow away very quickly. There is some fear that the trees could out-compete our native woodland trees such as oak, ash and beech, but fairly recent research by the Forestry Commission has shown that although this might be true in the short term, over a period of 200 years or so our native species gradually establish themselves and the sycamore becomes a minor part of the woodland.

When we planted a 6 hectare woodland on our very windy site in Cornwall, the Forestry Commission insisted that we include 10% sycamore, so that it would grow away quickly and provide shelter for the other woodland trees. Funnily enough, the sycamore has been one of the least successful trees in the woodland. In the first 3 years it only grew about 30cm in total and even the supposedly slow-growing oaks easily beat this. It has sped up in the last couple of years, though is still one of the poorer doers in the woodland. Although our land is very well-drained, the moisture-loving native alders (see the next entry) have put on more than 5 metres growth in just 5 years! We are just sorry that we planted over 1,000 sycamores and only 150 alders, it should have been the other way round.

***Alnus* species**. ALDERS are very fast-growing trees, most of which grow best in a moist or wet soil. They succeed even in severe maritime exposure and will show little sign of wind damage. Nitrogen nodules are formed on the roots due to the action of soil bacteria and, as well as helping the alder to grow more rapidly, also provide nutriment for other plants.

   A. glutinosa. A native alder, some of which we planted out when 15cm tall are now over 5 metres tall after just 5 growing seasons. Mature plants can reach up to 20 metres tall with a spread of 15 metres. Although our soil is too dry really for this species to thrive in the long term, by the time it dies it will have done its job of providing enough shelter in the woodland to allow the slower-growing but longer-lived trees to become established. This species has already been mentioned in the section on hedges above, though it could equally well fit in here.

   A. cordata. The ITALIAN ALDER is another good species to try, with an eventual height of about 25 metres and a spread of 8 metres. It tolerates much drier soils than most members of the genus and has put on about 5 metres of growth in 5 years with us.

   A. rubra. The RED ALDER is the fastest growing species we have to date. Some of these plants in an exposed position have put on 7 metres of growth in just 5 growing seasons whilst a couple in a more sheltered position were almost 9 metres tall in the same time. Their maximum height is said to be about 18 metres, though by the way they are growing they will quite possibly exceed that.

Amelanchier canadensis. A suckering tree growing about 6 metres tall and 3 metres wide. It tolerates quite considerable exposure, though will not be very happy in severe conditions. It produces a delicious edible fruit in July. See also page 38.

Fraxinus excelsior. Our native ASH TREE is quite fast-growing and capable of reaching a final height of about 30 metres with a spread of 20 metres. It comes into leaf very late in spring, has a light canopy and is also one of the first trees to lose its leaves in the autumn – this makes it quite a good top-storey tree for a woodland garden. However, it is also quite a greedy tree with surface roots so it will be difficult to establish other plants under a mature specimen. Although it grows well right by the coast, in severely exposed areas it will usually be wind-pruned.

   The wood of this tree is very strong and elastic which makes it excellent for the handles of hoes, axes and other garden tools. The wood is also a very good fuel when properly seasoned. Many books say that it burns well even when still green, but a friend who has a lot of experience with burning wood tells me that this is a myth.

***Populus* species**. POPLARS are in general fast-growing trees, many of which are wind tolerant though few are happy with maritime exposure or in exposed upland sites. They need a rich moist soil if they are to grow well. Their aggressive root system makes them unsuitable for planting near buildings though this can be turned to advantage on the right site since the root system is good for binding soils and preventing erosion.

   An extract of the shoots, made by soaking the chopped up shoots in cold water for a day can be used as a rooting hormone for all types of cuttings. The following species all do well in windy sites:

P. alba. The WHITE POPLAR is the only species fully at home with maritime exposure. It can be up to 20 metres tall and 12 metres wide. It thrives in much drier soils than other members of the genus and does well in both hot or cold summers.

P. nigra. The BLACK POPLAR is a native species that can reach 30 metres in height with a spread of 20 metres. The cultivar 'Italica' is commonly used as a windbreak tree though it is not a very suitable choice because it has fragile branches and is prone to basal rots which can cause sudden collapse. The cultivar 'Plantierensis' is much more suitable.

P. tremula. The ASPEN is another native tree. This species succeeds on poor soils and will eventually reach about 18 metres in height with a spread of 10 metres. It produces lots of suckers and forms thickets. The sub-species *P. tremula davidiana* is very tolerant of alkaline soils.

P. x canadensis. This can reach 40 metres tall with a spread of 12 metres. The cultivar 'Robusta' is most commonly used in shelterbelt plantings.

Salix **species.** Many WILLOWS are excellent in shelterbelts. Very fast-growing trees, they demand a moist fertile soil if they are to do well and their aggressive root systems are often used of to stabilise soils, especially along the banks of streams. The branches of all the species of willows mentioned below are very flexible and they are used in making baskets. Some species and hybrids are being used in biomass plantings to provide fuel for power stations or organic matter for the compost heap – they are normally coppiced annually for this purpose. Like the poplars mentioned above, an extract of the shoots is used as a rooting hormone.

The following species are growing very well with us:

S. alba. The WHITE WILLOW is a native species that can reach 25 metres tall with a spread of 10 metres. It is rather slow for its first year or two, but then grows away rapidly.

S. daphnoides. The VIOLET WILLOW reaches about 10 metres tall with a spread of 8 metres. It can put on 2 metres of growth in a year, even in its first year of growth from a cutting.

S. pentandra. The BAY WILLOW grows about 10 metres tall and wide.

S. purpurea. The PURPLE OSIER reaches about 5 metres tall and wide. Its bark is so bitter that rabbits will not touch it, so it can be woven into a living fence to serve as a barrier.

S. triandra. The ALMOND-LEAVED WILLOW can be 9 metres tall and 6 metres wide. It has slightly fragrant flowers, which is very unusual for a willow.

S. viminalis. The OSIER reaches about 6 metres in height with a width of 4 metres. This is one of the main basket-making species.

S. 'Bowles hybrid'. See Plate 41. A hybrid that has been exceptionally fast-growing with us, reaching 4 metres in height in 3 years from cuttings even though it is in a very exposed position. It will reach a final height of about 8 metres with a spread of 5 metres.

It is possible to plant out cuttings of willows direct into their permanent positions during the winter. Indeed, this is the easiest and most certain way of establishing the plants because they do not like root disturbance. Any size of cutting, from 30cm up to 2.5 metres can succeed – give the cuttings a good mulch so as to keep down weeds and then stand well back and watch them grow.

Sorbus **species** are discussed more fully on page 30. Two members of the genus are particularly good in shelterbelts:

S. aria. The WHITEBEAM grows about 12 metres tall and 8 metres wide. Very easily grown on most soils, though it does particularly well on chalky soils. A bit on the slow side, but it succeeds in all types of exposure.

S. aucuparia. The ROWAN is a very tough creature that can grow 15 metres tall and 7 metres wide, and will succeed in the most exposed sites. It will grow in most soils though is intolerant of shallow soils or drought.

EVERGREEN SPECIES

Cupressocyparis leylandii. LEYLAND CYPRESS has been much overplanted as a hedge for small gardens in recent years, especially when you consider its ultimate height might be as much as 60 metres with a width of perhaps 8 metres. However, as a shelterbelt tree on a large site it is excellent. Fast growing and standing up to almost anything the weather can throw at them, our trees have been increasing in height by about 80cm a year since we planted them.

Although this species does not offer much in the way of food for us or wildlife, recent studies have shown that Leyland cypress is a popular nesting site for many species of birds, simply because it can offer them a nice secluded place in which to shelter. We had birds building their nests in them just 3 years after planting them out.

Pinus **species**. Most PINES are fairly wind resistant though many of them are too slow to be used in a shelterbelt. The following species grow best on acid soils, preferring a light, well-drained gravelly loam. Once established they are very drought tolerant. They all succeed in maritime exposure. They are a bit anti-social with leaf secretions inhibiting the germination of seeds, thereby restricting the growth of other plants below them.

P. flexilis. The LIMBER PINE has a deep tap-root that anchors it firmly, it does very well on exposed mountain slopes. After a slow start, it grows fairly quickly in Britain with increases in height of over 30cm a year being recorded. It can eventually reach 25 metres in height. This is the only species in this list with a seed large enough to bother about for eating. It is up to 11mm long and 9mm wide and eaten raw it has a delicious flavour with a hint of resin. The seeds can also be ground into a flour and used in making bread, biscuits and as a thickener in soups.

P. muricata. The BISHOP'S PINE grows about 20 metres tall with a spread of 6 metres. It grows quickly on barren acidic sandy soils, with annual growths of 1.8 metres being recorded for young trees. Mature trees produce a broad heavy crown and are somewhat likely to be blown down in severe gales. This species is not hardy in the colder areas of the country, it tolerates temperatures down to about -10°C.

P. nigra. The AUSTRIAN PINE can grow 30 metres tall with a spread of 8 metres. This is one of the few pine species that succeeds on chalk. It is extremely resistant to maritime exposure and has survived winds of 150 kilometres per hour with no sign of damage.

P. radiata. The MONTEREY PINE can eventually reach 65 metres in height with a spread of 10 metres. It won't take that long to get there either, because young trees can put on 2.5 metres or more new growth each year in the milder areas of the country. It is a bit slower away from these milder areas and is not hardy in the colder parts of Britain. Mature trees produce a broad heavy crown and are somewhat likely to be blown down in severe gales. Plants can produce new shoots from reasonably old wood so the lower branches can be cut back if required to produce a hedge-like effect.

A number of other species with larger, edible seeds are discussed on page 34. In general they are not so suitable for use in shelterbelts.

Quercus ilex. Although slow growing, the HOLM OAK eventually reaches 25 metres tall and 20 metres wide. It makes a superb evergreen shelterbelt tree that is very tolerant of maritime exposure. See also page 36.

Chapter Ten

GROUND COVER

When people take up gardening, whatever methods they may use, their usual aim is to grow a wide range of plants very few of which would usually be found wild on their land. It is wise to try and use those species that are best adapted to the conditions of the particular site but, gardeners being gardeners, we generally want to try and grow a wider range of plants than this. This means that many of these plants are at a general disadvantage on the site and the tendency is for the native species to re-establish themselves. Thus begins the long preoccupation with weeding, the constant battle to maintain those plants we want to grow at the expense of the plants that want to grow there.

There are many ways of trying to control weeds or at least to be able to live with them. We could, for example, just leave all the plants to fight it out between themselves. Unless we introduced something like Japanese knotweed, the natives would almost certainly eventually win and, over a period of many years, the land would gradually revert to native woodland. This is a valid and very interesting method of gardening, and is certainly very beneficial to the native wildlife, but we normally want to exert more control over our land than this.

We can remove the weeds by pulling or hoeing them out, or by burning them with a flame gun. We can try to prevent them growing by putting down mulches. In the long term we can change the nature of the environment (by planting native or exotic trees for example) and thereby put the weeds at a disadvantage (though other weeds suited to the new environment will then find their way in). We can grow very vigorous plants and let battle begin between them and the weeds. Each of these methods has its advantages and disadvantages and each have situations where they are applicable. In this chapter we will look at another method of controlling weeds – by growing carefully selected plants that can spread to cover the ground and thereby prevent the weeds from being able to establish themselves.

Like other forms of weed control, ground cover has its advantages and disadvantages. Its primary advantages include:

1. By covering the ground with a carpet of vegetation it can greatly reduce or even prevent the germination of weed seeds.

2. When established, it can prevent the ingress of perennial weeds.

3. It protects the soil from erosion by wind or rain and water loss due to wind or evaporation. This can be particularly important on steep slopes.

4. It acts as an insulating cover for the soil, keeping it cooler in the summer and warmer in the winter. This can be especially useful for other plants, lilies for example, that we might want to grow through the ground cover.

5. One of the biggest problems with hoeing is that this promotes the breakdown of organic matter in the disturbed soil. A ground cover is a living mulch that helps to build up the organic content of the soil and reduces the leaching of nutrients.

6. It provides habitats and cover for beneficial insects and other predators.

7. It can be very attractive.

8. It can provide us with various other commodities such as food and thus make the ground more productive by allowing two crops to be grown on the same piece of land.

The main disadvantages include:

1. It can provide a habitat for slugs, snails and other pests. This is to a large extent mitigated by the beneficial creatures it also encourages, but it is best not to grow slug-susceptible plants in a ground cover if you normally have a problem with slugs.

2. It can compete with other plants for food and water. Where possible grow a ground cover that does not compete with the other plants you are growing. For example, if you have a ground cover with shallow roots (which is the case with most ground cover plants), grow it with deep-rooting plants.

3. If the ground cover is too vigorous it can overrun the plants you want to grow.

As long as the above factors are taken into account, it is possible to choose ground cover plants that will greatly reduce the work-load of weeding whilst also benefiting the other plants you want to grow.

One important point to remember about ground cover is that it is only an effective weed-suppresser once it is established. In virtually all cases you need to plant into a soil that is free from perennial weeds. You will also need to weed the plants until they are established, which is usually 1 - 3 growing seasons. As many gardeners (including myself) have found out to their cost, if you plant ground cover into a weedy soil you will actually increase your difficulties because you will then have to spend lots of time pulling out all the weeds by hand, often for a number of years until the ground cover can assert itself.

One fairly simple way around this is to put a barrier mulch on top of the soil and then plant into this. Choose a material such as newspaper that will break down after a couple of years, apply a **thick** covering of the newspaper and make sure you overlap it well – 8cm is a good minimum. Then put 5 - 10cm of well-rotted organic matter on top of the newspaper and plant into this. By the time the newspaper has broken down the weeds below it should have died off and the ground cover plant, which should be well established by now, will be rooting through the mulch and into the soil. The main disadvantage of this method is finding enough organic matter to cover the newspaper.

Ground cover plants can be deciduous or evergreen. Since they keep their leaves all year round, the evergreen species will tend to give a better protection to the soil whilst also being more effective at preventing the growth of weeds. Many deciduous species, however, produce such a dense growth in the summer that they will soon out-compete any seedlings that have tried to get growing during the winter. They can also have such vigorous root systems that other plants will fail to become established. The dead leaves of many deciduous species will also serve as an effective weed-suppressing mulch in the winter.

Spring is a good time for planting most of the species mentioned below. Planting distances depend upon the vigour of the plants – very fast-growing species can often be planted as much as 1 metre or more apart whilst slower plants might need to be 15cm apart. Most ground covers spread quite freely and are easily divided so, if the cost of planting out a large area is too prohibitive, it is possible to plant out a small section and then divide the plants annually so that you can quickly increase the size of the planted area.

In ideal circumstances the ground cover will be planted either at the same time as the other plants, or some time afterwards. There will be plenty of occasions when you will want to put a taller plant into an area where the ground cover is already well established. In such a situation it can be very difficult for the new plant to become established and so you might need to give it special attention. A good way of doing this is to carefully remove all the roots of the ground cover plant when digging your planting hole – make this hole a bit wider than normal. Then line the walls of the hole with a thick organic barrier such as newspaper. This will serve as a barrier for a few months to allow the new plant to become somewhat established.

Ground cover can be used in various situations. It is probably pre-eminently suitable under and around trees and shrubs and there is a very wide range of plants that can be used in such situations. Another good use is as a companion for bulbs. Lilies, for example, like the cooler soil conditions created by the ground cover and can easily grow through the carpet of vegetation if an appropriate ground cover has been chosen. Steep banks are another suitable position. The root system of the plants helps to bind the soil and this, together with the foliage, prevents soil erosion.

Ground cover can also be used with herbaceous perennials, though greater care is required here in the choice of plants in order to make sure that they do not out-compete the perennials. There are also successful methods of using ground cover with annuals (the Bonfils method of growing cereals for example) though in general I have found ground cover and annuals do not do well together.

Now we come to a list of species that can be used for ground cover. When I talk about a plant's edible and other uses in this list then remember that this is really a secondary use, ground cover and weed exclusion being the prime purpose.

In general you should not expect high yields from these plants – though there are exceptions of course. However, since you will be growing these plants amongst your other crops, then their yields can be seen as an added bonus.

This chapter contains a rather diverse collection of plants with a wide range of needs. I have divided up the lists below according to habitat, habit and size. If there are no cultivation notes then the plant will succeed in any reasonable well-drained soil.

PLANTS FOR SUNNY POSITIONS

The species in these lists grow best in a sunny position, though many of them will also tolerate at least some shade. This will be mentioned where appropriate. They are listed in order of the likely height they will attain, starting with the lowest growing species.

DECIDUOUS HERBACEOUS PERENNIALS

Mentha pulegium. PENNYROYAL is a low-growing member of the mint family, spreading fairly freely at the roots. It dislikes dry soils and grows best in a sunny position, though it is not too fussy.

The leaves have a pleasant spearmint flavour and can be used as a flavouring in salads or cooked foods. The leaves should not be eaten by pregnant women, however, because they can induce an abortion. The growing or dried plant is a good insect repellent and is said to be particularly effective against ants.

We have two quite distinct forms of this species. One is very upright, to 40cm tall, and does not spread very freely. The other is no more than 8cm tall even when in flower and spreads very well to form mats about 40cm across within its first growing season, though it can become bare in the centre. This is the form we would most recommend for ground cover.

Fragaria species. There are many species of STRAWBERRY that can be used for ground cover, just look for those species that make a lot of runners. Some of them have exquisitely flavoured fruits, though they are somewhat smaller than the cultivated strawberries and are often not borne freely. My favourites are:

F. moschata. The MUSK STRAWBERRY grows up to 45cm tall and spreads very freely. Plant it with a 30cm spacing in late summer and the ground will be covered by the end of the next growing season. The fruit ripens in July and is about 15mm in diameter. It is borne low down on the plant and so is rather fiddly to find. This is an ideal plant for getting rid of the children for an hour or so – simply tell them they can have as many strawberries as they want and let them loose amongst the plants.

F. viridis. The GREEN STRAWBERRY is similar to the above but only grows 30cm tall. The fruit is carried towards the top of the plant and so is easier to harvest.

Both of these species have deliciously aromatic fruits but these are not produced very freely. They fruit best in a sunny position but also tolerate some shade and grow well under shrubs.

The cultivated strawberries could also be used as a ground cover but, since they are likely to suffer from virus diseases after a few years, I would not recommend them for this purpose.

Rubus illecebrosus. The STRAWBERRY RASPBERRY has a large fruit up to 40mm long that, not surprisingly, looks rather like a cross between a strawberry and a raspberry. It ripens in mid to late summer and looks delicious. It is, however, rather bland raw, though the flavour is said to improve when it is cooked.

The plant grows about 50cm or more tall and spreads freely by suckers once it is established. Plant it about 30cm apart and it will fill the space in its third growing season. Although technically this is a shrub, it dies down completely in the winter and does not leave any woody stems above ground level. Therefore I have included it here. It has not proved a very effective weed suppresser with us yet, though I have seen it doing a better job in other gardens.

Houttuynia cordata. This is a rampant herbaceous plant, spreading rapidly by suckers and growing about 60cm tall. It dies right down in the winter and, although it makes a nice summer ground cover, it has not proved to be an effective weed suppresser with us. It succeeds in moist and wet soils as well as in shallow water. In drier soils it will not spread very freely.

According to reports that I have read, the plant has a smell reminiscent of rotten fish. Now I don't know what sort of nose the person who penned that report has, but the plants we are growing have a very strong and pleasant scent of oranges. It is not just my imagination (which can be quite vivid when it comes to alternative foods), since for the last year or so the plant has been compulsory smelling for any visitors to our land. The leaves can be eaten raw and are one of our favourite flavourings in mixed salads. They normally have a pleasant flavour of orange peel, though at other times the same plants are not so pleasant with a distinct bitterness. I have yet to work out why this should be, it is possibly because the ground we are growing them in is not moist enough.

There are a number of very ornamental forms with multi-coloured leaves, I have only tried eating 'Chameleon' so far and this also has a pleasant orange flavour. Perhaps some of the other cultivars smell of rotten fish!

Origanum vulgare. OREGANO is a very dense growing native perennial plant for sunny positions. It forms clumps about 60cm tall and makes a good ground cover though it is rather slow to spread and will need to be planted about 30cm apart. It will fill the space in its third growing season.

An excellent aromatic flavouring for cooked foods and salads, it is also a very good companion plant and is said to repel insects from its neighbours. An essential oil from the plant is used in soaps and perfumery and also as a food flavouring. The whole plant was formerly used as a strewing herb in order to make houses smell sweet whilst also repelling insects.

O. vulgare hirtum. A sub-species which comes from Greece and is considerably more aromatic – this is the form we prefer as a food flavouring.

The ornamental cultivar 'Aurea' has golden-yellow leaves. This is a lower-growing plant, to about 30cm tall. It also spreads more freely with us and planted at 30cm spacing can fill the ground in the second growing season.

EVERGREEN HERBACEOUS PERENNIALS

Mentha requienii. The CORSICAN MINT is no more than a centimetre or two tall even when flowering and forms a gradually spreading mat. When growing it for ground cover it should be planted about 25cm apart each way and will fill the space in its second year. It should be a suitable ground cover for growing bulbs through, though we have not tried this.

A deliciously aromatic plant, it can be used in the same ways as Pennyroyal, see *Mentha pulegium* earlier in this chapter.

Chamaemelum nobile. CAMOMILE is a superb companion plant that enhances the health of its neighbours whilst helping to repel insects. It is also very suitable for growing with many species of bulbs. See also Chapter 1.

The cultivar 'Treneague' is a non-flowering form that remains compact and spreads slowly by short runners to form a good evergreen ground cover in a sunny position. It grows about 2cm tall and should be planted no more than 15cm apart if growing it as a ground cover. It will need quite a bit of weeding until it is established, and fairly regular weeding even when established, since it never becomes dense enough to prevent seeds germinating or the ingress of perennial weeds. See page 142 for its use in lawns.

Sedum **species**. There are many members of this genus that can be used as low ground cover for sunny positions. They spread fairly freely at the roots and reach a height of 2 - 15cm. They are all very drought tolerant, growing well on hot dry banks and in poor soils. Many species of bulbs will grow well with them.

Their leaves are edible raw or cooked, but they are not the most appetizing leaves I have ever eaten. The following species are worth trying:

S. acre. COMMON STONECROP grows about 5cm tall and spreads fairly quickly. Plant it about 20cm apart and it should have filled the area by the end of its second growing season. The leaves have an acrid flavour, though they are rich in vitamin C. When dried into a powder they make a spicy seasoning. Introduce this species with some caution because it can become a pest and is very difficult to get rid of. Even a single leaf left behind is capable of producing roots and growing into a new plant.

S. spathulifolium. Growing to about 5cm tall. Plant them about 30cm apart.

S. spurium. Growing up to 15cm tall when in flower. Plant them about 30cm apart.

Campanula poscharskyana. This lovely little HAREBELL grows about 25cm tall and spreads very rapidly at the roots to form an excellent ground cover. It grows well in dry soils and is very drought tolerant. Planted 25cm apart, it will fill the ground in its second season.

The leaves are fairly small but they have a mild sweet flavour, are produced freely and can be harvested all year round to be used in salads. The texture is a bit tough, dry and powdery, though, so I only use it as part of a mixed salad. It is especially valuable for winter use. The flowers are sweet and tender, they make a very attractive addition to salads.

C. portenschlagiana. See Plate 42. This has smaller leaves than the above species, otherwise it has similar needs and uses. I feel that the flavour is inferior to the foregoing species, though it seems to be a tougher plant.

Peltaria alliacea. GARLIC CRESS grows about 30cm tall and spreads freely at the roots to form large clumps. It prefers a light soil and will also succeed in light shade. Planted 25cm apart each way, it should fill the space in its second growing season.

The leaves taste, not surprisingly, like a cross between garlic and cress with a slight but not unpleasant bitterness. They are available almost all year round, disappearing for a few weeks in the summer when the plant is in flower. At this time you simply use the flowers, since they have the same flavour as the leaves. They are too strong for most people to be able to eat them in quantity, but they make an excellent flavouring in salads or cooked foods. In hot or dry weather in the summer they develop a stronger, more bitter flavour. It is at this time that plants in the shade prove their value.

We have been growing this plant for a number of years from a division originally supplied to us. This has been a bit slow to spread, but in the spring of 1993 we obtained some seed from Liege Botanic Gardens. Most seedlings grew away well and we have found that there is a very wide range, both in the flavour of the leaves and in the speed with which plants spread. The best tasting plants are also the fastest growing, which is a very nice combination for us. These superior forms are spreading quickly and look as though they are going to be an excellent ground cover as well as a productive source of leaves. Garlic cress prefers a light soil and a sunny position.

DECIDUOUS SHRUBS

Vaccinium praestans. The KAMCHATKA BILBERRY grows about 15cm tall and spreads slowly by means of suckers to form clumps 30cm or more wide. It requires a moist but free-draining lime free soil, preferring one that is rich in peat or a light loamy soil with added leaf-mould. It succeeds in full sun or in light shade though it fruits better when growing in a sunny position. It requires shelter from strong winds. When growing as a ground cover, space the plants 25cm apart each way and they should fill in the gaps in their second or third growing season.

In Britain the plants grow better in northern England and Scotland, while in the south they need a position with plenty of light but little direct sun.

The fruit is about 12mm in diameter and ripens in mid to late summer. It is sweet and fragrant and has a delicious flavour that tastes somewhat like a strawberry.

EVERGREEN SHRUBS

Myrtus nummularia. Growing to about 10cm tall and forming a pretty carpet of growth 50cm or more wide. A fairly easily grown plant, it does well in dry soils and is tolerant of maritime exposure. It grows very well in London and in many other places in southern Britain, but is not hardy in the colder parts of the country. Plant it 45cm apart when growing it for ground cover. It will fill the space in its second or third growing season.

This plant only just made it into the book because I first came across its edible fruits in December 1996 just before sending the manuscript off to the publishers. This fruit is up to 10mm in diameter, it has a soft, juicy flesh and a sweet and agreeable slightly aromatic flavour. This is a fruit for the connoisseur. The plants are too small ever to produce abundantly but what a treat for the senses to be able to pick and eat a fruit of this quality fresh from the garden in early winter.

Arctostaphylos uva-ursi. BEARBERRY is a slow-growing plant reaching about 10cm tall and forming a spreading carpet that is eventually 1 metre or more wide. A good plant for sunny banks, it also tolerates light shade and requires an acid soil. Plant it about 50cm apart. It will be somewhat slow to get going, but will be providing a good cover in its third growing season.

The fruit is about 6mm in diameter and ripens from mid to late summer. Whilst it is edible, it is far from being exciting, having an insipid flavour with a dry and mealy texture. It becomes sweeter when cooked and has been added to soups and stews where it is said to be a good carbohydrate source. The dried fruits can be used in rattles and as beads, this is possibly a better use than eating them! The dried leaves make a pleasant tea and a yellowish-brown dye that is obtained from the leaves does not require a mordant in order to fix it. The form 'Massachusetts' is an especially prostrate, free-flowering and free-fruiting cultivar.

Rubus **species**. There are several members of this genus that can be grown for ground cover in sun or light shade and can also provide edible fruits. The following are some of the best for a sunny position.

Rubus nepalensis. The NEPALESE RASPBERRY is one of our favourite ground covers. The plant, which looks somewhat like a strawberry at first glance, is only about 10cm tall but spreads freely by rooting at intervals along the prostrate stems. It forms a good carpet that is fairly effective at excluding weeds so long as you remove the perennials first (which I did not do!). It requires shelter from strong winds and grows well in light shade. It strongly dislikes dry conditions.

There is some disagreement about its hardiness – some reports say that it is only hardy in the mildest areas of the country though I have seen it growing and thriving in Cambridgeshire, where the winters can be pretty cold. It will often lose its leaves in cold winters, but usually grows back strongly in the spring. Space it every 30cm when growing it for ground cover and it will fill the space in its second season.

The fruit is ripe from July to September and is somewhat smaller than the cultivated raspberry with a very pleasant acid flavour. In a good year the yields can be fairly high, though they are often a disappointment.

We have a number of different clones of this species. All of them flower well, some of them also usually produce a good crop of well-formed fruits but a number of the clones are very disappointing and only produce small misshapen fruits. Make sure you see the plant in fruit before you buy it.

R. calycinoides. Growing to about 10cm tall and spreading freely by suckers. A very tolerant and easily grown plant, it does well in dry conditions and in full shade. The plants are evergreen in most climates but they can lose their leaves in severe winters. Planted about 50cm apart each way, it soon makes a thickly matted carpet that is a very effective weed excluder.

This species is occasionally cultivated in some countries for its edible fruit, which ripens in mid summer. There are some named varieties. 'Emerald Carpet' is an ornamental thornless form with orange berries that resemble small raspberries.

Thymus **species**. THYMES are very drought tolerant plants for sunny positions, doing well in dry soils and spreading slowly by self-layering stems. Any of the species of low-growing plants can be used for ground cover, planted at about 25cm spacing. They should fill their allotted space in the second or third growing season. See also page 168.

Vaccinium vitis-idaea. The COWBERRY spreads by underground runners and, although it is rather slow at first, it will eventually reach about 25cm tall and up to 1 metre wide. It requires a sheltered position in an acid soil and does well in full sun or the light shade of a coniferous woodland. Planted at 30cm spacing, it should fill the space in its second or third growing season.

The fruit, which ripens in the autumn and is about 6mm in diameter, can be eaten raw or cooked. It has a pleasant acid flavour and is used like cranberries in preserves – indeed many people consider it to be superior to cranberries. The taste is better after a frost and the fruit hangs on the plant all winter if it is not picked. The cultivar 'Koralle' has large and conspicuous berries.

Empetrum nigrum. The CROWBERRY is a native evergreen shrub growing about 30cm tall and spreading slowly. It requires an acid soil and is very wind-resistant so does well in exposed positions, making a good ground cover when planted about 25cm apart each way.

The fruit is about 8mm in diameter, it ripens in early autumn and can hang on the plant all winter if the birds leave it alone. It is not highly flavoured when eaten raw, but is acceptable after a frost and can be used in making jams and drinks. A purple dye can also be obtained from it. You usually need to grow both male and female plants if fruit is required, though occasionally self-fertile plants with hermaphrodite flowers are found. Most, if not all, other members of this genus can be used in a similar way.

Vinca **species**. These plants do very well in full sun as well as in deep shade. Because they are woodland plants, they are discussed in the section below on plants for shade.

PLANTS FOR SHADE

The following species grow best in a shady position, though many of them will also succeed in fairly sunny positions. This will be mentioned where appropriate. They are listed in order of their likely height, starting with the lowest growing species.

DECIDUOUS HERBACEOUS PERENNIALS

Asarum canadense. SNAKE ROOT grows about 10cm tall with a spread of perhaps 50cm. It does well in the light shade of a woodland, though it will also succeed under shrubs in the garden. It spreads slowly at the roots and, planted 25cm apart, should fill the space in its second year. Snake root requires a moist humus-rich soil, but keep it away from the slugs since they regard it as a gourmet's delicacy.

Both the flowers and the fresh or dried root can be used as a ginger substitute. The root can be harvested all year round but is best in the autumn.

Chrysosplenium alternifolium and *C. oppositifolium*. GOLDEN SAXIFRAGES are native perennials for the bog garden or areas of constantly moist soil, preferring acid conditions. They grow 15 - 30cm tall and spread fairly freely at the roots. They make a good ground cover in wet woodlands and are best planted 30cm apart. See also page 136.

Hosta species. Most, if not all, HOSTAS can be used for ground cover. Their rosettes of leaves make an attractive carpet about 20cm tall, whilst their flowering stems range in height from 20 - 100cm. They form slowly spreading clumps and are best planted about 20cm apart each way. Although they die down in the winter, their summer growth is so vigorous that they are very effective weed suppressers. All the species succeed in woodland conditions (where they produce better foliage but don't flower so freely) as well as in sunny positions (where they flower better but the leaves can get scorched). The plants are rather susceptible to slug damage, especially when young – a mulch of well-rotted oak leaf-mould will help protect them.

The petioles (leaf stems) can be eaten raw or cooked. So far I have only eaten *H. crispula* and *H. longipes*, which are somewhat fibrous but have a sweet flavour.

Cornus canadensis. CREEPING DOGWOOD grows well in light acid woodlands, including amongst conifers. The plant grows about 25cm tall and spreads quickly at the roots when it is well-suited, but it does not like alkaline soils. Rather slow in its first year or two, the plant has been known to spread 60cm or more per year once established. Plant it at 50 - 100cm spacing according to your budget.

The fruit is about 6mm in diameter and ripens in late summer and early autumn. It has a pleasant taste, though it is not highly flavoured, and can be eaten raw or cooked. Rich in pectin, it is suitable for adding to low-pectin fruits when making jam. Pectin is also said to protect the body from the harmful effects of radiation so, with the depletion of the ozone layer, perhaps we should all be eating pectin-rich fruits.

Plate 33. *Orchis mascula*. The EARLY PURPLE ORCHID is a stunning flower with a highly nutritious bulb. But don't dig it up from the wild! See page 82. Photo: Tim Harland.

Plate 34. *A Flowering Lawn*. A lawn can be a play area, but it can be so much more...
A wide variety of pretty and edible plants can also be grown there. See Chapter 7.

Plate 35. *Physalis peruviana*. Growing in its own 'paper bag', the highly flavoured
fruit of the GOLDENBERRY makes a delicious dessert fruit. See page 163.

Plate 36. *Thymus serpyllum*. An aromatic ground cover loved by bees. The leaves are used as a health promoting flavouring in salads and cooked foods. See page 169.

Plate 37. *Elaeagnus cordifolia*. Producing early fruit in April and May, this hardy plant will thrive in almost any situation, including by the sea. See page 186.

Plate 38. *Elaeagnus parvifolia*. A highly productive nitrogen-fixing plant. The richly flavoured fruit is slightly astringent but is adored by children. See page 182.

Plate 39. *Hibiscus syriacus*. A beautiful autumn flowering shrub. The flowers make an attractive mild tasting salad and the leaves have a delicious nutty flavour. See page 189.

Plate 40. *Rosa rugosa*. Making a very wind resistant hedge, this plant produces very large hips bursting with vitamin C. See page 178.

Plate 41. *Salix 'Bowles hybrid'*. A fast growing wind resistant shrub. This four year old hedge is already providing excellent shelter. See page 194.

Plate 42. *Campanula portenschlagiana.* An evergreen ground cover plant that will thrive in very dry places. It has edible mild flavoured leaves and flowers. See page 203.

Plate 43. *Amaranthus caudatus.* Often grown as an ornamental plant, it has highly nutritious seeds and one of the most protein rich leaves known. See page 220.

Plate 44. *Chenopodium quinoa*. A very productive and easily grown grain crop. The seed can be used in all the same ways as rice. See page 221.

Plate 45. *Lupinus mutabilis*. The PEARL LUPIN has all the same uses as soya but in a temperate zone gives a higher yield. See page 225.

Plate 46. *Papaver somniferum*. The nutty flavoured seeds of the OPIUM POPPY are commonly used as a flavouring in breads and cakes. See page 226.

Plate 47. *Setaria italica*. Probably the highest yielding MILLET for cool temperate climates. See page 226.

EVERGREEN HERBACEOUS PERENNIALS

***Asarum* species**. *A. canadense* has been discussed above in the section on deciduous plants. The following species are evergreen. They both prefer acid conditions and grow about 10cm tall. Plant them at 30cm spacing for ground cover and they will fill the space in their second or third year.

A. caudatum. This does well in deep shade. The root can be used as a ginger substitute.

A. europaeum. ASARABACCA Also said to do well in calcareous soils. A vibrant apple-green dye is obtained from plant.

Viola odorata. SWEET VIOLET grows about 10cm tall and spreads freely at the roots to form large clumps. It makes a good ground cover in the dappled shade of trees though it will also succeed in full sun. Planted at 30cm spacing it will fill the gaps in its second growing season.

This species provides mild-flavoured salad leaves all year round and makes an excellent salad plant. See also page 81.

Montia sibirica. PINK PURSLANE is a short-lived perennial plant about 20cm tall that self-sows freely and thus forms a dense ground cover. A very tolerant plant, it requires a moist humus-rich soil for best results and, although it much prefers shady conditions, it can also succeed in sunny positions so long as the soil does not become dry. This is one of the few species that can succeed in the dense shade of a beech wood. Planted at 30cm spacing, it will fill the gaps in its second year.

This is a very productive salad plant that should be more widely grown. Both the leaves and the flowers can be eaten in salads or cooked like spinach. The leaves can be harvested all year round and have a mild flavour but with an aftertaste that is rather like raw beetroot – which is fine if you like raw beetroot but this leaf is not for me. In hot weather the leaves usually develop a bitter aftertaste, especially if grown in dry soils or sunny positions. The small pink flowers are produced from early spring until at least the middle of summer. They are milder tasting than the leaves and make an attractive garnish for salads.

M. perfoliata. MINER'S LETTUCE grows about 15cm tall and is an annual that self-sows so freely when in a suitable site that it can also be used as an evergreen ground cover. It prefers acid conditions and can succeed on poor or very dry soils. It is best sited in the shade of trees and can succeed in quite dense shade.

The leaves have a milder and, to my palate, a much more pleasant flavour than the previous species without the aftertaste of beetroot. This is a productive salad that can be used in quantity all year round. The small white flowers are also edible and are available from the middle of spring until the middle of summer.

Ajuga reptans. BUGLE is a good ground-cover for semi-shade, forming a carpet about 30cm high and rooting as it spreads. Fairly tolerant of soil conditions, it prefers a moisture-rich soil but will succeed in dry shade. Fairly fast growing but it does not always smother out weeds and can become bare at the centre if not growing in good conditions. Plant it at 30cm spacing. See also page 142.

Liriope graminifolia. Growing to about 30cm tall. It forms clumps and is rather slow to spread but eventually forms a good dense cover in a shady position and is very drought tolerant. It prefers a sandy soil and will also grow in full sun so long as there is plenty of humus in the soil. Plant it at 30cm spacing.

I have not yet tried eating this species, but the root is said to be eaten in China and Japan, where it is also used medicinally. Any other members of the genus can also be used for ground cover.

Pulmonaria officinalis. LUNGWORT grows about 30cm tall and wide. It does best in the light shade of a woodland though it also succeeds in deep shade and even in the sunless shadow of a building. If the soil is rich in humus and does not dry out, then lungwort will succeed in full sun, but the leaves will tend to wilt in hot or dry weather. It is slow to spread but makes a good weed-excluding carpet of vegetation. Plant it 30 - 50cm apart each way according to your budget, it should fill the space in the second or third year.

The bland-flavoured leaves can be added in moderation to mixed salads, though their texture is less than wonderful. The plant is sometimes cultivated as a medicinal herb, having a very beneficial effect on the lungs.

EVERGREEN SHRUBS

Rubus calycinoides. This species, which grows 10cm tall, has been discussed earlier when dealing with plants for sunny positions. It also does well in full shade, though will not fruit so freely in such a position.

Gaultheria procumbens. WINTERGREEN grows about 15cm tall and spreads freely by suckers when in suitable conditions. It requires a lime-free soil and succeeds in both deep shade and semi-shade. It forms a tuft-like carpet and is best spaced about 40cm apart when growing it for ground cover. It should fill the space in its second or third year.

The fruit is up to 15mm in diameter and ripens in late summer, it will hang on the plant for many weeks if not eaten by the birds. This is a highly aromatic fruit with an antiseptic germolene-like flavour that reminds you of a hospital waiting room! Some people, like my elder son, love them, whilst others, like my younger son who will normally eat anything, are a bit less sure! This species is dealt with in more detail on page 59.

Hedera helix. IVY is a superb ground cover for woodlands and other very shady places, though it does also succeed in full sun. When growing along the ground in deep shade it is no more than 20cm tall, though it sends out long stems that form new roots at intervals along them. A very effective weed suppresser, it can be planted as much as 1 - 2 metres apart if your budget is tight and will still fill in the spaces in its third or fourth growing season.

The cultivars 'Hibernica', 'Lutzii' and 'Neilsonii' have been especially recommended for ground cover. Plants do not usually flower or set seed when growing on the ground, especially when in deep shade. See also page 243.

Vinca minor. PERIWINKLE is an evergreen native shrub growing about 30cm tall spreading freely at the roots and by layering when established. A superb dense ground cover, it succeeds in sunny positions and also in dense shade. If grown in a shady position it is quite drought tolerant. When planted about 50cm apart it can form a dense ground cover by the end of the second year.

The pliable stems can be used in basket making and the plant has many valuable medicinal properties.

V. major. Somewhat larger but has similar uses.

Rubus tricolor. The CREEPING BRAMBLE is a very vigorous and effective ground cover for woodlands, succeeding in deep as well as dappled shade. It grows about 30cm tall and spreads rapidly by means of its prostrate self-layering stems. It should not be used with small plants since it will very quickly drown them. Plant it 1 metre apart for ground cover and it should fill the space in its second growing season.

The fruit is about 10mm or more in diameter and ripens over a period of several weeks in mid to late summer. A type of blackberry (but orange in colour), the flavour from a good form is very acceptable. Most plants do not bear very heavily, though we have come across some plants that produce quite large yields.

Mahonia repens. The CREEPING OREGON GRAPE grows up to 30cm tall and, once established, spreads freely by means of suckers. It does very well in dappled woodland shade, and in the shadier corners of a garden, though it also succeeds in full sun. The very young plants are rather susceptible to slug damage but, as they become established, their leaf-fall tends to discourage the slugs. Plant them about 75cm apart and they should fill the spaces in their third growing season.

The fruit ripens in mid summer and is about 9mm in diameter. When fully ripe it has a pleasant acid flavour, though it does contain rather a lot of seeds. The fruit goes really well in porridge or muesli and also makes a good jam that is reminiscent of blackcurrants.

M. nervosa. OREGON GRAPE grows about 60cm tall and spreads slowly by suckers. It has similar needs to the above species, but is more shade tolerant and does well in deep woodland shade. It is best to plant it about 30cm apart each way for ground cover and it should fill the gaps in its third growing season. The fruit is about 8mm in diameter and ripens in early summer. It has the same uses as the above species.

M. aquifolium. Another plant called OREGON GRAPE, and very similar to *M. nervosa*. It grows about 2 metres tall and spreads slowly by suckers. A very tolerant and easily grown plant, it succeeds in most situations from dense shade to full sun. The fruit is rather small but is easily harvested and is ripe in late summer. See also page 59.

Gaultheria shallon*.* The SALAL grows up to 1.2 metres tall and forms a slowly spreading clump 1 metre or more wide. It makes a very good ground cover in the shade of trees and is drought tolerant once established. Planted at 70 - 90cm spacing, it should fill the space in its second or third year.

The freely borne fruit is up to 10mm in diameter and is produced abundantly over a period of several weeks from mid to late summer. It has a sweet and pleasant flavour. See also page 59.

Prunus laurocerasus*.* CHERRY LAUREL is an easily grown tall evergreen shrub succeeding in full sun or in the dense shade of trees. It thrives in most well-drained soils except shallow chalk. It can have a negative effect on nearby plants and I would only use it under mature trees. Another disadvantage of this plant is that it can become rather aggressive in a woodland and prevent the regeneration of native trees, so plant it with caution.

There are some low-growing forms such as 'Cherry Brandy', 'Otto Luyken', 'Zabelina' and 'Schipkaensis' which make very good ground cover plants about 1 metre tall. They have excellent weed-suppressing properties and should be planted about 60cm apart each way.

The fruit is 10mm or more in diameter and ripens in early autumn. When fully ripe it has a pleasant sweet flavour reminiscent of almonds and can be eaten in moderation, though some reports say that it is poisonous. (Almonds contain the poison hydrogen cyanide, which is why it is not wise to eat many seeds if they are bitter. See Appendix 4 for more details.) An almond flavouring can be distilled from the leaves.

Chapter Eleven

A FEW ANNUALS
& BIENNIALS

There are people who feel that annuals and biennials have little or no part to play in a garden of low-labour perennial plants. Others think that there is always going to be a need for them and it is more a matter of finding a way to fit them into the perennial garden. I must admit to being more drawn to the first idea, and even my wife, who was an ardent supporter of conventional vegetables has been moving away from them in the past few years. The reason is quite simple – when you find the right sort of perennials then they are more productive and much less work than the annuals.

However, her support for the perennials is by no means unqualified. There are many annuals and biennials (to save time, I will call them all annuals for the rest of this chapter) for which there are no real alternatives at present. You also have a longer time lag with many of the perennials between sowing the seed and reaping the harvest. In exceptional circumstances this can be as much as 40 years, though it is usually far less than this.

One way of growing annuals with less effort that is often mentioned is the growing of species that self-sow. In this way, apart from the initial sowing, you can sit back and the plants will re-establish themselves year after year.

I have strong reservations about this since virtually all annuals, even the most aggressively self-sowing ones, are opportunists and will only be able to maintain themselves if they can find some disturbed ground in which to germinate. Just look at a field that used to grow annual crops but has been left to pasture for a number of years. There were plenty of annual weeds around whilst the ground was being cultivated but after just a few years without cultivation the annuals will have virtually disappeared and it will be almost all perennial species. As soon as the ground is ploughed again, however, there will be lots of poppies and other annuals germinating from seed that has been laying dormant in the soil.

In nature soil disturbance is caused by various events, such as a tree being blown down, a landslide, or a forest fire. There are also some environments, such as a very dry desert, that are so harsh they cannot support many perennial species. In this type of situation the annuals can grow rapidly, flower and produce their seed in the brief periods when growth is possible.

In most parts of the temperate zone, however, the vast majority of plants in an established ecosystem will be perennials of one type or another. These plants are in much less of a hurry to flower and set seed. Instead, they concentrate on forming a good root system and strong top growth that can cover the soil to out-compete neighbouring plants and prevent the successful germination of most seeds. When the annuals do germinate, there is so much competition from these established plants that they often cannot obtain sufficient moisture, sunlight and nutrients in order to thrive or even to survive. They thus become a very minor part of the ecosystem.

Most annuals are creatures of the sun and of disturbed soils. Of the 560 annual species on our database, 553 of them succeed in full sun whilst there are only 5 that will grow well in heavy shade. Of the 105 biennials, 100 of them will grow in full sun whilst only 6 will grow in heavy shade.

It is possible, on a garden scale, to encourage annuals to self-sow by hoeing areas of ground where the seed has been scattered by the plants, and this can be quite successful with species such as pot marigolds and poppies. You will not find it working for carrots however! To grow most of our traditional vegetables successfully you are going to have to give them a bit more attention than this. There are exceptions to every rule, of course, and spinach beet will maintain itself for years if you let it run to seed and provide disturbed ground for it to germinate in.

In the long term there are not many annuals that I would want to spend the necessary time and effort that is required to grow them, but they are very valuable in providing a stop-gap measure until the perennial crops begin to yield. If you do want to grow annuals, then you would be well-advised to concentrate on the conventional food crops first. This is where the vast majority of human effort in growing food has been directed, and therefore it is these that have been selectively bred for yield and flavour and so are adapted for our very restricted palates.

Over the centuries we have bred plants to be milder tasting and more succulent, and as we have altered these foods so has our appreciation of tastes changed. If you examine the diet of humans in this country two thousand or more years ago you will find that it included many bitter tasting leaves (such as dandelion) and acid fruits (such as crab apples). If you examine the nutritional value of these foods then you will usually find that they are far superior to the types of food we eat nowadays.

We have, to a large extent, lost the ability to enjoy the vast range of flavours that are available for us in nature, though it is not impossible to regain this ability. Children, for example, will often accept far more acid-tasting foods than adults. It is quite common for children to eat raw rhubarb, though there are few adults who would eat it. As I finish writing this book, my youngest son is 21/2 years old. He has been brought up in an environment where there is a huge amount of these alternative foods available. I thought that I had developed a fairly wide-ranging acceptance of flavours, but he beats me hands down and will often eat quite large quantities of foods that I find distasteful. It is going to be very interesting to see how his tastes develop over the years.

Some of the perennial plants advocated in this book have quite distinct flavours and are often an acquired taste. Most of them have never been selected for yields and thus are less productive than the cultivated annuals. However, I am going to stick with the perennials since their potential yields are greater than the annuals, they are generally more nutritious, often have a nicer flavour and are much easier to grow. (See the section 'A way forward' in the final chapter for more details.)

The accepted way of growing annuals, whether on the farm or in the garden, is to cultivate the soil and to grow blocks of individual species – on some of the large farms in this country these blocks can be 200 hectares or more in size!

Annual cultivation, especially if this means the soil being left bare over the winter, is extremely detrimental to the health of the soil. Organic matter breaks down more quickly, nutrients are leached from the soil, the soil is eroded by wind and rain, the structure is damaged and many of the creatures in the soil are killed. Even with the fairly stable soils we enjoy in Britain, it is impossible to maintain soil fertility without large inputs of organic matter.

Non-organic growers rely on chemicals to feed the soil, but over a period of time the land becomes more and more difficult to work as the organic matter and the soil disappears. Organic growers will make compost from garden waste, but this is not enough to maintain soil fertility and so they have to import organic matter from other sources.

There are methods of growing annuals without digging the soil, either by surface cultivation or by the use of mulches. These methods will help to preserve soil structure and reduce the other negative effects of cultivation.

With surface cultivation your main gardening tool is some type of hoe. The only time that you dig the soil is when you harvest root crops, otherwise you only hoe the surface and sow seeds or put plants direct into this.

It is important to avoid stepping on no-dig beds if at all possible to prevent compaction of the soil. One way of doing this is to make rectangular beds 1 - 1.5 metres wide and as long as it suits you, with paths 30 - 50cm wide on either side of them. The paths can be allowed to be covered in grass, which can then be mown regularly to provide more compost material. The main drawbacks with this is that you will forever be trying to prevent the grass growing into the beds, and the grass also offers cover for slugs. Alternatively, you can leave the soil bare and then hoe out all the weeds once a month during the growing season, using them as compost.

Both of those methods help to create additional organic matter in the garden. The third option is to mulch the paths to prevent anything growing on them. Overall this third option is the least labour-intensive, though it does use up organic matter, which is one of your major resources in the garden.

We follow a system of no-dig or minimal dig on our cultivated beds and it works well so long as there are no perennial weeds in the soil. Even the most persistent perennials will be killed off if you hoe often enough. With the most aggressive plants such as couch grass, it might be wise either to try and dig them out or to apply a thick light-excluding mulch for 18 months (including two summers) before setting up a no-dig system. An old carpet is ideal for this, but try to avoid those made from nylon or other materials that will not decay in the soil. In particular avoid foam backed carpets.

You will need a lot of organic material to set up a no-dig mulching system since you need to spread a layer of organic matter at least 5cm deep over the soil. This will soon disappear in humus-hungry soils and then you will need to top it up. With time though, as the soil becomes richer in organic matter, the mulch will last much longer before needing to be supplemented. You sow seeds direct into the mulch (which needs to be of fine well-rotted materials if you are sowing small seeds) and you can also grow certain root crops such as potatoes in the mulch without having to dig the soil to harvest them.

After a few years of following no-dig methods you will notice many changes in your soil. It will, for example, be a lot firmer than organically-cultivated soil that is regularly dug. If you dig up a spadeful of this soil you will notice that it contains lots of air channels formed by worms. These and the many other creatures that live in the soil will be working hard on all the organic matter you have applied in order to produce a rich, fertile environment for themselves to live in. This does, of course, also help the soil to grow much healthier plants for you to eat! Because of all the aeration provided by these creatures, the soil will drain well even in very wet weather. The wealth of organic matter means that it will also hold more moisture and therefore will not dry out so quickly when there is no rain.

On a garden or allotment scale it is not necessary to grow all the plants of one species in a block, you can spread the plants around, grow them amongst perennials or on the sunny sides of shrubs. Remember that the greater the diversity of plants that you grow, and the more that you spread them around, then the greater chance you have of avoiding pests and diseases, or at least of minimizing their effects.

I am not going to talk about the common garden vegetables in this chapter, there are plenty of good gardening books where you can find information about them. There are a number of less well-known annuals and biennials however that, despite the extra work, are very exciting plants to grow. The following is a selection of them. Unless stated otherwise, they all need a sunny position and a well-drained soil. They will not normally maintain themselves by self-sowing (even in disturbed ground) unless the text says otherwise. They are normally sown in situ in the spring, though many of them, especially those that self-sow, can also be sown in the autumn and will then produce an earlier and often larger crop the following year. All the plants are annuals unless the text says otherwise.

A few more annual species will be found scattered throughout the book when they seem to fit in well to a particular habitat.

LEAF CROPS

Amaranthus **species**. These plants are dealt with below under seed crops. They also produce a large quantity of leaves that make an excellent spinach substitute.

Anthriscus cereifolium. CHERVIL is a reasonably well-known biennial herb growing about 50cm tall and 25cm wide. It prefers a well-drained moisture retentive soil and dislikes hot dry summers It is best to grow summer crops in a cool shady position and give winter crops a sunny position.

The edible leaves have a mild aromatic taste with a hint of aniseed and can be added to salads or used as a flavouring. Fairly fast growing, the plant can be harvested on a cut and come again basis and is ready about 8 weeks after germinating. From successional sowings the leaves can be harvested all year round, particularly if some protection is given in the winter. Stored seed can be rather slow or difficult to germinate but once you have the plant in your garden it will often self-sow or you can collect your own seed and sow it whilst it is still fresh.

Chervil is said to be a good companion plant for growing with carrots and radishes, the radishes becoming hotter and crisper. When grown with lettuces it is said to protect them from aphids and ants. The plant is also said to repel slugs, though I would have some doubts about this.

Atriplex hortensis. ORACH is a fast-growing and productive plant that reaches about 1.5 metres tall and 25cm wide. A trouble-free and easily grown plant, it will yield more heavily in a rich moisture-retentive soil but is not too fussy and grows well in saline and very alkaline conditions. It usually self-sows freely in the garden.

The leaves are available in the summer and make a very acceptable though rather bland spinach substitute. They are traditionally mixed with sorrel leaves in order to modify the acidity of the latter.

There are red and bronze-leaved forms of this plant. They have the same flavour as the green-leaved forms and are sometimes grown in the ornamental garden.

Borago officinalis. BORAGE is often grown in the herb garden, it can be up to 60cm tall and wide and does well in dry soils. It tolerates quite poor soils, but is much more productive in more fertile conditions.

The leaves are rather hairy and have an unpleasant feel in the mouth, but if chopped up very small and added to mixed salads they are reasonably acceptable. They have a slightly salty, somewhat cucumber flavour. The flowers are much nicer and make a very decorative and tasty addition to salads. You can also get a blue dye from the flowers and this has been used to colour vinegar, though why anyone wants blue vinegar is quite beyond me.

The seed is one of the more interesting uses of this plant. It contains 30% of an edible oil, 20% of which is gamma-linolenic acid. This is the essential fatty acid that is found in evening primrose oil and has been shown to have many beneficial effects on the body. Amongst other things, this oil helps to regulate the hormonal systems and lowers blood pressure – it has been shown to be of benefit in the treatment of various diseases including multiple sclerosis. The main problem is in harvesting the seed because a few seeds ripen each day and fall from the plant as soon as they are ripe. Collecting seed of this species is one of the frustrations of my life – I always seem to get there the day after a lot of seed has ripened and fallen off, and a day before the next lot of seed will be ready! Fortunately the plant usually self-sows freely so long as there is disturbed ground for it.

Calendula officinalis. POT MARIGOLD is another herb that is often grown in the garden. Plants grow about 60cm tall and wide and flower better in a poor soil. They usually self-sow freely.

The leaves can be eaten in salads. They are somewhat sweet when first put in the mouth but soon develop a strong, penetrating flavour and are a bit too strong for me to enjoy. They are said to be very nutritious, though. The petals are more acceptable and add a nice colour to salads. When dried, they can be used as a flavouring in cakes and soups in much the same way as saffron, in fact a yellow dye can be obtained from the petals that is a saffron substitute.

Pot marigold is an excellent companion plant to grow in the garden. The flowers attract hoverflies to the garden, the young of which are fairly efficient eaters of aphids. The growing plant acts as an insect deterrent and is said to have root excretions that reduce the soil eelworm population. This makes it an excellent companion plant for tomatoes. The flowers are an alternative ingredient of 'Quick Return' herbal compost activator.

Chrysanthemum coronarium. CHOP SUEY GREENS can grow up to 1.2 metres tall and 60cm wide. This plant is often grown as an ornamental in Europe, but in the Orient they have developed many varieties for their edible leaves. It prefers a well-drained fertile soil and tolerates light shade in the summer. It does not grow well at temperatures above 25°C, tending to become bitter in hot weather.

The young shoots and stems can be eaten raw or cooked. They are strongly aromatic and not to everyone's taste, including mine! They can be added to mixed salads or used as a vegetable or as a flavouring in cooked foods. The leaves will become bitter if they are overcooked at a high temperature. The leaves quickly wilt once they have been picked so it is best to harvest them as required.

A very fast-growing plant, it takes just 4 - 5 weeks from sowing the seed to the first harvest when plants are grown on the cut and come again principle.

There are reports that this is a good companion plant, protecting neighbouring plants from caterpillars and reducing the population of nematodes in the soil. It is another plant that will self-sow freely if given disturbed ground.

Eruca vesicaria sativa. ROCKET grows about 60cm tall and 25cm wide. A very easily grown plant, it prefers some shade in the summer and will often self-sow freely. If some seed is sown in late summer in a sheltered, sunny position, it can provide leaves throughout mild winters.

Rocket became something of an 'in' salad in 1993 with large prices being paid in specialist markets for small bunches of the stuff. I find it quite distasteful, though many people seem to enjoy its unique spicy flavour. The leaves develop a hotter flavour as they become older. The flowers can also be eaten with flavour similar to the leaves.

The ground-up seeds are a mustard substitute. An oil obtained from the seeds becomes edible if it is stored for 6 months. This oil can also be used as an illuminant in lamps.

Malva **species**. This genus of very easily grown and tolerant plants provides us with some of our favourite salad leaves. A number of perennial species have been mentioned in Chapter 4, the following annuals are also very useful salad plants. They both self-sow in suitable conditions.

M. pusilla grows about 30cm tall and perhaps 25cm wide. The leaves have a pleasant mild flavour and can be used in quantity in salads. This is possibly the best flavoured member of the genus though it is much lower yielding than *M. verticillata 'Crispa'* (see below) or the perennials *M. alcea* and *M. moschata* (see page 94). The seed can also be eaten raw or cooked.

Best used before it is fully mature, the seed has a pleasant nutty taste but it is rather small and very fiddly to harvest.

M. verticillata. The CHINESE MALLOW (*see photograph overleaf*) grows about 1.5 metres tall and 30cm wide. Whilst the books say that it prefers a sunny position, the best plants I have ever seen of this species were growing in fairly shady conditions in Robert Hart's forest garden where it was self-sowing freely.

This is a salad plant par excellence. It yields well and has very large leaves that are easy to pick – some of the leaves can be over 30cm wide. It produces leaves for most of the summer and into the autumn if it is picked regularly and prevented from flowering. The flavour is mild and good, the texture smooth and rather mucilaginous. Definitely a leaf you can add in quantity to a salad, it also makes a very pleasant thirst-quenching munch when working in the garden.

Their is at least one named form of this species. 'Crispa' is very similar in size and productiveness but has attractive wavy edges to the leaves which make it look more decorative in salads. It is often mistakenly called *Malva crispa*.

Portulaca oleracea. PURSLANE is actually a perennial, growing to about 25cm tall and wide. It is not winter-hardy in Britain, though it can be grown here as a spring-sown annual. It requires a moist light rich well-drained soil in a sunny position and will not produce good quality leaves when growing in dry conditions.

Purslane is occasionally cultivated for its edible leaves and there are some named varieties. The plants take about six to eight weeks to produce a crop from seed and can then be harvested on a cut and come again principle, providing edible leaves for most of the summer. These mild-flavoured leaves are nice in salads and can also be cooked – when added to soups and stews they will act as a thickening agent in much the same way as okra.

The plant has been attracting some attention from nutritionists because the leaves are fairly rich in omega-3 fatty acids. These play an important role in preventing heart attacks and strengthening the immune system. However, many seeds such as walnuts are much richer sources.

The small seed is also edible but is not produced in sufficient quantities in cool-summer climates to make collection worthwhile.

P. oleracea sativa. This form has golden-green leaves and adds a nice colour contrast to green leaves in salads.

ROOT CROPS

Arctium lappa. BURDOCK is a native biennial that can grow up to 2 metres tall and 1 metre wide. It succeeds in most soils, but the best roots are obtained when grown on light well-drained soils. It also does well in semi-shade.

There are several named forms in Japan where burdock is cultivated for its edible root. Seeds of these named forms are sometimes also available in British catalogues. The wild plant can be rather bitter, but the following reports refer to the cultivated form.

Malva verticillata. The large mild flavoured leaves of the CHINESE MALLOW
make a superb and plentiful salad with a curiously sensuous texture.

The very young root can be eaten raw, but older roots are normally cooked. These roots can be up to 120cm long and 2.5cm wide at the top, but they are best harvested when no more than about 60cm long since they are apt to become woody at the core. Young roots have a mild flavour, but this becomes stronger as the root gets older.

I've only ever eaten the roots, but there are also the following reports of edibility. The young leaves can be eaten raw or cooked and have a mucilaginous texture. The young stalks and branches can be cooked like asparagus or spinach and they taste best if the rind is removed. The pith of the flowering stem can be eaten raw in salads, boiled or made into confections. There is a report that the seeds can be sprouted and used like beansprouts, but the seed is so slow to germinate that I doubt if it would be very useful for sprouting.

A. minus. This is a related native plant growing about 1 metre tall and 50cm wide. It has similar uses, but is rather bitter.

The seed of both of these species is rather slow to germinate. It is probably best sown in the autumn, though should be sown as late as possible to prevent the plants running straight to seed in the spring without forming decent roots. Spring-sown seed is best pre-soaked for 12 hours in water and only just covered by soil.

Burdocks are some of those antisocial species that attack you with their seeds. These seeds are contained in small spherical seed cases with burrs. These burrs will attach themselves to your clothes at the slightest excuse and will be more than a little difficult to remove. Ideal as a strategy by the plant for getting its seeds taken to a new site, but rather a nuisance at times. One word of warning, the tiny hairs in the seed cases of both species can cause health problems, so wear a mask if you are harvesting the seed in any quantity.

Campanula rapunculus. RAMPION is a biennial plant that grows up to 1 metre tall and 30cm wide. An easily grown plant, it prefers a moist but well-drained rich sandy loam, though it succeeds in most good soils. The books say it can be grown in a meadow, though I don't know how good the roots would be in this case.

Rampion used to be cultivated for its edible root. Though rather on the small side, it has a very nice sweet almost nutty flavour and can be eaten raw or cooked. You will get better quality roots if you prevent the plant from flowering. The leaves are bland but acceptable raw whilst the young shoots in spring can be blanched and cooked like asparagus.

Chaerophyllum bulbosum. TURNIP-ROOTED CHERVIL grows up to 1.2 metres tall and about 25cm wide. This easily-grown biennial succeeds in most soils, though it prefers moist conditions.

Occasionally cultivated for its edible root, this is about the size of a small carrot, is aromatic, floury and sweet with a peculiar flavour that is said to be excellent and unlike any other vegetable. I find it a very pleasant munch raw, and have yet to try it cooked. Peeling the root it is said to ruin the flavour. Harvested in late summer when the plant dies down, it can be stored like potatoes for later use.

There are some problems associated with growing this plant. The seed either has a very short viability or, according to another report, it becomes dormant if allowed to dry out and will not germinate for a year. It is best, therefore, to sow the seed in early autumn as soon as it is ripe. If stored for a spring sowing it should be kept in damp sand in a cold but frost-free place and then sown in situ in March.

SEED CROPS

Amaranthus **species**. There are many members of this genus and they all have edible leaves and seeds, indeed many of them are occasionally cultivated as food plants. The leaves have a pleasant mild flavour and are best cooked like spinach, though they can also be eaten raw. One word of warning – if the plants are grown with a lot of chemical fertilizers they can concentrate nitrates in their leaves. There is some evidence that these nitrates can cause stomach cancers and the blue baby syndrome. The answer is simple – grow the plants organically (but even then do not overdo the nitrogen).

The seed is small but is very nutritious and often produces abundantly. It is also very easy to harvest. When ground into a flour it can be used to thicken soups. Bread made from a mixture of wheat and amaranth flour will be richer in protein and nutritionally very superior to an all-wheat loaf. The seed can also be cooked and eaten, but make sure that you chew it thoroughly since the seed is so small that it can easily be swallowed whole and will then pass straight through the body without being digested.

Amaranths are potentially very productive crops in this country, especially if global warming raises our average temperatures by a couple of degrees or so. Most, if not all members of the genus photosynthesize by a more efficient method than the majority of plants. Called the 'C4 carbon-fixation pathway', this process is particularly efficient at high temperatures, in bright sunlight and in dry conditions.

These fast-growing plants are frost-tender and so need to be sown outdoors in May or, preferably, sown in a greenhouse in April and planted out after the last expected frosts. Keep them growing well if you start them off in pots. If allowed to go short of nutrients they will soon become stunted and will then produce very little in the way of seeds or leaves. They need a hot summer if they are to do well and are drought resistant once established.

Some of the more productive species to grow include:

A. caudatus. See Plate 43. The familiar LOVE LIES BLEEDING of the flower garden. Not only is it very ornamental, but it can be very productive in this country. A well-grown plant can be 2 metres tall and 50cm wide with a yield of up to 100,000 seeds. One report states that there are some forms that can tolerate a pH as high as 8.5, but it did not name any cultivars.

A. cruentus. Growing up to 2 metres tall and 50cm wide, this species will tolerate a pH as low as 4 and will also succeed in chalky soils.

A. hybridus. ROUGH PIGWEED grows up to 1 metre tall and 40cm wide. It ripens its seed earlier so is more reliable in this country.

A. hypochondriacus. PRINCE'S FEATHER grows about 1.2 metres tall and 50cm wide. This species is often cultivated, especially in tropical areas, for its edible leaves and seeds, there are many named varieties. This is the most robust and highest yielding of the grain amaranths, though it is late maturing and therefore less suitable for northern areas.

A. viridis. One of the better species for leaf production. It has grown about 1 metre tall on our windy site and has often self-sown.

Chenopodium quinoa. See Plate 44. QUINOA (pronounced Keen-wa if you want to sound authentic) is an amazing grain crop from South America. It has recently been heralded as a new wonder crop, but has been grown in the Andes for thousands of years and was also being grown in Victorian gardens in Britain over a century ago. It is amazing how quickly things can be lost or forgotten.

Quinoa grows about 1.5 metres tall and 25cm wide, though there are many named varieties and these are often less tall. For optimum seed production grow the plants about 15cm apart in rows 30cm apart. This is an easily grown plant, it requires a rich moist well-drained soil and a warm position if it is to do really well, but it also succeeds in less than optimum conditions. It tolerates moderate soil salinity, is fairly wind resistant and is drought tolerant once established.

The plants tolerate light frosts at any stage in their development, except when flowering. This means that it is possible to sow the seed directly outdoors in mid spring and then harvest the crop in August. Young plants look remarkably like the common garden weed FAT HEN (*Chenopodium album*), so be careful not to weed the seedlings out in error.

The plant is sensitive to the amount of daylight hours in a day and many varieties fail to flower properly away from equatorial regions. Those varieties coming from the south of its range in Chile are more likely to do well in Britain.

Quinoa can outcrop cereals on light land in Britain and has an excellent potential as a commercial crop in this country. I don't often grow this plant in quantity but in 1991 obtained a yield of 150 kilos from 250 square metres. This works out at about 6 tonnes per hectare and compares very favourably with the yields of wheat that would be obtained from a similar plot.

The seed itself is very easy to harvest by hand on a small scale and is usually ripe in August. Cut down the plants when the first ripe seeds are falling easily from the flower head, lay out the stems on a sheet in a warm dry position for a few days and then simply beat the stems against a wall or some other surface. The seed will fall out easily if it is fully ripe and then merely requires winnowing to get rid of the chaff. It will store for a number of years if kept cool and dry.

The seed is about the size of millet and is very nutritious. It contains an excellent quality protein that has the same biological value as milk and so does not need complementing with other plant proteins. This makes it an ideal food for a vegetarian or vegan diet. Totally free of gluten, it is a good cereal substitute for people such as coeliacs with a gluten intolerance. The seed is also a good source of carbohydrates. It can be used in all the ways that rice is used, either as a sweet or a savoury dish.

The seed is covered with a coating of bitter-tasting saponins (see Appendix 4), but these are easily removed by soaking the seed for 12 - 24 hours and then rinsing thoroughly until the rinse water is free of suds. Commercially the seeds are put in large drums that are then rotated in order to abrade the saponins.

The presence of saponins on the seed means that, unlike cereals, it is not eaten by birds. Another benefit is that the soak water can be sprayed over plants that are being eaten by birds and will act as a deterrent until washed off by the next rain.

C. nuttalliae. HUAUZONTLE is a related species growing about 60cm tall. It has a longer growing season and so is a less reliable crop in Britain. It has grown well with me in Cornwall, ripening a reasonable crop in September. The seed has a similar flavour and the same uses as quinoa.

Both of these species are related, and superficially similar, to our native weed FAT HEN, *C. album*. This plant also has edible seeds, although they are much smaller and less freely borne.

The leaves of all three species can be eaten raw or cooked and make an acceptable spinach. Only eat the raw leaves in small quantities, since they have been known to cause stomach upsets.

Cicer arietinum. CHICK PEAS are normally thought of as a tropical crop, but they are surprisingly hardy and some varieties have been known to tolerate temperatures down to -25°C when covered by snow. The plants grow up to 60cm tall. They grow best in a light fertile soil and require a hot, sunny position for best results. They have a 4 - 6 month growing season and can be grown successfully in Britain as long as the summers are reasonably dry and warm. They do not grow well in maritime areas, however, because the hairy seedpods tend to collect dew, this encourages the growth of moulds and then the seeds rot inside the pods.

The seeds are delicious cooked with a flavour that reminds me of baked chestnuts and they are the major ingredient of 'humous'. This is a Greek food made from liquidised chickpeas, sesame seeds and garlic, that it is becoming increasingly popular in this country. The seed can also be sprouted and used in salads or roasted and used as a coffee substitute.

Fagopyrum esculentum. BUCKWHEAT grows about 1.5 metres tall and 30cm wide. A very easily grown plant, it prefers dry sandy soils but succeeds in most conditions including poor, heavy or acid soils, and can even be grown in sub-soils. It prefers a cool moist climate, but also succeeds in dry and arid regions. The plants are not very frost-tolerant, so the seed should not be sown before April.

Buckwheat is frequently cultivated for its edible seed and leaves, it can produce a seed crop in 100 days from sowing and a crop of leaves in 8 weeks. The seed ripens irregularly over a period of several weeks, however, so it is difficult to harvest.

The seed can be eaten raw or cooked. It has a mild, slightly nutty flavour but rather a gritty texture. It can be sprouted and added to salads or used as a cereal. Dried and ground into a flour, it can be made into pancakes, noodles, breads and so on, or it can be used as a thickening agent in soups. Like the quinoa mentioned earlier, it is free of gluten and can therefore be used by people intolerant of wheat.

Whilst the leaves can be eaten raw they are rather less than wonderful. They are, however, rich in rutin. This substance has been shown to have a very beneficial effect on the blood circulation and is a treatment for arthritis and high blood pressure. The cooked leaves are somewhat nicer and can be used like spinach.

Buckwheat is an excellent green manure for restoring the structure of soils and if allowed to flower will prove to be a magnet for hoverflies whose larvae are such good aphid eaters.

There is also a perennial species of buckwheat with similar uses. This is discussed on page 111.

Helianthus annuus. SUNFLOWERS are one of the most amazing of annual plants, capable of growing up to 5 metres or more tall in just one growing season. They are often grown as ornamental plants, and there are, fortunately, many varieties that are much lower growing.

An easily grown plant, the sunflower succeeds in most soils though it grows best in a deep rich soil. It prefers a sunny position, but will also tolerate light shade. Established plants are drought tolerant. The young growth is a real magnet for slugs and so the seedlings might need some protection if you have a slug problem. This is a very greedy crop, the plants tend to impoverish the soil if they are grown too often in the same place.

Sunflowers are often grown for their edible seeds, though they are not a reliable commercial crop in Britain as yet. New cultivars are being developed, however, that should do well in this country. There are two distinct types of seed crop, one with smaller black seeds which is grown mainly for oil, whilst the other has larger striped seeds and is grown more for its edible seed. 'Dwarf Russian' is one of the better cultivars to try in Britain as a seed crop whilst 'Rostov' is one of the most reliable oil crops.

The seed can be eaten raw or cooked and has a delicious nut-like flavour. A seed yoghurt can be made if the seed is blended with water and left for 12 - 24 hours in a warm place to ferment. The seed is rich in oil, this can be extracted and used for food, as a lubricant, for making candles and soaps. The seeds can also be roasted and used as a coffee substitute. Young flower buds can be steamed and served like globe artichokes, which is all right if you like globe artichokes and don't mind eating something that is even more fiddly!

If the list of edible uses is not enough for you then how about the following other uses: a blotting paper is made from the seed receptacles; a fibre from the stem is used to make a fine quality cloth; a high quality writing paper is made from the inner stalk; the pith of the stems is used to make slides for microscopes; the dried stems make an excellent fuel, the ash that remains is rich in potassium and makes a good fertiliser; a yellow dye is obtained from the flowers and a purple-black dye is obtained from the seed of certain varieties; the plant can be grown as a spring-sown green manure that produces a good bulk of organic material which can either be dug into the soil or added to the compost heap.

Lens culinaris. LENTILS are sprawling plants that grow about 45 cm tall and wide. They are easily grown plants that prefer a sandy soil in a warm, sheltered position, though also succeed in clay. Seed production is best in soils that are not overly rich.

Lentils are a reasonably well-known food but many people do not realise that they can be grown successfully in this country. Indeed, there are many named varieties and some of these are surprisingly hardy. One called 'WH2040', for example, can withstand temperatures as low as -23°C in the seedling stage and so has the potential to be grown as an autumn-sown crop. The cultivars 'Chilean' and 'HarLen' should also be suitable in Britain.

Plants are grown in much the same way as peas, and take the same time to mature, so they are a potential commercial crop for Britain and yields of up to 2 tonnes per hectare are possible.

The seeds can be orangey-brown or green in colour. When cooked, they provide a good quality easily digested protein. They are said to be more nutritious and more digestible when sprouted and eaten raw in salads – they have a slight sweetness when used this way and also contain more vitamins and minerals. I have grown this crop on occasions but it has small seeds with no more than two of them in a pod and this makes it a rather fiddly plant to harvest by hand.

Linum usitatissimum. FLAX or LINSEED used to be widely grown in Britain for its fibre, oil and edible seed but then went out of favour. In recent years it has staged something of a comeback and fields of its blue flowers can once again be seen in this country.

It prefers a light well-drained moderately fertile humus-rich soil in a sunny sheltered position and prefers a cool moist climate, so it does best in the western half of the country. It is a very greedy plant, depleting the soil and requiring a rich, well prepared soil if it is to do well. It is said to be a good companion plant for potatoes and carrots.

There are two basic types of flax. The first branches quite freely and is grown mainly for its oil-rich edible seed. The plants are grown at 5 - 10cm spacings in order to encourage branching.

The seed contains 30 - 40% oil, and this is made up mainly of linoleic and linolenic essential fatty acids. It also contains cyanogenic glycosides, or prussic acid. In small quantities these glycosides stimulate respiration and improve digestion, but in excess can cause respiratory failure and death (See Appendix 4). Cultivars low in these glycosides have been developed and large quantities of the seed would need to be eaten to achieve a harmful dose. 'Foster' is one cultivar that makes very good eating, it has a mild nutty flavour. The seed is used in breads and cereals, it can also be sprouted and used in salads.

An edible oil can be extracted from the seed, though it needs to be properly refined before it can be eaten. This oil is very beneficial to the health because of its content of fatty acids, but it is very unstable and easily goes rancid. The healthiest way of eating it is in the form of the whole seed. The oil is of a very high quality for industrial use. It is perhaps best known as an ingredient of paints, as a wood preservative and as an ingredient of linoleum.

The second type of flax does not branch much and is grown mainly for its high quality fibre which is used in making cloth, sails, nets, paper, insulating material etc. This is grown at less than 5cm spacings in order to discourage branching.

Lupinus **species**. LUPINS have a long history of being cultivated for their edible seeds. Usually these seeds have a bitter flavour due to the presence of toxic alkaloids, and need to be soaked for 12 - 24 hours in a few changes of water prior to cooking in order to leach out these toxins. There have been a number of varieties developed this century, however, that are free of the toxic alkaloids and have a sweet flavour.

Lupin seeds are about the same size or larger than soya beans. They can be used in all the ways that cooked beans are used, they can also be ground into a flour and used to enhance the nutritional value of cereals when making bread. The sweet varieties can also be sprouted and then cooked or eaten raw. Lupin seeds are very nutritious, they are good sources of easily-digestible protein and carbohydrate and also contain some oil.

Lupins prefer a light acid soil but are not too fussy, though they will not be happy in alkaline soils. All the species listed below can also be used as spring-sown green manure crops, they grow quickly and fix a good quantity of atmospheric nitrogen.

Some of the species worth trying are:

L. albus. The WHITE LUPIN grows about 1.2 metres tall. Try to get hold of the variety 'Kiev' which is alkaloid-free.

L. angustifolius. The BLUE LUPIN is about 1 metre tall. Try and get hold of the sweet variety 'Uniwhite' and let me have some seeds if you do.

L. mutabilis. See Plate 45. The PEARL LUPIN grows about 1.5 metres tall. The seed of this South American species has a very similar nutritional value to soya beans but the plant is much higher yielding than soya in Britain. It can be used in all the ways that soya is used, including as a meat substitute, as a source of edible oil and as an oil for industry. This species is currently receiving a lot of attention as a possible commercial crop in temperate areas that are too cool for soya production.

Nigella damascena. LOVE-IN-A-MIST is an easily grown and tolerant plant often found in the ornamental garden. It is up to 60cm tall and 20cm wide, flowering for most of the summer. It will often self-sow freely. The plant is said to be a poor companion in the garden, in particular it seems to inhibit the growth of legumes.

The seed is freely produced and easy to harvest. It can be used as a condiment and has the flavour of nutmeg.

Two other members of this genus have useful seeds. They are also very easily grown in most soils:

N. arvensis. WILD FENNEL grows about 30cm tall. The seeds are used as a flavouring in cakes and bread.

N. sativa. BLACK CUMIN grows about 35cm tall. The seed is normally used as a flavouring on bread, cakes, curries and pickles and is a very popular spice from the Mediterranean to India. The immature seed is bitter, but when fully ripe it is aromatic with a spicy, fruity taste. The seeds can also be sprinkled in the linen cupboard in order to repel moths.

Papaver somniferum. See Plate 46. The OPIUM POPPY does not produce enough opiates in the British climate to make it a worthwhile pharmaceutical crop. It is, however, a very ornamental flower that grows about 60cm tall and 20cm wide, and is easily obtained from most seed catalogues.

It prefers a rich well-drained sandy loam in a sunny position, grows well on chalk but dislikes wet clay soils. It usually self-sows freely.

Although the seed is small, it is produced in abundance and is very easy to harvest – just pick off the capsules as they dry, place them in a cloth or paper bag, leave them until fully dry then shake and all the seed will fall out in the bag. The seeds do not contain any of the narcotic principles, but are very nutritious with a pleasant nutty flavour. They are used as a flavouring in bread and cakes. An edible oil can also be extracted from the seed, it is particularly good when used as an illuminant in lamps.

P. rhoeas. Our native CORN POPPY has similar uses, though it is lower yielding. Both species usually self-sow freely, *P. rhoeas* is the more successful at this. Poppy seed is very long-lived and can remain viable in the soil for 70 years or more. Little wonder that there is the saying 'One year's seed, seven years' weed'.

Setaria italica. See Plate 47. There are several MILLETS that can be grown in Britain but they do not normally yield well except in very hot summers. This species, the FOXTAIL MILLET, has been the most reliable for us in Cornwall so far. Plants grow about 50cm tall and are very drought-resistant once established. Sow them in situ in the middle of spring or, preferably, start the plants off in a greenhouse a few weeks earlier and plant out after the last expected frosts. Give them a very sunny sheltered position and, so long as the later part of summer is not cool and wet, you should get reasonable yields. The seed is very easy to harvest from the plant but, as with most cereals, removing the husks is more complicated. Don't expect the same sort of yields as wheat and most other cereals because millets are relatively low-yielding even in the tropics.

Millet can be used in all the ways that rice is used, either in sweet or savoury dishes, and it can also be ground into a flour then made into porridge, cakes and puddings. I find the taste rather boring but the sprouted seed is somewhat sweeter. Millet is perhaps the most nutritious of the cereals. It is very easy to digest and is gluten-free, so it can be eaten by coeliacs and other people who are gluten-intolerant. It also contains a good quality protein and is a source of vitamin A.

FRUITS

Physalis ixocarpa. The TOMATILLO is a spreading plant that grows about 1.2 metres tall. It is sometimes cultivated in southern North America for its edible fruit which is about the size of a tomato and is enclosed in a papery husk. The fruit turns a light yellow when fully ripe, usually with some purple markings, and is a delicious flavouring in savoury dishes. I use it in all the ways that cooked tomatoes can be used and find it very superior to that fruit. Tomatillos can also be eaten raw but are not so nice that way.

The plants are not frost hardy and so are best started off in spring in a greenhouse, or on a window sill, in much the same way as tomatoes and can then be planted out after the last expected frosts. Tolerant of most soils, they grow best in a rich, light soil and do well in hot, dry years. Yields are normally good so long as the summer is not cold and wet – in a wet year beware of slugs. Harvest any unripe fruits in the autumn before the first expected frosts and store them, still in their papery husks, in a cool place such as an unheated bedroom. They will ripen slowly over the next few months, indeed the books say that they can store for up to 12 months though ours never have.

There are some named varieties, but I do not know of a source of seed for them in Britain. If you find a supply, then try and get hold of 'Rendidora' since this ripens earlier than other cultivars and so is likely to crop better here.

All members of this genus have potentially edible fruits. Make sure it is fully ripe before trying any though, because in a few of the species the unripe fruit is poisonous.

The following are particularly worth trying:

P. philadelphica. WILD TOMATILLO is said to be the parent of *P. ixocarpa*. It is very similar to that species, though both the plant and the fruit are smaller. Once again, there are some named varieties with superior yields if you can get hold of them.

P. pruinosa. The STRAWBERRY TOMATO grows about 50cm tall with branches spreading from its base. The small yellow fruits are delicious raw with a bitter-sweet flavour. They can also be cooked.

P. peruviana. The GOLDENBERRY is a tender perennial, but if you live outside the milder areas of Britain you might consider growing it as an annual. The fruit is similar to *P. pruinosa*, but is rather larger. See also page 163.

Chapter Twelve

THE WILD
OR CONSERVATION GARDEN

Throughout this book we have been looking at various plants and their habitats with the primary concern of seeing what foods and other commodities they can provide for us. Although the gardening methods advocated here do bring about many benefits to the wider environment, so far these have been seen more or less as an added bonus. In this chapter we are going to reverse the position. Now we are going to look at plants and habitats specifically for the benefit they will provide to the non-human creatures who share this planet with us. Whilst most of the plants listed here can also provide us with foods and other commodities, this is only seen as a side benefit of growing them.

That the world is becoming increasingly polluted and less capable of supporting life can hardly be disputed since almost daily we hear new stories of rain forest destruction, holes in the ozone layer, acid rain... It is important to realise that this is not only happening in other countries. In Britain the tiny remnants of our own ancient woodland continue to be destroyed. Current agricultural practices mean that top soil is being lost at an alarming rate. The daily weather forecast now includes details on air quality and warnings as to how long we can remain in the sun without too much danger of getting skin cancer. It all makes depressing reading and we can only too easily become despondent with a feeling of powerlessness. Yet, of course, we can all make positive contributions towards cleaning up the planet and by our own actions we can try to encourage others to follow suit.

If we examine our own lifestyles then we will almost certainly find many areas where we can make changes that will benefit the environment. Using the car less is one obvious example whilst refusing to buy disposable plastic items is another. This book has been showing you how to grow more of your own food and other commodities, and to do this in as harmonious a manner as possible. By doing this you take more responsibility for your own life and also have a very direct positive effect on the environment.

There are also many ways in which we can make a positive change in our surrounding environment for the benefit of the other creatures that share this planet with us. In the August 12th 1994 edition of *The Guardian* newspaper there was an article about the declining population of some of our commonest species of birds. Apparently, in the period between 1969 and 1991 tree sparrow populations declined by 85%, corn bunting by 76%, grey partridge by 73%, turtle doves by 75% and skylarks by 50%. The article went on to blame current agricultural practices that have seen hedgerows destroyed, meadows ploughed up and fields harvested before the birds had a chance to finish rearing their young. It said that the dawn chorus, that enchanting time of the morning when the air is alive to the sound of bird song, is heard no more in many parts of East Anglia, where an eerie silence now greets the dawn.

Apart from changes in agricultural practices, the article suggested that the bird tables of urban gardens are now one of the last hopes of many birds. This is the only point where I disagree with the article. It is a rather sick joke that much of the food found on urban bird tables has actually been grown by using the very practices that have destroyed the birds' habitats. It would be far better to grow species of food-bearing plants in our gardens for the birds to eat. This is much healthier for them and does not make them dependant on the capricious nature of humans. It is all too easy for us to forget to put out food for the birds, to go away on holiday for a couple of weeks, or to move away from the area – the net result is no food for birds that have become dependent on this feeding. If, however, you are growing food plants for them, then the food will be there even if you are not.

If you have sufficient space then you might decide to dedicate some of your ground specifically for providing habitats for native plants and animals. If space is tighter then you might have to choose whether to concentrate on wildlife plants or on food production. Whichever you choose, the one need not completely rule out the other.

By introducing a wide range of plants and habitats to our gardens and farms we will also attract a wide range of insects, birds, amphibians, mammals and other creatures. This diversity leads to a much better stability in the ecosystem, thereby greatly reducing the incidence of pests and diseases. Instead of being locked into the concept of seeing nature as an enemy who is trying to oppose our attempts to grow plants, we can start working in harmony with her. Surely it is better to open your garden or farm to hedgehogs, frogs, slow-worms and the like than to use slug pellets with all the attached risks of killing other creatures in the food chain, as well as your own pets.

However, before getting too carried away with diversity, it is important to realise that the best plants for native wildlife tend to be native plants. These are the species best adapted to the local environment and also the species that the local wildlife has adapted to. Most of this chapter will be looking at plants native to Britain. If you garden in a different country then you should try to adapt the list to cover your own native species.

We also need to understand just what a native plant is – and it has nothing to do with national frontiers. If you want to grow a native plant then you should try to obtain that plant from stock growing in your **local** area. A species growing in one area will often have subtle differences to the same species growing elsewhere. These differences are a result of the plant adapting to the local environment.

If you buy some oak trees, for example, that have been grown in Holland (as many of the trees we buy in garden centres are) then this oak will most likely have been bred from seed of trees growing in Holland. Thus we are effectively introducing a different geno-type to the area. The same would be true, of course, if we gardened in the north of Britain and bought the trees from a nursery in the south of the country.

Any relatively stable habitat is only stable because all the different species are working in harmony with each other. If you introduce a subtly different plant this can upset that balance. For example, the introduction might be more vigorous than the indigenous forms of that species growing wild in the area. It will therefore grow more strongly and reproduce more effectively than the indigenous plants. Some other plant species are likely to suffer as a result of this increased competition and therefore the various creatures dependent upon that other species will also suffer.

It is impossible to say just what the end effect of introducing these different genotypes will be, but we can try to avoid any difficulty by buying our native species from local nurseries. It is important to make sure, of course, that they obtained the plants from local stock. We can also go out and collect the seed ourselves – but make sure that you obtain any necessary permission and do not collect from locally rare plants.

Because we are encouraging diversity, in a wildlife garden there will usually be a higher proportion of insect-damaged plants – though more often than not this damage will be superficial. It is far better to lose a few leaves or even a few plants to insects or slugs and end up with a food that is healthy and nutritious than it is to eat a pristine-looking food that contains various toxic chemicals that will poison you as well as any other creature that tries to eat it.

TREES & SHRUBS

Assuming you have the space, the most important step you can take is to plant trees and shrubs. If you want these plants to have the maximum benefit for the wildlife then you should concentrate on native species, and ideally a mixture of those species that are found in your local woods (or those species that would have been in your local woods if the woods were still there!). Of course, trees take up a lot of space, which is fine if you have a large tract of land but not if all you have got is a small back yard. There are, however, many quite small trees or shrubs that can be grown in situations such as this. Where space is tight, you will have to decide whether to make wildlife or food production the priority, but even with a wildlife garden you will still obtain some food for yourself, as I hope the lists of plants will demonstrate.

Trees provide habitats for insects, birds and mammals. Their roots go deep into the earth bringing up nutrients and water that would otherwise be lost from the garden. Their dead leaves can be turned into leaf-mould which is an excellent soil conditioner, trees extract carbon dioxide from the atmosphere, converting it into wood and giving out oxygen, thus helping to counter global warming. Trees can provide us with fruits, nuts, edible leaves and many other products as well as looking so beautiful.

Incidentally, if you are going to plant out a new native woodland, then there are various grants available to help you do this. For relatively small woodland plantings of up to half a hectare, for example, it is often possible to obtain free trees from your local council. For larger plantings there are grants available from the Forestry Commission. The only commitment you have to make is to grow the trees to maturity. When we planted our woodland in 1991, we made it clear to the

Forestry Commission that the first priority for the woodland was to provide a habitat for wildlife. Thus, as well as the various timber trees, we also put in a large proportion of smaller trees such as the crab apple, and shrubs such as the guelder rose. What will hopefully develop from this planting over the next 50 years and more is a fairly natural mixed woodland that will be self-sustaining and provide a wide range of habitats for other native plants and animals.

COPPICE

Assuming you have the space, one of the very best methods of growing trees is to coppice them. This involves chopping a tree down virtually to the ground at regular intervals ranging from every year for some species such as willows to perhaps once in every 50 years with oak trees, with every 10 years being the average. Assuming the right species are chosen, then the trees will send up very vigorous growth from their base in the year after they were cut down, with some species producing shoots that can reach 3 metres or more in their first year. Many broad-leaved trees respond well to coppicing, though most conifers are unable to regrow if cut down.

Coppice wood has a very wide range of uses, ranging from fuel, posts, construction, paper making and furniture-making. You will also be able to get many other commodities from coppice woodland including edible leaves, a small supply of fruits and nuts, fibres for making clothes and shredded bark for mulching.

From the wildlife point of view, a coppiced woodland offers a wide range of habitats. Assuming a 10 year rotation, one tenth of the land each year will be cleared woodland. This will allow a wealth of seeds that are lying dormant in the soil to germinate, and in the following years there will be an abundance of foxgloves, primroses, bluebells etc.

As the woodland regrows in subsequent years most of these plants will gradually be shaded out, though their seeds will be in the soil waiting for the next time that the trees are coppiced. By the end of 10 years growth, the coppiced area will be very dense woodland, offering good habitats for many creatures who can then take advantage of the plants growing in the more open areas of the coppice. Thus a coppiced woodland can be an exceedingly rich habitat for our native species.

Of our native species, some of the best to grow for coppicing are *Alnus glutinosa*, *Carpinus betulus*, *Corylus avellana*, *Fraxinus excelsior*, *Populus nigra*, *Populus tremula*, *Quercus petraea*, *Quercus robur*, the various *Salix* species and *Tilia cordata*. These trees are discussed later on in the chapter.

HEDGES

If you don't have space for a woodland, you might be able to grow a hedge of native trees and shrubs. This will bring many of the benefits of the woodland but in an area that can be as small as a few metres long and a metre or two wide. Many of those native species suitable for hedging are indicated in the list of trees and shrubs below.

For those people who have a large plot of land then I would strongly recommend that, as well as planting out a woodland of native trees, you also plant some mixed native hedges. These will act as pathways along which many creatures and plants will be able to travel. Make sure that this hedge joins up with your woodland and, where possible, try to ensure that it joins up with other native hedges or woodlands. It is also a good idea to allow a few of the hedgerow trees to grow into specimen plants instead of trimming them. This will make the hedge look more attractive as well as providing yet more habitats for the wildlife.

Try not to trim all of the hedge every year. Instead set up a rotation and trim one third of it each year, preferably in the winter when most of the food it can provide has been eaten and before the birds begin to build their nests. This will ensure that the hedge can flower and produce fruit in the years when it is not cut and it will also provide sufficient protection for birds who want to nest in the hedge.

The hedge trimmings will be rather thicker than from annually trimmed plants, but you can put them through a shredder to produce an excellent mulch material. Alternatively you can pile them up in a quiet corner in order to create another habitat. Insects will soon be attracted to this pile and will live under the bark of the wood. Other creatures including hedgehogs will be attracted to nest in the woodpile. The hedgehogs will then join forces with the frogs in your ponds in eating every last slug in the neighbourhood (or at least a good proportion of them).

Chapter 2 should have given you plenty of ideas on useful trees to grow, though most of these were not native. Listed below are many of our native species of trees and large shrubs. All are deciduous unless it says otherwise. They are arranged according to the habitat they would occupy in a woodland (this is explained more fully in Chapter 2). This does not mean, of course, that you need to grow them in a woodland. Any of them can be used as specimen plants, or be integrated with non-native species in the garden.

To help give some idea of the plants most suited for your situation, the native habitat of each species is given. When grown in a similar habitat, the plants should be able to maintain themselves by self-sowing. Most of these species will also succeed in other habitats, as the text should explain, but when grown in other habitats they are less likely to maintain themselves.

When discussing these plants there will often be a comment about the number of insect species associated with the tree. This is a very important indicator of the value of trees to wildlife. The more insect species a tree supports then the more it will be able to support the other creatures in the intricate web of life that is found in a woodland.

PIONEER SPECIES

Alnus glutinosa. ALDER grows up to 25 metres tall and 10 metres wide. It is found in wet ground in woods, near lakes and along the sides of streams. Alder is very amenable to trimming and can be grown as a tall hedge or as coppice.

This is an important food plant for the caterpillars of many butterfly and moth species and also for small birds in winter. There are 90 insect species associated with this tree. The plant is discussed more fully on page 193.

Betula pendula. The SILVER BIRCH grows wild in open woodland and on heaths, usually in acid soils. Very rarely it is found on chalk.

B. pubescens. The DOWNY BIRCH grows in open woodland and heaths, usually on acid soils, from sea level to 830 metres.

These two species are often amongst the first trees to find their way to land that is reverting to woodland. Very tough and fast-growing trees that can reach 18 metres tall and 10 metres wide, they succeed in most soils and situations, though they prefer acid conditions. They are not so happy in strong maritime exposure, and will often be severely wind-shaped in such a situation. There are 229 insect species associated with these trees.

Birch has been widely utilised for food and other commodities in the past and I will list just a few of these uses here. A pleasant drink can be made from the sap, it is not as sweet as sugar maple but is a much more reliable crop in this country. A tea is made from the leaves and another tea is made from the essential oil in the inner bark.

The bark is waterproof, durable, tough and resinous. It can be used to make drinking vessels, canoe skins and roofing tiles. Only the outer bark is removed and, if this is done carefully, it will not harm the tree. A tar-oil obtained from the white bark in spring has fungicidal properties and is also used as an insect repellent and a shoe polish. A glue is made from the sap. A medicinal oil similar to 'Oil of Wintergreen' is obtained from the inner bark, it is especially good for treating muscular aches and pains. The young branches, which are very flexible, are used to make whisks and besoms and are also used in thatching.

Hippophae rhamnoides. SEA BUCKTHORN is usually found near the coast on fixed dunes and sea cliffs. A fast-growing shrub, it can grow up to 6 metres tall and suckers freely to form thickets. It demands a sunny position in a well-drained soil, growing well in maritime exposure and in sandy soils. The vigorous root system has been used for stabilising sand dunes along the coast. Since the plant forms nitrogen nodules on its roots, it also serves to improve soil fertility.

The acid fruit, which is produced in abundance if at least one male plant is grown for every 5 -6 females, is a very good source of vitamin C. It is loved by the birds though not many people would enjoy eating it raw. It does become less sharp after a frost or if it is cooked, and when sweetened it makes a good fruit juice. This is an ideal fruit to add to sweeter fruits when making juices, adding a delicious taste as well as an abundance of minerals and vitamins. Recent research in Sweden has shown that this is perhaps the most nutritious fruit that can be grown in the temperate zone.

There are some superior fruiting forms from northern Europe where it is occasionally cultivated as a fruit crop. 'Leikora' is a free-fruiting form that is occasionally available here, but I do not know of any other cultivars that are available in this country yet.

Sea buckthorn is very thorny and can be grown as a hedge that gives protection from the elements as well as from two and four-legged creatures.

Populus nigra. The BLACK POPLAR, grows up to 30 metres tall and 20 metres wide. It is found mainly in moist soils, especially by streams, and does best in the south and east of Britain.

P. tremula. The ASPEN grows 18 metres tall and 10 metres wide, producing suckers freely. It is found in open woodlands and scrubby heathland, usually on poorer soils where it is sometimes dominant. Over 90 insect species are associated with this tree and it is a food plant for the green hairstreak butterfly.

Both of the above species can be coppiced. Because they are very fast growing, they can be cut back as often as every year if required for fuel – though there are much better fuel woods around. See also page 193.

Salix species. WILLOWS are very valuable sources of nectar for bees in the spring. These trees and large shrubs require a moist fertile soil if they are to grow well, their aggressive root system means that they should not be planted within about 12 metres of buildings or drains. When grown for basket making or fuel, willows are normally coppiced annually, though sometimes they are left for two years in order to provide stouter stems.

The following species are native. They are discussed more fully on pages 24 and 194:

S. alba. The WHITE WILLOW is found growing by streams and rivers, marshes, woods and wet fens on richer soils. Growing up to 25 metres tall and 10 metres wide, it has over 200 associated insect species.

S. fragilis. The CRACK WILLOW is found by streams and rivers, marshes, fens and wet woods. It is more tolerant of poor soils than *S. alba*. It can be 15 metres tall and wide. The crack willow gets its name from the ease by which small pieces of branch will break off the tree. These small branches can form roots when they lie on the ground and so this is one of the ways in which the tree reproduces itself. This habit, though, does make it the least useful willow for basketry out of the species listed here.

S. pentandra. The BAY WILLOW grows wild along the sides of streams, in marshes, fens and wet woods in northern Britain. It can be 10 metres tall and wide.

S. purpurea. The PURPLE WILLOW grows in wet places in lowland areas, preferring neutral or alkaline soils. It is sometimes locally dominant in fens. The plants grow up to 5 metres tall and wide.

S. triandra. The ALMOND WILLOW grows along the sides of rivers and ponds and marshes. It is common in England, less so in Wales and very local in Scotland. It can grow up to 9 metres tall and 6 metres wide.

S. viminalis. The COMMON OSIER is found by rivers and streams, also on deep moist alluvial soils, avoiding very acid soils. It grows up to 6 metres tall and 4 metres wide.

Sambucus nigra. ELDER grows wild in hedgerows, scrub, woods, roadsides and waste places, especially on disturbed base-rich and nitrogen rich soils. It is very resistant to the ravages of rabbits. It grows up to 6 metres tall and wide.

This species is a must in any conservation garden and is also suitable for hedging. See also page 183.

TALL TREES

Carpinus betulus. HORNBEAM is found in woodlands and hedgerows on sandy or clay loams, preferring heavier soils. It grows 25 metres tall and 20 metres wide. An easily grown and very tolerant plant, it prefers a heavy soil and dislikes very acid conditions. It has a very dense canopy and therefore casts a heavy shade.

Hornbeam is very tolerant of trimming and makes an excellent medium to large hedge. If cut once a year in late summer it will retain its dead leaves all winter and thereby provide more shelter. The tree can also be coppiced, usually at intervals of 10 years or more depending on the size of wood you want. It has 28 associated insect species.

Fagus sylvatica. BEECH grows wild in woodlands, where it is often the dominant species, and strongly favours chalky soils. It grows up to 30 metres tall and 15 metres wide, succeeding in almost any soil. It has a very dense canopy and casts such a heavy shade that few species are able to grow in a beech woodland. It has 64 species of associated insects.

Suitable for hedging and providing edible leaves and seeds, it is dealt with more fully on pages 28 and 182.

Fraxinus excelsior. ASH forms woods on calcareous soils in the wetter parts of Britain, it is also often found on acid soils as well as in oakwoods, scrub and hedges. It can be up to 30 metres tall and 20 metres wide. It has 41 associated insect species. Ash coppices very well and its hard, resilient wood can be used for many purposes including as tool handles and for fuel. See also page 193.

Pinus sylvestris. The SCOT'S PINE can be the dominant species in woodlands in mountainous areas and on acid, sandy soils. It is probably only genuinely native in Scotland, though it grows well in sandy soils in all parts of the country. A tall evergreen tree growing up to 25 metres tall and 10 metres wide, it tolerates chalky soils but grows better and lives longer on acid sands. It is very tolerant of exposure and can be grown to provide shelter from the wind. There are over 50 species of associated insects.

Turpentine can be obtained from resin in the tree but it is not present in economic quantities.

Prunus avium. The WILD CHERRY is found in better soils in hedgerows and woods, especially in beech woods. It can grow up to 18 metres tall and 7 metres wide. It prefers a sunny position with some lime in the soil.

The fruit is up to 2cm in diameter and can be sweet or bitter. It is often quite pleasant, but the birds will usually beat you to it.

P. padus. The BIRD CHERRY grows wild by streams and in moist open woods, usually on alkaline soils, though it is also found on acid soils in upland areas. Up to 15 metres tall and 8 metres wide, it succeeds in most soils and grows well on the sunnier edges of a woodland.

The fruit is about the size of a pea, it is usually fairly bitter but the birds don't seem to mind this and eat it as voraciously as they eat the wild cherry.

Quercus petraea. The SESSILE OAK is often the dominant tree in woodlands, especially on acid soils and in the western and northern parts of Britain. It grows up to 35 metres tall and 25 metres wide.

Q. robur. The PEDUNCULATE OAK is more commonly found in the east and south of the country, where it is often the dominant woodland tree, especially on clay and basic soils, but avoiding acid peat and shallow limestone soils. It can grow up to 35 metres tall and 30 metres wide.

If you have space for them, oaks are the conservationist's tree par excellence in this country, they have 284 associated insect species. They both prefer fertile soils on the heavy side and are fairly tolerant of exposure.

The seed is rich in carbohydrate and can be roasted then used as a caffeine-free coffee substitute. It is also possible for us to eat the seed, indeed I once knew a young lad who would often munch on them when we were out walking together, but they do really need to be leached of bitter tannins before being used. This will also remove a good proportion of the minerals and vitamins from the seed, unfortunately, which leaves you with the starch and very little else. The seeds can be leached by grinding them into a flour and then rinsing this thoroughly until the bitterness has gone (which can take a few hours).

A slower but easier method is to put the seeds into a cloth bag and immerse this in a stream or other running water for a few months. The North American Indians would often bury the seeds in boggy ground over the winter and then dig them up in the spring when they were starting to germinate. At this stage they are almost sweet and have retained more vitamins and minerals so they are also more nutritious.

There is considerable variation in the tannin content of our native oaks, so it might be worth your while trying some acorns from different trees to see if you can find some low in tannin. If you really want to eat acorns and would rather not have all that hassle, then why not grow *Q. ilex* (see page 36) and leave our native acorns for the many other creatures that can enjoy them bitterness and all.

Oak trees have many other uses, including the following. The well-rotted leaves make one of the best leaf-moulds I know and a mulch of it repels slugs, grubs etc. – but don't use fresh leaves since these can inhibit plant growth. The bark is an ingredient of 'Quick Return' herbal compost activator. An ink is made from the oak galls mixed with salts of iron.

Oaks respond very well to coppicing. Because they are slow-growing, though, this is on a longer term than many other species, often at intervals of 50 years.

The wood is hard, tough and durable even under water and is highly valued for furniture-making and construction. Oak is occasionally grown as a hedge, but is not really very suitable for that purpose and will often become bare at the base after some years.

***Sorbus* species**. This genus of easily grown trees can provide an abundance of fruit for wildlife (see also page 30). The following species are native:

S. aria. The WHITEBEAM grows in woods and scrub, usually on chalk or limestone, mainly in the south of Britain. It can be up to 12 metres tall and 8 metres wide. This is a very tolerant tree that succeeds in heavy clays, shallow chalky soils and acid sands, as well as in very exposed positions.

S. aucuparia. The ROWAN grows in woods, scrub and mountain rocks, mainly on lighter soils. It is rare or absent on clays or soft limestones. It grows up to 15 metres tall and 7 metres wide. This is a very tough plant, it grows at higher elevations than any other native tree and succeeds in some of the bleakest and most windswept areas of the country. Birds absolutely adore this fruit and will usually leave your apples alone if they can eat this instead. It has 28 associated species of insects.

S. devoniensis. Only found wild in Devon, Cornwall and southern Ireland, where it grows in old woods. It can be up to 12 metres tall and wide.

S. domestica. The SERVICE TREE grows in woods and bushy places. It can be 15 metres tall and wide.

S. torminalis. The WILD SERVICE TREE grows as an occasional tree in woods, usually on clay and sometimes on limestone, in the southern half of the country. It can be up to 20 metres tall.

Tilia cordata. SMALL-LEAVED LIME grows in woods on most fertile soils, especially limestone, and is commonly found on wooded limestone cliffs. It grows up to 30 metres tall and 12 metres wide.

T. platyphyllos. There is some doubt over whether the LARGE-LEAVED LIME is a genuine native of Britain. It is found wild in woods on good calcareous or base-rich soils and on limestone cliffs, especially in the Midlands and Welsh borders, though it is widely planted elsewhere. It grows up to 30 metres tall and 20 metres wide.

T. x vulgaris. COMMON LIME is very doubtfully native, though it self-sows and is also widely planted. It can grow up to 35 metres tall and 15 metres wide. All three species of lime are very amenable to coppicing and provide a valuable white wood that is excellent for carving. It is often used for making kitchen implements because it is virtually without odour and so does not taint the food.

There are 31 species of insects associated with lime trees, though there are also potential problems with bees. See also page 31.

Ulmus glabra. The WYCH ELM is found in woods, hedges and by streams. It is commoner in the west and north of the country. It grows up to 30 metres tall and 25 metres wide.

U. procera. The ENGLISH ELM grows in hedgerows, by woods and along the sides of roads. It is less frequent in the north of the country.

These stately trees are very fast-growing and will succeed in maritime exposure. Unfortunately they have been decimated by Dutch elm disease and a mature specimen of the English elm is now a rare sight. Plants of this species will often regrow from suckers when the top growth is killed off, but then as soon as the trunk is large enough along comes the beetle and re-infects the tree. The wych elm has been less affected by the disease, though it is far from immune.

There is some hope now that the disease is on the decline, but it is much too early to recommend anything other than small trial plantings. When we planted our woodland in 1992 the Forestry Commission asked us to put in 50 young trees of the English elm to see how they would fare. Let us hope that they are still growing strongly in another 100 years time.

You can eat young elm leaves, they have a mild flavour and are somewhat mucilaginous, making a nice addition to salads. They look superficially similar to hazel leaves, as my wife found out many years ago. She soon discovered the difference when the bitter-tasting hazel leaves attacked her palate! The immature fruits, used just after they are formed, can be eaten raw and have an aromatic, unusual flavour that leaves the mouth feeling fresh and the breath smelling pleasant. A fibre obtained from the inner bark can be used for making mats and ropes. Let us hope that it will not be too many years before these useful trees can grace our countryside again.

SMALLER TREES

Acer campestre. FIELD MAPLE grows up to 15 metres tall in open deciduous woods, hedgerows and scrub, usually on basic soils. It is most common in south, east and central England.

Field maple makes an excellent hedge, growing fast when young but then slowing with age. See also page 180.

Ilex aquifolium. HOLLY is found wild in most well-drained soils in scrub, hedges and woodland, where it is often the dominant under-storey shrub. A slow-growing evergreen shrub or small tree, it can eventually reach 9 metres tall with a spread of 5 metres. It is very tolerant of pruning, however, and there are also many smaller growing cultivars, so this is a plant that can be fitted into most small gardens. An exceedingly tolerant plant, it can be grown in most soils and situations including deep shade and maritime exposure. It makes a very good hedge that will keep out most unwelcome visitors, though you will need to have the patience to wait for it to grow.

The fruit is a good winter food for birds as long as you grow plants of both sexes. There are many named varieties in garden centres and these are usually marked as to whether they are male or female. These named varieties, of course, cannot really be considered native plants. One male is enough to fertilize 5 - 6 females.

Malus sylvestris. The CRAB APPLE is found wild in woods, scrub and hedges, especially in oak woods, on neutral to calcareous soils. It grows up to 10 metres tall and 6 metres wide. An easily grown tree, it does well in most soils, including heavy clays, and is well suited to the sunny edges of a woodland. It is very ornamental when flowering in the spring. There are 90 associated insect species.

The fruit varies considerably in size and quality, from 2 - 4cm or more in diameter. It is edible, but is usually rather acid and astringent, which makes it good for mixing with sweeter apples when making cider or apple juice. The fruit is rich in pectin, which does make it very useful for mixing with pectin-low fruits such as raspberries when making jam.

Occasionally you can come across forms of crabs with quite acceptable fruits, this is often because there has been hybridisation with a cultivated apple. Various forms of crabs are sometimes grown as pollinators in commercial apple orchards.

Taxus baccata. YEW is an evergreen tree that grows wild in woods and scrub, usually on limestone. It sometimes forms pure stands in sheltered sites on chalk in south-east England and on limestone in the north-west. It is tolerant of considerable shade.

Very amenable to trimming, it makes an excellent hedge. See also pages 44 and 188.

SHRUBS

Cornus sanguinea. DOGWOOD grows up to 3 metres tall in woods and scrub on calcareous soils and also grows well in a mixed hedge. It is occasionally locally dominant in chalk scrub. The flowers have a rather unpleasant smell to most people, though they are attractive to insects. When coppiced annually, the plant throws up lots of straight stems that can be used in basket making. See also page 180.

Corylus avellana. HAZEL grows wild in woods and hedgerows, especially on the slopes of hills and often on calcareous soils. It is often the dominant shrub-layer in lowland oak woods and sometimes also in ash woods. It grows up to 6 metres tall and 3 metres wide and makes a good hedge.

Hazel is an excellent shrub to grow in a coppiced woodland. It is usually cut down every 7 - 12 years and the wood has a very wide range of uses. It is, for example, used to make fencing, baskets, pea sticks and small items of furniture. The new growth will take about 5 - 7 years before it is mature enough to start producing nuts so the longer the interval between coppicing the more nuts you are likely to harvest. See also page 189.

Crataegus monogyna. The HAWTHORN is a very common plant in scrub, woods, hedges and thickets. It is found in most soils and is rare only in wet peat and poor acid sands.

C. laevigata. The MIDLAND HAWTHORN is much less common and is more a woodland species, being found mainly in eastern England. Where found in hedges it is often as a relict of ancient woodland.

The hawthorns are very undemanding shrubs or small trees, growing up to 6 metres tall and wide, and succeeding in most soils and situations. They have 149 associated insect species.

The plants are very amenable to trimming and make good hedges, indeed they are widely used for this purpose in country areas and make a good stock-proof barrier, especially if they are layered occasionally.

Amongst their other uses, the young shoot tips have a pleasant nutty flavour and make a nice addition to salads. The fruit is 8 - 10mm in diameter and is also edible but is rather less than wonderful with a bland flavour and a mealy texture, but is well known for its tonic effect upon the heart and also as a treatment for high blood pressure. The roasted seeds are used as a coffee substitute and a tea is made from the dried leaves.

Euonymus europaeus. The SPINDLE TREE grows in woods, scrub and hedges, usually on calcareous soils. Very tolerant of soil conditions, it does particularly well in dry shade and also succeeds on chalk. Growing up to 6 metres tall, it is very amenable to trimming and can be grown in a hedge.

All parts of the plant are poisonous but there are several non-food uses. An oil from the seed is used in soap-making. The baked and powdered berries or the leaves have been used to remove lice from the hair and as an insecticide. The wood is very hard, it is used for making spindles, skewers, knitting needles, toothpicks and also for carving. A high quality charcoal obtained from the wood is used by artists. This plant often harbours blackfly, so it might be wise not to grow it near broad beans or other susceptible plants.

Juniperus communis. JUNIPER is an evergreen plant that is found in a wide variety of soils ranging from the chalk downs of southern England in sites where there is least sunshine and most rain, to the heaths, moors, pine and birch woods in the north of Scotland on acid peat. It is often the dominant component of scrub on chalk, limestone and slate. Very variable in size, it can be up to 9 metres tall and 4 metres wide. See also page 54.

Ligustrum vulgare. PRIVET grows up to 3 metres tall in hedges and scrub, especially in calcareous soils. It makes a very good hedge, though needs constant trimming. Plants can form dense thickets and make good bird cover. This is also an important food plant for many caterpillars, including the larvae of the privet hawk moth. See also page 188.

Prunus spinosa. SLOES grow wild in hedgerows and woods, usually in sunny positions, on all soils except acid peat. Up to 4 metres tall, it suckers freely and can form extensive thickets.

This is a very easily grown species that succeeds in all soils except very acid peat. It does well in light shade but fruits better in a sunny position and is very resistant to maritime exposure.

The sloe is an important food plant for the caterpillars of several species of butterfly, especially the larvae of the brown and black hairstreak butterflies. When allowed to form dense thickets, it makes an ideal nesting site for many species of birds, especially nightingales.

The fruit is about 15mm in diameter and can be eaten raw or cooked. It is very astringent in the early autumn, mellowing with the autumn frosts, but never becoming exactly pleasant. Many children seem to like it, and it can also be used for making preserves and sloe gin, but this is a fruit I am happy to leave for the birds.

The bark is a good source of tannin and is used to make an ink. The juice of unripe fruits is used as a laundry mark that is almost indelible.

The sloe is an exceedingly tough plant and succeeds in very exposed positions. It is one of the major components of hedgerows in Cornwall, making a good stock-proof hedge if it is well maintained. It is rather bare in the winter and, unless the hedge is rather wide, it is not a very good shelter from the wind at this time.

Rhamnus cathartica. COMMON BUCKTHORN is found wild on fen peat, in scrub, hedges, ash and oak woods, on calcareous often dry soils. It is most common in the south, east and the Midlands, and is absent from much of the extreme west and Scotland. It grows up to 6 metres tall and 3 metres wide and prefers a calcareous soil but is not too fussy. It grows well on the woodland edge but don't grow it near cereals because it often bears a stage in the life-cycle of the disease 'crown rust' of oats. Common buckthorn is a main food plant for the brimstone butterfly.

Amenable to trimming, it can be grown as a formal or informal hedge. A green dye is obtained from the immature fruit and a yellow dye from the bark.

R. *frangula*. The ALDER BUCKTHORN grows in swamps and damp places, usually on moist heaths and damp open woods, preferring a peaty soil. It is found in most of England and Wales, but is absent from Scotland. Up to 5 metres tall and 4 metres wide, it is easily grown in most soils though it dislikes dry conditions and exposed sites. It has very similar uses to the above species.

Viburnum opulus. GUELDER ROSE is commonly found in hedges, scrub and woodland, usually on damp soils. This is a large shrub for the woodland edge, growing 5 metres tall and wide. Very tolerant of soil conditions, it grows well on chalk though it dislikes soils that are poor, dry or very acid.

The fruit is edible but rather less than pleasant to my taste. It can also cause diarrhoea, especially if eaten raw, or in large quantities or when not fully ripe. It does, however, make an excellent tasting jam. In general, the birds will enjoy it much more than you and might even leave your apples alone whilst they are eating it. A red dye and ink can be obtained from the fresh or dried fruit. The plants have also been grown as a hedge though they tend to become bare at the base and do not afford much shelter in the winter.

V. *lantana*. The WAYFARING TREE is found in open woodland and woodland edges, especially on calcareous soils. Growing 5 metres tall and 4 metres wide, it has similar needs to the above species. Its fruit is even less acceptable to our stomachs and palates but the stems can be used as a twine.

WOODLAND & HEDGEROW PLANTS

When planting a native hedge or woodland, don't forget that many other native plants can be grown amongst the shrubs and trees. The following list is a selection of the possibilities and a walk through your local woods will show you other plants that can be used. All the plants listed here are perennial unless otherwise stated. They will provide food and shelter for the wildlife, thus adding to the diversity of creatures that are able to live in and near the hedge and woodland. Assuming the soil and situation are suitable, they should all maintain themselves without further input from you. If you have any favourites, though, you could always mollycoddle them by spreading their seed around and perhaps removing some of the growth from neighbouring plants.

Alliaria petiolata. GARLIC MUSTARD is a biennial growing up to 1 metre tall. Growing best in alkaline soils, it succeeds on both the sunny and shady sides of a hedge. It is an important food source for the orange-tip butterfly.

    If you like a taste that is like a cross between garlic and mustard then try adding some leaves to your salads in late winter and early spring. We have often used them and they do add a rather pleasant flavour.

Allium ursinum. WILD GARLIC grows exceedingly well in a shady position. Reaching a height of 30cm, when well-sited it usually forms carpets of growth many metres wide. Wild garlic is often found growing in quite wet soils, though it is also found in drier parts of the woodland and in hedgerows. See also page 76.

Aquilegia vulgaris. COLUMBINE grows up to 1 metre tall. It likes growing on the sunnier edges of a woodland or hedgerow. See also page 89.

Conopodium majus. PIGNUT grows about 30cm tall and grows well in semi-shade. It dislikes alkaline soils but is otherwise not too fussy. See also page 78.

Geum rivale. WATER AVENS grows about 30cm tall, doing best in a moist humus-rich soil and a shady position.

    The fresh or dried root can be used to make a chocolate-like drink or is used as a seasoning – it was once used to flavour ales. The dried root can also be used as a moth repellent.

Geum urbanum. WOOD AVENS grows up to 50cm tall and does best in a humus-rich soil in a shady position.

    It was widely cultivated as a potherb in the 16th century. The young leaves can be cooked whilst the root is used as a spice in soups and stews. It can be used as a substitute for cloves and also has a hint of cinnamon.

Hedera helix. IVY is a superb plant for wildlife and is so adaptable that it took me quite a while to decide which chapter to put it in. I finally put the main entry here with other notes on pages 158 and 208. This vigorous evergreen climber succeeds in sun, dense shade and in most soils. It can be grown as a climbing plant, a hedge or as ground cover, and provides dense shelter for birds and spiders, a late supply of nectar for insects and a supply of berries for the wildlife during late winter and early spring. It is also a food plant for the larvae of many species of butterfly.

Some of the more direct uses for us include: a yellow and a brown dye are obtained from the twigs; a decoction of the leaves is used to restore black fabrics and as a hair rinse to darken the hair; if the leaves are boiled with soda they can be used as a soap substitute for washing clothes.

Contrary to what some people think, ivy is not a parasite and will cause little or no harm to any healthy tree into which it is growing. It is rather vigorous, however, and can climb into the crown of an ailing tree, a small tree or a young slow-growing tree and will then shade out and possibly kill it.

Humulus lupulus. Our native HOP can climb up to 6 metres tall, though it usually goes sideways as much as it goes up. This is a plant for a fairly sunny position on the woodland edge or in the hedgerow. It will support itself by twining around other plants. Hops have a very wide range of uses as described on page 68.

Hyacinthoides non-scriptus. BLUEBELLS (or HAREBELLS if you live in Scotland) grow well in the semi-shade of a woodland, even if the soil is dry. They also succeed in full sun. Plants grow up to 30cm tall and can form huge carpets of growth in suitable conditions.

An excellent paper glue is obtained from the sap in the bulb and stem. You simply cut open a bulb and rub it quite hard over one piece of the paper, then press the two pieces of paper together and leave them to dry. The resultant join is very strong, in fact if you try and pull it apart the paper will tear before the join breaks.

Malva moschata. The MUSK MALLOW is an excellent salad plant which grows about 75cm tall and thrives in light shade or full sun in a hedge or along the woodland edge. See also page 94.

Oxalis acetosella. WOOD SORREL is a salad plant which forms a gradually spreading clump about 8cm tall and 30cm wide. It thrives in the deep shade of a woodland and will also succeed in sunnier positions. See also page 74.

Rubus fruticosus and *R. idaeus.* BLACKBERRIES and RASPBERRIES should be too well known to include in this book. Just a reminder that it is not only humans who like the fruits, so plant some in the hedgerow or along the woodland edges. The plants will also provide some very good nesting sites for birds and small mammals.

Rumex acetosa. SORREL is a delicious salad plant which grows about 60cm tall and does well in the sunnier parts of a hedge or woodland. See also page 80.

Saponaria officinalis. SOAPWORT grows about 1 metre tall and can spread freely at the roots. It succeeds in most soils in sun or light shade. The flowers are an absolute magnet for moths and will attract them from miles away.

A gentle and very effective soap can be obtained by infusing the macerated plant in warm water. The root is especially effective and can be dried for later use. The soap is especially suitable for cleaning old and delicate fabrics, indeed it is used to clean the Bayeaux Tapestry because it is the only cleaner that will remove the dirt from this ancient fabric without removing the colours at the same time. The soap is also very good for the skin. Because it does not remove the body's natural oils, it is a very useful soap for anyone with delicate skin.

Symphytum officinale. COMFREY is a very useful species which grows about 1.2 metres tall and grows well in a sunny position or light shade in the woodland. See also pages 12 and 80.

Tussilago farfara. COLTSFOOT grows about 20cm tall and spreads very freely at the roots. See also page 146.

Urtica dioica. The STINGING NETTLE is well known to anyone who has had a brush with it! Growing up to 1.2 metres tall, it prefers a rich soil though is not too fussy. Especially when growing in rich soils, the plant can spread vigorously and is then very difficult to eradicate. If you really need to get rid of it, then it is said that cutting the plant down three times a year for three years will kill it.

Nettles are one of the most undervalued of economic plants. They have a wide range of uses, for food, medicines and fibres and are also a very important plant for wildlife. There are at least 30 species of insects that feed on it and the caterpillars of several butterfly species are dependent upon it for food. There is also a species of aphid that is specific to nettles. This aphid is active early in the year and therefore forms a food supply for the various aphid predators, which can then move onto other plants in the garden to eat aphids there.

Nettles have a long list of other uses, a few of which I will detail here. The leaves are extremely rich in vitamins and minerals. They make a very nutritious spinach substitute that is liked by many people, though the smell of fish as it cooks puts me off. Only use the young leaves since older ones develop gritty particles called cystoliths which act as an irritant to the kidneys. The leaves can also be used in making tea and nettle beer.

The stems contain a strong flax-like fibre which can be used for making string, cloth and paper – the stems are best harvested as the plant begins to die down in early autumn and they are then treated like flax in order to obtain the fibre. The plant is an essential ingredient of 'Quick Return' herbal compost activator and the leaves are also an excellent addition to the compost heap. See Chapter 1 for details of making a liquid feed from nettles – this feed is both insect repellent and a good foliar feed. The growing plant increases the essential oil content of other nearby plants, thus making them more resistant to insect pests.

I have often seen recommendations to grow nettles amongst the soft fruit in order to stop the birds from eating all your fruit. Whilst this might work, it will also stop you from picking the fruit unless you are happy to be stung. I have found that allowing the grass to grow up around the soft fruit in July works just as well, but make sure that you have given the fruit bushes a good weed-excluding mulch around their roots so that the grass does not out-compete them.

Finally, a hair wash is made from infused nettle leaves and this is used as a tonic and anti-dandruff treatment. Incidentally, one of the more effective dandruff treatments that I have heard about is to bathe the hair in fresh urine. Apparently this works quite well and also sorts out who your true friends are!

Viola odorata. SWEET VIOLET is a productive winter salad plant which grows about 10cm tall and spreads freely to form clumps 1 metre or more wide. It succeeds in most soils in sun or shade and does well on the woodland edge or in a hedgerow. See also page 81.

PONDS

A pond can really enhance a garden – it can also provide a home for frogs who will then more than pay their rent by eating many of the slugs in the garden. Ponds will also attract many other creatures to the garden – one of my favourite summer occupations is watching the swallows fly over one of our ponds, either catching some of the many insects which fly over the water, or dipping down and taking a mouthful of water as they fly across.

The pond can range in size from just a few square feet to as large as you like. An old bath can be buried in the ground or you can buy pond liners or pre-formed ponds. It is best not to have fish in a pond if you want amphibians since many species will eat the spawn and the tadpoles. There are, however, many useful plants that can be grown in a pond. The subject is dealt with in more detail in Chapter 6.

WILDFLOWER MEADOWS

A meadow of wild flowers is a wonderful and sadly rare sight in Britain today. The flowers attract a wealth of butterflies, moths, bees and other insects and these in turn will bring along many species of birds. Whilst few of us will have enough land to be able to create a full-size meadow, most of us will have gardens and most of these gardens will have a lawn. It is a fairly simple matter to seed or plant an area of this lawn with native wild flowers and then only cut it from August onwards once the plants have set seed. It will soon become a wonderful miniature wildflower meadow for bees and butterflies and will also be a focal point for the garden in spring and early summer.

It is best to choose a sunny site, since this will encourage heavier flowering. It is also important that the soil is not too rich otherwise you will end up with a very vigorous growth of grass and very little in the way of pretty flowers. Don't cut the grass until the flowers have set seed and make sure that you remove all the mowings in order to keep soil fertility low since this will encourage the flowers and discourage too lush a growth of grass. These mowings, of course, can provide an excellent source of organic matter for the compost heap, so try to site your meadow somewhere near the compost in order to reduce the need for carting it about.

You can just walk over the area sowing a mixture of wildflower seeds – this can be very effective if the seed mixture contains grasses and you are sowing into bare earth, but is very wasteful of seed if grass is already established. If you want to convert an existing area of grass into a meadow then it is better to sow the seed in trays, grow them on in pots and plant them out in the autumn or spring – although this is much more work, you will have much better results.

It is very important to take all factors into account when planning a garden, farm or whatever. When designing our land a few years ago I wanted to do everything right. The compost bins were sited in the middle of the most intensely cultivated part of the land, I wanted the meadow to be somewhere nearby and so I chose a convenient site that bordered this area. In the autumn I went out and planted lots of wild flower plants, then sat back and waited for them all to flower the following summer. I waited, and waited and am still waiting! I could not find even one of the plants growing there – there was plenty of lush grass growth but no wild flowers. In satisfying one criteria for siting a wildflower meadow I had completely overlooked another. The site I had chosen was almost the lowest point on the land and consequently had received all the nutrients and soil being washed down the hill as a result of many years of intensive agriculture. It was probably the richest soil on the land – no wonder the grass was growing so well! So well, in fact, that it completely smothered the flowers. The moral of the story? Don't ask a former bus driver to design your land.

It is possible to reduce soil fertility by cutting the grass every few weeks in the growing season and removing all the mowings, though this can take a few years to be effective if the ground is very fertile. It might make more sense to move the site of the meadow, a conclusion I am reluctantly coming to terms with.

Many of the species mentioned in Chapter 7 can be grown in a meadow, the following perennial species could also be included:

Bunium bulbocastanum. PIGNUT grows up to 60cm tall and prefers growing on alkaline soils in the wild, though it is not too fussy in cultivation.

The root matures in late summer and has a delicious taste very like sweet chestnuts, though it is rather small and fiddly and only one tuber is formed by the plant. There is a potential to improve the size by cultivation so perhaps this species should have been included in Chapter 5. The seed and flowers can be used as a cumin substitute and the leaves as a garnish and flavouring in much the same way as parsley.

Cardamine pratensis. CUCKOO FLOWER is also much liked by the orange-tip butterfly. Growing about 45cm tall, it requires a moist soil and prefers a sunny position. The leaves and flowers have a hot and pungent cress-like flavour. They go well as a flavouring in mixed salads.

Filipendula ulmaria. MEADOWSWEET is a plant for moist or wet meadows. It grows 1.2 metres tall and requires a humus-rich moist soil, succeeding in full sun only if the soil is reliably moist throughout the growing season. It dislikes acid soils, though it grows well in heavy clay soils.

Meadowsweet has a long and proven history of medicinal use. The dried leaves are used as a flavouring or as a herb tea, they can also be used as a sweetener in other herb teas. The flowers are used as a flavouring in various alcoholic beverages and in stewed fruit, they are also made into a syrup which can be used in cooling drinks and fruit salads. An essential oil obtained from the flower buds is used in perfumery and the whole plant was formerly used as a strewing herb.

Filipendula vulgaris. DROPWORT grows about 75cm tall and grows wild in calcareous meadows. It prefers a well-drained moisture retentive soil, though it also does well in dry conditions. The young leaves can be eaten raw or cooked.

Galium verum. LADY'S BEDSTRAW grows about 60cm tall and spreads very freely at the roots. It prefers a loose moist leafy soil in some shade, but it tolerates a position in full sun. It will also succeed in dry conditions, but does not thrive in a hot climate. It is a food plant for the caterpillars of several butterflies.

The plant has many uses. These include a yellow dye from the flowering stems that is used as a food colouring. The roasted seed makes a very acceptable coffee substitute. The flowering tops are used in the preparation of a refreshing acid beverage. A red dye is obtained from the root. The dried plant has the scent of newly mown hay and it was formerly used as a strewing herb and for stuffing mattresses where it also acts to repel fleas.

Rumex acetosella. SHEEP SORREL grows about 30cm tall. It succeeds in most soils, preferring a moist moderately fertile well-drained soil in a sunny position. Although it is found wild on acid soils, it can tolerate some alkalinity. It is a food plant for the caterpillars of several butterflies.

The acid flavoured leaves are a delightful addition to a mixed salad, and also make a thirst-quenching munch on a summer's day. If the winter is not too severe they can be available all year round. They should not be eaten in large quantities, though, because they contain oxalic acid. See Appendix 4 for more information.

Trifolium pratense. RED CLOVER is an excellent plant for the meadow, growing up to 60cm tall. It prefers a moist, well-drained circum-neutral soil in full sun and tends to be short-lived, though it will self-sow successfully if growing in a suitable site. It is a very important food plant for the caterpillars of many butterfly and moth species and will also draw in plenty of bees.

It grows well in an apple orchard, the trees will produce tastier fruit that stores better. It should not be grown with camellias or gooseberries because it harbours a mite that can cause fruit drop in the gooseberries and premature budding in the camellias.

The young leaves and young flowering heads can be eaten raw or cooked. They taste vaguely of peas and, as leaves go, they are a good source of protein.

My wife likes them, but I have eaten nicer saladings. The seed can be sprouted and used in salads, it has a crisp texture and more robust flavour than alfalfa, but harvesting the seed by hand is very time consuming. A delicate sweet herb tea is made from the fresh or dried flowers. The dried leaves impart a vanilla flavour to cakes. The plant is sometimes used as a green manure, because it fixes atmospheric nitrogen.

EXOTIC SPECIES

So far in this chapter we have been talking about growing native plants in native habitats. Now I would like to issue a little warning of the potential dangers of introducing plants from other countries. It may seem strange to talk about this when the greatest part of the book has been dedicated to extolling the virtues of so many non-native species. There are a number of plants that have been introduced into this country that have subsequently found the environment so much to their liking that they have spread freely and become well established.

Sometimes this can be mainly beneficial. The buddleia, for example, is an excellent plant for butterflies, juneberries provide fruits for birds and the sweet chestnut feeds a range of birds and mammals. On some occasions, however, the introduced plant becomes a menace and threatens existing environments. ***Rhododendron ponticum*** is a prime example of this. It has become naturalized in woodlands and is preventing the regeneration of native trees.

We should not just introduce new species willy-nilly, but need to carefully consider the potential of the plant in this country. There are very few restrictions on importing plant seed into this country and this is generally beneficial since Britain is quite poor in native species, but we do have to exercise discrimination. As far as possible we should try to protect our native plant habitats since these have the proven track-record for our area.

It is as well to remember, though, that had it taken a thousand years or more longer before the land bridge between Britain and the rest of Europe was cut off by rising sea levels, there would have been a lot more native species in this country. There is a school of thought which suggests that given time any introduced species will become adapted to the environment and the native species of plants and animals will become adapted to it, so that there will be an overall increase in diversity and stability of the ecosystem.

As an example of this, we can look at ***Polygonum japonicum***, the JAPANESE KNOTWEED. This is an extremely invasive species, so much so that it has been known for a plant growing on one side of a motorway to send its roots all the way under the road to put up new shoots on the other side. Once established in a suitable location it is virtually impossible to eradicate and will soon out-compete virtually any other plant growing nearby. There have been various horror stories of it taking over completely in this country and destroying our native wildlife habitats.

A report on the BBC Radio 4 'Natural History Programme' in September 1994 stated that this plant is becoming a very valuable habitat for spiders, frogs, grass snakes and many other creatures. What is happening is that many species of insects have discovered that the hollow stems of the plant are an excellent winter-hibernation home. Thus the plant has become a haven for insects. In due course, various insect-eaters have discovered this food-rich habitat and moved into the area. Frogs, in particular, have thrived. Right behind the frogs have come the grass snakes, who like nothing better in life than to swallow a frog or two for breakfast. One site in north Wales is now a primary habitat for grass snakes and is seen as an excellent wild life haven.

It is not just as a wildlife habitat that this plant has shown its value. The young shoots can be cooked and eaten in the spring, they have a pleasant acid taste and can be used as a rhubarb substitute in pies, fruit stews and jams. The older stems and shoot tips can also be cooked, they taste like a mild version of rhubarb. The seed can be ground into a flour and used with wheat when making bread, though it is rather small and fiddly to use. The plant is also a potential source of biomass and can be used to make compost or as a mulch.

Whilst I would not recommend people to introduce this plant, if it is already growing on your ground then it would be worthwhile studying it carefully to see just how many species of insects, amphibians and reptiles are living on it before trying to eradicate it. In the meantime at least you will be able to make some use of it.

All this does go to show that no plant is without value and also that, given time, so-called pest species of plants can become a positive attribute to the environment. Perhaps there is still hope for the rhododendron!

GARDEN PLANTS

There are lots of well-known non-native plants that grow quite happily in our gardens and do not in general pose a threat to native habitats. Many of these are very attractive to bees and butterflies, others can provide fruits or seeds for birds and small mammals. A few of these species are listed below. Your own observations in the garden will soon tell you which other plants attract the wildlife.

Agastache foeniculum. The flowers of ANISE HYSSOP are very attractive to bees and butterflies. See also page 86.

Amelanchier species. JUNEBERRY fruits will bring in birds from miles away in mid summer. See also page 37.

Berberis species. Many species of BARBERRIES produce prolific crops of fruits for you and the birds to share. See also pages 53 and 185.

Borago officinalis. BORAGE flowers for most of the summer and will provide lots of nectar for the bees. See also page 215.

Buddleia davidii. The BUTTERFLY BUSH flowers for much of the summer and, as its common name suggests, will attract clouds of butterflies to the garden. See also page 165.

Cotoneaster species. These evergreen and deciduous shrubs will succeed in most soils and situations. The fruit is a good food for birds in the autumn and winter.

Elaeagnus **species**. The birds absolutely adore the fruits and by careful selection of species it is possible to have ripe fruits in the garden for about 6 months of the year. See also pages 181 and 187.

Hyssopus officinalis. HYSSOP flowers will attract bees and butterflies. See also page 167.

Monarda didyma. BERGAMOT grows up to 1 metre tall and 50cm wide, and is a delightful herb for a moist soil in a sunny position or light shade. The flowers are rich in nectar and are a great favourite with the bees. The young leaves can be used as a flavouring in salads and cooked dishes. They have a strongly aromatic flavour. When dried, the leaves make an excellent tea and are an ingredient of Earl Grey tea. They can also be used as an ingredient in potpourri. An essential oil used in perfumery is obtained from the leaves.

Oenothera biennis. EVENING PRIMROSE is a drought-resistant biennial plant that grows up to 1.2 metres tall and 60cm wide. It prefers a dryish, well-drained sandy loam and a sunny position, though it will succeed in most soils including very poor ones and is drought tolerant.

The fragrant flowers, which are an absolute magnet for moths, have a sweet flavour and can be used as a garnish in salads. The root can be eaten cooked, it is fleshy, sweet and succulent with a slightly peppery flavour that somewhat resembles salsify or parsnips. It is said to be very wholesome and nutritious and many people do seem to like it, though I am not one of them.

Perhaps the most exciting part of this plant is the oil obtained from its seed. This oil is rich in gammalinolenic acid, an essential fatty acid that is not found in many plant sources and has numerous vital functions in the body. When added to the diet it has proved to be beneficial in the treatment of many diseases such as arthritis, multiple sclerosis, premenstrual tension and hyperactivity.

Rosa rugosa. The birds and mice absolutely adore the fruit and seeds of this plant in mid to late summer. See also page 178.

Sedum spectabile. The ICE PLANT grows about 40cm tall and wide. It flowers in late summer and is one of the best butterfly and bee plants that I know. This is one of the most tolerant plants you can grow in the garden, withstanding almost total neglect, poor soils and drought, though it does not like wet soils or much shade. Even I have difficulty killing this plant! The leaves can be eaten raw or cooked, but there are many that are nicer.

GARDENING METHODS

Whilst a reasonable standard of hygiene should be maintained in the garden, if you want to attract wildlife then it is a good idea not to be too fastidious. Dead flowering stems have their own beauty in winter and you will be entertained by seed-eating birds swaying on the stems as they seek out every last seed – mind you, be a bit selective as to which seedheads you leave in the garden since the birds will also be scattering a good portion of the seeds around and you could be blessed with hundreds of unwanted self-sown plants. The dead flower stems will also offer a home for ladybirds and other insects to hibernate on or in, thus making sure that they survive the winter and are ready in the spring to get on with the job of eating your aphids.

Leave a few weeds growing. Once again you have to be selective, but the occasional dandelion, apart from providing food for us and various birds also looks quite pretty.

It is surprising how useful some weeds can be. As an example, SHEPHERD'S PURSE (*Capsella bursa-pastoris*) has edible leaves that can be eaten raw or cooked. The plant is cultivated for these leaves in some countries, apparently it responds well to cultivation and gives reasonable yields. Its seed is relished by birds but we can also eat them and, although rather fiddly to harvest, they can be ground into a meal and used in soups. The fresh or dried root is used as a ginger substitute. The seed, when placed in water, attracts mosquitoes. It has a gummy substance that binds the mosquito's mouth to the seed and it also releases a substance toxic to the larvae – half a kilo of seed is said to be enough to kill 10 million larvae. Shepherd's purse can also be grown on salty or marshy land in order to reclaim it by absorbing the salt and 'sweetening' the soil. If that doesn't make you treat the plant with a bit more respect then nothing will.

There are many other ways of enhancing farms and gardens for the wildlife, but those above are some of the major ones that involve plants. See the booklist in Appendix 1 if you want to study the subject in more detail.

Chapter Thirteen

FUTURE POSSIBILITIES

Having spent the greatest part of this book talking about plants that I have had at least some experience of, in this the last chapter I would like to look at some of the many plants that I would love to get hold of and try out. If you happen to be growing any of the plants on this list then I would love you to get in touch with me and let me know how they are doing and, if possible, let me have some seed or a plant or three.

Many of the plants mentioned here are not, as far as I know, being grown in this country. Nor is there much information as to whether or not they can succeed here. In these cases I have included the plant's native range and habitat in order to give some idea of its climatic needs.

LEAVES

Leaves are one thing we are not short of when looking at alternative foods. With just a little planning there is quite simply a huge range to choose from, even in the depths of winter. When showing visitors around, I normally offer them tasters of various plants. This is mainly leaves, since these are what we have in greatest abundance at present, and the range in flavour that they offer is amazing. Some taste like lemons, others like oranges, liquorice, garlic or onions. They can be sweet, salty, acid or bitter. Some have a very mild flavour whilst others are much stronger.

Now I am not the greatest convert to leaf-eating (though perhaps my wife is) but even I cannot fail to be impressed with what can be grown in Britain. We have a very wide range of plants with edible leaves on our land and, with very little difficulty, can enjoy fresh salads all the year round from the open garden (and all this without an annual lettuce to be seen). There is, however, one leaf that I particularly want to get hold of and this, rather surprisingly, is grown as an annual.

Stevia rebaudiana. Having rather a sweet tooth, I have been fascinated by this South American plant for a number of years. A perennial plant in its native Brazil and Paraguay, it is not very frost-hardy in Britain though it can be grown as an annual crop. It requires a light, well-drained soil in a warm sunny position.

One report says that the leaves contain 'stevioside', a substance that is 300 times sweeter than sucrose. Other reports say that they contain 'estevin' a substance that, weight for weight, is 150 times sweeter than sugar. Either is good enough for me!

The dried leaves can be ground and used as a sweetener or soaked in water and the liquid used in making preserves. The powdered leaves are also added to herb teas. The leaves are sometimes chewed by those wishing to reduce their sugar intake and they can also be cooked then eaten as a vegetable.

ROOTS

We are already growing a wide range of edible roots but there are many more with excellent potential that I would dearly love to get my hands on. My wife really likes eating carrots, but over the past few years has been moving more and more away from growing annual crops. In 1996, for the first time in many years, she did not grow any annual roots, not even carrots. One of my main objectives now is to find a perennial root that is nice raw or cooked and that can be used as a carrot substitute.

Whilst carrots and carrot-substitutes are nice sweet-tasting roots for raw eating, there are also a number of other perennial plants in this list with roots that are good sources of carbohydrate and so could be used as a potato substitute.

Arracacia xanthorrhiza. ARRACACHA comes from the mountains of northern South America and is unlikely to be very hardy in this country, though it should be possible to grow it in much the same way as potatoes. It is said to grow best in a sandy loam with a pH in the range of 5 to 6, in areas with about 1,000mm of rain a year, and requires a minimum rainfall of about 600mm.

Often cultivated for its edible root in South America, attempts in the 19th century to cultivate it as a commercial crop in Europe were unsuccessful – but that does not mean of course that we should not have another try.

The plants have two main drawbacks. Firstly, they take about 120 - 240 days from planting to produce a crop – this latter figure especially is too long for many temperate climates. In South America the plants are often left in the ground for more than a year in order to produce a heavier crop, but this would not be possible in areas with winter frosts.

The other drawback is that plants might be sensitive to day length, possibly requiring short days to initiate tuber production, and so they may not be suitable for temperate climates, especially in areas with early frosts.

This can be a highly productive crop – yields of 2 - 3 kg of edible roots per plant and total yields of 40 tonnes per hectare are possible. The tuber is said to be very palatable and easily digested, its flavour is between that of parsnips and sweet chestnuts with a hint of sweetness that increases in storage.

Astragalus pictus-filifolius. This plant comes from the sand dunes and prairies of western North America, where it grows about 30cm tall. It is likely to require a well-drained light soil in a warm sunny position. The root is eaten raw and what particularly interests me is a comment from one book which says that in America the root is dug up after rain and eaten as sweets.

Balsamorrhiza sagitatta. OREGON SUNFLOWER grows about 30cm tall and requires a very well-drained soil in a sunny position. I have obtained seed of this plant on a couple of occasions but failed to get it to germinate. The plant is hardy enough to be grown in most of Britain, tolerating winter temperatures down to about -25°C and the seed should germinate within a few days of sowing, so perhaps the seed I obtained was not viable.

The roots can be eaten raw or cooked and are said to have a sweet taste when cooked. The young shoots can also be eaten raw or cooked, whilst the larger leaves and leaf stems can be boiled and eaten. Mind you, I am not sure I would want to eat the older leaves because another report says that the large hairy leaves are used as an insulation in shoes to keep the feet warm! The young flowering stem can be peeled and eaten raw like celery. The seed can be eaten raw or cooked and when roasted is a coffee substitute.

A number of other members of the genus have similar uses, they include **B. deltoidea**, **B. hookeri** and **B. incana**.

Claytonia megarrhiza. The ALPINE SPRING BEAUTY is a very cold-hardy plant for a sunny position in moist but well-drained peaty soils. It dislikes chalk.

The root is said to be long, fleshy and up to 2.5cm thick, which is a very good size for a wild root. It can be eaten raw but is normally peeled, then boiled or baked. The leaves and flowering tops can be eaten raw or cooked and are succulent, juicy and mild in flavour

Cymopterus acaulis. Coming from western North America, where it is found as far north as Alberta, this plant grows about 10cm tall on dry flat or sloping land on the plains and in valleys.

The root is said to have a pleasant taste, the young roots in spring are the best. Another report says that only the young roots should be used whilst there is also a report that the water from boiled older roots can be used as an insecticide. This makes me rather reluctant to eat older roots. Mind you, the roots of parsnips have also been used to make an insecticide (not that I am particularly fond of parsnip either). The leaves and young shoots can be eaten raw or cooked.

A number of other members of the genus are also worthy of more investigation. These include **C. bulbosus**, **C. fendleri**, **C. montanus** and **C. purpurescens**.

Lomatium cous. Coming from western North America, this plant grows on dry often open rocky slopes and flats. It is often found with sagebrush, is most common in foothills and lowland areas but is occasionally found high in the mountains above the treeline.

The root is eaten cooked, it can also be dried and ground into a flour and can then be mixed with cereal flours or added to soups. When dug up in the spring, it is said to have a parsnip-like flavour.

I would also be interested in obtaining any other members of this genus, in particular **L. geyeri** and **L. macrocarpum**. Known as BISCUIT ROOTS, they have celery-flavoured roots that can be eaten raw or cooked. The North American

Indians dried and ground them into a flour and then either mixed it with cereal flours or added it to soups. They also mixed the flour with water, flattened it into cakes then sun-dried or baked them for use on journeys, the taste is said to be somewhat like stale biscuits.

Megacarpaea gigantea. This tall plant comes from the grassy but not stony slopes of central Asia. The root is rich in starch and is said to be delicious cooked. The report goes on to say that it contains enormous quantities of nutritious substances.

M. megalocarpa. This comes from central Asia where it is found in saline semi-deserts, deserts, dry clayey and saline steppes, occasionally growing on rocks and stony slopes. It requires a light well-drained soil in a sunny position. The root, which is said to be starchy, thick and nutritious, is up to 3cm thick.

Microseris scapigera. YAM DAISY is about 30cm tall, it grows in grassland and open places on North, South and Stewart Islands in New Zealand and in loamy soils or moist clay up to the montane and sub-alpine zones in Australia. Another report says that it is also found on salt pans. It is unlikely to be hardy in the colder areas of Britain.

The root is said to be sweetish and moist with a coconut flavour. Another report says it tastes like a sweet potato with an occasional hot taste. The root is between 2 and 8cm long and is a favourite food of the Australian Aborigines, who eat it in quantity. The root can be harvested all year round but it tastes bitter at certain times of the year, especially in early winter.

M. nutans and *M. procera* from western North America might also be worthy of investigation.

Oenanthe sarmentosa. WATER DROPWORT grows up to 1 metre tall in low wet places in western North America from British Columbia to California. In cultivation it is likely to require a moist or wet fertile soil in a sunny position.

Although many members of this genus and family are poisonous, the roots of this species are said to have a sweet floury flesh and to be highly esteemed in the areas where it is eaten. Another report says the root has a cream-like taste when boiled, with a slight parsley flavour. Be quite sure of the plant's identity before trying to eat it because it is very similar to many poisonous plant's in this family.

Orogenia linearifolia. INDIAN POTATO grows about 15cm tall on open mountain sides and ridges, often in sandy or gravelly soils, and especially near vernal snowbanks where it blooms as soon as the snow melts. It is found in much of western North America.

The root has a pleasant crisp taste, though the outer skin has a slightly bitter taste. Available at almost any time of the year, its only drawback is that it is a bit small and fiddly to harvest in quantity.

Osmorhiza **species**. A number of plants in this genus are of interest. They are all woodland plants in their native environments so should be good candidates for a permaculture forest garden. They should succeed in any deep moisture-retentive soil in full sun or dappled shade.

Their roots can be eaten raw whilst their aromatic leaves and seeds are often cooked or used as a flavouring. Those species of most interest include:

O. aristata. Found in hills and low mountains all over Japan, this species grows about 60cm tall.

O. chilensis. This grows up to 75cm tall in deciduous *Nothofagus* forests and amongst moist shaded cliffs to 200 metres elevation in southern Chile. It is said to be hardy to about -20°C.

O. claytonii. WOOLLY SWEET CICELY grows up to 1 metre tall in woods and on wooded slopes in eastern North America. It is said to be hardy to -20°C.

O. longistylis. ANISE ROOT grows up to 1.2 metres tall in rich, often alluvial woods and thickets. It is hardy to -20°C. The root is said to be very sweet, aromatic and fleshy with a spicy flavour similar to aniseed.

O. obtusa. Growing about 1 metre tall in shady or partly shady areas, often on slopes and in valleys, from Alaska to California, the root is said to be a cross between parsnip and aniseed in flavour.

Perideridia gairdneri. YAMPA is a famous North American Indian food, it grows up to 1.2 metres tall in woodland, dry and wet meadows and mountains from Saskatchewan to California.

This is the one root crop that I most want to get hold of. It is fairly small, about 5 - 8cm long, but must have potential for increased size by selective breeding. The root is said to have a very pleasant sweet and nutty taste and can be eaten raw or cooked in quantity. It can also be dried for later use or ground into a flour and used in porridge and cakes. The flavour is said to be somewhat like a superior parsnip and the dried root is said to be so nice that it is an almost irresistible nibble. The seed is used as a caraway-like seasoning, or can be parched and eaten in porridge.

Psoralea esculenta. BREADROOT is another of the famous North American Indian foods. It grows about 30cm tall in rocky woods and prairies, on calcareous soils. It has been grown in Britain and is said to be perfectly hardy in this country. It requires a sunny position and succeeds in most soils so long as they are well-drained.

The root can be eaten raw, cooked or be dried for later use. The dried root can also be ground into a flour and used in cakes and porridge. Starchy and glutinous, the raw root is said to have a sweetish turnip-like taste. The plant has in the past been recommended for commercial cultivation and has the potential to be high yielding.

Stellaria jamesiana. This plant is related to our common garden weed, chickweed. It grows up to 50cm tall in moist woodland in North America westwards from Wyoming and Texas. The root is said to be sweet and pleasant.

Valeriana obovata. TOBACCO ROOT is found in western North America where it grows up to 1.2 metres tall in open moist sites, moist meadows, ditches, swamps and prairies, sometimes on saline soils.

This is a root that I would dearly love to try simply because I have heard such positive and also negative reports about it. The root is said to have a very strong and peculiar taste. Some people, it seems, would literally rather starve to death than put it in their mouths, whilst others find it a very agreeable flavour. The North American Indians used to slow-bake it for about 2 days in earth ovens (see *Camassia esculenta* in Chapter 4) and this cooked root could also be dried and used as a flour. There is a report that the **raw** root might be poisonous, so it needs to be cooked thoroughly.

FRUIT

Fruit is another food of which there is no shortage of potentially good species, indeed a very wide range has already been mentioned in this book. Apart from trying to obtain more species from certain genera such as *Actinidia, Crataegus, Elaeagnus* and *Prunus*, as well as obtaining named cultivars of various unusual fruiting species such as the deciduous *Elaeagnus* species, then I am fairly content with the fruits I already know about and grow. It is more a matter of waiting until they reach fruiting size. One fruit does puzzle me though...

Ziziphus jujube. JUJUBE is a deciduous tree growing about 10 metres tall. It is native to China and Japan where it grows on dry gravelly or stony slopes of hills and mountains. I am really not sure why I never seem to come across this tree in my travels, it certainly sounds like a potential fruit for Britain. It succeeds in most soils, including alkaline and poor soils, so long as they are well-drained. It prefers an open loam and a hot dry position and is said to be hardy to about -20°C.

Often cultivated in warm temperate zones for its edible fruit, there are many named varieties and, because it is fast-growing, it can fruit in 3 - 4 years from seed. The fruit is said to have a sourish-sweet flavour with a mealy texture and is meant to be nicest when dried.

SEED CROPS

Producing edible seeds from perennial crops in Britain is no real problem, but if you want to grow seeds that can be eaten in quantity to form a staple part of the diet then things become more complicated.

NUTS

The staple crops from seeds can be divided into 3 categories: nuts, legumes and cereals. As long as we have the patience then I do not think that, in the long term, nuts will pose a problem in this country since there are a number of very promising species to choose from.

Many examples can be found in Chapter 2: most notably *Araucaria araucana*, *Castanea* species, *Cephalotaxus* species, *Corylus* species, *Juglans* species, *Pinus* species, *Quercus ilex* and *Torreya* species. The main problem with nuts is the time it takes before the trees come into bearing, with some species taking up to 40 years. The answer, of course, is to grow annual crops such as sunflowers until the trees are mature.

Legumes and cereals are more problematic. There are many suitable annual species but it is the perennials that most interest me, especially if these can be grown as a part of a self-sustaining system.

LEGUMES

Amongst the legumes, *Caragana arborescens* has been mentioned on page 46, *Amphicarpaea bracteata* on page 67, *Phaseolus coccineus* is on page 119 and *Medicago sativa* on page 11. The following species also seem to be very promising.

Desmanthus illinoensis. PRAIRIE MIMOSA is a herbaceous perennial growing about 1.3 metres tall. It requires a moist but well-drained soil in full sun and should be hardy in virtually all parts of Britain. I only obtained this plant in the spring of 1996, so it will be a few years before I can get a true picture of its potential. It certainly has a good write-up.

The seed is rich in protein and has a bland flavour when cooked. The following report is what whetted my appetite. "This plant is being evaluated by the Land Institute of Salina, Kansas, as an edible legume for growing with perennial grains in a non-tillage permaculture system." Then when another report said that it was suitable for the wild garden or other naturalistic plantings and that in favourable situations it can self-sow to the point of nuisance, I was sold. This report obviously indicates that it can produce a good crop of seeds, and the fact that it has a bland flavour is an advantage since this means that it can be eaten in quantity. All you have to do is add the flavouring that you fancy – and there are plenty of flavourful plants you can grow in this country.

The seed is rather small, about the same size as alfalfa seed. This does mean that it is probably going to be a fiddly crop to harvest by hand. However, the seed germinates freely and, like alfalfa, could be sprouted and eaten raw.

That is a grand total of just 5 species of legumes to use as staple foods. This is far too small a number for us to depend on, especially since we are not yet always sure of potential yields. There are a few other possibilities worthy of further research but they all have drawbacks. The following are some of the more interesting amongst them:

Caragana species. We already know about *C. arborescens* (see also page 46), but there are a number of other species in this genus worthy of research into the edibility of their seeds. **C. brevispina**, for example, has a larger seed than *C. arborescens* though it has a distinct bitterness. I have seen plants growing in eastern Britain that produce very good crops on a regular basis.

C. boisii and **C. fruticosa** are both closely related to *C. arborescens* so probably also have edible seeds. Many other species might also be worthy of further investigation.

Desmodium species. There are some Chinese and Japanese members of this genus that should succeed outdoors at least in the milder areas of the country but I have very little information on their needs. Their seeds are eaten cooked. All are herbaceous perennials, though in mild climates they might become shrubs. Their roots will probably require some winter protection, such as a good organic mulch.

D. dunnii. This comes from China.

D. oldhami. Growing up to 1.2 metres tall in woods and thickets in central and southern Japan.

D. oxyphyllum. Growing up to 1.2 metres tall in oak groves and shrubby thickets, and in gravelly soils of mountain slopes. It is found in China, Japan, Korea and the Himalayas.

Gleditsia species. This genus of deciduous trees contains some very interesting species that grow well in Britain. They need a warm, sheltered, sunny position and a well-drained soil if they are to do well. Established trees are very tolerant of drought and the pollution of cities. The young trees, and young shoots of older trees, are usually rather frost-tender, but they become hardier with age and several members of the genus can be grown in most of Britain. The trees are rather late coming into leaf, have a light canopy and are also some of the first trees to lose their leaves in the autumn. Their light shade makes them excellent canopy trees for a forest garden – they should be very good companions for the conventional fruit crops such as apples and plums.

G. japonica. Growing up to 20 metres tall and 12 metres wide, though it is usually smaller in Britain.

This tree has been bearing good crops of seed on a fairly regular basis at Kew Gardens in London. Reports say that the seed is roasted, dehusked, soaked until soft and then boiled and eaten with sugar but I have yet to try it.

The pulp surrounding the seed can be used as a soap substitute. There is also one report that soap can be obtained from the seed. This suggests that the seed contains saponins which would explain the long process in preparing them for eating. See Appendix 4 for more details.

G. triacanthos. The HONEY LOCUST grows up to 20 metres tall and 15 metres wide. It is very cold-hardy, tolerating temperatures down to about -30°C once it has got through its early years, though grows better in the hotter parts of the country. It is also said to be tolerant of saline conditions. Unlike most plants in this family, honey locusts do not fix atmospheric nitrogen.

The honey locust is often cultivated in warm temperate zones for its edible seeds and seedpods. Trees start to bear when about 10 years old and produce commercial crops for about 100 years. The trees are shy to flower and therefore do not often produce a worthwhile crop in Britain due to our cooler summers. I have seen the cultivar 'Nana' produce good crops on a number of occasions at Kew gardens, but only after good summers.

The seeds are produced in long pods up to 40cm long and 4cm wide. Individual seeds are about 8mm long and can be eaten raw or cooked. They have a sweet flavour, indeed the young seeds taste rather like raw peas.

The pulp surrounding the seed is sweet and can be eaten raw or made into sugar, though the pulp in older pods turns bitter.

G. caspica, **G. macracantha** and **G. sinensis**. These are other species worthy of attention because they have yielded well on several occasions at Kew, even in cool summers. I have yet to find any reports for the first two species of their seed being edible, but all of them are very likely to have the potential of becoming a food crop.

Lathyrus japonicus maritimus. The BEACH PEA is a native of Britain. The plant has conflicting reports on edibility, with some saying that it is an excellent food crop and others that it is very bitter. The main problem with plants in this genus is that several species have been shown to cause 'Lathyrism', a disease of the nervous system that can disable or kill. Apparently it is safe to eat the seeds so long as they do not comprise more than 30% of the diet, but I would want further research to be carried out before committing this seed to my stomach.

CEREALS

Much more research is needed to enable us to find good perennial cereals. There are a number of potential species but either their yields are very low, or the seed is very small and fiddly to harvest. Many species suffer from both of these disadvantages. There is much room for judicious selective breeding here.

There is some research being carried out in the USA, where they are particularly looking at ways of growing perennial cereals with perennial legumes. Whilst this research has uncovered some plants with exciting potential, it is too early yet to be able to recommend trying any of the species.

To date, the only perennial grass we grow that has a reasonable sized seed and good yields is **Secale montana**, which is discussed in Chapter 5. Other grasses with potential mentioned in the book are **Triticum turgidum** in Chapter 5 (but this is a very short-lived perennial) plus **Beckmannia eruciformis** and **Glyceria fluitans** in Chapter 6 (these two species have very small and fiddly seeds). The other species that I would like to look more closely at are detailed below.

Elymus species. There are a number of species in this genus that have been used for their edible seed. I have grown **E. canadensis** and **E. glauca**, both of which have very small seeds. I would quite like to get hold of **E. condensatus** and **E. triticoides**, which were widely used as a food by the North American Indians. Both of these species are likely to have small seeds that are difficult to utilize.

Oryzopsis hymenoides. INDIAN MILLET is unlikely to be hardy outside the milder areas of the country. Growing about 60cm tall, the seed of this species is about the size of a small millet and it is fairly easy to harvest. Yields will be much lower than conventional cereals, though. The seed is said to have a pleasant taste and to be very nutritious, it is rich in starch and can be ground into a flour and then used in making bread, cakes, or as a thickener in soups.

   O. asperifolia. A related species from eastern North America with similar uses, the seeds of this species are said to be larger than *O. hymenoides*.

SEEDPODS

Last but not least, I wouldn't mind this plant coming my way.

Astragalus crassicarpus. The GROUND PLUM grows about 50cm tall, though the stems are sometimes prostrate. It comes from the prairies and plains of North America and requires a well-drained soil in a sunny position. It is said that many members of this genus can be difficult to grow, and that this may at least be due partly to a lack of their specific bacterial associations in the soil.

   The thick fleshy unripe seedpods, which resemble green plums in appearance, are about 25mm in diameter. They are eaten raw or cooked and are said to be highly esteemed. This is a highly variable plant, and is divided into several different species by some botanists. The form that is sometimes called *A. mexicanus* has larger seedpods up to 35mm in diameter.

A WAY FORWARD

Obtaining the plants is only part of the story, you then have to successfully grow them and then eventually obtain a yield from them. This is often a simple matter if it is the leaves that you are after, but some of the trees we are growing for their seeds can take 40 years or more before they will start to crop – and it is quite possible that at the end of those forty years we will either find out that the seed is not that pleasant, or that the tree does not yield well in this country. Fancy waiting 40 years to find out you have been wasting your time!

   When people moved from a hunter/gatherer mode of living to agriculture, they were quite naturally drawn towards those crops that responded most readily to cultivation. This was obviously going to be annual plants since these produce a new generation every year and thus allow selective breeding to show an effect much sooner than from perennials. There was also far less incentive to cultivate tree crops since a large percentage of the land was woodland, there was no ownership of this land and thus the fruits and seeds of the woods were there for the taking.

It is important to remember that most of the foods we take so much for granted today are actually the result of well over 2,000 years of selective breeding. At first this might have been a chance by-product of cultivating the plants, but as time went by people became more aware of the potential for selective breeding and our cultivated plants have changed quite dramatically. I wonder how many of those foods from 2,000 years or more ago we would want to eat today?

Just as we have gradually adapted the plants we are growing, so too have our palates adapted to these foods. The taste of foods used to be much stronger than they are now. Leaves were more bitter, fruits more acid. Plants were also less productive and tougher than they are now. My wife loves carrots (in case you didn't already know) but I do not think she would like them anywhere near as much if they were like the wild carrot from which they have been bred. The wild carrot has very little flesh, most of the root consisting of the fibrous core, yet this was the carrot our ancestors ate (and presumably enjoyed). Similarly, our cultivated apples have been bred from small acid crab-apples and lettuces have been developed from a bitter-tasting poisonous plant.

It is not only the tastes of plants that have been altered by breeding, yields and size have also improved dramatically. Compare the size of a wild to a cultivated carrot, of a crab to a cultivated apple. Yields of potatoes were extremely low when they were first introduced into this country, average yields of wheat have increased by a factor of three or more in the last century.

Most of the plants contained in this book have never been selected for flavour or yield, yet a number of them taste at least as nice if not much nicer than the plant foods most people are used to. What is needed is a programme of selective breeding aimed mainly at improving yields.

This breeding needs to be carried out with more awareness than was given to it in the past. The wild ancestor of the lettuce is a very hardy plant that is not unduly bothered by pests and diseases. Selective breeding might have produced a more productive plant with milder-tasting leaves, but it has also led to a loss of the plant's natural resistance to pests and diseases. Cultivated lettuces are also much more demanding of good growing conditions and nitrogen-rich soils. Thus selective breeding has been a rather mixed success.

Quite often it is the very qualities we try to breed out of a species that are the main reason the plant becomes weaker and more difficult to grow. In the case of the lettuce, the bitterness of the leaves was the plants natural defence against being eaten, either by us or by insects. It is as well to be aware of this when breeding plants, to try and make sure that we do not weaken the species.

It is quite interesting to look at the origins of selective breeding and perhaps we could consider how the apple has developed. It is most likely that earlier hunter gatherers, when harvesting apples, would have concentrated on gathering from trees with larger and tastier fruits. These are the ones that would have been taken back to the settlement for eating. It is possible that the people threw the apple cores away somewhere near the settlement, although it is more likely that they would have eaten the core and then defecated somewhere near the settlement.

Unless they had been chewed, most of the seeds would have passed through the digestive system unharmed. Indeed, the gastric juices in the stomach would have started to eat away at the seed coating, making it easier for the seed to germinate once it had been defecated. Not only that, but it would also have been supplied with a handy pile of manure in which to grow. These seedlings would have tended to be similar to the trees from which they had been harvested, with some worse and perhaps a few that were larger or better-flavoured. The people would then have been attracted to the larger and better flavoured fruits and the cycle would have started over again.

Over a period of time there would be a considerable improvement in the size and flavour of the apples. However, all the trees would still have had to survive in the wild, they would not have been cossetted and protected like many of our modern food crops. Thus the weaker trees would have perished, even if they produced a superior fruit. This is an excellent example of how different species adapt together. As the flavour of the apple improved, so the humans became used to this improved flavour and over the generations gradually lost their appreciation of the older, more bitter tastes.

The situation changes considerably when we cultivate the plants. If, when selecting for improved characteristics, we do not take into account any other effects this might have on the plant, then we might very well end up with a weaker plant. This will need more attention when we are growing it, will be more susceptible to pests and diseases, and will also quite possibly be less nutritious. The process can be insidious and happen without us realising it, but over the generations the plant gradually becomes more difficult and so we adapt more specialised methods of growing it.

The wild tomato in South America is about the size of a cherry, but this small fruit contains more minerals and vitamins than the large watery tomato you buy from a supermarket. Similarly, many of our other cultivated foods are actually less rich in nutrients than their wild counterparts. The human race evolved on these wild, nutrient-rich foods, and it is only very recently in our evolution that we have moved on to these relatively nutrient-poor foods. Perhaps this is one of the reasons that, although we live longer nowadays, few of us manage to do so healthily. If we are eating nutrient deficient foods, then is it not also likely that we will become nutrient deficient? In order to obtain all the nutrients our bodies need, we either have to eat larger quantities of food or use some of the many vitamin and mineral supplements that are sold in increasing quantities each year.

When selecting for improved yields, flavour and texture it is important to monitor the other changes this might bring about to the plant. We need to see the effect this selection has on the plant's natural resistance to pests and diseases plus its general robustness, we also need to check the nutritional value of the food we obtain from the plant to make sure that we are not losing out in this way. What is the point of doubling yields if at the same time you lose many of the nutrients in the food?

FOREST GARDENS
THE FARMS OF THE FUTURE

Trees and shrubs in particular have a huge potential for providing food for us and they are also a lot less work than growing annuals. Once established, a tree can produce its crop year after year with very little effort required from the grower. No preparing the soil, no sowing seed, no battle to keep the seedlings ahead of the weeds and slugs. Just come along at the appropriate time of the year and harvest the crop. Of course, it isn't really quite that easy in practice, but I am sure you get the picture.

Another thing about trees is that they require far less inputs. Whilst most of the cultivated annuals that we grow need to be pampered and cossetted in a rich soil if they are to yield well, a properly planned tree system is much more resilient and to a very large extent self-sustaining. Not only that, but you can also grow various other crops under and into the trees, allowing the land to be much more productive than any system of growing annuals.

A dear friend of mine, Robert Hart planted a forest garden over 20 years ago on his Shropshire farm. This is the most mature forest garden that I know of in Britain and a visit there is inspiring. It is a place of peace and great beauty, as well as being a productive food garden. Due to an accident in early 1996, Robert was unable to put much energy into looking after the garden that year. When I visited him in late summer, the garden was literally dripping with fruit and there were plenty of green leaves there for the eating. This to me was the final proof of the forest garden. How much food would have been available from a garden of annual vegetables if the gardener was unable to dig it, sow the seeds and weed it in the spring?

You may well ask why, since it all sounds so wonderful, there are not lots of people already growing their food this way. Whilst the system of forest gardening using a very wide range of useful plants as advocated in this book is quite new in this country, there have been many systems in the past that have tried to make more than one use of the land at a time. There are many true examples of forest gardening abroad, especially in the tropics. However, the trend in farming both here and abroad has been towards specialisation and mechanisation. A complex forest garden does not respond to such methods, it requires more individual attention.

At this point many people might start to get worried. "Haven't modern farming methods freed us from all the hard work on the land? One person in a tractor can accomplish so much more on a farm than the dozens of people who would have had to work long hard hours outdoors in all weathers in the past. I certainly do not want to become a slave of the soil!"

This sort of reasoning misses the point. Even apart from the fact that machine-intensive methods of farming the land are unsustainable in the long term, there is no reason to believe that the integrated systems mentioned in this book will mean lots of extra work in order to obtain all our food. An average person in Britain probably spends about an hour or two of their working day earning enough money to buy their food for that day, they also have to spend time going to get the food plus more money for the expenses of collecting it and travelling to work.

All too often they are employed in some job that they would really rather not be doing and do not find much satisfaction in their work.

Once an integrated forest gardening system has been established then I believe that no more than 2 hours work a day on average would be required from one person in order to obtain their food – so there really is not much difference in the total time involved. Coupled with that, there is the satisfaction of seeing a job through from beginning to end instead of just being one very small cog in a large machine. The catch, of course, is in establishing the system. This does take time and it is much more labour intensive in the early days especially if you start with degraded land. However, if we don't make a start then our children will be left with the same problems that face us.

Many people nowadays are not prepared to work for some future that they personally might not receive the benefits from. We all want immediate results and we want to benefit from them now. I once read about a man in the 18th century who wanted to get married. As was the custom, he went to the parents of his beloved and asked for permission to marry their daughter. Their reply was to ask him if he had planted any walnut trees. What they meant by this was that, if he was to be a worthy husband for their daughter, then he would have to make good provision for any children. Walnut trees take many years to come to maturity and he would receive little if any financial return from planting them – but his children would reap the benefit.

We need to look more to the future. We need to examine our current lifestyles and see if they are sustainable and we should also try to ensure that when we leave this world we leave it a richer place than when we arrived. Establishing integrated forest gardens is one way of doing this – ensuring sustainable cropping of foods for our futures and also for our children's futures.

There are a few working forest gardens that have been established in this country in recent years and there are also a number of people who are carrying out research into long-term sustainable gardening, but most projects are still in their infancy and much remains to be done. We need to set up forest gardens in many parts of the country, to keep careful records of the plants used, how well they grow and yield and how much we like them.

Whereas forest gardens can be sustainable in the long term with very little input from the grower, this can never be the case for modern methods of agriculture which depend on large annual inputs of fertilizers, sprays and fossil fuels. The time will come when we are no longer able to apply the huge inputs that are necessary to maintain the high yields. The time will also come when the land itself cannot tolerate the treatment it is being given. Year by year we are seeing more top soil being eroded than the land is capable of replacing and a loss of organic matter in the soil that makes the land increasingly difficult to work. Unless farming methods are changed then future generations are going to be left with a very impoverished soil that will not be able to grow many crops. I often wonder what our grandchildren are going to think of this generation.

This book is not about knocking existing methods – it is more interested in offering alternatives. I hope that the preceding chapters have demonstrated the potential that exists for us to implement new and sustainable growing methods. What needs to be done now is to put this potential into practice.

FURTHER READING

CONSERVATION

Butterflies and Moths in Britain and Europe
Carter. D.; Pan; 1982; 033026642X
An excellent book on Lepidoptera, it also lists their favourite food plants.

Garden Plants Valuable to Bees
International Bee Research Association; 1981
The title says it all.

Planting Native Trees and Shrubs
Beckett. G. and K.; Jarrold; 1979
An excellent guide to native British trees and shrubs with lots of details about the plants.

Waterways and Wetlands
Brookes. A.; British Trust for Conservation Volunteers; 1987; 0950164380
A very practical 'how to' manual, packed with information and sources.

EDIBLE & OTHER USEFUL PLANTS

A Dictionary of Plants Used by Man
Usher. G.; Constable; 1974; 0094579202
Forget the sexist title, this is one of the best books on the subject. Lists a very extensive range of useful plants from around the world with very brief details of the uses. Not for the casual reader.

A Field Guide to North American Edible Wild Plants
Elias. T. and Dykeman. P.; Van Nostrand Reinhold; 1982; 0442222009
A very readable guide.

Alternative Enterprises for Agriculture in the UK
Carruthers. S. P. (Editor); Centre for Agricultural Strategy, Reading University; 1986; 0704909820
Some suggested alternative commercial crops for Britain. Readable. Produced by a University study group.

Cornucopia – A Source Book of Edible Plants
Facciola. S.; Kampong Publications; 1990; 0962808709
Excellent. Contains a very wide range of conventional and unconventional food plants (including tropical) and where they can be obtained (mainly North American nurseries but also research institutes and a lot of other nurseries from around the world.

Dictionary of Economic Plants
Uphof. J. C.; Weinheim; 1959
An excellent and very comprehensive guide but it only gives very short descriptions of the uses without any details of how to utilize the plants. Not for the casual reader.

Edible and Medicinal Plants
Launert. E.; Hamlyn; 1981; 0600372162
Covers plants in Europe. There is a drawing of each plant, plus quite a bit of interesting information.

Edible and Useful Wild Plants of the United States and Canada
Saunders. C. F.; Dover Publications; 1976; 0486233103
Useful wild plants of America. A good pocket guide.

Edible Native Plants of the Rocky Mountains
Harrington. H. D.; University of New Mexico Press; 1967; 0862303439
A superb book. Very readable, it gives the results of the authors experiments with native edible plants.

Edible Wild Fruits and Nuts of Canada
Turner. N. J. and Szczawinski. A.; National Museum of Natural Sciences; 1978
A very readable guide to some wild foods of Canada.

Famine Foods of the Chiu-Huang Pen-ts'ao
Reid. B. E.; Southern Materials Centre; 1977
A translation of an ancient Chinese book on edible wild foods.
Full of information and fascinating.

Food For Free †
Mabey. R.; Collins; 1974; 0002190605; £9.00 inc. p&p
Edible wild plants found in Britain. Fairly comprehensive, very few pictures and rather optimistic on the desirability of some of the plants.

Lost Crops of the Incas
Popenoe. H. et al; National Academy Press; 1990; 030904264X
An excellent book. Very readable, with lots of information and a few good pictures of some lesser known food plants of South America.

Native Edible Plants of New Zealand
Crowe. A.; Hodder and Stoughton; 1990; 0340508302
A very well written and illustrated book based on the authors own experiments with living on a native diet.

Nuts
Howes. F. N.; Faber; 1948
Rather dated but still a masterpiece. The book contains sections on tropical and temperate plants that have edible nuts plus a section dealing with nut plants in Britain. Very readable.

Plants for Human Consumption
Kunkel. G.; Koeltz Scientific Books; 1984; 3874292169
An excellent book for the dedicated. A comprehensive listing of Latin names with a brief list of edible parts.

Sturtevant's Edible Plants of the World
Hedrick. U. P.; Dover Publications; 1972; 0486204596
Lots of entries, quite a lot of information in most entries and references. Some of the information is rather questionable, though, with a number of very poisonous plants said to be edible.

Tanaka's Cyclopaedia of Edible Plants of the World
Tanaka. T.; Keigaku Publishing; 1976
The most comprehensive guide to edible plants I've come across. Only the briefest entry for each species though and, as can be expected from a work of this size, some of the entries are more than a little dubious. Not for the casual reader.

The Book of Edible Nuts
Rosengarten. Jnr. F.; Walker & Co; 1984; 0802707699
A very readable and comprehensive guide. Well illustrated.

Wild Fruits of the Sub-Himalayan Region
Parmar. C. and Kaushal. M.K.; Kalyani Publishers, New Delhi; 1982
Contains lots of information on about 25 species of fruit-bearing plants of the Himalayas, not all of them
suitable for cool temperate zones.

FLORAS

A Field Guide to the Common and Interesting Plants
of Baja California
Coyle. J. and Roberts. N. C.; Natural History Publishing Co.; 1975
A very readable pocket flora with good illustrations, it gives quite a few plant uses.

A Manual of Indian Timbers
Gamble. J. S.; Bishen Singh Mahendra Pal Singh; 1972
First published over 100 years ago but still a classic, giving a lot of information on the uses and habitats of
Indian trees. Not for the casual reader.

Flora Europaea
Cambridge University Press; 1964
An immense work in 6 volumes (including the index). The standard reference flora for Europe, it is very
terse though and with very little extra information. Not for the casual reader.

Flora of Canada
Livingstone. B.; National Museums of Canada; 1978; 0660000253
In 4 volumes, it does not deal with plant uses but gives descriptions and habitats.

Flora of Japan (English translation)
Ohwi. G.; Smithsonian Institution; 1965
The standard work. Brilliant, but not for the casual reader.

Flora of the British Isles
Clapham, Tootin and Warburg; Cambridge University Press; 1962
A very comprehensive flora, the standard reference book but it has no pictures.

Flora of the USSR
Komarov. V. L.; Israel Program for Scientific Translation; 1968
An immense (30 or more large volumes) and not yet completed translation of the Russian flora.
Full of information on plant uses and habitats but is probably too heavy going for casual readers.

Flora of Tierra del Fuego
Moore. D. M.; Anthony Nelson; 1983; 0904614050
Standard work for this part of S. America. Excellent details of habitat and a few notes on plant uses.

Flowers of Europe – a Field Guide
Polunin. O.; Oxford University Press; 1969; 0192176218
An excellent and well illustrated pocket guide for those with very large pockets. Also gives some details
on plant uses.

Flowers of Greece and the Balkans
Polunin. O.; Oxford University Press; 1980; 0192176269
A very good pocket flora, it also lists quite a few plant uses.

Flowers of the Himalayas
Polunin. O. and Stainton. A.; Oxford University Press; 1984
A very readable and good pocket guide (if you have a very large pocket!) to many of the wild plants in the Himalayas. Gives many examples of plant uses.

Flowers of the Mediterranean
Polunin. O. and Huxley. A.; Hogarth Press; 1987; 0701207841
A very readable pocket flora that is well illustrated. Gives some information on plant uses.

Flowers of the Southwest Mountains
Arnberger. L. P.; Southwestern Monuments Ass.; 1968
A lovely little pocket guide to wild plants in the southern Rockies of America.

Gray's Manual of Botany
Fernald. M. L.; American Book Co.; 1950
A bit dated but good and concise flora of the eastern part of North America.

Vascular Plants of the Pacific Northwest
Hitchcock. C. L.; University of Washington Press; 1955
A standard flora for Western N. America with lots of information on habitat etc. Five large volumes, it is not for the casual reader.

GENERAL TOPICS

A - Z of Companion Planting
Allardice.P.; Cassell Publishers Ltd.; 1993; 0304343242
A well produced and very readable book.

A Colour Atlas of Poisonous Plants
Frohne D. & Pfonder J.; Wolfe; 1984; 0723408394
Brilliant. Goes into technical details but in a very readable way. The best work on the subject that I've come across so far.

Climbers and Wall Shrubs
Davis. B.; Viking; 1990; 0670829293
Contains information on 2,000 species and cultivars, giving details of cultivation requirements. The text is terse but informative.

Commonsense Compost Making
Bruce. M. E.; Faber; 1977; 0571099904
Excellent little booklet dealing with how to make compost by using herbs to activate the heap. Gives full details of the herbs that are used.

Companion Planting for Successful Gardening
Riotte. L.; Garden Way, Vermont, USA; 1978; 0882660640
A good guide to the subject.

Complete Guide to Water Plants
Muhlberg. H.; E. P. Publishing Ltd.; 1982; 0715807897
Deals with a wide range of plants for temperate areas (and indoor aquaria) with quite a lot of information on cultivation techniques.

Fertile Waste †
C.A.T. Publications; 1994; £4.50 inc. p&p
Shows how human effluent can be safely used to increase soil fertility and thus reduce pollution.

Forest Gardening †
Hart. R.; Green Books; 1996; £13.00 inc. p&p
A classic, it is written by one of the pioneers of woodland gardening in Britain.

Green Manures
Woodward. L. & Burge. P.; Elm Farm Research Centre; 1982
Green manure crops for temperate areas. Quite a lot of information on a number of species.

Growing Unusual Fruit
Simmons. A. E.; David and Charles; 1972; 0715355317
A very readable book with information on about 100 species that can be grown in Britain (some in greenhouses) and details on how to grow and use them.

Hedges and Screens
Shepherd. F.; Royal Horticultural Society; 1974; 0900629649
A small but informative booklet giving details of all the hedging plants being grown in the R.H.S. gardens at Wisley in Surrey.

How To Make A Forest Garden †
Whitefield. P; Permanent Publications; 1996; 1856230082; £17.00 inc. p&p
A detailed and inspiring explanation of how to design and create your own forest garden with details of over 100 edible perennials.
Very readable and informative.

Introduction to Permaculture †
Mollison. B. and Sley. R. M.; Tagari Publications; 1991; £16.50 inc. p&p
Clearly laying out the principles of permaculture.

Oriental Vegetables †
Larkcom J.; John Murray; 1991; 0719547814; £18.00 inc. p&p
Well written and very informative.

Permaculture – A Designer's Manual †
Mollison. B.; Tagari Publications; 1991; £33.00 inc. p&p
The standard reference work on permaculture, bursting with information.

Permaculture in a Nutshell †
Whitefield. P.; Permanent Publications; 1993; 1856230031; £5.00 inc. p&p
An excellent small introduction to the concept of permaculture.
Well written and very readable.

The Permaculture Plot †
Pratt. S. (Compiler); Permanent Publications; 1996; 1856230104; £5.50 inc. p&p
A regularly update guide to permaculture plots that can be visited in the U.K..

Plants for Ground-Cover
Thomas. G. S.; J. M. Dent & Sons; 1990; 0460126091
A comprehensive guide to the subject.

Plants for Shade
Knight. F. P.; Royal Horticultural Society; 1980; 0900629789
A small but informative booklet listing plants that can be grown in shady positions with a few cultivation details.

Rare Vegetables for Garden and Table
Organ. J.; Faber; 1960
Unusual vegetables that can be grown outdoors in Britain. A good guide.

Salads all the Year Round
Larkcom. J.; Hamlyn; 1980
A good and comprehensive guide to temperate salad plants, with full organic details of cultivation.

Shelter Trees and Hedges
Rosewarne Experimental Horticultural Station; Ministry of Agriculture, Fisheries and Food; 1984
A small booklet packed with information on trees and shrubs for hedging and shelterbelts in exposed maritime areas.

Successful Gardening Without Digging
Gunston. J.; The Garden Book Club; 1960
Written by a man who practiced what he preached, the photos look very dated but the advice is as good as ever.

The Dry Garden
Chatto. B.; Dent; 1982; 0460045512
A good list of drought resistant plants with details on how to grow them.

The Milder Garden
Taylor. J.; Dent; 1990
A good book on plants that you didn't know could be grown outdoors in Britain.

PLANT PROPAGATION

Hardy Woody Plants from Seed
McMillan-Browse. P.; Grower Books; 1985; 0901361216
Does not deal with many species but it is very comprehensive on those that it does cover. Not for casual reading.

Plant Propagation
McMillan-Browse. P.; Mitchell Beazely; 1992; 1857329031
A very well illustrated general guide.

Propagation of Trees, Shrubs and Conifers
Sheat. W. G.; MacMillan and Co; 1948
A bit dated but a good book on propagation techniques with specific details for a wide range of plants.

The Reference Manual of Woody Plant Propagation
Dirr. M. A. and Heuser. M. W.; Varsity Press; 1987; 0942375009
A very detailed book on propagating trees. Not for the casual reader.

GENERA & GROUPS OF PLANTS

Alliums – The Ornamental Onions
Davies. D.; Batsford; 1992; 0713470305
Covers about 200 species of Alliums. A very short section on their uses, good details of their cultivation needs.

Bulbs
Phillips. R. and Rix. M.; Pan Books; 1989; 0330302531
Superbly illustrated, it gives brief details on cultivation and native habitat.

Conifers
Rushforth. K.; Christopher Helm; 1987; 074702801X
Deals with conifers that can be grown outdoors in Britain. Good notes on cultivation and a few bits about plant uses.

Gourds
Organ. J.; Faber; 1963
Deals with squashes and their relatives. Interesting and readable, it gives cultivation techniques and some details of plant uses.

Growing Lilies
Fox. D.; Croom Helm; 1985
A lovely and very readable book dealing with the cultivation of the genus *Lilium*.

Hemerocallis – Day Lilies
Erhardt. W.; Batsford; 1992; 0713470658
A comprehensive book on the genus with a short section on edible uses.

Ornamental Shrubs, Climbers and Bamboos
Thomas. G. S.; Murray; 1992; 0719550432
Contains a wide range of plants with a brief description, mainly of their ornamental value but also usually of cultivation details and varieties.

Perennials Volumes 1 and 2
Phillips. R. & Rix. M.; Pan Books; 1991; 0330309369
Photographs of over 3,000 species and cultivars of ornamental plants together with brief cultivation notes, details of habitat etc.

Shrubs
Phillips. R. & Rix. M.; Pan Books; 1989; 0330302582
Excellent photographs and a terse description of 1900 species and cultivars.

The Book of Bamboo
Farrelly. D.; Sierra Club; 1984; 087156825X
Very readable, giving lots of information on the uses of bamboos, both temperate and tropical.

The New RHS Dictionary of Gardening 1992
Huxley. A.; MacMillan Press; 1992; 0333474945
Excellent and very comprehensive, though it contains a number of silly mistakes. Readable yet also very detailed.

The RHS Gardener's Encyclopedia of Plants and Flowers
Brickell. C.; Dorling Kindersley Publishers; 1990; 0863183867
Excellent range of photographs, some cultivation details but very little information on plant uses.

Trees and Shrubs Hardy in Great Britain. Vol 1 - 4 and Supplement
Bean. W.; Murray; 1981
A classic with a wealth of information but poor on pictures.

† Titles available by mail order from:

PERMANENT PUBLICATIONS (PF)
Hyden House Ltd., Little Hyden Lane,
Clanfield, Hampshire PO8 0RU, England
Tel: (01705) 596500 Fax: (01705) 595834
Email: permaculture@gn.apc.org
WWW: www.permaculture.co.uk/

Ask for your FREE copy the Permanent Publications *Earth Repair Catalogue* of over 250 books and videos on permaculture and other ecological subjects.

Appendix 2

USEFUL ADDRESSES

I have restricted this list to those nurseries and seed companies with whom I have dealt in the past. A small comment on each is included, where a plant species is mentioned in this comment it is because this is the only nursery I know of that supplies the plant in question.

Please note that many of these nurseries do not sell plants by post. Most of them also charge for their catalogues and none of them are open 24 hours a day seven days a week. Since times and charges can vary from year to year I have not entered individual details of this for each nursery. However, before ordering catalogues or visiting nurseries please phone or write to them for details of charges, times of opening etc.

If you are unable to find the plant you are looking for from these nurseries, then there are a couple of other options to try. Firstly, there is an excellent publication called, *The Plant Finder* that is issued each year by the Royal Horticultural Society. This book lists over 65,000 species and cultivars of plants together with the nurseries in this country that supply them. If this book does not list the plant you are seeking, then you could try contacting Plants for a Future, whose address is given in the lists below.

PLANT SOURCES

Arbor Exotica. The Estate Office, Hall Farm, Weston Colville, Cambridgeshire CB1 5PE.
Tel: (01223) 290328
Many trees including *Juglans ailanthifolia cordiformis* and *Zanthoxylum americana*.

Burncoose and South Down Nurseries. Gwennap, Redruth, Cornwall TR16 6BJ.
Tel: (01209) 861112
Very good general range with many unusual species.

Cally Gardens. Gatehouse of Fleet, Castle Douglas, Scotland DG7 2DJ.
Not on telephone.
Unusual perennials and some rare shrubs including *Aralia cordata* and *Cyperus esculentus* in their 1994 catalogue, though the range varies each year.

Clive Simms. Woodhurst, Essendine, Stamford, Lincolnshire PE9 4LQ.
Tel: (01780) 55615
An excellent range of unusual fruiting plants and nut trees.

Drysdale Garden Exotics. Bowerwood Road, Fordingbridge, Hampshire SP6 1BN.
Tel: (01425) 653010
A good range of exotics, including *Ephedra* species and a huge range of bamboos.

Greenway Gardens. Churston Ferrers, Brixham, Devon TQ5 0ES.
Tel: (01803) 842382
Smilax aspera plus many unusual trees, especially from South America.

Hall Farm Nursery. Harpswell, Gainsborough, Lincolnshire DN21 5UU.
Tel: (01427) 668412
Wide range of shrubs and trees including *Berberis lycium* and *Crataegus arnoldiana*.

Hardy Exotics. Gilly Lane, Whitecross, Penzance, Cornwall TR20 8BZ.
Tel: (01736) 740660
A good range of plants for mild counties, there is also a more limted range for gardens nationwide.

Hartshall Nursery Stock. Hartshall Farm, Walsham-le-Willows, Bury St. Edmunds, Suffolk IP31 3BY.
Tel: (01359) 259238
Wide range of trees and shrubs including *Malus baccata mandschurica* and *Pinus cembroides*.

Hoecroft Plants. Severals Grange, Wood Norton, Dereham, Norfolk NR20 5BL.
Tel: (01362) 844206
170 species and cultivars of grasses including *Elymus canadensis*.

Jacques Amand Ltd. The Nurseries, Clamp Hill, Stanmore, Middlesex HA7 3JS.
Tel: 0181-954 8138
Rare and unusual bulbous plants including *Dentaria diphylla*, *Lilium* species and *Streptopus roseus*.

Jungle Giants. Plough Farm, Wigmore, Herefordshire HR6 9UW.
Tel: (01568) 86708
An excellent range of bamboos.

Kenwith Nursery. The Old Rectory, Littleham, Bideford, Devon EX39 5HW.
Tel: (01237) 473752
Good range of conifers including *Pinus albicaulis*.

Kingsfield Conservation Nursery. Broadenham Lane, Winsham, Chard, Somerset TA20 4JF.
Tel: (01460) 30070
Native plants and seeds including *Conopodium majus* and *Glyceria fluitans*.

Langthorn's Plantery. High Cross Lane West, Little Canfield, Dunmow, Essex CM6 1TD.
Tel: (01371) 872611
A wide range of plants including *Fagopyrum dibotrys* and *Lycium barbarum*.

Mallet Court Nursery. Curry Mallet, Taunton, Somerset TA3 6SY.
Tel: (01823) 480748
A wide range of trees and shrubs including *Cephalotaxus harringtonia nana*.

Mickfield Fish and Watergarden Centre. Debenham Road, Mickfield, Stowmarket, Suffolk IP14 5LP.
Tel: (01449) 766425
Pond and bog garden plants including *Zizania aquatica*.

Mount Pleasant Trees. Rockhampton, Berkeley, Gloucestershire GL13 9DU.
Tel: (01454) 260348
An excellent range of trees including *Crataegus azerolus* and many cultivars of *Ginkgo biloba*. This nursery produces very high quality native trees for woodland plantings.

Mrs Susan Cooper. Firlands Cottage, Bishop's Frome, Worcestershire WR6 5BA.
Tel: (01885) 490358
Many rare and unusual trees including *Gleditsia japonica*, *Pinus armandii* and *P. cembra edulis*.

Plants For A Future. The Field, Penpol, Lostwithiel, Cornwall PL22 0NG.
Tel: (01208) 873554 (daytime). (01208) 873623 (evenings).
Growing most of the plants contained in this book and can supply many of them on request.

Poyntzfield Herb Nursery. Balblair, Black Isle, By Dingwall, Ross & Cromarty, Scotland IV7 8LX.
Tel: (01381) 610352
An excellent range of herbs, medicinal plants and seeds.

Reads Nursery. Hales Hall, Loddon, Norfolk NR14 6QW.
Tel: (01508) 46395
Excellent range of Citrus fruits and other uncommon plants including *Bomarea edulis*.

Salley Gardens. Flat 3, 3 Millicent Road, West Bridgeford, Nottingham NG2 7LD.
Tel: (01602) 821366
An excellent range of herbs and medicinal plants including several *Asclepias* species and
Osmorhiza claytonii.

Spinners. Boldre, Lymington, Hampshire SO41 5QE.
Tel: Not known
A wide range of plants, their list has included a hermaphrodite form of *Actinidia deliciosa*, *Dioscorea
japonica*, *Diospyrus lotus*, *D. virginiana*, *Hydrangea serrata amagiana* and *Smilax china*, though some of
these might not be available at present.

Stone House Cottage Nurseries. Stone, Kidderminster, Worcestershire DY10 4BG.
Tel: (01562) 69902
A good range of climbing plants which can be seen growing in their gardens.

Thornhayes Nursery. St. Andrew's Wood, Dulford, Cullompton, Devon EX15 2DF.
Tel: (01884) 266746
A good range of fruiting trees including *Crataegus arnoldiana*, *C. durobrivensis*, *C. schraderiana*,
Sorbus devoniensis and many West Country apple varieties.

Trevor Scott. Thorpe Park Cottage, Thorpe-le-Soken, Essex CO16 0HN.
Tel: (01255) 861308
A good range of grasses including *Beckmannia eruciformis*, *Elymus canadensis* and
Hierochloe odorata.

Westwood Nursery. 65 Yorkland Avenue, Welling, Kent DA16 2LE.
Tel: 0181-301 0886
Hardy orchids.

The Royal Horticultural Society's Plant Centre. RHS Garden, Wisley, Woking, Surrey GU23 6QB.
Tel: (01483) 211113
A very wide and constantly changing range of plants.

SEED SOURCES

Most of the sources shown here do not specialise in food and other useful plants, but their lists contain
many of the plants included in the book. As with the plant nurseries, many of the seed puppliers make a
charge for their catalogue. Please ring them to check the cost, or send an SAE and some stamps.

Abundant Life Seed Foundation. PO Box 772, 1029 Lawrence Street, Port Townsend, WA 98368, U. S. A.
An excellent range of non-hybrid vegetables plus many unusuals and native North American wild foods.
It is easy to obtain seed from them by using a credit card for payment.

B & T World Seeds. Whitnell House, Fiddington, Bridgwater, Somerset TA5 1JE.
An amazing list of over 25,000 species and varieties, the list is rather expensive to obtain though.

B & D Davies. 2 Wirral View, Connah's Quay, Deeside, Clwyd, Wales CH5 4TE.
An excellent range of coniferous trees.

Chiltern Seeds. Bortree Stile, Ulverston, Cumbria LA12 7PB.
Over 4,000 species of plants in a descriptive catalogue. One of my favourite catalogues.

Chris Chadwell Seeds. 81 Parlaunt Road, Slough, Berkshire SL3 8BE.
A botanist who can supply a range of seeds from various countries in the world. It is also possible to obtain wild-collected seeds by subscribing to one of his expeditions.

Deep Diversity (Seeds of Change). PO Box 15700, Santa Fe, New Mexico 87506 - 5700, U.S.A.
A very good range of seed of unusual food plants.

Future Foods. PO Box 1564, Wedmore, Somerset BS28 4DP.
This company specialise in alternative food plants and have an excellent range of seeds and tubers.

SOCIETIES

It is also possible to obtain the seeds of many interesting species by joining many of the specialist gardening societies. Apart from the many other benefits that the following societies offer, they also produce excellent seed lists.

Alpine Garden Society. AGS Centre, Avon Bank, Pershore, Worcestershire WR10 3JP.

American Rock Garden Society. PO Box 67, Millwood, New York, 10546, U.S.A.

Hardy Plant Society. Little Orchard, Great Comberton, Near Pershore, Worcestershire WR10 3DP.

RESEARCH BODIES

Agroforestry Research Trust. 17 Arden Drive, Chelston, Torquay, Devon TQ2 6DZ.
Looking at systems of growing food and other commodities in woodland gardens. They produce an excellent quarterly magazine.

Henry Doubleday Research Association. Ryton Garden, Ryton, Coventry CV8 3LG.
The best organic research centre in Britain for traditional fruits and vegetables. Try and visit their gardens near Coventry.

Permaculture Association. PO Box 1, Buckfastleigh, Devon TQ11 0LH.
Encourages methods of growing plants on a sustainable basis with a strong emphasis on perennials and especially trees.

Plants For A Future. The Field, Penpol, Lostwithiel, Cornwall PL22 0NG.
Looking at all aspects of useful plants that can be grown in temperate climates. It holds a database of over 6500 species and can offer advice on suitable species for any locations. It also gives full details on how to grow and utilize the plants. As mentioned in Chapter One of the book, further information on any of the species contained in the book can be obtained by writing to this address. A charge of 10p per species is charged to cover costs of copying etc.

Appendix 3

PLANTS FOR SPECIFIC HABITATS

These tables are for guidance only, please refer to the entry for each plant in order to see its cultivation needs in more detail.

Plants for Heavy Clay Soils

Acer species 192, 239
Alchemilla vulgaris 142
Allium schoenoprasum 88, 153
Alnus species 23, 193, 233
Amelanchier species 38, 193, 250
Arbutus unedo 42
Berberis species 53, 180
Betula species 23, 234
Camassia species 96, 147
Carpinus betulus 236
Chaenomeles species 56
Cornus canadensis 206
Cornus species 47, 180
Crataegus species 40, 181, 240
Cynara cardunculus 93
Cyperus esculentus 114
Elaeagnus pungens 187
Fagopyrum dibotrys 111
Fagopyrum esculentum 222
Ficus carica 162
Filipendula species 248
Fragaria vesca 'Semperflorens' 99
Hedera helix 158, 208, 243
Hemerocallis fulva 79, 93
Hosta species 206
Ilex aquifolium 239
Juniperus communis 54, 241
Leontodon hispidus 143
Ligustrum species 188
Mahonia species 59, 209
Malus mandschurica 42
Malus sylvestris 240
Melilotus officinalis 144
Mentha pulegium 200
Mentha requienii 202
Monarda didyma 251
Pinus cembra 35
Populus species 193, 235
Prunus cerasifera 189
Prunus laurocerasus 210
Pulmonaria officinalis 208
Quercus ilex 36, 196

Quercus petraea 237
Rheum x cultorum 120
Rosa species 50, 178
Rumex patienta 113
Salix species 194, 235
Sambucus species 5, 25, 183, 235
Sorbus species 31, 195, 238
Symphytum species 8, 80
Tagetes species 4
Taxus baccata 44, 188, 240
Tussilago farfara 146
Ulmus glabra 238
Viburnum species 242
Vinca minor 209

Plants for Poor Sandy Soils

Acer pseudo-platanus 192
Achillea millefolium 141
Amaranthus caudatus 220
Arabis caucasica 164
Aralia cordata 77
Artemisia abrotanum 175
Atriplex species 153, 178
Baccharis patagonica 179
Berberis species 53, 185
Betula species 23, 234
Borago officinalis 215
Broussonetia papyrifera 38
Buddleia davidii 165, 250
Calendula officinalis 215
Caragana arborescens 46
Caragana brevispina 260
Cardamine hirsuta 154
Carpobrotus species 165
Castanea species 25
Cercis siliquastrum 39
Chamaemelum nobile 5, 142, 202
Crambe maritima 110
Crataegus monogyna 181, 240
Cynara cardunculus 93
Elaeagnus species 181, 187
Eleutherococcus sieboldianus 182
Elymus species 261
Fagopyrum dibotrys 111
Fagopyrum esculentum 222
Ficus carica 162
Gaultheria procumbens 59, 208
Gleditsia triacanthos 260
Hedera helix 158, 208, 243
Helianthus tuberosus 115
Hippophae rhamnoides 234

Hippophae salicifolia 23
Ilex aquifolium 239
Juniperus communis 54, 241
Lens culinaris 224
Ligustrum ovalifolium 188
Lupinus arboreus 24
Lupinus mutabilis 225
Lycium barbarum 177
Mahonia nervosa 209
Medicago sativa 11
Melianthus major 102
Montia sibirica 74, 154, 207
Oenothera biennis 251
Origanum vulgare 201
Physalis peruviana 163
Pinus species 35, 195, 236
Polymnia edulis 118
Populus tremula 194, 235
Pseudosasa japonica 190
Rhus species 49
Rubus fruticosus 244
Ruta graveolens 167
Satureia montana 167
Saxifraga stolonifera 168
Sedum species 202
Thymus vulgaris 168, 205
Tilia x vulgaris 32, 238
Trifolium species 146, 248
Tropaeolum majus 95
Ulex europaeus 25
Vaccinium macrocarpon 57
Yucca species 100
Ziziphus jujube 258

Plants for Acid Soils

Amaranthus caudatus 220
Amelanchier laevis 38
Apios americana 67
Arctostaphylos uva-ursi 204
Berberis darwinii 185
Betula species 23, 234
Castanea species 25
Chrysosplenium species 78, 136, 206
Corylus avellana 189, 240
Crataegus monogyna 181, 240
Crataegus opaca 40
Empetrum nigrum 205
Fagopyrum esculentum 222
Fagus sylvatica 28, 182, 236
Fraxinus excelsior 193, 236
Gaultheria species 59, 208
Glyceria fluitans 133
Hydrangea species 48
Ilex aquifolium 239

Juniperus communis 54, 241
Lupinus species 225
Montia sibirica 74, 154, 207
Myrica gale 137
Myrica pensylvanica 183
Physalis peruviana 163
Pinus edulis 35
Pinus muricata 195
Pinus sylvestris 236
Quercus petraea 237
Rhexia virginica 138
Rubus fruticosus 244
Rumex acetosa 80, 155
Rumex acetosella 248
Sorbus aria 31, 195, 238
Sorbus aucuparia 5, 31, 195, 238
Taxus baccata 44, 188, 240
Ulex europaeus 25
Vaccinium species 57, 203

Plants for Alkaline Soils

Acer campestre 180, 239
Amaranthus caudatus 220
Anthemis tinctoria 164
Atriplex species 153, 178, 215
Beckmannia eruciformis 136
Buddleia davidii 165, 250
Bunium bulbocastanum 247
Caragana arborescens 46
Carpinus betulus 236
Cercis siliquastrum 39
Chenopodium quinoa 221
Cornus capitata 27
Cornus mas 47, 181
Cornus sanguinea 180
Corylus avellana 189, 240
Crataegus species 40, 181, 240
Dentaria laciniata 73
Elymus condensatus 261
Euonymus europaeus 241
Fagus sylvatica 28, 182, 236
Filipendula vulgaris 248
Fragaria vesca 'Semperflorens' 99
Glyceria fluitans 133
Hedera helix 158, 208, 243
Juniperus communis 54, 241
Lavandula angustifolia 167
Ligustrum vulgare 188
Orchis mascula 82, 148
Orchis morio 148
Physalis peruviana 163
Pinus nigra 196

Rumex scutatus 121, 167
Ruta graveolens 167
Salvia officinalis 60
Satureia montana 167
Secale montana 120
Sedum species 202
Sempervivum tectorum 168
Setaria italica 226
Taxus baccata 44, 188, 240
Thymus herba-barona 169
Thymus praecox arcticus 169
Ulex europaeus 25
Vinca minor 209
Yucca species 100
Ziziphus jujube 258

Plants Tolerant of Atmospheric Pollution

Acer campestre 180, 239
Arbutus unedo 42
Broussonetia papyrifera 38
Buddleia davidii 165, 250
Chaenomeles species 56
Crataegus tanacetifolia 41
Elaeagnus multiflora 182
Eleutherococcus sieboldianus 182
Fagus sylvatica 28, 182, 236
Fraxinus excelsior 193, 236
Ginkgo biloba 28
Gleditsia species 260
Hedera helix 158, 208, 243
Ilex aquifolium 239
Ligustrum species 188
Populus x canadensis 194
Prunus laurocerasus 210
Salix viminalis 194, 235
Sambucus species 5, 25, 183, 235
Sorbus aria 31, 195, 238
Sorbus aucuparia 5, 31, 195, 238
Taxus baccata 44, 188, 240
Ulmus glabra 238

Plants for Windy Sites

(an 'M' denotes tolerance to maritime exposure and a 'W' tolerance to strong winds.)

Acer campestre W 180, 239
Acer pseudo-platanus M 192
Alnus species M 23, 193, 233
Amelanchier canadensis W 38, 193
Araucaria araucana M 32
Arbutus unedo M 42
Asparagus officinalis M 120
Asphodeline lutea M 90
Atriplex species M 153, 178, 215
Baccharis patagonica M 179
Berberis darwinii M 53, 185
Berberis x stenophylla M 185
Betula species W 23, 234
Buddleia davidii M 165, 250
Caragana arborescens W 46
Caragana brevispina W 260
Carpobrotus species M 165
Castanea sativa M 25
Ceanothus thyrsiflorus M 185
Chenopodium quinoa W 221
Cornus capitata M 27
Cornus mas W 47, 181
Corylus avellana W 189, 240
Crambe maritima M 110
Crataegus species W 40, 181, 240
Cupressocyparis leylandii M 195
Cynara species W 92
Elaeagnus species M 181, 187
Elymus species M 261
Empetrum nigrum W 205
Eriobotrya japonica M 162
Eruca vesicaria sativa W 216

Escallonia rubra macrantha M 179
Fagus sylvatica W 28, 182, 236
Feijoa sellowiana M 162
Foeniculum vulgare W 111, 154
Fraxinus excelsior M 193, 236
Glycyrrhiza glabra W 121
Helianthus tuberosus W 115
Hippophae rhamnoides M 234
Hippophae salicifolia M 23
Hydrangea species M 48
Ilex aquifolium M 239
Juniperus communis M 54, 241
Lathyrus japonicus maritimus M 261
Laurus nobilis W 43, 163
Lavandula species W 167, 176
Ligustrum ovalifolium M 188
Ligustrum vulgare M 188
Linum usitatissimum W 224
Lonicera angustifolia W 48
Lonicera involucrata W 48
Lupinus arboreus M 24
Lupinus mutabilis W 225
Lycium barbarum M 177
Malva moschata W 94
Malva pusilla W 216
Melianthus major W 102
Mespilus germanica W 42
Myrica cerifera W 183
Myrtus ugni W 60
Origanum vulgare W 201
Oxalis triangularis W 95
Phormium tenax M 188
Phragmites australis M 134
Pinus species W 35, 195, 236
Plantago species M 144
Pleioblastus simonii M 190
Populus alba M 194
Populus species W 194, 235

Potentilla anserina M 118
Prunus cerasifera W 189
Prunus laurocerasus W 210
Prunus maritima M 49
Pseudosasa japonica M 190
Quercus ilex M 36, 196
Quercus petraea W 237
Rhus glabra W 50
Rhus typhina W 49
Ribes aureum W 57
Rosa canina W 50
Rosa rugosa M 178, 251
Rosmarinus officinalis M 60
Rubus fruticosus W 244
Rumex acetosella M 248
Rumex scutatus W 121, 167
Salix species M 24, 194
Sambucus canadensis W 52
Sambucus nigra M 5, 183, 235
Sambucus racemosa W 52
Sanguisorba minor M 145, 155
Secale montana W 120
Sedum species M 202
Semiarundinaria fastuosa M 190
Sorbus aria M 31, 195, 238
Sorbus aucuparia M 31, 195, 238
Sorbus devoniensis W 31, 238
Sorbus domestica W 30, 238
Sorbus latifolia W 31
Sorbus torminalis W 31, 238
Taraxacum officinale M 113, 145, 155
Taxus baccata W 44, 188, 240
Thymus species W 168, 205
Tilia cordata W 31, 238
Tilia x vulgaris W 32, 238
Trifolium pratense W 248
Tussilago farfara M 146
Ulex europaeus M 25
Ulmus species M 238
Urtica dioica W 245
Vaccinium myrtillus W 58
Yucca species W 100

Appendix 4

PLANT TOXINS

This book contains information on a very wide range of edible plants, many of which will be completely new to most readers. Whilst it is all to easy to get carried away about the possibility of poisoning oneself with a strange new plant, there are surprisingly few plants that will actually cause you much harm if you eat reasonable quantities of them – and the majority of these tend to have an unpleasant flavour and so are unlikely to be eaten.

It is probably true to say that most, if not all, foods contain at least some deleterious substances. Runner bean seeds, for example, are poisonous raw but make a nutritious protein-rich food when cooked. Cabbages, when eaten in large quantities, can cause goitre and there have been occasional cases of people being killed by eating very large amounts of onions.

It is also true that these deleterious substances in plants are often beneficial to the body in small quantities. It really comes down to a matter of dose. Many of our medicines, for example, are made from plant substances that in larger concentrations can be lethal.

This appendix looks at some of the more common toxins found in plants and explains how they can be harmful, or beneficial, to the health.

ALKALOIDS

Some of the most toxic plant poisons are alkaloids, though fortunately these substances have a bitter taste and can be recognised by the tongue quite easily. They are found in a few edible plants, particularly in the pea and bean and the potato families. Apart from the edible tubers, for example, all parts of the potato plant are rich in alkaloids and highly poisonous to humans.

It is believed that plants produce alkaloids as a protection from being eaten, although this strategy is by no means totally successful because many creatures have evolved an ability to eat certain alkaloids. Indeed, some insects are able to concentrate these alkaloids inside their own bodies, making themselves poisonous to any potential predator.

Alkaloids are often totally missing from some parts of plants. The opium poppy (*Papaver somniferum*), for example, is very rich in many toxic alkaloids, but the seeds are totally free of alkaloids and are a very nutritious addition to the diet. Many alkaloids are used as medicines, examples include morphine from the opium poppy and quinine, which is used in the treatment of malaria.

CALCIUM OXALATE

This substance is closely related to oxalic acid (see below), but is much more antisocial in its action on the body. It is contained in the plant in the form of small crystals and, if ingested, it will give an extremely unpleasant sensation to the mouth and any other mucous surfaces it comes into contact with. Basically, there is a burning sensation and it feels as though hundreds of small needles are being stuck into you. Fortunately calcium oxalate is easily destroyed by thoroughly cooking or drying the plant. If eating foods that contain calcium oxalate, be very sure that you have thoroughly cooked it, or you will regret the experience. Whilst it is unlikely to kill you, I speak from personal experience when I say that the discomfort caused by the small crystals is very substantial and will persist for a few hours.

COUMARIN

Coumarins are found in a number of plants, in particular many grasses and members of the genus *Gallium* which includes the herb Lady's bedstraw. They can be recognised by the delicious smell of new-mown hay that is given off by the dried plant.

Coumarins are often used in medicine, one of their main properties is that they thin the blood and reduce its ability to coagulate. This can be very useful for people suffering from thrombosis or various other complaints of the circulatory system. However, in the wrong dose, they can prevent the blood from coagulating when the person is cut, and it is then possible to bleed to death. Indeed, they have been used with great success in the rat poison 'Warfarin', causing the rat to bleed to death from even a small cut.

Coumarins are most dangerous if the plant material is dried and then becomes mouldy. When eating foods that contain coumarins therefore, it is safest to only use the fresh plant.

ESSENTIAL OILS

Many plants produce aromatic substances that are known as volatile or essential oils. These substances have been shown to have a deterrent effect on many insect pests, and so plants rich in essential oils have been traditionally used in companion planting schemes.

Essential oils have a wide range of uses and, in small doses, are generally beneficial in the diet. They are found in many herbs, for example, and are therefore often used as food flavourings. They also have a wide range of medicinal applications and are used in perfumery, aromatherapy etc. They often have a marked antibiotic effect and have also been used to make insecticides and fungicides.

It is when essential oils are distilled that they are most likely to cause problems. They are very potent, even one drop of the oil of some species has been known to cause skin irritations. When using the distilled oils, therefore, be very careful not to exceed the recommended dosage.

GLYCOSIDES

Glycosides are found in a wide range of plants and are widely used medicinally, though they are some of the most toxic plant substances known. There are three main groups:

Cyanogenetic glycosides (in particular hydrogen cyanide, which is sometimes called prussic acid.) These substances are found in a number of well-known food plants – particularly in the leaves and seeds of members of the rose family, including apples, pears, almonds, plums and peaches. In small quantities these glycosides have been shown to stimulate respiration and improve digestion, they are also claimed to be of benefit in the treatment of cancer. In excess, however, they can cause respiratory failure and death.

Anthraquinone glycosides are often used medicinally for their laxative effect, though in larger doses they can be fatal. Probably the best known food plant they are found in is the roots of rhubarb.

Cardiac glycosides are some of the most poisonous plant substances known. They are widely used medicinally for their effect on the heart, but this should only be done under expert supervision because it is all too easy to take too large a dose, which is invariably fatal. One of the best known plants containing these substances in Britain is our native foxglove, *Digitalis purpurea*.

OXALIC ACID

Oxalic acid is found in a wide range of foods, including many common foods such as spinach and rhubarb. It can often be detected by the acid, lemony flavour it imparts to the food. Although it is perfectly safe for most people to eat in small quantities, oxalic acid-rich foods should not be eaten in large amounts since oxalic acid can bind up the body's supply of calcium leading to nutritional deficiency. People with a tendency to rheumatism, arthritis, gout, kidney stones and hyperacidity should take especial caution if including this plant in their diet since it can exacerbate the symptoms of these diseases.

SAPONINS

These are another group of toxins that are often met in food plants. Those best known are probably various beans, alfalfa and fenugreek.

Saponins are very poisonous substances if they get into the bloodstream, where they break down the white blood cells causing anaemia and, in severe cases, death. However, they are very poorly absorbed by the human body and so most pass straight through the digestive system without causing any harm. Thus, although not recommended as part of the diet, they are fairly safe to ingest when contained in leaves or whatever.

They can be removed very easily by a number of methods. Very often they form a coating on the outside of seeds, in this case it is a simple matter to soak the whole seeds overnight and then rinse them thoroughly until the rinse water is no longer soapy. When contained in the seeds, saponins can be removed by carefully leaching the seed or flour in running water. Saponins are not very heat-stable and so thorough cooking, and perhaps changing the cooking water once, will also normally remove most of them.

Saponins are much more toxic to some creatures, particularly cold-blooded animals such as fish and frogs. Hunting tribes have traditionally put large quantities of them in streams, lakes etc. in order to stupefy or kill fish.

The most interesting use of saponins is as a soap. See the entry for *Ceanothus americanus* in Chapter 2 for more details of this. Saponins are also used externally to kill body parasites.

TANNINS

These are a variety of astringent compounds that have the ability to precipitate proteins. They are, therefore, often used medicinally. When applied to cuts, they coagulate the blood and therefore help to stop the bleeding. They can also be taken internally in the treatment of internal bleeding and diarrhoea.

Tannins are particularly valuable in making dyes. On their own they make brown to red colours, and can also be used as a mordant to help fix less permanent dyes.

They are found in a wide range of plants, perhaps the best known is in oak trees and it is these substances that give acorns their bitter flavour. A moderate use of tannin should not be a problem to the body, though in the long term they have been shown to be carcinogenic.

THIAMINASE

The enzyme thiaminase is found in a number of plants, especially ferns and many other non-flowering plants. It reacts strongly with thiamine (vitamin B1), breaking it down and thereby depriving the body of this essential vitamin if it is eaten regularly in the diet. Whilst small amounts of thiaminase in the diet will not cause any problems to a person who is eating a well-balanced diet with plenty of vitamin B1, when taken in excess it can cause anaemia and even death. Thiaminase is destroyed by heat so the plant is perfectly safe to eat if it is well cooked.

Appendix 5

NATIVE PLANTS

NATIVE SPECIES

Acer campestre	Field maple	180, 239
Achillea millefolium	Yarrow	141
Ajuga reptans	Bugle	142, 207
Alchemilla vulgaris	Lady's mantle	142
Alliaria petiolata	Garlic mustard	243
Allium oleraceum	Field garlic	147
Allium schoenoprasum	Chives	88, 153
Allium ursinum	Ramsons	76, 243
Allium vineale	Crow garlic	147
Alnus glutinosa	Alder	23, 193, 233
Althaea officinalis	Marsh mallow	88
Aphanes arvensis	Parsley piert	164
Aquilegia vulgaris	Columbine	77, 89, 243
Arabis hirsuta		165
Arctium lappa	Great burdock	217
Arctium minus	Burdock	219
Asparagus officinalis	Asparagus	120
Barbarea vulgaris	Yellow rocket	153
Bellis perennis	Daisy	142
Betula pendula	Silver birch	23, 234
Betula pubescens	White birch	23, 234
Brassica oleracea	Wild cabbage	108
Bunium bulbocastanum	Pig nut	247
Butomus umbellatus	Flowering rush	132
Buxus sempervirens	Box	176
Calluna vulgaris	Heather	176
Campanula rapunculoides	Creeping bellflower	91
Capsella bursa-pastoris	Shepherd's purse	251
Cardamine hirsuta	Hairy bittercress	154
Cardamine pratensis	Cuckoo flower	247
Carpinus betulus	Hornbeam	236
Chamaemelum nobile	Camomile	5, 142, 202
Chenopodium album	Fat hen	221
Chenopodium bonus-henricus	Good King Henry	109
Chrysosplenium alternifolium	Golden saxifrage	78, 136, 206
Chrysosplenium oppositifolium	Golden saxifrage	136, 206
Cichorium intybus	Chicory	109, 143, 154
Conopodium majus	Pignut	78, 243
Cornus sanguinea	Dogwood	180, 240
Corylus avellana	Hazel	189, 240
Crambe maritima	Seacale	110
Crataegus laevigata	Midland hawthorn	181, 240
Crataegus monogyna	Hawthorn	181, 240
Cyperus longus	Galingale	132
Empetrum nigrum	Crowberry	205
Euonymus europaeus	Spindle tree	241
Fagus sylvatica	Beech	28, 182, 236
Filipendula ulmaria	Meadowsweet	248
Filipendula vulgaris	Dropwort	248
Fragaria vesca	Wild strawberry	166
Fragaria vesca 'Semperflorens'	Alpine strawberry	99

Fraxinus excelsior	Ash	193, 236
Galium verum	Lady's bedstraw	248
Geum rivale	Water avens	243
Geum urbanum	Wood avens	243
Glyceria fluitans	Floating manna grass	133
Hedera helix	Ivy	158, 208, 243
Hierochloe odorata	Holy grass	137
Hippophae rhamnoides	Sea buckthorn	234
Humulus lupulus	Hop	68, 244
Hyacinthoides non-scriptus	Bluebell	244
Hypochoeris radicata	Cat's ear	143
Ilex aquifolium	Holly	239
Juniperus communis	Juniper	54, 241
Lathyrus japonicus maritimus	Beach pea	261
Leontodon hispidus	Rough hawkbit	143
Ligustrum vulgare	Privet	188, 243
Malus sylvestris	Crab apple	240
Malva moschata	Musk mallow	79, 94, 244
Malva sylvestris	Mallow	95
Mentha pulegium	Pennyroyal	200
Menyanthes trifoliata	Bogbean	133
Muscari neglectum	Grape hyacinth	148
Myrica gale	Bog myrtle	137
Myrrhis odorata	Sweet cicely	79, 155
Nasturtium officinale	Watercress	130
Nuphar lutea	Yellow water lily	129
Nymphaea alba	White water lily	130
Nymphoides peltata	Water fringe	130
Ophrys apifera	Bee orchid	148
Orchis laxiflora	Marsh orchis	148
Orchis mascula	Early purple orchis	82, 148
Orchis morio	Green-winged orchid	148
Origanum vulgare	Oregano	201
Oxalis acetosella	Wood sorrel	74, 244
Papaver rhoeas	Corn poppy	226
Phragmites australis	Common reed	134
Pinus sylvestris	Scot's pine	236
Plantago lanceolata	Ribwort plantain	144
Plantago major	Common plantain	144
Plantago media	Hoary plantain	144
Polygonum bistorta	Bistort	142
Polygonum persicaria	Red leg	142
Populus nigra	Black poplar	194, 235
Populus tremula	Aspen poplar	24, 194, 235
Potentilla anserina	Silverweed	118
Prunella vulgaris	Self-heal	144
Prunus avium	Wild cherry	236
Prunus padus	Bird cherry	237
Prunus spinosa	Sloe	241
Quercus petraea	Sessile oak	237
Quercus robur	Pedunculate oak	237
Rhamnus cathartica	Common buckthorn	242
Rhamnus frangula	Alder buckthorn	242
Ribes alpinum	Alpine currant	175

Rosa canina	Dog rose	50
Rosa villosa	Apple rose	51
Rubus fruticosus	Blackberry	244
Rubus idaeus	Raspberry	244
Rumex acetosa	Sorrel	80, 155, 244
Rumex acetosella	Sheeps sorrel	248
Sagittaria sagittifolia	Arrow head	131
Salix alba	White willow	24, 194, 235
Salix fragilis	Crack willow	235
Salix pentandra	Bay willow	194, 235
Salix purpurea	Purple osier	194, 235
Salix triandra	Almond-leaved willow	194, 235
Salix viminalis	Osier	24, 194, 235
Sambucus nigra	Elderberry	5, 25, 183, 235
Sanguisorba minor	Salad burnet	145, 155
Saponaria officinalis	Soapwort	244
Scirpus lacustris	Bulrush	134
Sorbus aria	Whitebeam	31, 195, 238
Sorbus aucuparia	Mountain ash	5, 31, 195, 238
Sorbus devoniensis	French hales	31, 238
Sorbus torminalis	Wild service tree	31, 238
Symphytum officinale	Comfrey	8, 80, 245

Taraxacum officinale	Dandelion	113, 145, 155
Taxus baccata	Yew	44, 188, 240
Thymus praecox arcticus	Wild thyme	169
Thymus serpyllum	Wild thyme	146, 169
Tilia cordata	Small leaved lime	31, 238
Tilia platyphyllos	Large leaved lime	32, 238
Trifolium pratense	Red clover	248
Trifolium repens	White clover	3, 146
Tussilago farfara	Coltsfoot	146, 245
Typha angustifolia	Small reed mace	134
Typha latifolia	Reedmace	134
Ulex europaeus	Gorse	25
Ulmus glabra	Wych elm	238
Ulmus procera	English elm	239
Urtica dioica	Stinging nettle	8, 245
Vaccinium myrtillus	Bilberry	58
Vaccinium oxycoccus	Small cranberry	58
Vaccinium vitis-idaea	Cowberry	58, 205
Valerianella locusta	Corn salad	155
Viburnum lantana	Wayfaring tree	242
Viburnum opulus	Guelder rose	5, 242
Vinca minor	Lesser periwinkle	209
Viola odorata	Sweet violet	81, 96, 155, 207, 246
Viola riviniana	Wood violet	81
Viola tricolor	Heartsease	96

MORE OR LESS
NATURALIZED SPECIES

Acer pseudo-platanus	Sycamore	22, 192
Acorus calamus	Sweet flag	132
Allium sativum	Garlic	106
Allium triquetrum	Three-cornered leek	76
Amelanchier canadensis	Juneberry	38, 193
Amelanchier laevis	Allegheny shadberry	38
Amelanchier lamarckii	Apple serviceberry	46
Angelica archangelica	Angelica	77
Anthemis tinctoria	Yellow camomile	164
Anthriscus cereifolium	Chervil	214
Aponogeton distachyos	Water hawthorn	129
Arabis caucasica	Rock cress	164
Asarum europaeum	Asarabacca	207
Atriplex halimus	Sea orach	153, 178
Atriplex hortensis	Orach	215
Barbarea verna	Land cress	154
Berberis buxifolia		53
Berberis vulgaris	Barberry	180
Borago officinalis	Borage	215, 250
Buddleia davidii	Buddlia	165, 250
Bunias orientalis	Turkish rocket	108
Calendula officinalis	Pot marigold	215
Campanula persicifolia	Harebell	91
Campanula rapunculus	Rampion	219
Carpobrotus acinaciformis	Hottentot fig	165
Carpobrotus edulis	Hottentot fig	165
Castanea sativa	Sweet chetsnut	25, 191
Chaenomeles speciosa	Japanese quince	56
Cornus mas	Cornelian cherry	47, 181
Cydonia oblonga	Quince	41
Eruca vesicaria sativa	Rocket	216
Fagopyrum esculentum	Buckwheat	222
Ficus carica	Fig	162
Foeniculum vulgare	Fennel	111, 154
Fragaria moschata	Hautbois strawberry	166, 200
Gaultheria procumbens	Checkerberry	59, 208

Gaultheria shallon	Shallon	59, 210
Helianthus annuus	Sunflower	223
Helianthus tuberosus	Jerusalem artichoke	115
Hemerocallis fulva	Common day lily	79, 93
Hemerocallis lilioasphodelus	Yellow day lily	93
Hyssopus officinalis	Hyssop	167, 176, 251
Juglans regia	Walnut	29
Lathyrus tuberosus	Earthnut pea	117
Levisticum officinale	Lovage	121
Linum usitatissimum	Flax	224
Lycium barbarum	Box thorn	177
Mahonia aquifolium	Oregon grape	59, 209
Malva alcea		94
Malva pusilla		216
Malva verticillata	Chinese mallow	79, 217
Medicago sativa	Alfalfa	11
Melilotus officinalis	Melilot	144
Melissa officinalis	Lemon balm	79
Mentha requienii	Corsican mint	202
Mespilus germanica	Medlar	42
Montia perfoliata	Miner's lettuce	74, 154, 207
Montia sibirica	Pink purslane	74, 154, 207
Myrica pensylvanica	Northern bayberry	183
Nigella arvensis	Wild fennel	225
Nigella damascena	Love-in-a-mist	225
Oenothera biennis	Evening primrose	251
Papaver somniferum	Opium poppy	226
Phormium tenax	New Zealand flax	188
Phytolacca americana	Pokeweed	112
Pleioblastus simonii	Medake	190
Pontederia cordata	Pickerel weed	137
Populus alba	White poplar	24, 194
Portulaca oleracea	Green purslane	217

Index 1

PLANT USES

Fruit

Gelatine Substitutes

Leaves

Seedpods

Annuals	*Melilotus officinalis*	144
Climbers	*Tropaeolum majus*	95
Perennials	*Apios americana*	67
	Asclepias species	89
	Astragalus species	262
	Phaseolus coccineus	119
	Trifolium repens	146
	Tropaeolum minus	96
Shrubs	*Caragana arborescens*	46

Stems

Bamboos	*Phyllostachys* species	70
	Pleioblastus simonii	190
	Pseudosasa japonica	190
	Semiarundinaria fastuosa	190
Biennials	*Angelica archangelica*	77
	Arctium species	217
Perennials	*Acorus calamus*	132
	Aponogeton distachyos	129
	Aralia cordata	77
	Asparagus officinalis	120
	Balsamorrhiza species	255
	Crambe maritima	110
	Cryptotaenia species	78
	Cynara cardunculus	93
	Darmera peltata	133
	Foeniculum vulgare	111
	Gunnera tinctoria	136
	Hosta species	206
	Levisticum officinale	121
	Phragmites australis	134
	Rheum x cultorum	120
	Saxifraga stolonifera	168
	Symphytum species	80
	Typha species	134
	Zizania latifolia	135
Shrubs	*Yucca* species	100
Trees	*Yucca brevifolia*	101

Sweeteners

Annuals	*Stevia rebaudiana*	253
Perennials	*Asclepias* species	89
	Filipendula ulmaria	248
	Glycyrrhiza glabra	121
	Phragmites australis	134
	Typha species	134
Shrubs	*Hydrangea* species	48
	Melianthus major	102
Trees	*Acer pseudo-platanus*	192
	Hovenia dulcis	41
	Juglans regia	29

Tea Substitutes

Perennials	*Althaea officinalis*	88
	Chamaemelum nobile	5
	Filipendula ulmaria	248
	Levisticum officinale	121
	Melissa officinalis	79
	Monarda didyma	251
	Symphytum species	80
	Trifolium pratense	248
	Tussilago farfara	146
	Urtica dioica	245
Shrubs	*Aloysia triphylla*	160
	Arctostaphylos uva-ursi	204
	Ceanothus americanus	55
	Crataegus species	240
	Eleutherococcus sieboldianus	182
	Gaultheria procumbens	59
	Hyssopus officinalis	167
	Lavandula species	167
	Lycium barbarum	177
	Myrica gale	137
	Rosa species	50
	Rosa rugosa	178
	Rosmarinus officinalis	60
Trees	*Betula* species	234
	Sassafras albidum	42
	Tilia species	31

NON EDIBLE USES

Adhesives

Bulbs	*Allium sativum*	106
	Chlorogalum pomeridianum	97
Perennials	*Althaea officinalis*	88
	Eremurus spectabilis	151
	Phormium tenax	188
Trees	*Betula* species	234

Basketry

Climbers	*Akebia* species	157
Perennials	*Acorus calamus*	132
	Cyperus esculentus	114
	Cyperus longus	132
	Hierochloe odorata	137
	Phormium tenax	188
	Phragmites australis	134
	Scirpus lacustris	134
	Typha species	134
Shrubs	*Calluna vulgaris*	176
	Cornus sanguinea	180
	Ligustrum vulgare	188
	Vinca species	209
	Vitex agnus-castus	52
	Yucca species	100

Trees	*Corylus avellana*	189
	Salix species	194
	Salix fragilis	235
	Yucca brevifolia	101

Beads

Shrubs	*Arctostaphylos uva-ursi*	204

Biomass

Perennials	*Cichorium intybus*	143
	Helianthus tuberosus	115
	Polygonum japonicum	249
	Symphytum species	80
	Typha species	134
Trees	*Salix* species	194

Broom

Perennials	*Phragmites australis*	134
Shrubs	*Calluna vulgaris*	176
Trees	*Betula* species	234

Charcoal

Shrubs	*Euonymus europaeus*	241
Trees	*Tilia* species	31

Companion Plants

Annuals	*Calendula officinalis*	215
	Chrysanthemum coronarium	216
	Tagetes species	4
Perennials	*Achillea millefolium*	141
	Chamaemelum nobile	5
	Origanum vulgare	201
	Tagetes lucida	4
	Trifolium pratense	248
	Trifolium repens	146
	Urtica dioica	245
Shrubs	*Artemisia abrotanum*	175
	Hyssopus officinalis	167
	Rosmarinus officinalis	60
	Ruta graveolens	167
	Salvia officinalis	60
	Thymus species	169
Trees	*Laurus nobilis*	43
	Morus nigra	30

Compost

Perennials	*Symphytum* species	80
	Urtica dioica	245
Trees	*Quercus* species	237

Disinfectant

Shrubs	*Calycanthus* species	46
	Rosmarinus officinalis	60

Dyes

Annuals	*Borago officinalis*	215
	Calendula officinalis	215
	Fagopyrum esculentum	222
	Helianthus annuus	223
Climbers	*Hedera helix*	243
	Humulus lupulus	68
Perennials	*Anthemis tinctoria*	164
	Chamaemelum nobile	5
	Galium verum	248
	Gunnera tinctoria	136
	Phormium tenax	188
	Phragmites australis	134
	Phytolacca americana	112
	Prunella vulgaris	144
	Rumex acetosa	80
Shrubs	*Arctostaphylos uva-ursi*	204
	Buddleia davidii	165
	Caragana arborescens	46
	Ceanothus americanus	55
	Cornus sanguinea	180
	Empetrum nigrum	205
	Hibiscus syriacus	189
	Ligustrum vulgare	188
	Myrica gale	137
	Rhamnus species	242
	Rhus typhina	49
	Rosmarinus officinalis	60
	Ruta graveolens	167
	Ulex europaeus	25
	Viburnum opulus	242
	Vitex agnus-castus	52
Trees	*Alnus glutinosa*	180
	Juglans regia	29
	Sassafras albidum	42

Essential Oils

Perennials	*Acorus calamus*	132
	Chamaemelum nobile	5
	Cyperus longus	132
	Filipendula ulmaria	248
	Foeniculum vulgare	111
	Hierochloe odorata	137
	Monarda didyma	251
	Origanum vulgare	201
	Viola odorata	81
Shrubs	*Aloysia triphylla*	160
	Lavandula species	167
	Myrica gale	137
	Rosa species	50
	Rosmarinus officinalis	60
	Salvia officinalis	60
	Thymus species	169
Trees	*Betula* species	234
	Sassafras albidum	42

Fibre

Annuals	*Helianthus annuus*	223
	Linum usitatissimum	224
Bulbs	*Chlorogalum pomeridianum*	97
Climbers	*Humulus lupulus*	68
Perennials	*Althaea officinalis*	88
	Asclepias species	89
	Boehmeria nivea	102
	Cyperus longus	132
	Phormium tenax	188
	Typha species	134
	Urtica dioica	245
Shrubs	*Caragana arborescens*	46
	Yucca species	100
Trees	*Broussonetia papyrifera*	38
	Tilia species	31
	Ulmus species	238
	Yucca brevifolia	101

Fire Retardants

Perennials	*Carpobrotus* species	165
	Sempervivum tectorum	168

Fungicide

Bulbs	*Allium sativum*	106
Shrubs	*Sambucus nigra*	183
	Thymus species	169
Trees	*Betula* species	234

Green Manures

Annuals	*Fagopyrum esculentum*	222
	Helianthus annuus	223
	Lupinus species	225
Perennials	*Medicago sativa*	11
	Trifolium pratense	248

Hair Care

Climbers	*Hedera helix*	243
	Schisandra chinensis	159
Perennials	*Chamaemelum nobile*	5
	Urtica dioica	245
Shrubs	*Artemisia abrotanum*	175
	Hibiscus syriacus	189
	Juniperus communis	54
	Rosmarinus officinalis	60
	Salvia officinalis	60
	Yucca species	100
Trees	*Castanea sativa*	25
	Yucca brevifolia	101

	Foeniculum vulgare	111
	Galium verum	248
	Geum rivale	243
	Hierochloe odorata	137
	Melissa officinalis	79
	Mentha species	200
	Origanum vulgare	201
	Tagetes lucida	4
	Urtica dioica	245
Shrubs	*Aloysia triphylla*	160
	Artemisia abrotanum	175
	Berberis species	5
	Calycanthus species	46
	Hyssopus officinalis	167
	Juniperus communis	54
	Lavandula species	167
	Myrica gale	137
	Rosmarinus officinalis	60
	Ruta graveolens	167
	Salvia officinalis	60
	Sambucus species	52
	Sambucus nigra	183
	Santolina chamaecyparissus	177
	Satureia montana	167
	Thymus species	168
	Viburnum opulus	5
Trees	*Betula* species	234
	Juglans regia	29
	Laurus nobilis	43
	Quercus species	237
	Salix purpurea	194
	Sassafras albidum	42
	Sorbus aucuparia	5

Resin

Shrubs	*Juniperus communis*	54
Trees	*Pinus sylvestris*	236

Roofing Materials

Perennials	*Gunnera tinctoria*	136
Trees	*Betula* species	234

Rooting Hormone

Trees	*Populus* species	193
	Salix species	194

Soap

Bulbs	*Chlorogalum pomeridianum*	97
Climbers	*Hedera helix*	243
Perennials	*Phytolacca americana*	112
	Saponaria officinalis	244
Shrubs	*Ceanothus americanus*	55
	Ceanothus thyrsiflorus	185
	Yucca species	100
Trees	*Gleditsia japonica*	260
	Yucca brevifolia	101

Soil Stabilization

Perennials	*Darmera peltata*	133
	Hierochloe odorata	137
	Phragmites australis	134
Shrubs	*Caragana arborescens*	46
	Hippophae rhamnoides	234
	Rhus typhina	49
Trees	*Populus* species	193
	Salix species	194

Starch

Perennials	*Plantago* species	144

Strewing Herbs

Perennials	*Acorus calamus*	132
	Chamaemelum nobile	5
	Filipendula ulmaria	248
	Foeniculum vulgare	111
	Galium verum	248
	Hierochloe odorata	137
	Origanum vulgare	201
Shrubs	*Hyssopus officinalis*	167
	Juniperus communis	54
	Salvia officinalis	60

String

Perennials	*Phormium tenax*	188
Shrubs	*Viburnum lantana*	242

Stuffing Material (for toys, mattresses etc.)

Perennials	*Galium verum*	248
	Tussilago farfara	146
	Typha species	134
Trees	*Fagus sylvatica*	28

Tooth Care

Perennials	*Althaea officinalis*	88
	Glycyrrhiza glabra	121
Shrubs	*Salvia officinalis*	60
Trees	*Fagus sylvatica*	28
	Juglans regia	29

Thatching Materials

Perennials	*Phragmites australis*	134
	Scirpus lacustris	134
	Typha species	134
Shrubs	*Calluna vulgaris*	176
Trees	*Betula* species	234

Wax

Shrubs	*Myrica* species	183
	Myrica gale	137

Index 2

PLANT NAMES